Sillon de Talbert
Île de Bréhat
Paimpol
Plage Bonaparte
Plouha
Baie de St Brieuc
Cap Frehel
Fort la Latte
Hydro-elect Barrage
Le Val-André
Erquy
Bienassis
St Cast
Rothéneuf
Cancale
Baie du Mont St Michel
St Brieuc
Matignon
Dinard
St Malo
Le Guildo
Mont-Dol
Polders
Mont St Michel
Lamballe
Corseul
Dol
Moncontour
Dinan
DU - NORD
Combourg
R. Rance
ILLE-
La Hardouinais
Fougères
Loudéac
R. Ille
St Aubin du Cormier
Liffré
R. Oust
ET-VILAINE
Concoret
Comper
RENNES
R. Vilaine
Forêt de Paimpont
Vitré
Josselin
Colonne des Trente
Paimpont
I H A N
Coëtquidan St Cyr
Les Rochers
Ploermel
St Marcel
Malestroit
R. Oust
Vannes
Redon
Châteaubriant
R. Vilaine
La Roche Bernard
Saffré
La Grande Brière
Guérande
LOIRE-
Croisic
La Baule
St Nazaire
ATLANTIQUE
NANTES
R. Loire

BRITTANY
AND THE BRETONS

BY THE SAME AUTHOR:

THE COMPANION GUIDE TO
KENT AND SUSSEX

BRITTANY
AND THE BRETONS

by

KEITH SPENCE

LONDON
VICTOR GOLLANCZ LTD
1978

ISBN 0 575 02494 1

Printed in Great Britain at
The Camelot Press Ltd, Southampton

To my mother

CONTENTS

LIST OF ILLUSTRATIONS

The photographs listed below are all by Keith Spence, unless otherwise specified.

PREFACE

My earliest memories of Brittany go back before the war. I remember the hot beach at Dinard (in those far-off summers the sun shone continually), the little ferry across the Rance to Saint-Malo, my attempts at swimming in a rubber ring, an Algerian called (I think) 'Pauvre Georges', who tramped along the beach attempting to sell carpets to sunbathing holiday-makers. I remember feeling solemn when my father said 'There's going to be a war', and we cut short our holiday and got back home in time for September 3, 1939. After that I did not see Brittany again for twenty years; but since 1959 I have been back with my own family almost every year, staying mainly at camp sites up and down the country. During those years Brittany has been steadily increasing in popularity as a tourist centre, and with the opening of the Brittany Ferries routes from Plymouth to Roscoff, and Portsmouth to Saint-Malo, not to mention the establishment of a network of motorways, the gentle tourist stream may soon become a flood. Brittany is a large and empty land, and can comfortably welcome vast numbers of visitors, except in July and August on the coast; but then this proviso applies to the whole of Europe. If you go only a few miles inland you can always find somewhere to stay, even at the height of the season. Those responsible for the future development of the country are aware of this, and are encouraging visitors to hire cottages inland and are attempting to bring prosperity to the most depressed areas by setting up national parks, with emphasis on nature conservation and the encouragement of traditional crafts and industries.

In a single book it is impossible to do justice to all the aspects of a country as large as Brittany, which is about 170 miles long by ninety or so wide and is thus comparable in size to Denmark. In fact, it is hard to give more than a partial outline of even a single aspect. Thus the reader who loves a particular spot in Brittany may well find that I have not mentioned it at all; while as far as the sailing aspect is concerned, my interest in the sea is confined to staggering thankfully ashore at Saint-Malo or Roscoff, while still capable of admiring the picturesqueness of flotillas of boats under sail dancing across the bays of Douarnenez or Quiberon. What I have tried to do is to follow my natural curiosity about matters left in the air by all the people I have spoken to and all the books I have consulted. For example, you cannot visit Nantes—or most other towns, for that matter—without coming across references to the Duchesse Anne de Bretagne; she was even quoted at me by an elderly boatman of the Grande Brière, rather as though a Norfolk fenman were to start talking about Good Queen Bess. So I have devoted a complete chapter to her life, which incidentally has a great bearing on the finest religious art and architecture produced in Brittany, and also, at some remove, on today's nationalists, since it was by Anne's marriage to two successive French kings that Brittany was eventually united to France. Similarly the overwhelming impact of the remains of the Atlantic Wall on the whole coastline led me to investigate the life led by the Bretons under the Nazi Occupation. Here again any attempt at a summary leads inevitably to the present day, as Brittany's current political situation owes much to the confusions and divided loyalties that stemmed from the alternatives of resistance or collaboration. Then I have devoted a good deal of space to Breton writers hitherto unknown to me: to poets like Tristan Corbière, of Roscoff, to Max Jacob, of Quimper, and above all to Hersart de la Villemarqué, who virtually created Breton literature single-handed (or who got the credit for doing so, which is perhaps much the same thing).

This book does not attempt to be a substitute for the *Michelin Green Guide*, which describes every place of importance in alphabetical order and, with its maps and lists of annual events, is an essential part of any visitor's luggage. For those who can read French, by far the best reference book is the *Guide de Bretagne*, published by the Brittany newspaper *Ouest-France* and written by a team of experts under the editorship of Michel Renouard. Like the *Michelin Guide* it is arranged alphabetically, and is especially rich in descriptions of churches, chapels and their furnishings. Then there is the series of monographs on Brittany published by Jos le Doaré, of Châteaulin, each heavily illustrated and devoted to a single subject, such as traditional furniture, or legends of the sea. Joseph Chardronnet's *Histoire de Bretagne* is a lucid and readable introduction; while Pierre-

Jakez Hélias's prizewinning autobiography, *Le Cheval d'Orgueil*, describes in minute detail what it was like to grow up in a remote corner of Brittany between the wars.

For the immense number of saints, and the places named after them, I have used two different styles: for the saints themselves, the English abbreviation St, as in St Malo; for the place, the French style, spelt out and hyphenated, Saint-Malo. Thus it should always be clear whether the person or the place is involved. Except where otherwise acknowledged, all the translations are my own, as are the photographs.

Among the many people who have helped me with information, hospitality or both over the past two years I would like to thank especially Bernard de Parades, of Quimper, for whom no question of mine has been too trivial and who has put his unrivalled knowledge of Breton folklore and music at my disposal; Erwan le Bris du Rest, of the Musée de Bretagne in Rennes, who introduced me to the ramifications of modern Breton politics; Dan Lailler, Director of the Saint-Malo Museum, an expert on corsair history; Annick Eschermann, founder of the Peintres de Bretagne; Fanch Gourvil and Donatien Laurent, authorities on the Breton literary revival; Per Denez, of Rennes University; Mme Léone Jarnet-Auffret, Director of the Brière National Park; and Toby Oliver, of the Brittany Information Bureau. Finally I would like to thank my wife Penny, who has come with me on nearly every trip to Brittany, and who has endured my Brittanomania with the minimum of complaint.

Tonbridge, Kent
October 1977

BRITTANY
AND THE BRETONS

CHAPTER I

The Land and the People

BRITTANY IS A stone goddess with many faces. There is the tourist face, often the only one the visitor sees: the Brittany of the beaches of Dinard and La Baule; of uncertain weather, when no two days are the same, and a chilly rainswept morning may be followed by a brilliant afternoon; the Brittany of cider, pancakes and mead; of heavy horsedrawn caravans trundling through the national parks; of lazy days pottering along the country's rivers and canals. This is the Brittany of the land-based holidaymaker; while for the small-boat sailor there is an entirely different face, and one which has its dangers. Every little creek round the whole coastline, from Cancale in the north to Le Croisic in the south, is a natural lure for boats; but the sea round Brittany is always unpredictable, with sudden fogs blanketing the coast, savage reefs and islets where even experienced sailors can run aground, and dangerous currents off Ushant, the Pointe du Raz and at the mouth of the Gulf of Morbihan. Then there is the monumental face of Brittany—the prehistoric alignments of Carnac, with their silent regiments of standing stones; the thousands of calvaries by the roadside; the parish enclosures with their carved figures, produced in a flowering of the sculptor's art without parallel elsewhere in Europe.

There is the folklore Brittany of the great annual festivals at Quimper and Concarneau and smaller gatherings all round the country, where for days on end the Bretons play on bagpipe and oboe and dance their hearts out under the open sky. There is the religious Brittany of the *pardons*, those penitential assemblies, now adapted somewhat for the tourist, which until a few generations ago were as much statements of local pride and patriotism as professions of faith. Finally there is what might be called the veiled face of Brittany, the Brittany that shares its roots with the other Celtic countries of Europe, and whose devotees range in attitude from the fanaticism of out-and-out nationalists to a benevolent interest in preserving the culture of their native land. This is the Brittany that it is the hardest for the outsider to pin down, or even to come into contact with, though its most raucous manifestations shout at you everywhere from slogans painted on walls and hoardings.

To the Bretons of past ages their country had only two faces: Armor, meaning 'the sea', from which the Romans took the name Gallia Armorica for the far west of Gaul; and Argoat, 'the woods'. Like the sea itself Armor's name lives on into the present, familiar to cross-Channel tourists as the name of the ferry *Armorique*. But Argoat has almost vanished, surviving precariously here and there in forests scattered around the centre of the country, which can still conjure up distant memories of the days when kings hunted through the endless woodland, when wild boar and wolf lurked in the undergrowth, and hermits, retiring from the world, built solitary huts in clearings beside springs and forest streams. In both Armor and Argoat, the stone bones of Brittany are never far to seek. A geologist could spend a lifetime studying the rocks that line the Breton coast. There are tremendous bastions like Cap Fréhel and Cap Sizun, where gulls and cormorants wheel and the sea crashes at the cliff's foot hundreds of feet below. There are strange lunar landscapes, such as the Pointe du Château in the extreme north, where black outcrops jut like rotting fangs above the seaweed-covered boulders; and the shattered coastline round from Aber-Wrac'h, in the furthest corner of Finistère, where wreckers once hung lanterns on the horns of their cattle to lure ships on to the rocks. There are curiosities like the pink granite boulders of Ploumanac'h and Trégastel, worn into extraordinary shapes—an elephant, a tortoise, a hat—by thousands of years of wind, rain and sea spray; and the Sillon de Talbert, the Chesil Bank of Brittany, a natural breakwater of rounded stones, where seakale and samphire flourish, and seaweed is collected and rotted down as fertiliser for the neighbouring farms.

Most stretches of coast have acquired romantic names, from the Emerald Coast—the best known of all—which stretches from Cancale to Le Val-André, taking in Saint-Malo and Dinard on the way, right round to La Baule in the south, where the beaches have been christened the Coast of Love, either in desperation at the lack of local natural phenomena, or in tribute to the effects of the greater warmth of the summer sun in that part of the world. When inventiveness fails, the givers of names fall back on a simple Côte Sauvage, as they have done along the Atlantic coast of the Quiberon peninsula, where the jagged foreshore is constantly battered and eroded by rollers that have nothing to stop their force between Brittany and the coast of America; yet on the other side of the peninsula, only a mile or so away, oysters can be gathered at low tide from the sand flats, such is the normally calm state of Quiberon Bay.

By contrast, the landscape of Argoat has little in the way of spectacular rock scenery. Its 'mountains' are hardly more than gentle hills, and the highest point—the Montagne Saint-Michel, in the Monts d'Arrée—is only 384 metres (1,250 feet). These hills are all that is left of the Armorican Massif, which, along with the Massif Central, formed the Hercynian Fold, heaved up from the sea-bed in a geological cataclysm about 500 million years ago. The Alps are comparative newcomers on the mountain scene, being only about one-tenth of that immense age. So old are Brittany's mountains that over much of the country the massif has been completely worn away, leaving exposed even older rocks that are among the most ancient on the whole face of the earth. If Argoat is deficient in dramatic mountains, the granite is never far from the surface, as inland farmers have found to their cost since agriculture was first practised in Brittany, and as the enormous number of quarries large and small bear witness. In two places shattered rocks, lakes and trees form the kind of landscape you might expect to find in Austria or elsewhere in the foothills of the Alps: round the pretty little town of Huelgoat, in the Monts d'Arrée; and on a more spectacular scale round the sinuous Lac de Guerlédan, which I saw in March, when it glinted like steel below the brown and leafless hills. To my mind the most dramatic rock formation in Argoat is off the beaten track, in wild country north of Rostrenen—the Gorges du Toul Goulic. In this wilderness of giant rounded boulders, some as big as cottages and many of them covered with a skin of soft green moss, the River Blavet disappears for several hundred yards below the tumbled boulders, roaring like an underground train. Erosion, or the hand of man, has carved one of the rocks with two dish-like hollows, ready for sacrifice to the subterranean god, and many of the overhangs of the Toul Goulic were surely used by prehistoric man as primitive shelters.

With such a wealth of stone lying ready to hand, it is not surprising that virtually every building in Brittany, from the medieval to the modern, is stone-built. Until recently, it would have been impossible to tell the date of a farmhouse or cottage, as stone dictated its own design of thick wall and massive fireplace, and the basic four walls were virtually indestructible. It is only in the last few years that the pattern has been broken, with pointless asymmetries of wall and gable, in the kind of house that invariably has a bogus menhir (standing stone) in the front garden. Yet even these places are built of great stone blocks, white-painted and slate-roofed; for stone is still the cheapest as well as the only suitable material for Breton houses. Nowadays stone comes from the quarries; but the earliest small houses were made from stones gathered up as the fields were cleared, the blocks unsuitable for building going to make up the *talus* round each little field. These stone walls, several feet high and with sloping sides, were covered with earth and soon became overgrown so that they looked like part of the natural scene, and became reservoirs of plant and animal life. Today they are neglected over much of the countryside; the trees planted along them to supply firewood, and once regularly pollarded, have grown to unmanageable size, and when they fall they often tear down a stretch of *talus* entangled in their roots. Elsewhere the *talus* has been bulldozed away, as our own hedges have been grubbed up, in the interests of larger units and supposedly greater efficiency. But where this happens, I was told, the field drainage pattern of centuries is altered, the ground loses its moisture-retaining capacity, and the ancient wisdom of the *talus*-building farmer is vindicated.

A land of granite breeds a granite race; and the Bretons, like the Auvergnats of the Massif Central, have a reputation for dourness. But one cannot generalise about them, any more than one can about any other nationality. And it must be remembered that the Bretons are a nation, as are the Welsh, in spite of centuries of gradual assimilation to the central power, both by deliberate French policy, and by the natural process of intermarriage, and living and working together. The Breton's fierce local patriotism is expressed in its most extreme form in the motto of the people of Saint-Malo, the Malouins, which runs 'A Malouin first, a Breton perhaps, a Frenchman if there's anything left over' ('*Malouin d'abord, breton peut-être, français s'il en reste*'). Bretons also have the reputation of being slower-witted than the typical Frenchman, and Breton jokes in France are as common as Irish ones in England, and as ill-founded. Much of the mutual incomprehension springs from the different cultures of Breton and Frenchman, reaching its most extreme form in their different languages; it is even said that Bretons were shot as spies in the First World War because they could not understand a challenge given to them in French. And the language barrier cuts Brittany itself into two halves: the western section of the country, Basse-Bretagne, is the Breton-speaking half (*bretonnant*); while the eastern section, Haute-Bretagne, is French-speaking.

The Bretons brought their language with them when they fled from Great Britain in the fifth century AD, driven out of Wales and Cornwall by the Angles and Saxons, and settled across the Channel in Little Britain—Petite Bretagne, soon shortened to simple Bretagne. Breton is still very similar to Welsh; a good many of the terms used to describe places are identical, or virtually so. *Aber* means 'estuary' in both languages; the Welsh *ynys*, island, is *enez* in Breton; *mynydd*, mountain, is *menez*; and so on. Many of Brittany's army of saints came from Wales, and where they settled they founded small religious communities whose names begin with the prefix Lan-, the Welsh Llan- with a single L. However, a certain amount of nonsense is talked about the way in which Bretons can understand Welshmen, and vice versa; and the same has been said about Bretons and those who still speak the ancient Cornish language. It has been claimed, for example, that when the first of the 'onion-Johnnies' from the Roscoff area landed in Cornwall soon after the war, they managed to make themselves understood by the first Cornish-speakers they met; and the same applied when they crossed the Bristol Channel into Wales. I have heard it irreverently suggested that this story was put about by the onion men themselves, who learnt a few words of Welsh in order to improve the sale of Brittany onions in the Valleys. I was also told that the onion-Johnnies brought back the habit of tea-drinking from Britain to Brittany, and that it is served round Roscoff incredibly strong, with a slug of red *vin ordinaire* in it to give it extra body. Fortunately, perhaps, I have never been offered this particular brew.

The Celtic countries are not renowned for their cooking, unless you count such fringe foods as haggis and laver bread; and Brittany is no exception. The marvellous meals that can certainly be eaten there owe more to the quality of the raw materials than to any cunning in the invention of new recipes—ingredients such as young lamb from the saltings on the Bay of Mont Saint-Michel, oysters from Cancale and the Morbihan, *langoustines* and mussels from almost anywhere on the coast, eels from the Grande Brière, artichokes from the farms round Roscoff. The best of the Breton fare is also the cheapest: if you are really hungry, you cannot do better than go to one of the *crêperies* that specialise in pancakes garnished with every flavour from fish to strawberry jam, order a couple of *crêpes* and wash them down with a litre or so of the local cider (the flat cider, *cidre bouché*, corresponding to the scrumpy of the West Country). The only wine produced in Brittany is Muscadet, a dryish white wine that comes from the Nantes region. As an apéritif there is mead or *hydromel*, usually sold as Chouchen, which is too heavy and sickly for my taste. However, the ancient Gauls are said to have performed wonders in battle after drinking mead, so it no doubt has its positive qualities. Traditional peasant *cuisine* is undergoing a revival at the moment in Breton homes, though it has not yet spread to the restaurants. The only dish I have tried is a stew of ham, dumplings and vegetables called *kig ha fars*, which is immensely filling, and the kind of meal that could see a Breton farmer through a hard afternoon's work in the fields.

Until roughly the beginning of this century Breton culture—meaning not only language and food, but clothing, furniture, music and dance—formed a remarkably homogeneous whole. The modern Breton writer Pierre-Jakez Hélias sums it up in the expression '*savoir-vivre*', an extension of the term '*savoir-faire*' to every aspect of life. Certain elements of this totality have been taken out of context, as it were, to form the current cultural revival, in which the music of *bombarde* and *biniou* (Breton oboe and bagpipe), traditional dances and the wearing of the old regional costumes on festive occasions play the major part. The fixtures and fittings of the houses—the box-bed (*lit-clos*), the bench-cum-chest (*banc-coffre*), the table-cum-larder (*table huche*), the marriage chest and the dresser—can all be seen in the local museums; as can the elaborate embroidered costumes, and the lace head-dresses (*coiffes*) still worn by a few old women here and there as part of their everyday attire. What has vanished without trace is the mental background of which all these were the outward manifestations: the terrors of death and the afterlife, the belief in a twilight world where a man going about his everyday tasks might stumble on the *korred* (elves), or even the sorcerer Merlin, where dreams and omens were closely scanned and interpreted, and where a dogged devotion to religion went hand in hand with the most irrational superstititions.

Superimposed on this ground-bass of everyday existence is the historical Brittany, bound up for at least 2,000 years with the major events of the outer world, beginning with Caesar's conquest of Gaul in 56 BC, and continuing with Romanisation and the influx from Britain in the last days of the Roman Empire. In the ninth century Nominoë welded the haphazard association of Breton clans into a kingdom, after defeating the Frankish army under Charles the Bald in 845—'the first date to remember in the history of Brittany,' says Joseph Chardronnet, 'and one scarcely found in textbooks on the history of France'. The monarchy lasted little more than sixty years, to be succeeded by the anarchy of the Norman invasions of the early tenth century, and then by the dukedom, which was Brittany's golden age. In 937 Alain Barbe-Torte, 'Alan of the Curly Beard', defeated the Normans outside Nantes and established the Duchy of Brittany, which lasted for nearly 600 years. It is not surprising that many Bretons look back with nostalgia to the days of the Dukes; after all, for a period as long as from the battle of Agincourt to the present day Brittany was autonomous, owing allegiance to no other sovereign or state. Since 1532, when the union of Brittany and France was finally accomplished, Brittany has been just another large region in a major nation state, chafing at her subordinate role and on one occasion, in 1675, flaring into active revolt. The Revolution abolished the States of Brittany—a legislative body which met only irregularly but which gave the Bretons a certain amount of control over their own affairs; and nineteenth-century educational reforms did their best to weld the whole of France into a unity. At the moment it seems unlikely that Brittany will win much in the way of self-determination from the central government in France. But among her many faces is a face set firmly towards survival; and in their ability to endure Brittany and the Bretons are still as one.

Until France's local-government reorganisation during the 1960s Brittany had five Départements or administrative regions. In the reshuffle, the Département of Loire-Atlantique, with the splendid city of Nantes as its capital, was removed from Brittany, to form part of the new Pays de la Loire region. But Nantes has played such a major part in Breton history and culture that it cannot possibly be left out of any book on Brittany. The four remaining Départements are Ille-et-Vilaine, with its capital (*préfecture*) at Rennes, which is also the capital of the whole of Brittany; Côtes-du-Nord (capital, Saint-Brieuc); Finistère (capital, Quimper); and Morbihan (capital, Vannes). Apart from Morbihan, which means in Breton 'Little Sea' (Mor Bihan), from the Gulf which forms its heart, all the other departmental names are purely functional, and reflect the bureaucratic minds of those who doled them out after the Revolution. Thus the Ille and the Vilaine are two rivers that meet at Rennes; while Côtes-du-Nord and Finistère mean simply 'North Coasts' and 'Land's End'. Pre-Revolutionary Brittany was divided along quite different lines, according to the bishoprics that dated back to the first days of Christianity in the country, prefixed by the word *Bro*, meaning 'land'—Bro Dreger for the Tréguier diocese, Bro Zol for Dol, Bro Naoned for Nantes, Bro Gwened for Vannes. Some old regional names have died out, like Domnonea for the north central section, and Waroch—the name of an early warlord—for the south-east of Brittany. But one name has survived all the changes of fashion, perhaps because it has no exact geographical reality. Kerne or Cornouaille, the Breton Cornwall, with all its resonances of myth and legend back to the days of good King Gradlon of Quimper, still lives as powerfully as ever.

CHAPTER II

Villages of the Dead

THE GREAT MEGALITHIC civilisation that, between about 3000 and 1500 BC, erected its standing stones grouped or in isolation round the Atlantic seaboard of Europe left behind in Brittany its most extensive memorials. These are the immensely long rows of stones known as the *alignements* of Carnac, which run for miles across the heath a little way inland from the seaside delights of Carnac Plage. I have seen the alignments in the rain, when the scene was indescribably depressing; and on a summer's day so hot that all one could do was find a convenient clump of trees and picnic in its shade. On those two occasions the stone rows had no mystery about them at all. But the third time I saw them was on a misty October evening, when whatever sun had shone during the afternoon had vanished into the murk. A few yards from the road and I was lost, on ground that resonated eerily under foot, among the dank grey stones that stretched into infinity like an army of ghosts.

The stones of Carnac are of two types: the menhirs, or single standing stones (from the Breton *men*, stone, and *hir*, long); and the dolmens, which consist of two uprights and a horizontal laid across them (from *dol*, table, and *men*, stone). These are the remains of burial chambers, and were originally covered with earth to form tumuli or burial mounds. England's main megalithic monuments, Stonehenge and Avebury, are stone circles and have nothing to equal them in Brittany; though there are circles of less impressive dimensions at the end of the Carnac alignments. Carnac's menhirs, taken individually, are not particularly impressive; there are many far larger ones scattered over the uplands of Brittany. It is their sheer number that overwhelms you. As you drive past the alignments—or preferably walk along them—you are staggered by the magnitude of the ten or eleven striding lines, and you wonder what colossal powers of organisation set them there, and to what purpose.

It is generally thought nowadays that the megalith builders were a caste of priest-kings, and that their constructions were set up as giant observatories linked to the movements of the heavenly bodies. With exclusive knowledge of the correct dates for sowing and harvesting, such priests would be in a position of commanding authority among a primitive farming population. Early writers peopled the stones with Druids carrying out ghastly rituals of human sacrifice; yet for all the modern research into azimuth lines, and the rising and setting points of various stars 4,000 years ago, we are not much nearer certainty than our ancestors. A facetious Breton once remarked to me that the menhirs were put there to enable Stone Age man to get away from sabre-toothed tigers by shinning up them; and when Gustave Flaubert described the site in 1847 he had similar fun at the theorists' expense. The stones mark the graves of warriors who died in battle; they are laid out in the shape of the Python worshipped at Delphi; they are a Druid temple used also for great gatherings, and the rows of stones are streets between which the Druids built their huts; finally, they were erected by Caesar's troops as giant tentpegs to stop their tents blowing away in the Brittany gales. With a final grand gesture, Flaubert reaches his own conclusion: '*irréfutable, irréfragable, irrésistible*'. The stones of Carnac are large stones!

Like all the most awe-inspiring places, Carnac can make you take refuge in the kind of cheeky irreverence in which Flaubert indulged. In our own day, the world of ancient Gaul has been satirised in the Astérix books of Goscinny and Uderzo, which narrate in strip-cartoon form the adventures of Astérix himself, the Druid Panoramix, the tribal chief Abraracourcix, Obélix, who never goes anywhere without a menhir on his back, and a large supporting cast of Gauls and Romans. Obélix himself has his origins in Breton legend, where the elves known as the Korred are said to have brought the menhirs to Brittany on their backs. Nancy Arrowsmith gives an account of the Korred's habits and physical appearance in *A Field Guide to the Little People*. They are magicians and dancers, and know the secrets of the treasures buried under the standing stones. They help ordinary mortals with the loan of oxen, and will sharpen knives and scythes left out overnight. They are from one to three feet tall, and are startling to look at. 'The Korred's bodies are hunched, their skin black, their hair dark and shaggy, and their eyes, set far back into their heads, are the colour of burned rubies. Instead of fingers, the Korred have cats' claws, as well as goats' hooves in the place of feet. Their voices are cracked and muffled but they have an extraordinarily loud laugh.' (The name of the Korred still survives in place-names such as Concoret, on the edge of the Forest of Brocéliande.)

The Korred have vanished long ago from Carnac, driven into hiding (though where can they hide?) by the tourist crowds. And the hordes of children who used to offer to guide you round the alignments have vanished, as has the old lady who welcomed us years ago with the incantation '*Soyez les bienvenus au pays de menhirs*' ('Welcome to the land of the standing stones'). At the height of the season the alignments swarm with people, walking among the stones, and even climbing up them with no one taking any particular notice. A number of the menhirs are now suffering badly from the onslaught; and it cannot be long before they are fenced off, as at Stonehenge, though at Carnac the problems of fencing and patrolling such a vast area would be far greater. Not only are the alignments themselves jammed in high summer to bursting-point: the narrow roads that run alongside are packed solid with cars; and at a busy weekend it can take half an hour to drive through the little village of Carnac itself. As for Carnac's small museum, the crowds shuffling between the cases make it impossible to get more than a glimpse of the exhibits, apart from the carved stones on the walls. So do not go to Carnac, if you can possibly help it, in either July or August. When the crowds have gone, the museum is well worth a visit, partly for the exhibits—the arrowheads and axes, the skeletons, and most fascinating of all the stones carved with dots, whorls and crosses, filled in with red ochre—and partly because since it was first founded it has been very much a family concern. Its origins are summed up in its name, which is the Musée J. Miln-Z. Le Rouzic, named jointly after its founder, and the man who ran it for almost sixty years.

James Miln was a Scottish amateur archaeologist who began work at Carnac in 1874; Zacharie Le Rouzic was his chief assistant, taking over the excavations and the collection that forms the nucleus of the museum when Miln died suddenly in 1881. Miln published two books on his findings: the first in 1877, on a group of field mounds called Le Bossenno, which he discovered to be the remains of a substantial Roman villa; and the second, which appeared posthumously in 1881, on the alignments of Kermario. This second volume includes a brief sketch by his publisher, David Douglas, of Miln's life. He was born in Forfarshire in 1818, and as a young man travelled widely in India, China, New Zealand and other remote parts of the world. 'Naturally observant and reflective,' wrote Mr Douglas, 'the knowledge which he thus acquired of different races of men in different stages of culture and civilisation, drew him gradually to the study of archaeology, to which he finally devoted himself with a degree of energy and ardour but rarely exhibited.'

Fortunately Miln had the money to indulge his passion—at one time, he tells us, he even thought of buying the land on which Le Bossenno was situated—and he made Carnac's Hôtel des Voyageurs his headquarters from 1873, when he first arrived in Carnac, until 1880. He died while seeing his second volume through the press, a few days after learning that his services to archaeology had been recognised by the Société Polymathique du Morbihan—a learned society at Vannes—who had elected him vice-president. His books consist largely of lists and meticulous drawings of the objects he unearthed; but what distinguishes them from today's dry treatises is the occasional glimpse of the local peasant way of life, which was vanishing before his eyes as surely as the Stone Age civilisation had vanished thousands of years before.

Miln was in fact far more interested in Roman remains than in evidence of earlier cultures. As to the origin of the alignments, he was aware of astronomical theories but inclined more to some kind of burial tradition, largely on the grounds that the name Kermario means in Breton 'the village of death'. He did in fact find plenty of Roman objects at the western end of the alignments, inside a quadrilateral arrangement of massive walls that were almost certainly a Roman camp, used in later centuries as a place of temporary defence. So the story of Caesar's tentpegs may not have been so far from the truth after all, especially in view of the fact that Miln discovered a number of menhirs built into the Romans' wall. Elsewhere he found that one of the stones had been overturned at an early date to form a crude fireplace, and his own workmen 'frequently, during showers, found a good shelter round the fireplace under this menhir, where they had relighted the fire extinguished for many centuries'. In other respects too his discoveries linked generations remote from each other. Of a pottery fragment found at Kermario, he noted that 'vases of this form are still made at Quimper, and are used for carrying food to the working classes by their wives and children'. Moreover, to judge from the smallness of the fingerprints on some of the fragments, the everyday items of pottery were made by women, and Miln found that in local potteries this was still the case; the men made only the really large bowls and dishes.

Though the Kermario excavations are of greater relevance today, since they relate to what can still be seen on the ground, Miln's work at Le Bossenno was far more interesting, and he describes it with much greater excitement and enthusiasm. He excavated eight mounds altogether, and found that together they formed an extensive Gallo-Roman villa complex, which included a small dwelling-house, a larger dwelling with bath-house adjoining it, a blacksmith's workshop with forge, and a small temple or *lararium*. The bath-house ceiling was originally brilliantly decorated in multi-coloured stripes and lozenges, with shells—oysters, whelks, snails and cockles—embedded in regular patterns, so that the interior must have looked like an eighteenth-century shell grotto. Among the finds were knives and brooches, sinkers for fishing lines or nets, and round pieces of tile that Miln's workmen identified as discs for the game of *palet*, a kind of quoits they played themselves.

The most fascinating of all the objects was a small bronze statuette of an ox. When it was unearthed, the workmen crowded round excitedly and told Miln that they had discovered 'the ox of St Carnély'. Carnély or Cornély (Cornelius) is the patron saint of Carnac, and on September 13 every year a cattle festival is still held in his honour. In Miln's day it was a full-scale *pardon*, with a fair for the sale of animals, booths, merry-go-rounds, and the usual files of pilgrims proceeding round the church on their knees. The date, September 13, is nearly that of the autumn equinox, which no doubt sets the festival right back in pagan times. Miln describes a far more curious ritual concerned with cattle, which also must be pagan. When sick cattle had been cured, they were driven in solemn silence from the farm to the church, and from there to the fountain of St Cornély, where water was poured over them. Then in the same silence the journey was reversed, and they were driven back past the church and so home. The cattle were also made to pass through the smoke of the bonfires on Midsummer Eve (June 24), which was believed to keep them from disease during the following year. The biggest fire of all was lit on the tumulus of Mont Saint-Michel, outside Carnac, and from Miln's account it sounds as though he himself was asked to light it. 'When it is desired to honour a stranger, he is asked to set fire to the huge pile of furze, which, blazing up in an instant, lightens up the whole hill and neighbourhood, amidst shouts of joy from the spectators.'

Cornelius is an odd kind of patron saint—and fittingly so, as Carnac is a very odd kind of place. He is said to have been one of the early popes, martyred in 252 or 253 under the Emperor Decius, and he is always portrayed with the papal tiara on his head. The explanation of how he got from Rome to Brittany is far-fetched enough. Fleeing from Rome from the menace of the pagan armies, he headed north and then west through Italy and Gaul, on a chariot drawn by two oxen. With his pursuers hard on his heels he reached Carnac, where he turned and saw the army marching towards him in regular columns. Whereupon he uttered a tremendous curse, and the troops were immediately turned to stone; they have been standing there, rank on rank, ever since. The link between saint, horned beasts and standing stones must put the origins of Cornély back in the Stone Age, or at least in the period of the Druids. His figure looms through the murk of swirling peoples and fluctuating religions, whose only surviving relics are Carnac's lines of petrified figures.

A further curiosity about Carnac, or at least about its church, is that the main entrance is on the north side, in the direction of the menhirs, instead of on the southern side, as is almost universal in church-building. It has been suggested that for countless generations pilgrims had made the southward journey through the lines of megaliths, and that when Christianity took over, the walk was continued a little further, right to the door of the church. In Miln's time the peasants still had the habit of building a stone axe or celt into the chimney, where it was supposed to ward off lightning; and as late as the nineteenth century stone axes are said to have been used locally in a far more sinister ritual. According to the *Guide de la Bretagne Mystérieuse*, the peasants carried out a form of primitive euthanasia by means of neolithic axe heads, which they called 'the blessed hammer' ('*er mel beniged*'). To spare the dying any further agony, they were speeded on their way by a blow on the head from a stone axe. And to this day the Roman Catholic Church's ritual contains a gentler version of this grim practice: when a pope dies, he is struck three times on the skull with a silver hammer by the senior cardinal, as a faint echo of the final rites submitted to by the pontiffs of the Neolithic Age.

As to the derivation of the name Carnac, I have always had a hope that it would prove to derive directly from the Egyptian Karnak, one city of stone at the centre of the ancient world giving its name to another cruder city on the very edge of it. And Miln gives a grain of support to the theory by his statement that the decoration on some of the pottery fragments found at Le Bossenno was of Egyptian type. The fourth-century *Notitia Dignitatum* (a kind of Imperial Roman *Who's Who*) mentions the '*prefectus militum Maurorum Venetorum Venetis*' (commander of the Moorish troops at Vannes of the Veneti); and Miln comments that the similarity of pottery might be accounted for 'by the fact of African soldiers having been stationed in the Morbihan and in Finistère'. Entertaining though the thought of Negro or Arab legionaries on the Breton coast may be, the theory does not really hold up beside the two other alternatives: that the syllable *Carn-* is either the Breton *karn-*, meaning 'horn', and having to do with cattle; or that it is the same as 'cairn', and means a mound of stones on a tumulus. The termination *-ac* is one of the commonest place endings in Brittany.

After Miln's death in 1881, Zacharie Le Rouzic took over the excavations. He must have been the youngest professional archaeologist of all time, as he was born in 1864 and was thus only ten when he became Miln's chief assistant, and eleven when he was put in charge of the collection of objects excavated by Miln. From 1881 until his death in 1939 he was the uncrowned king of Carnac archaeology. In his book *Lascaux and Carnac*, Professor Glyn Daniel has fond memories of the old man, who helped him greatly when he was an undergraduate in the 1930s. The family tradition is carried on at Carnac Museum, where Le Rouzic's son-in-law, M. Maurice Jacq, took over from Le Rouzic as Curator. In a letter he kindly wrote to me, M. Jacq described the old man as *un grand chercheur*—'a great searcher who explored the whole of Brittany to compare the other megalithic monuments with those of the Morbihan. There is not a scrap of ground that was not excavated and explored by this great archaeologist (*ce grand fouilleur*).' The present Curator is Mme Bailloud, M. Jacq's daughter and Le Rouzic's grand-daughter.

There are three main alignments near Carnac. Those of Ménec and Kermario are each over a kilometre long and average about 100 metres wide; while the Kerlescan alignment is shorter, at about 880 metres, and wider, at about 140 metres. If one assumes that the alignments have astronomical significance, then perhaps each one represents a successive refinement of observational techniques, or a shift in the major constellations, making it necessary to lay out a new enfilade of stones. The general direction of all of them is east-north-east, with the circles and the largest of the menhirs at the western end.

The finest of the dolmens are those of Kercado, near the alignments, and the massive construction known as the Table des Marchands, across the Crach river near Locmariaquer. The gigantic capstone of this chamber tomb is twenty feet long by thirteen wide; old photographs show it perched precariously on three or four slender uprights, which gave it the look of a table for giants or Stone Age gods to eat off. In recent years it has been walled in, as it was originally. A few carvings can still be made out on the granite roof. Not far away is the smashed menhir called the Grand Menhir Brisé. Now in four pieces, it originally stood about sixty feet above ground and weighed an estimated 330 tons—almost as tall as Cleopatra's Needle and nearly twice as heavy.

The whole of the lozenge-shaped stretch of land, from the mouth of the Etel to the narrow strait that leads into the Gulf of Morbihan, is thick with dolmens and menhirs, looming among the holiday cottages and giving a superhuman dimension to what would otherwise be a dreary area of heathland. Of the centuries of endeavour that went into their building, no other evidence remains. If one could imagine a world where the technology of Jodrell Bank was combined with the religious symbolism of Westminster Abbey, one might begin to understand the significance of those enigmatic fields of stone.

Beyond Locmariaquer, with its flat black oyster boats and neat little church, the land tapers away to the Pointe de Kerpenhir. At the very end of the promontory, overlooking the fast-flowing channel beyond which lies the Presqu'Ile de Rhuys, is an incongruity that typifies this odd corner of Brittany. A German blockhouse, still containing the rusty remains of a gun, squats on the headland ready to blow anything that moves out of the water, while below on the rocks a statue of the Virgin gives her protection to the yachts dancing in and out of the gulf.

It was in these waters that Julius Caesar in 56 BC defeated the fleet of the Gauls. The previous year he thought he had pacified the country, but the Veneti, with their capital at Vannes, detained and imprisoned the Roman envoys sent to them, and set about stirring up a general revolt. The Veneti, Caesar tells us in the *Gallic War* (translation by S. A. Handford), 'are much the most powerful tribe on this coast. They have the largest fleet of ships, in which they traffic with Britain; they excel the other tribes in knowledge and experience of navigation; and as the coast lies exposed to the violence of the open sea and has but few harbours, which the Veneti control, they compel nearly all who sail those waters to pay toll.' The Gauls were used to sailing the open waters of the Atlantic, and their ships were very similar to medieval or Spanish galleons. 'Exceptionally high bows and sterns fitted them for use in heavy seas and violent gales, and the hulls were made entirely of oak, to enable them to stand any amount of shocks and rough usage. The cross-timbers, which consisted of beams a foot wide, were fastened with iron bolts as thick as a man's thumb. The anchors were secured with iron chains instead of ropes. They used sails made of raw hides or thin leather.'

During the winter Caesar ordered boats to be built on the Loire—traditional boats of Roman type, propelled by oars, and in normal conditions on the open sea no match for the Veneti's dreadnoughts. The only advantage the Romans had was that of speed. In all other respects the Gauls' ships were superior: better in stormy conditions, impossible to ram because they were so solid, and too high for grappling or boarding. After he had wasted some weeks capturing a few coastal strongholds, Caesar decided on a full-scale naval battle. The exact locality is disputed, but it is generally thought to have been off Port-Navalo, opposite the Pointe de Kerpenhir. The battle was fought under the eyes of Caesar and the whole army; the actual vantage-point has never been decided. However, south of Port-Navalo is a tumulus, covered in gorse and bracken, called the Butte de César (Caesar's Mound) which answers well enough; there is no need to assume that popular tradition is necessarily wrong. From the Butte there are tremendous views in one direction over the sea and in the other over the Gulf of Morbihan. It would have been much too far to exercise direct control over the fleet: presumably Caesar had his throne carried to the top of the tumulus, kept his fingers crossed, and waited. In the event, he had both tactics and luck on his side. The Gauls put to sea with no fewer than 220 of their massive craft, and to begin with the Roman admiral Brutus was unsure how to deal with them. Eventually the day was won by a very simple device: the Romans hooked the Gauls' rigging by means of large hooks fixed on long poles; the ropes were pulled taut, and then snapped when the galleys rowed hard away. The Gallic ships were virtually becalmed, and when the wind fell altogether there was nothing they could do. The Romans took one ship after another, and the Veneti were routed. Without ships, they could no longer defend their strongholds, and so they surrendered.

Caesar's treatment of them was merciless. 'He resolved to make an example of them in order to teach the natives to be more careful in future about respecting the rights of ambassadors: he had all their councillors executed and the rest of the population sold as slaves.' Like Alexander the Great in the lands that he conquered, the resonances of Julius Caesar's name lingered on down the ages in Brittany. Below the tumulus of Saint-Michel at Carnac, where Miln and later excavators discovered remains from the Roman period, the body of Caesar was said to lie in a golden coffin, with stones piled in a mound above him.

Roman remains above ground in Brittany are few and far between. The best-preserved Gallo-Roman walls to be seen are those of the so-called Temple de Mars, a little south of Corseul, not far from Dinan. They stand isolated in the middle of a field, beyond a farm, and bear little resemblance to any other fragment of a temple I have ever seen. What survives looks like part of an octagonal apse from some much larger building, made of a double 'skin' of small granite bricks, with stone rubble filling between. It is the kind of place that would repay systematic excavation, and it is surprising that it never seems to have been seriously investigated. The Temple de Mars is a prosaic mystery, suitable for the God of War. But the Goddess of Love is a different being altogether; and it is to be expected that Brittany's Venus should be far more elusive and evocative. The so-called Vénus de Quinipily is back in the direction of Carnac, west of the little town of Baud. She is marked clearly enough on the Michelin map; nevertheless, it needs a good deal of application to track her down. You follow the 'Camping' sign down a small road that runs out at a farm. A painted notice in the orchard bears the single word 'Vénus'; a few yards down a track, and there she stands, on top of a stone canopy and above what appears to be a huge stone bathtub. She is quite unlike the beautiful Venus you might expect: squat-bodied and thin-limbed, she is naked except for a headband and a scarf that falls below her waist. She looks Egyptian, even Red Indian, and has been identified variously as Cybele, as Isis, as an unknown goddess of the Gauls, or as a fake. Until the seventeenth century she stood on a hill a few miles to the north at Castennec, once the site of a settlement of the Gauls called Sulim. She was known as the Iron Woman (*Ar Gwreg Houarn*), and was venerated by the local peasants to such a degree that the Bishop of Vannes had her torn down and thrown in the River Blavet. In 1696 the Seigneur de Quinipily retrieved her, eroded by water but more or less in one piece, and set her up where she now stands, gazing across a fertile little valley towards a jumble of grey stone farm buildings. Venus or Isis, what does it really matter? She is yet another calm stone enigma of this extraordinary region.

CHAPTER III

Saint of Action, Saint of Law

THE ANCIENT TOWN of Dol is the first place of any consequence in Brittany reached by road from Cherbourg or the Pas de Calais, and a delightful introduction it is. The main street is lined with medieval stone houses, many of them with upper storeys that jut so far that they form arcades underneath; as a cross-Channel tribute, no doubt to the exiled James II, it is called the Grande Rue des Stuarts. Overlooking a square just off the Saint-Malo road is Dol's granite cathedral, the most austere, impressive and strange of all Brittany's cathedrals. Built mainly in the thirteenth century, it has two west towers, one of which looks as though a giant hand has snapped off its top; though it was in fact never completed. The windows still retain some of their medieval stained glass, illustrating episodes from the life of St Samson of Dol, one of the two dedicatees of the cathedral, and a Welshman, as was St Magloire, the other dedicatee.

Of all Brittany's reputed 7,847 saints—the strange-looking number is in fact the sum total of seven thousand, seven hundred, seven score and seven—Samson is probably the one of whom we know the most. He is one of the seven at the top of the league, as it were—the 'Seven Founding Saints' ('*Sept Saints Fondateurs*'), along with Sts Malo, Brieuc, Tugdual, Paul-Aurelian, Corentin and Patern. While the lives of most other Breton saints have come down to us as written transcriptions of a distant oral tradition, the anonymous *Life of St Samson* was written fairly soon after his death, within half a century at the most. Samson was probably born about 490, in North Wales, where his father was a court official. He was educated at one of the most famous seats of learning in Wales, the monastery of Llantwit, in Glamorgan, founded by St Illtyd, who was still abbot when Samson went there. At Llantwit he was a fellow-pupil of St Paul-Aurelian (St Pol), and was renowned at this early age for the intensity of his learning and the enthusiasm of his fasts. Illtyd must have been an excellent and sympathetic teacher, if we are to believe the *Life*. Young Samson learnt the alphabet in a day and could read in a week, and Illtyd had to discourage him from ruining the health of his growing frame by excessive fasting.

Abbot Illtyd was 'a most wise magician, who had knowledge of the future' ('*magicus sagacissimus et futurorum praescius*'), and on the strength of this remark the suggestion has been made that he was a Druid, either by birth or by descent. If this is so, then he was by no means the last great teacher who has had one foot in two opposing idealistic camps; and in the fifth and sixth centuries Christianity was still in a precarious state on the western fringes of Europe. A century later, Gregory of Tours could write pessimistically that 'after the missionary preaching of the bishops, the earlier generations were converted from their pagan temples and turned towards the churches; now they are busy plundering those same churches' (Lewis Thorpe's translation). And on their missions Samson and his fellow Welshmen were to find how hard it was to make many permanent conversions.

As a star pupil, Samson inspired envy among his less talented fellows, especially after he had cured one of the monks of snake-bite, and even more so when a miraculous dove sat on his shoulder during the whole service when he was ordained deacon. Illtyd's two nephews were so concerned that Illtyd would bequeath the monastery to Samson instead of to themselves that they tried to poison him. Samson, however, drained the poisoned cup they gave him 'without the slightest twinge of heartburn', and the brothers were finally driven to admit the error of their envious ways. Like all the most respected saints, Samson killed a fire-breathing dragon early in his career. This particular dragon not only breathed fire, but it tore up clods of earth and threw them in the Saint's face; however, when Samson advanced on it singing psalms it rolled itself into a ball and began to eat its own tail. The account of the dragon's death shows Samson using magic practices that he had no doubt learned from Illtyd. Drawing a circle round it with his staff he placed a crucifix within the circle; the dragon crept round and round the cross, unable to escape from the magic circle. Finally Samson called on it to die in the name of Christ.

It stood on its tail, lifted up its head, made an 'absurd' loop of its body (*inepte*, says the writer of the *Life*), spat out its poison and fell dead.

By now Llantwit was becoming too small for St Samson, and he set out on the first of his journeys. He went to Ireland, in the company of some learned Irishmen who were returning home from Rome. In Ireland he cast a devil out of an abbot who had lost his reason; then he returned to Britain, where he became a hermit in a cave beside the Severn. He was persuaded to leave this retreat, and was appointed first abbot and then bishop, probably about AD 520. Then, commanded in a vision to preach the Gospel beyond the seas, he crossed the Bristol Channel and landed in Cornwall. The *Life* gives a circumstantial account of an episode that took place in Tricurius, which has been identified as the Hundred of Trigg, and illustrates the way in which the early missionaries adapted the worship of standing stones to their own religion, rather as Cortes a thousand years later was to do with the Aztec temples. The local inhabitants were worshipping the stone

> after the custom of the Bacchantes, by means of a play in honour of an image. Thereupon St Samson beckoned to his brothers that they should stand still and be silent while he himself, quietly descending from his chariot to the ground and standing upon his feet and observing those who worshipped the idol, saw in front of them, resting on the summit of a certain hill, an abominable image. On this hill I myself have been and have adored and with my hand have traced the sign of the cross which St Samson with his own hand carved by means of an iron instrument on a standing stone. When St Samson saw the image, selecting two only of the brothers to be with him, he hastened quickly towards them, their chief, Guedianus, standing at their head, and gently admonished them that they ought not to forsake the one God who created all things and worship an idol.
>
> (Thomas Taylor's translation)

The Cornishmen were furious, and told St Samson to mind his own business, saying that they had a perfect right to follow the practices of their ancestors. For the word I have translated 'practices' the *Life* has the curious word *mathematicum*; in late Latin this meant 'astrology' rather than 'mathematics' in the strict sense. No doubt the men of Trigg were performing some Druidic ritual concerned with standing stones. Whatever they were doing, a miracle was at hand to serve the saint's purposes. One of the young men of the tribe was thrown from a horse and appeared to have broken his neck, but Samson prayed over him and brought him back to life. There and then the chief and all his tribesmen threw themselves at Samson's feet and destroyed their idol.

Even more fascinating in its religious implications is a confrontation that took place earlier in Samson's life, in a remote Welsh forest. On this occasion his antagonist was an old sorceress (*theomacha*, literally 'woman who fights against God'), dressed in rags and brandishing a trident, who had half-killed a young deacon travelling with Samson. When the saint caught up with her, she dropped her trident and stood rooted to the spot. He asked her who she was, and she told him: 'I am a sorceress, and the women of my race have until now sinned against you and yours, and now no one of my race is left in this forest except for me. For I have eight sisters and my mother is still alive, and they do not live here but in a wood still more remote, and I have been left in this wilderness by my husband, and my husband is dead, and for this reason I cannot leave the forest.' The saint asked her to bring the monk back to life, but she refused, saying that she had been brought up to do evil and was not going to start doing good at this late stage in her life. So Samson prayed for her to die, whereupon she dropped dead of a heart attack; and Samson revived the deacon by giving him the kiss of life.

This may be evidence of a cult even more ancient than the male-dominated religion of the Druids: a survival of the earlier worship of the Mother Goddess, driven into the remotest places by Druidism, as Druidism was itself driven by Christianity; and still served by a few hereditary priestesses, roaming the forests with their tridents like a coven of ancient and bloodthirsty Britannias.

St Samson has left traces of his passage through Cornwall in a village named after him near Fowey. Surprisingly, the *Life* gives no indication of what he did between the time he left

Cornwall and the time he arrived at Dol, apart from stating that he cured a man's leprous wife and possessed daughter at the spot where he landed. It could have been anywhere on the north coast; there is a village of Saint-Samson just north of Dinan, which would have been more or less on any direct route east towards Dol. All we are told is that, 'going from thence, having God for his guide, he discovered a most suitable spot in these parts and founded a famous monastery which to this day, by an appropriate use of language, is called Dol. From that place he planted the seed of many works of a wonderful character and founded many monasteries throughout almost the entire province, which, if all of them were described, one by one, we should be led to exceed the task we undertook' (Thomas Taylor's translation).

As Bishop of Dol, Samson must have spent an enormous amount of time and energy organising the rudimentary Church in North Brittany, but there is no indication of this in the *Life*. The few chapters that are devoted to those years concentrate on his relations with Childebert, King of the Franks, who died in 558, which means that Samson must have been a power in the land well before that date. We are told that Comorrus, with the connivance of Childebert, had usurped the throne of Brittany after killing Jonas, the rightful ruler, and handed over Jonas's son and heir, Judual, to Childebert. Hearing that Childebert proposed to put Judual to death, St Samson went to the Frankish court in Paris to persuade the king to change his mind. If we are to believe the account in the *Life*, Childebert was a mere pawn, manipulated by his evil queen, who tried to eliminate Samson in a variety of unpleasant ways; though not until Samson had threatened that the Franks would be dishonoured through their children (*degenerari a suis seminibus*) if Judual was not handed over to him. Abusing the saint in the vilest language, 'which it is not fit to repeat', the queen tried to poison him; but the cup broke in the cupbearer's hand and cut him to the bone. Next, she chose a wild horse for him to ride, hoping that it would throw and kill him, but he tamed it with the sign of the Cross. Finally, as a last resort, she ordered the keepers to provoke a captive lion and release it against him. When Samson advanced unswervingly towards it, the lion turned tail, pursued by the saint invoking the name of Christ and hurling javelins at it 'as though from a spiritual catapult'. This combination of physical and moral assault was too much for the lion, which fell dead on the spot. Childebert and his wicked queen had a change of heart; and Judual was released and returned with Samson to Brittany, where he overthrew Comorrus and took his rightful place on the throne.

For all its fanciful elaborations, the encounter with the lion shows that sixth-century bishops were men of iron rather than gentle pastors. The spears that Samson carried were his 'usual weapons' ('*solitis armis*')—a tradition of the warrior-prelate that was still going strong five centuries later, when Bishop Odo of Bayeux wielded his mace against the Saxons at the Battle of Hastings. In general physical appearance St Samson, St Pol, St Magloire and the rest must have looked far more like Mohican braves than like the elderly men of learning who wear the bishop's mitre today. Describing the Irish saints of the sixth century—and from the religious viewpoint Ireland, Wales and Brittany were virtually indistinguishable—Gerhard Herm writes in *The Celts*: 'The world in which they lived was a copy of that known to us from the sagas; monasteries resembled large ring forts and became associated with others in centrally directed federations. Spear-carrying abbots preferred the "Johannes tonsure" as well: they did not cut out a circular patch at the back of the head but shaved from ear to ear, leaving the hair long at the back—in the Druid style, as many interpreters have suggested.' The reference to ring forts makes sense of the final summary of the life's work of St Samson, which says that he 'built and fortified catholic churches' both inside and outside Brittany.

The date of his death or his age are not recorded: Père Albert Le Grand, the seventeenth-century chronicler of the lives of the Breton saints, says that he died in 615, aged 120, or in 607, aged 112. But Le Grand is not renowned for his chronological accuracy. Assuming that Samson was born about 490, and that eighty was an enormous age for those days, he would have died in about 570. This would fit in with the suggested date of 610–615 for the *Life*, which, according to its anonymous author, is derived from an account written by St Samson's nephew, who handed it on to his own nephew in turn. The author amplified the written account by talking to this great-nephew and to monks from Llantwit. Whatever the date of Samson's death, 'having finished his course, a course good and beyond measure, he left his wasted body to be embalmed and buried in the sacred mound in the monastery at Dol'.

Though the *Life* is so circumstantial, it gives little clue to St Samson's character, apart from the fact that he liked to have his own way. The virtues listed are negative ones. First, he was chaste. 'From the first flower of his youth until his blessed end he happily and completely conquered the incentive to lust, alike in respect of the male and the female sex.' Second, he was a vegetarian. 'He never throughout his whole life tasted the flesh of any animal or winged creature' (though fish is not mentioned). But the greatest stress is laid on his sobriety. 'No one ever saw him drunk, nor did any kind of drink injure him in any way, either by making his mind wander or his steps totter, to the smallest degree.' Perhaps by stressing the negative virtues, the author was tacitly rebuking the clergy of his own day.

Before the sixth century Brittany can hardly be said to have existed at all, except as the remote Roman province of Armorica. The colonisation of 'Little Britain' had begun during the previous century, after the Roman emperor Honorius had pulled the legions out of Great Britain in 410, with the dismissive remark that henceforth the British must look to their own defence. Throughout the fifth century Norse and Danish raiders harried the eastern seaboard of Britain, driving the British inhabitants west into Wales and Cornwall. As the pressure from the east built up, enormous numbers of emigrants took ship across the Channel to Brittany—an exodus that lasted altogether about 150 years. In the process, the original tribes of Armorica were swamped by the newcomers. That brief period saw the end of the old tribal groupings—the Veneti centred on Vannes, the Redones on Rennes, the Namnetes on Nantes, the Curiosolitae with their capital at Corseul near Dinan, the Osismi who inhabited what was to become Finistère, with their capital at Vangium (Carhaix). In their place were three rough groupings of Bretons—in the north the Dumnonii, in the south-west the Cornovii, and in the south-east a people known simply as Bretons. To the native inhabitants the British invasion was as overwhelming as the coming of the horned warriors from the north was to the Britons themselves, though it seems to have been more peaceable. And instead of contenting themselves largely with hit-and-run raids, as the Norsemen did, the Britons were there for good.

Presumably the newcomers had some primitive form of organisation; but it was left to the saints to give it a definitive form, that of bishoprics, which were fixed by the end of the sixth century. St Samson established the bishopric of Dol about 530 and St Paul-Aurelian that of Saint-Pol-de-Léon at roughly the same date. St Tugdual and St Corentin, both second-generation Bretons, founded the bishoprics at Tréguier and Quimper respectively; as did St Brieuc (Brioc), from Cardigan, and St Malo, from Gwent, the bishoprics named after them. Nominally the old Armorican Church was still controlled from Rome, or at least from Tours, but the new Celtic bishops took no notice of that. There were in fact three Armorican bishoprics, Nantes founded about 370, Rennes in 461 and Vannes in 465. When the Welshmen and the Bretons set about founding their own, they did not even bother to consult the Archbishop of Tours, and though successive Archbishops tried to exercise some kind of control over the Breton Church, for all practical purposes it was independent from the sixth to the ninth centuries.

Among the Breton bishoprics, that of Dol gradually rose to pre-eminence. When Duke Nominoë became the first ruler of an independent Brittany in 845, he raised Dol to the status of an archbishopric, and an archbishopric it remained until 1199, when the Pope reduced it once more to an ordinary bishopric. In 1799, exactly six centuries later, the bishopric of Dol was finally suppressed, having lasted almost 1,300 years.

A vestige of Brittany's ecclesiastical independence survives in the titles given to the parish clergy. In Brittany alone the priest is not called the *curé*, as he is everywhere else, but the *recteur*, the ruler rather than the tender of his flock; and his curate is the *curé*, whereas in the rest of France the curate is the *vicaire*.

I have not been able to discover whether St Samson's monastery was located in Dol itself, or on the top of Mont Dol, an isolated granite outcrop a little north of the town and the only hill of any consequence in the neighbourhood. It is reputed to have been a Celtic holy place, and Christian hermitages were established on it. St Michael's footprint is said to be visible on one of the rocks on the summit, as is the Devil's claw mark; I looked hard but could not find either. Mont Dol today is given over to litter and courting couples, with little evidence of titanic struggles between Satan and the Archangel.

The tower on Mont Dol, now turned into a chapel, was built as a telegraph station, one of fifty-five such stations used to transmit strategic information between Paris and Brest. The line went from Montmartre to Dreux and Avranches; to Mont Saint-Michel, where the signalling apparatus was erected on top of the abbey church, whose spire had not yet been built; to Mont Dol, then via Saint-Malo and Saint-Brieuc to Brest. The telegraph was invented by Claude Chappe in the early years of the Revolutionary period, and its urgent importance to the authorities is shown by the fact that the whole line from Paris to Brest was set up in only seven months during 1794. Thomas Carlyle described Chappe experimenting in Vincennes Park: 'He has scaffolding set up, has posts driven in; wooden arms with elbow joints are jerking and fugling in the air, in the most rapid mysterious manner!' The Chappe telegraph consisted of an upright, to which was attached a cross beam (the regulator) that could be pivoted vertically to a number of different positions. At each end of the regulator was a smaller beam known as the indicator, looking rather like an old-fashioned railway signal, which could also be pivoted. The combination of various positions of regulator and indicators enabled thousands of different words to be visually transmitted; however, the apparatus was useless at night or in fog, and was superseded by the electric telegraph in the 1840s. Under Napoleon the telegraph was not only used to transmit military information: it also signalled the winning numbers of the Loterie Nationale. Chappe himself came to a sad and untimely end. In 1805, aged forty-two, he threw himself down a well at the telegraph headquarters in Paris.

The telegraph lines were only one aspect of Napoleonic long-distance transmission of messages. They were complemented by the semaphore system, which was put up in about 1803 along the whole Channel and Atlantic coastline of France from

Flushing to Bayonne. In Brittany the *arrondissements* or divisions into which the coast was divided were Saint-Servan, Cap Fréhel, Ile de Bréhat, Ile de Batz, Brest, Audierne, Penmarc'h, Lorient and Le Croisic.

Most visitors to Dol make the pilgrimage to Mont Saint-Michel, the Holy of Holies on this stretch of the coast. And no one writing on Brittany can ignore it entirely—though it is no longer officially in Brittany but in Normandy, since the River Couesnon that divides the two provinces changed its course after an exceptionally high tide in some past century. An old rhyme refers to this piece of geographical incompetence:

Le Couesnon par sa folie
Mit Saint-Michel en Normandie

—which has meant, of course, that Mont Saint-Michel has been extensively dealt with by Peter Gunn in his Normandy volume in this series. To me it is a place to be appreciated from a distance. I last saw it at about four-thirty on a summer's morning, as I drove down the steep hill from Avranches to the plain below. The Abbey on its rock rose from the sea-mist like a vision of the Cathédrale Engloutie emerging from the waves, or like the Egyptian pyramid to which Victor Hugo compared it in a poem (*Chéops de l'Occident, pyramide des mers*). Seen close to, the magic of Mont Saint-Michel gradually dissipates, as you struggle to find a space in the seething car-park, and then plod up the hill at a quarter of a mile an hour wedged in by the tourists of a hundred nations, diving every few minutes into one of the crêperies or ice-cream parlours that charge double for everything, since this is Mont Saint-Michel. But I have a favourite way of cheating on the Sacred Mountain. About half way up the climb there is a small wooden door that leads into a peaceful garden. From here you can contemplate infinity across the sands of the bay, or gaze upwards in relaxed self-satisfaction at the queues shuffling behind the Abbey windows high overhead.

Mont Saint-Michel has been a place of pilgrimage since the eighth or ninth century. It was a refuge from the invading Norsemen, was besieged in the Hundred Years War, and was turned into a prison for 300 recalcitrant priests in 1793. The great general Bertrand du Guesclin was given command of the garrison there in 1357; his wife, Typhaine de Raguenel, who must have been a formidable bluestocking, spent her time on the Mount engaged in astronomy and the study of philosophy. Earlier still, the long-distance lure of Mont Saint-Michel was well proved in the case of an eleventh-century German called Othbert. One Christmas Eve, Othbert and his friends spent their time singing and dancing instead of attending church. Their village priest put a curse on them, and for a whole year they were compelled to carry on with the dance until they collapsed, and lay motionless on the ground for three days and three nights. Not surprisingly, Othbert saw the error of his ways, took up the pilgrim's staff and trudged to Mont Saint-Michel, where he wrote out an account of his misadventures for the good monks of the Abbey.

The countryside between Dol and the Bay of Mont Saint-Michel would have looked very different in St Samson's time from the way it does today. Now the area is known as the Marais (Marshland) of Dol, and consists of rich agricultural land, rather like Romney Marsh, reclaimed from the sea; towards Mont Saint-Michel the district is called by the Dutch name Polders. But the Marais and much of the Bay was once covered by the trees of the Forêt de Scissy, until at an unknown date, possibly in the eighth or ninth century, the sea poured in, covering the trees whose fossilised stumps are sometimes turned up in the soil.

Like Dol, Tréguier is a fine old town, not as visited as it might be considering the good things to be found in it; and it would surely be as well-known as Dinan if it were more accessible. As at Dinan, streets of ancient houses rise steeply from a boat-lined river bank towards the town centre. Tréguier is dominated by the tall stone spire of the cathedral, pierced with holes of all manner of shapes and sizes to lessen the force of the Brittany wind. The patron saint of the cathedral is Tugdual, founder of the bishopric in the sixth century, but his shadowy figure is obliterated by the magnificent ghost of a very different and far later saint, the lawyers' patron St Yves. Yves is the only Breton saint of any consequence who dates from medieval or post-medieval times; thus, though he was responsible for his share of miracles, his life was run-of-the-mill compared with the highly-coloured careers of Samson and the other missionary saints.

In the sonorous phrases of Albert Le Grand, Yves was the 'mirror of ecclesiastics, ornament of his century, lawyer and father of poor widows and orphans, universal patron of Armorican Brittany, but especially of the See of Tréguier'. Yves Hélory was born in the manor-house of Ker-Martin, at Minihy on the outskirts of Tréguier, on October 17, 1253. His mother was an extremely pious woman, and from his earliest years told him that he should live like a saint; to which he would answer, somewhat priggishly, that sainthood was the goal he hoped to attain. At the age of fourteen he went to Paris University, where he studied logic, scholastic theology and canon law. After ten years in Paris he moved on to the University of Orléans to read civil law; and after finishing his course there he returned to Brittany, to Rennes, where he carried on further religious studies with a Franciscan monk and decided to enter the priesthood. His first clerical post was as the *Official* (ecclesiastical judge) of the Archdeacon's Court, where he built up such a reputation as a lawyer that the Bishop of Tréguier, Messire Alain de Bruc, summoned him back to his native city and made him his own *Official*, appointing him also rector of a near-by parish. We are told that he never passed sentence 'without the tears running down his cheeks, when he reflected upon his own life and how one day he would himself be judged'.

The most famous of his Solomon-like judgments is portrayed wherever St Yves is carved or painted. In Tréguier Cathedral there is a naïve wood carving showing him with a poor man on his right and a rich man on his left. The story goes that the rich man had sued the poor man on the grounds that he only kept body and soul together by the smells wafting in from his own kitchen. Whereupon Yves asked for a coin and made it ring in the rich man's ear, giving as his judgment that the sound would pay for the smell. According to Le Grand, most of his clients were poor people for whom he would waive any fee. He would appeal on their behalf against unjust sentences, would take their part against the '*grands Seigneurs*', and would sensibly try to dissuade them from going to court at all. But his legal activities were only one side of his life, and in St Yves' eyes no doubt a comparatively minor side. His pastoral work among the poor of Tréguier was his main concern. He built a hostel at Ker-Martin, where he took in paupers, feeding them, giving them his own clothes, washing them and even greasing their shoes. He looked after the local orphans and paid for their apprenticeships.

As a preacher St Yves was tireless, and on one Good Friday he preached in seven different churches. His sermons were usually in Breton, sometimes in Latin but never in French, which must make him something of a pioneer among Brittany's clergy. He had a short way with members of the congregation who tried to leave before the sermon. Once when he was preaching in Locronan he saw a local squire, a well-known ladies' man, sidling out of church as he was climbing the pulpit. Yves was on him like a flash. 'If there were three or four girls here with the devil's trumpet'—presumably he meant a *bombarde* for dancing to—'he would have stayed, but not to hear the word of God. I pray God to punish him in this life and not to reserve the penalty for his offence to the next.' The squire immediately became paralysed; which seems a harsh punishment for doing what most of the congregation would no doubt have done if they had had the nerve. Fortunately the paralysis was not permanent, and the squire was cured after St Yves' death by a pilgrimage to his tomb.

Yves practised what he preached, and his asceticism was a byword. He always wore a hair shirt and would soak his outer tunic in water to make it more uncomfortable. He never rode anywhere on horseback, even on ceremonial occasions. His diet was mainly bread made from barley, oats or rye, and vegetable soup; he never ate meat, and fish only occasionally. He spent most of the night in prayer or meditation, and would sleep a little before dawn, lying on a clay bed with straw spread over it, and with the Bible or a stone for a pillow. Or he would sleep on a bench in the sacristy of Tréguier Cathedral, to make sure that the Duke of Brittany's officers did not walk off with any of the church treasures. On one occasion an officer tried to storm the sacristy with drawn sword, but Yves kept him away and was wounded in the hand.

In May 1303, at the age of only forty-nine, St Yves fell

mortally ill, more worn out by work and austerities, says Albert Le Grand, than by old age—'*tout cassé & usé, plus de travaux & austeritez que de vieillesse*'. On May 19 he died at Ker-Martin; from there his body was taken in state to the Cathedral at Tréguier. The crowd was enormous. 'Some kissed his feet, others, who could not get so close, touched the body with their rosaries, prayerbooks or sacred medallions, which they kept ever afterwards with great reverence. But the pity was to see the poor widows, beggars and other wretches flocking to prostrate themselves before the coffin, lamenting the loss of the father who fed them, their lawyer and consoler in time of need.' Almost as soon as Yves was buried posthumous miracles began; Le Grand lists over thirty, most of which are to do with rescue from drowning at sea, in rivers or in millstreams, of people in danger who invoked his name. He was canonised in the remarkably short time of forty-four years, largely through the exertions of Duke John III, who set the papal wheels in motion. And every year on May 19, the anniversary of his death and canonisation, a congregation of lawyers, not only from France but from all over the world, walk in solemn procession from Tréguier Cathedral to Ker-Martin, led by the skull of St Yves in its jewelled casket.

The honesty of this extraordinary and lovable man was made the subject of a Latin jingle soon after his death:

Sanctus Yvo erat Brito,
Advocatus et non latro,
Res miranda populo.

('St Yves was a Breton, a lawyer and not a crook, a matter of wonder to the people.') The same characteristic was the subject of a medieval joke, which has a distinctly Irish—which is presumably to say Breton—flavour. St Yves turned up at the Heavenly Gates in the company of a large group of nuns. 'Who are you?' St Peter asked one of them. 'A nun,' she answered. 'You can wait outside,' he said. 'We have quite enough in Paradise.' 'And who are you?' he asked St Yves. 'A lawyer.' 'You're the first one we've had,' said St Peter. 'Come on in.'

Tréguier's other patron saint would certainly have disclaimed the title. The bulky statue of Ernest Renan, the nineteenth-century philosopher and freethinker, sits slumped in front of the Cathedral, below the trees that line the square. The last time I was in Tréguier the town was getting ready for a *fest-noz* (evening festivity), and Renan was surrounded by platforms full of *bombarde*-players tootling away and dancers trying out their steps, neither of them activities of which his serious soul would have approved. Born in 1823, Renan scandalised orthodox Roman Catholicism with his *Vie de Jésus* (1863), in which he insisted that Christ was a man like any other—an 'incomparable man', but human none the less. His birthplace, a solid timber-framed house just off the square, is now a museum, full of portraits and maps of his journeys. In the attic is his school desk, and a report from the Ecole Ecclésiastique de Tréguier which gives his behaviour '*à l'église*' as '*souvent distrait*'. How ironic that Renan the doubter should actually have visited the Holy Land, while St Yves, the believer of all believers, hardly ever set foot outside his native parish!

CHAPTER IV

Châteaux

Of the vast forests that once covered the whole of central Brittany, only traces now remain—a few miles of greenery shadowing the road, like the Forêt de Rennes outside the capital, or the Forêt de Carnoët south of Quimperlé. The one remaining heavily wooded area of any consequence is the Forêt de Paimpont, which stretches round the little town of that name. It has an enchanted feeling, as all good forests should have; once off the road and a few minutes' walk down one of the rides and you are in the ancient silent world of trees, a world that has changed little since the Druids practised their rites under its oaks. The Druids typify the half-mythical forms that linger in the Forêt de Paimpont; but there are other ghosts even more evocative of a legendary past. For this was the ancient Forest of Brocéliande, whose ruler was King Arthur, and whose spiritual lord was Merlin, the Welsh magician Myrddin. As reputed son of the Devil and a British Christian, Merlin's ancestry set him astride both paganism and its successor. But even his magical powers failed when he fell into the clutches of the beautiful enchantress Viviane, who bewitched him with a charm he himself had taught her, shutting him in a magic castle from which there was no escape, so that he would stay by her for ever.

This turning of the tables on the sorcerer by his apprentice is said to have taken place at the Fontaine de Barenton, a little spring hidden among the trees in the high forest. It is hard enough to find: I was told in the Syndicat d'Initiative in Concoret, a town on the edge of the forest, that it is no use asking for directions to the Fontaine de Barenton—you just have to come upon it by chance. However, it is possible to be more precise; and it is marked (spelt Baranton) on the large-scale Michelin map of the area. To reach it, you branch off in the village of La Saudrais to a hamlet called Folle-Pensée. From there the fountain is signposted, and is about a quarter of an hour's walk up the hill. It is a peaceful and friendly spot, especially on a hot and dusty day. Some young oak trees (fifty or so years old, by the look of them) have been planted beside it, to give it suitably Druidic connections, and their trunks have been well initialled over the past few decades. The fountain basin is coffin-shaped and lined with stone—just the right size and shape for total immersion, if the Druids indeed carried out such a ritual. The water is at a constant temperature of 10 deg C (50 deg F), which would make baptism a chilly business at any time of the year. It is rich in carbonic acid; and though it does not have the unpleasant medicinal or rusty taste of many spa waters, it is said to be good for the treatment of rickets and mental disorders. Hence no doubt the name of 'Folle-Pensée' ('Mad Thought') for the hamlet below.

Barenton was a centre of Druid teaching. To become a Druid took twenty years of studying history, law, astronomy and medicine as the main subjects. If a candidate was successful in the final exam, he was given a cloak of feathers (the forerunner of the academic gown) and was entitled to sit in a bardic chair. Merlin himself is said to have suffered from a nervous disorder and to have been treated at the Druids' psychiatric clinic; and it was while he was sleeping by the fountain that Viviane got him into her power. At the fountain's edge is a large square stone, looking like the plinth of a statue, which is presumably the stone traditionally called the '*Perron de Merlin*' ('Merlin's Threshold'). In past centuries a cup was attached to the stone by a chain; and if a passer-by scooped up a few drops of water and sprinkled them on the stone, there would immediately be a downpour of rain. In his *Contes des Anciens Bretons*, Hersart de la Villemarqué describes how this ritual was still being carried out in his own day. 'In August 1835, all the inhabitants of the parish of Kon-kored (the Valley of the Fairies)'—now Concoret—'which gets its name from the valley watered by the fountain, went to the fountain in procession headed by crucifix and banners, singing hymns and ringing bells, to pray the heavens for rain. When they got there, the parish *curé* blessed the water, dipped in the sprinkler, and tipped out a few drops on the near-by stones. But'—adds the sceptical author—'no one told me whether he succeeded in gathering the storms clouds together.'

In the Middle Ages and earlier, however, no one doubted the efficacy of this procedure. A fifteenth-century writer tells how every time the Seigneur de Montfort visited the fountain and tipped water on the *perron*, 'no matter how hot it was, it rained so abundantly on the land, that the earth and all the crops upon it were watered, and great was their profit (*moult leur proufitte*)'. Chrétien de Troyes, who in the twelfth century chronicled the exploits of the Knights of the Round Table in thousands of lines of verse, mentioned the magical powers of the fountain; but the fullest and most poetic account occurs in the Welsh *Mabinogion*, in the story called *Owein, or the Countess of the Fountain*. Owein sets out from King Arthur's court at Caerleon and comes to a magic fountain, which has been described earlier in the story. (The translation is by Jeffrey Gantz, in the Penguin Classics series.)

> Take the path at the head of the clearing and climb the slope until you reach the summit; there you will see a vale like a great valley, and in the middle a great tree with branches greener than the greenest fir. Beneath that tree is a fountain, and beside the fountain a great stone, and on the stone a silver bowl, and a silver chain so that bowl and stone cannot be separated. Take the bowl and fill it and throw water on the stone, and you will hear a tremendous thundering, such that you will expect heaven and earth to shake with the noise, and after that a cold shower which you will barely survive. Hailstones will fall, and when the weather clears, the tree will not have one leaf that the shower has not carried away. A shower of birds will come and sit in the tree, and in your own country you have not heard such singing as theirs, but when their song is most pleasant to you a great moaning and groaning will come to you through the valley, and you will see a rider on a pure black horse dressed in pure black brocade, with a standard of pure black linen on his spear. He will attack you at once; if you flee he will overtake you, and if you stand mounted he will leave you on foot, and if you do not find trouble in this you will never find it as long as you live.

Needless to say, Owein succeeds in killing the Black Knight, marries his wife, the beautiful Countess of the Fountain, and takes on the role of defender of the fountain against all comers. It is impossible to disentangle such a twisted jumble of legend. But may there have been some sort of ordeal by battle that took place at Barenton, whose winner gained the favours of the priestess of the fountain, before he too was slain or deposed by a stronger successor?

Other Arthurian knights more famous than Owein have left their traces in the Forêt de Paimpont. Between Beignon and Plélan-le-Grand the road crosses the little River Aff at the Pont du Secret, where Queen Guinevere confessed her love to Sir Lancelot; while all the knights are gathered together in the small church at Tréhorenteuc, in a large and rather crude painting, which shows the Holy Grail appearing to the startled King Arthur and the assembled company. On the northern edge of the forest is the Château de Comper, beside the wide, still lake from which Sir Lancelot took the name Lancelot du Lac. The present château is largely a nineteenth-century reconstruction, but is a fine place for all that. Only one room deep, its pinky-mauve granite walls and lichen-covered slate roof blend marvellously with the rocks that jut through the grass around the lake. The first castle here is said to have been built by Diana the Huntress—unlikely on the face of it, though moon-worship is a religion that would not be out of keeping in Brocéliande. Some massive medieval walls survive, now incongruously used as shelters for tractors, oil drums and the rabbits that feed the park warden's family. The château is owned by a builders' firm, who use it for storage and hire out the main rooms for weddings and other formal occasions. The old *garde* there told me that he and his father had been *gardes* in succession at Comper since 1897, and that the Duke of Westminster used to visit the château before the war to hunt the wild boar. During the war the Germans used the large walled garden enclosure as a prison camp.

Comper's lake is one of the loveliest of the many *étangs* that ring the forest, and on a fine day the banks are a lure for fishermen and picnickers. Somewhere below its surface lies Merlin's Castle, to which the enchantress Viviane swam, holding under her arm the infant Lancelot whom she had found by the roadside. Thus water, rock, trees, magician and the flower of knighthood all coalesce into a single unity at this placid spot.

Paimpont itself is a neat little town, just a single street of granite houses, with a medieval gate at one end and a war memorial at the other. Its big church, with the Mairie attached, seems disproportionately large.

On the southern edge of the forest is a wild expanse of heathland, which the French army has taken over for training today's army officers—tanks and armoured cars, in succession to hauberk, lance and sword. A minor road (south of the main Plélan-Ploërmel road) runs right through the training ground, passing the modern blocks of Coëtquidan Saint-Cyr, France's Sandhurst. After the war Saint-Cyr moved from Paris to Brittany, and the new establishment was inaugurated in 1959. At the entrance a statue of General Leclerc commemorates one of the Free French heroes of the Second World War. Coëtquidan's prefix Coët-, meaning woodland, is naturally common enough round Paimpont; and John Fowles makes use of it in his short novel *The Ebony Tower*. The story is a reworking in modern terms of the medieval 'shuttle' theme—a knight shuttles in search of knowledge from wife and home to adventures and strange women, before returning home again. *The Ebony Tower* is full of the sun-dappled atmosphere of the Forêt de Paimpont; the hero, a young artist, makes his way to Coëtminais, the domain of an ancient Merlin-figure and his two Viviane-like mistresses, seeks and acquires knowledge, and goes back to England and the familiar domestic scene.

If Comper is more the shadow than the reality of a castle, lost in a myth-haunted countryside, the Château de Suscinio away to the south is anchored solidly in the world of medieval warfare. The most uncompromisingly pugnacious of all the Breton castles, it stands near the shore of the windswept Presqu'Ile de Rhuys—so near in fact that when it was built its moat filled and emptied with the tides. The name is said to derive from the old French '*souci n'y ot*', meaning '*sans-souci*' or 'without care'; if so it is certainly a misnomer, as the château has had its fair share of troubles. Suscinio was built between the thirteenth and sixteenth centuries, which accounts for the contrast between the stark grandeur of the external walls and the luxury of the accommodation within: each bedroom, for example, has its own window seat, fireplace and lavatory annexe. The whole complex is now being restored as far as possible to its original form. The fourteenth-century War of Succession left an inescapable mark on the castle, in the form of a stretch of wall built in grey stone, in contrast to the mottled brown and yellow on either side. Known as the 'Breach of Du Guesclin', it was made in 1373 by the great French general during his recapture of the castle from the English. Suscinio's medieval ups and downs are listed on a notice below the gatehouse, in a curious medley of English and presumably German: '1380. Retaking hof the castle which was held by spanischmen. 1399–1442. The distrorungs hare restored.' During the Revolution it was used as a stone quarry, and was held for a time by Cadoudal's Royalist Chouans (see page 216) during the Quiberon campaign of 1795. Suscinio has a slender link with the legendary world, for the fairy Mélusine is said to haunt its subterranean tunnels—Mélusine who, like Viviane, was no doubt a Celtic water goddess.

A few miles away is Sarzeau, an attractive little market town and the only place of any consequence in the Rhuys peninsula. The church has some curious capitals, several of them decorated with bird motifs, and two good painted statues of saints—Isidore, dressed as a Breton peasant, wearing breeches and carrying crops and a sickle, and Corneille (known at Carnac as St Cornély), the patron saint of farm animals. Sarzeau's main literary figure, the playwright and novelist Alain-René Lesage (1668–1747), author of *Gil Blas,* is commemorated by a portrait bust in the main square; but he is cast into the shade by a man of genius from a previous age, Peter Abelard, who came against his will to Rhuys in the twelfth century.

The bare outlines of the love story of Heloise and Abelard are well known and have been elaborated into countless stories and romances. Nothing could be simpler than the summary by Villon in his *Ballade of the Women of Former Times*:

Où est la très sage Héloïs,
Pour qui fut chastré et puis moyne
Pierre Esbaillart à Sainct-Denys?
Pour son amour eut cest essoyne.

('Where is the wise Heloise, for whom Peter Abelard was

castrated and became a monk at Saint-Denis? For his love he suffered so greatly.') What is not so well known is that Abelard was by birth a Breton, and spent several years of his life as abbot of a Breton monastery. At the age of about fifty-three he wrote his autobiography, *The Story of My Misfortunes* (*Historia Calamitatum*), in which he set down the trials of his life with an almost clinical detachment. The eldest child of a Breton nobleman, he was born in Le Pallet, a small town between Nantes and Clisson, in 1079. In his youth he became a wandering scholar and then a teacher, specialising in dialectic and rhetoric, and setting up his own school in Paris, where pupils flocked to his lectures. Among them was Heloise, more than twenty years younger than he was and the niece of Fulbert, one of the canons of Notre Dame. 'In looks she did not rank lowest, while in the extent of her learning she stood supreme,' says Abelard (*The Letters of Abelard and Heloise*, translated by Betty Radice in the Penguin Classics series); and in order to gain easier access to her, he took lodgings in Fulbert's house.

Once Abelard was installed under Fulbert's roof, the couple gave themselves up night and day to lovemaking. Abelard admits that his teaching suffered. 'As my interest and concentration flagged, my lectures lacked all inspiration and were merely repetitive'; instead of studying philosophy, he wrote love songs. Inevitably Heloise became pregnant, and Abelard smuggled her away to his sister's house in Brittany. Here she had a son who was given the curious name Astrolabe, chosen by Heloise herself. Canon Fulbert had trusted Abelard absolutely, and had previously disbelieved the rumours about him and Heloise; but Astrolabe's birth drove him to fury. To placate him, Abelard agreed to recall Heloise from Brittany and marry her—though he ran into opposition from Heloise herself. She tried to dissuade him from marriage, quoting the Christian Fathers and domestic disturbance as reasons against it. In a passage with an astonishingly modern ring she asked: 'Who can concentrate on thoughts of Scripture and philosophy and be able to endure babies crying, nurses soothing them with lullabies, and all the noisy coming and going of men and women about the house? Will he put up with the constant muddle and squalor which small children bring into the home?' But

Abelard insisted, and they were married, with Fulbert as one of the witnesses.

Fulbert wanted the marriage to be publicised as widely as possible; on the other hand, Abelard tried to keep it hushed up and packed Heloise off to a convent. Assuming wrongly that Abelard had forced her to become a nun, and had thereby repudiated the marriage, Fulbert's anger revived. Together with his friends and relatives, he 'took cruel vengeance on me of such appalling barbarity as to shock the whole world: they cut off the parts of my body whereby I had committed the wrong of which they complained.' Nothing can give a greater idea of the gulf that separates us from the medieval world than the immediate aftermath of Abelard's tragedy. To us such an event would be a matter for private commiseration; but this was not the case in twelfth-century France. 'Next morning the whole city gathered before my house, and the scene of horror and amazement, mingled with lamentations, cries and groans which exasperated and distressed me, is difficult, no, impossible, to describe. In particular, the clerks and, most of all, my pupils tormented me with their unbearable weeping and wailing until I suffered more from their sympathy than from the pain of my wound.' He was also distressed by the Old Testament strictures against castration: 'A eunuch is such an abomination to the Lord that men made eunuchs by the amputation or mutilation of their members are forbidden to enter a church as if they were stinking and unclean.' However, such sanctions were not applied to Abelard; he entered the monastery of Saint-Denis, where he continued to teach, while Heloise stayed in her convent.

These events took place in 1119. Seven years later, after troubles at Saint-Denis and elsewhere, Abelard accepted the post of abbot at Saint-Gildas-de-Rhuys, which in those days was in the uttermost wilds of Brittany. To judge by the account in the *Historia Calamitatum*, his physical sufferings in Paris were nothing to his spiritual difficulties at Saint-Gildas. 'The country was wild and the language unknown to me'—this suggests that the brothers spoke only Breton, not French—'the natives were brutal and barbarous, the monks were beyond control and led a dissolute life which was well known to all.' These were the monks that Abelard had to bring back under the discipline of the monastic rule, and he found it an impossible task. The local lord levied taxes on the monks so heavy that they had to steal to pay them, the entire population was beyond the rule of law, and 'outside the monastery wall that tyrant and his minions never ceased to harry me'. As the period covered by the *Historia* comes near to the present (about 1132), Abelard changes into the present tense. The monks have tried to poison him on a number of occasions, and he has been forced to move from the abbey and live in a separate cell; they have bribed robbers to murder him on the road; and he has tried to control them by excommunication, but without avail. He expelled the worst offenders and returned to the abbey, but the remaining monks were even worse. 'They did not deal with poison but with a dagger held to my throat. . . . I am still in danger, and every day I imagine a sword hanging over my head, so that at meals I dare scarcely breathe. . . . This is my experience all the time: a poor monk raised to be an abbot, the more wretched as I have become more wealthy, in order that my example may curb the ambition of those who have deliberately chosen a similar course.'

Abelard's account of his time at Saint-Gildas has a paranoid ring to it; yet there must have been more to his complaints than a pent-up imagination working on petty grievances. Whatever his reasons, it is clear that he was not suited to Saint-Gildas, nor Saint-Gildas to him. In spite of his troubles, he found time during his exile to set up the convent of the Paraclete, near Troyes, on a proper footing, with Heloise as its abbess. During the 1130s he returned to Paris and his career as a teacher, came into conflict with St Bernard of Clairvaux over his theological beliefs, and died at Cluny in 1142, leaving as his literary testament not only his autobiography but a series of long letters to Heloise and numerous Latin hymns, of which a handful survive. In one of her letters to Abelard, Heloise looks back twenty years or so to their life together, in a sentence that brings these passionate beings before us after more than eight centuries. 'God is my witness that if Augustus, Emperor of the whole world, thought fit to honour me with marriage and conferred all the earth on me to possess for ever, it would be dearer and more honourable to me to be called not his Empress but your whore.' Heloise survived Abelard by twenty years, dying in 1163 or 1164. Their bodies were buried side by side at the Paraclete, and are now together in a single sarcophagus in the cemetery of Père-Lachaise, in Paris.

The reputation of Heloise lived on in Brittany in a garbled and misleading form—that is, if we can take as genuine the poem about her in the *Barzaz-Breiz*, which La Villemarqué claimed to be authentic. The poem makes Heloise out to be a Breton, like Abelard; she follows him to Nantes, learns how to read and write, and engages in black magic:

The first spell that I conjured with my dear Abelard
From a crow's eye we made it, mixed with a toad's cold heart.

Heloise boasts how she blighted the abbot's crops with her spells, and how she feeds a brood of vipers on the blood of murdered babies. Finally,

If I can live with Abelard, my soul's light and my dear,
If we can be together for yet another year,
For two or three years only, my sweetest love and I,
We'll make the world run backwards, we'll overturn the sky.

These four lines may be bogus; yet they sum up the whole story.

Saint-Gildas today is a pretty little tourist town, with good beaches near by and a small harbour a mile or so down the hill. Much of the abbey church is Romanesque, built in the eleventh and twelfth centuries, and is no doubt much as Abelard would have known it; the cloisters are bright with flowers; and the abbey buildings (of more recent date) are occupied not by recalcitrant monks, but by nuns and the staff of an 'Institut Médico-Pédagogique'. Abelard himself does not seem to be commemorated in any way (though during the Revolution the town was briefly re-christened 'Abelard'); however, as a compensation two saints have their tombs in the church, below some fine modern stained glass—St Goustan (from whom a suburb of Auray takes its name), and St Gildas, buried behind the high altar. Reliquaries in the church treasury contain Gildas' mortal remains—a leg, a forearm, part of his skull—in sumptuous caskets and coffers.

Gildas is an elusive figure, especially since there were at least two Celtic saints of that name. According to Albert Le Grand, he was born in Cornwall about 499, and is not to be confused with another Gildas, who wrote an account of British sufferings at the hands of the Saxons, *De Excidio Britanniae* (*On the Destruction of Britain*). Crossing the Channel as a young man, Gildas seems first to have set up an oratory on the small island of Houat, off the Quiberon peninsula, before going to the mainland and establishing himself beside the Blavet river. Here he acted as intermediary between Waroch, Count of Vannes, and the notorious Comorrus (Comorre), Count of Cornouaille, with whom St Samson also became involved. Gildas negotiated a marriage between Triphine, Waroch's daughter, and the brutal Comorrus, a Breton Bluebeard who murdered his wives when they became pregnant. Hoping to avoid this fate, Triphine fled from her husband as soon as she found herself with child and made for Vannes, where she hid in a thicket on the outskirts of the town. All to no avail: despite her pleas for mercy Comorrus dragged her from her hiding-place and cut off her head. Waroch laid out Triphine's body in state, found Gildas and told him the whole story; the enraged saint went straight to Comorrus's castle, prayed for divine aid, and hurled a handful of dust against the castle wall. The castle collapsed on the spot, seriously injuring Comorrus, and Gildas returned to Vannes, where he placed Triphine's head back on her shoulders and brought her back to life. The grateful Waroch presented Gildas with the monastery on Rhuys, in his own domains. Fortunately, Comorrus did not pass on his brutal character to his heirs: the restored Triphine gave birth to a son, Trémeur, who took instruction from Gildas and became a saint in his turn. Gildas died on Houat about 570; his body, pushed out to sea in an otherwise empty boat, made its own miraculous way to land at Rhuys, where it lies to this day.

If Suscinio is the king of Breton castles in its ruined grandeur, then Josselin, well inland, is surely the queen; but a queen who has withstood the passage of time a good deal better. The original château was attacked by the English in the 1160s and largely destroyed; the present tremendous walls, with their striding trio of pointed towers, were built by Olivier de Clisson towards the end of the fourteenth century. Clisson's exploits in the Hundred Years War gained him the title of 'Butcher of the English'. In 1380 he was appointed Constable of France, in command of all the armed forces of the realm, and his motto, '*Pour ce qui me plest*' ('I do as I please') reveals the scope of his arrogance and power. When first built, the castle rose sheer from the river, instead of from the road, as it does today, and must have been even more impressive. Clisson's self-display was outdone by his successors, the Rohans, who married into his family and own Josselin to this day. In about 1500, Jean de Rohan built the spectacular internal *corps-de-logis*, an early-Renaissance (or late-Gothic) showpiece of narrow gables, fretted pinnacles and decorative stonework balustrades. If you look closely at the carving, you can see in several places the Rohan motto '*A plus*' (meaning 'Even more', or 'To excess'), together with the initial 'A' of Anne de Bretagne, and the crown of the King of France, to whom she was married. More often than not the letters are carved in the shape of writhing sea monsters. The device of initials and '*A plus*' motto were carried over into the interior, notably above the fireplace in the Grand Salon, where they are picked out in gold on a red background. After the Revolution the château fell into disrepair, until major restoration in the nineteenth century brought it back to life again.

It was from Josselin that in 1351 Beaumanoir set out with his Breton knights to fight the famous 'Combat des Trente' against the English; and it was to Josselin that they returned in triumph. As La Villemarqué put it:

> Only a foe to Brittany
> Would not have leapt with joy to see
> Our men to Josselin coming home,
> Their helmets crowned with yellow broom.

Josselin is still a town full of flowers, though now grown in the window boxes of its half-timbered houses rather than worn in the helmets of warriors. Its chief legend concerns another plant, the bramble (*ronce*), which gives its name to the Pardon of Notre-Dame-du-Roncier, held every year early in September. The legend dates back to the ninth century, when a peasant is said to have found, beside the River Oust, a miraculous bramble bush that kept its leaves even in the depths of winter, and in the centre of the bush an archaic wooden statue of the Virgin. He took the statue home, but the next morning he found that it was back in the thicket. After this had happened several times, he realised that the statue was no ordinary effigy; and a chapel was built to house it on the site of the bush. It was eventually kept in the town's main church, but it was burnt in 1789 as an object of superstition. A few fragments were rescued from the flames and are now kept in a reliquary; a new statue was made in 1868. The Josselin Pardon was also known as the '*Pardon des Aboyeuses*' (the Pardon of the Barking Women), from the epileptics who attended it in the hope of a miraculous cure. The story goes that one day a beggar woman asked the housewives of Josselin to let her drink at the fountain where they were washing. They chased her away and set their dogs on her, which was a foolish as well as an unkind thing to do, as the beggar woman was the Virgin Mary travelling incognito. She put a curse on them, which made them and their descendants howl like dogs once a year, at Whitsun, as an annual reminder of their want of charity.

In the far north of Finistère, west of Morlaix, is the lonely Château de Kerjean—the only castle in that region remotely approaching Suscinio or Josselin in quality. Like Suscinio, it is undergoing a leisurely process of restoration. A bare granite Renaissance castle, with powerful battered walls, pierced for cannon, rising from a dry moat, Kerjean is largely a hollow shell, burnt out by a disastrous fire early in the eighteenth century. However, a few rooms are open to the public, including a crypt with recumbent warrior figures, a chapel with wooden statues of saints, and various rooms with a sparse collection of traditional furniture. Kerjean still keeps a sense of informality that belongs to a past tourist age. When you ring the bell, a dog bays somewhere far within; hens, goats and sheep roam about the courtyard; and the occasional workman chipping idly at a stone mullion will obviously make the work last for years, if not decades.

Restoration work of unusually high quality can be seen at the Château de la Roche-Jagu, set high on a bluff above the Trieux river, south of Lézardrieux. Named originally after an eleventh-century Breton called Jagu, the present château is

Above, The prehistoric stone alignments (menhirs) at Carnac

Below left, St Cornély, the patron saint of Carnac, with menhirs, the village fountain and church, and farm animals which came under his protection

Below right, A nineteenth-century peasant couple who have visited a Christianised menhir as a cure for childlessness

Above, The Stone Age urban surroundings: menh and dolmen in Sai Nazaire

Left, The so-called Temp de Mars, Gallo-Rom remains near Corseul

Above, Lunar landscape in North Brittany: low tide at the Pointe du Château

Below left, Massive boulders of the Gorges de Toul Goulic, near Rostrenen, where the River Blavet flows underground

Below right, The Fontaine de Barenton, a spring with Druidic associations in the Forêt de Paimpont

The little rock-cut harbour at Saint-Gildas-de-Rhuys

Above, Centre of the capital: the *quais* of Rennes and the River Vilaine

Below, The turrets and walls of Fougères and Josselin

Above, The Château de Comper, in the Forêt de Paimpont

Left, The Château de Suscinio, in the Rhuys Peninsula

Above, Saint-Malo, largely destroyed during the Second World War and since reconstructed

Right, The inner yacht basin at Saint-Malo, with the town's ramparts behind

Naval and military memorials. *Above left*, The corsair Duguay-Trouin, at Saint-Malo. *Above right*, La Tour d'Auvergne, the 'First Grenadier of France', at Carhaix. *Below left*, The Napoleonic hero Cambronne, at Nantes. *Below right*, Resistance monument to the *maquis* of Saffré, in the Morbihan an austere fifteenth-century building, dating from the period when the fortified castle was giving way to the well-appointed country mansion. What is remarkable about the restoration, which was carried out in the 1960s, is the superb carpentry: the massive beams and smaller rafters were the work of a local shipwright, and reveal in every curve and joint the love of a master-craftsman for his material. La Roche-Jagu is used in the summer for exhibitions and entertainments, such as evenings of music and poetry round the giant fireplace in the kitchen. A few miles to the west, and a little south of Lannion, is the Château de Tonquédec, built a generation or two earlier than La Roche-Jagu and now mouldering quietly away in a romantic setting above a rushing stream. We spent a night below its massive tree-sprouting walls, but saw and heard nothing more ghostly than a pair of owls.

On the eastern side of the country a chain of frontier towns guards Brittany's approaches from France proper; though the invaders are now tourists rather than the warring armies of the Middle Ages. From north to south the main fortresses are those of Fougères, Vitré and Châteaubriant, with the most splendid coming first. The phenomenal strength of Fougères is best appreciated from the ramparts that lead to the upper town. The mighty walls rise sheer from the gardens that now fill this section of the moat, and above them again are the pointed turret roofs—the Tour Raoul, the Tour Surienne, and loftiest of all the Tour Mélusine and the Tour du Gobelin—with their multi-coloured pennons fluttering in the wind. The plan of the castle is largely due to Raoul II, Baron de Fougères, who rebuilt it in 1173 after it had been destroyed in the previous decade by Henry II of England; while the towers that are its chief glory date mainly from the fourteenth and fifteenth centuries. The site is oddly chosen, down in a valley and dominated from the high ground where the main town now stands; but the rock outcrop on which the castle is built was originally surrounded entirely by water, except for a narrow neck of land at the main entrance where the gatehouse stands. Before the invention of artillery Fougères must have been almost impregnable.

The lower town is a good place to wander about in, from the waterwheels by the castle, past half-timbered houses to the fine old church of Saint-Sulpice, across the moat from the castle. Fougères and Suscinio are linked by the legendary presence of Mélusine. Fougères she haunts above ground, Suscinio below.

The castles of Vitré and Châteaubriant are less magnificent, but they are more closely linked with their respective towns, since they contain administrative buildings and are not just historic showpieces. Vitré's castle is a perfect triangle in shape and dates mainly from the late fourteenth and early fifteenth centuries. The massive outer walls are mainly grey, chequered with brown ironstone; but the internal effect is marred by the incongruous pseudo-Gothic town hall, built inside the castle in the early years of this century. There is a well-laid-out little museum in one of the towers (the Tour Saint-Laurent), including a galleried walkway lined with old photographs of the town. A revealing plan shows how the Paris–Brest railway, laid out in the middle of the last century, brutally destroyed a great swathe of medieval Vitré; fortunately there are still a good many ancient buildings left in the '*secteur sauvegardé*' round the castle.

At Châteaubriant the castle is mainly occupied by the *Sous-préfecture* for the region. The lower storey of a medieval tower survives; but the main building is the full-blown Renaissance château, built during the 1530s by Jean de Laval, Comte de Châteaubriant. Laval married a child bride, Françoise de Foix, when she was only eleven, and took her off to live in his château, far from the temptations of the capital. Rumours of Laval's cloistered wife reached the ears of François I, who asked for her to be summoned to court. Laval temporised; but François found out the secret signal agreed between Laval and Françoise that would bring her to him whenever he needed her. The signal was given; Françoise joined her husband, met the king and duly became his mistress. When the king grew tired of her she was sent back to the country, and is rumoured to have been found mysteriously dead in a darkened room in the château, murdered by her husband. However, it now seems probable that she died of natural causes in 1537, the year in which the château was completed. A stone set into the castle wall commemorates the twenty-seven hostages shot by the Germans in October 1941 (see also page 301); there is a monument to them near the Laval road on the outskirts of the town.

Life among the fleshpots of seventeenth-century Vitré has been vividly recorded by Mme de Sévigné, whose letters are to the France of Louis XIV what Pepys' diaries are to the England of Charles II. When Mme de Sévigné—in full, Marie de Rabutin-Chantal, Marquise de Sévigné—was not in Paris, she spent months on end at her château of Les Rochers, a few miles south of Vitré; and her letters written from there reveal her as an ardent country-lover and beautifier of her estate, with a romantic's love of solitude and the natural scene. Born in 1626, she married in 1644 the Marquis de Sévigné, who was consistently unfaithful to her and was killed in a duel in 1651. (One of his mistresses, the renowned Ninon de Lenclos, is reputed to have become in due course the mistress first of Sévigné's son and finally of his grandson—a record of service to three successive generations surely unrivalled in history.) Mme de Sévigné never remarried, bringing up her two children Françoise and Charles with the help of her uncle, the Abbé Christophe de Coulanges, referred to affectionately in the letters as '*le bien Bon*'. Françoise married M. de Grignan, the governor of Provence; and it was to Françoise, banished to a windswept château in the far south, that Mme de Sévigné wrote most of her most intimate and revealing letters.

Les Rochers has hardly changed at all since Mme de Sévigné lived there. It is still surrounded by trees, which make it easy enough to miss the entrance from the road (the D88, between Vitré and Argentré). You would hardly call Les Rochers beautiful, but it is full of character, and consists of three buildings of utterly different individuality—the main fifteenth-century château, with plenty of sharply pointed turrets, which she inherited; a detached octagonal chapel, which she built; and a fine classical stable block, built in the following century. When I went there in May the rain was pouring down and I was the only visitor. To summon the *gardien* as instructed, I rang a rusty bell on the end of a chain, and an enormous Dobermann loped round the side of the chapel; fortunately it only wanted me to throw a dead bird it had in its mouth for it to retrieve. I followed it into the garden and found the *gardien* (or rather the *gardienne*) planting large daisies in a flowerbed. As a true horticultural descendant of Mme de Sévigné she made me wait in the rain until she had finished her planting (which the

Dobermann proceeded to dig up), before showing me what little of Les Rochers is open to the public. The chapel was built in the 1670s by Mme de Sévigné and is decorated in grey, blue and gold; the benches, chairs and other furniture were designed by her. The other room on view is her workroom, where she wrote endlessly at a desk with a view of the garden. It is now set out as a small museum; its most notable relic is a small chamber-pot, looking like a gravy-boat with a lid, which Mme de Sévigné used when the sermons in the chapel got too long.

The gardens that were her joy still have their well-kept rows of pleached limes and their alleys leading into the woods. Her letters from Les Rochers are full of the delights of watching a garden take shape. In 1671 she writes to her daughter: 'My little trees are of surprising beauty. Pilois trains them towards the clouds with admirable integrity. Everything is good, but nothing is as beautiful as these alleys that you have seen being born.' (The Pilois she mentions was Jacques Pilois, head of the workmen at Les Rochers. On another occasion she wrote that she preferred his conversation to that of any *chevalier* at the Rennes parliament.) Four years later she remarks on how her trees have grown. 'I find these woods of an extraordinary beauty and sadness: all these trees that you have seen so small have become tall, straight and in the perfection of beauty; they have been pruned and give a delightful shade; they are forty to fifty feet high.' She was practical as well, and enjoyed supervising her workmen. 'I am enjoying myself cutting down some large trees; the bustle of the scene is exactly like those tapestries depicting the tasks of winter: trees being felled, men sawing, others piling up logs, others loading a cart, and myself in the middle of everything.'

Among the friends she made at Les Rochers was Mme de Chaulnes, wife of the Duc de Chaulnes, the governor of Brittany who was to acquire a reputation for savage repression after the Papier Timbré revolt of 1675 (see page 81). While walking in the woods, Mme de Sévigné and Mme de Chaulnes were caught in a typical Brittany summer downpour—'the rain set about drowning us, with water pouring off every bit of our clothes. The leaves were saturated one moment, and our clothes were saturated the next. We started to run; we shouted, we fell, we slipped, at last we got home, we lit a great fire; we changed blouses, skirts; I supplied everything; we had our shoes wiped dry; we split our sides laughing. That's how the governor's wife was treated in her own domain.' That summer (1671) the Duc de Chaulnes was still well liked in Brittany; the States (periodic assembly of administrators) were held at Vitré; and Mme de Sévigné attended the ceremonies from her town house, known as La Tour de Sévigné. The Duke and Duchess opened the proceedings with a sumptuous dinner, which shocked Mme de Sévigné's frugal mind. 'The good cheer was excessive; the roast joints were removed as though they had not been touched; and as for the pyramids of fruit, the doors should have been made higher to let them through.' But ostentation was punished: the pyramid with its twenty porcelain dishes crashed over at the door, drowning the sounds of violins, oboes and trumpets. The States seemed to have engaged in more celebration than legislation: 'the whole of Brittany was drunk that day', writes Mme de Sévigné, before returning with relief to '*ma solitude*' at Les Rochers. And in the October mornings that followed she describes herself as up to her knees in dew laying out fresh alleys in her peaceful park.

Thirty-five miles north-west of Vitré, towards Saint-Malo, is Combourg, a château whose literary resonances are far greater than those of Les Rochers. Mme de Sévigné had her moments of introspection in the midst of her all-embracing interest in the outside world; but Chateaubriand, who spent his formative years at Combourg, was the high priest of self-communing romanticism. With a mind steeped in Rousseau's myth of the Noble Savage, brought up on the ballads of Ossian and the poems of Thomas Gray, his works have a brooding intensity that was to inspire later authors like Flaubert and Victor Hugo. François-René de Chateaubriand was born in Saint-Malo in 1768, and the windswept granite of his birthplace shaped the active side of his nature. But it was at Combourg, where he lived claustrophobically with his parents and his adored elder sister Lucile, that his attitudes were formed and his introspection given full rein. In his brilliant autobiography, *Mémoires d'Outre-Tombe* (*Memoirs from Beyond the Grave*)—written at intervals throughout his life, and only completed in 1846, two years before his death—Chateaubriand paints a sombre picture of life at the château with his terrifying old father. 'His usual state was a deep melancholy that increased with age, and a silence broken only by his outbursts of rage. Greedily hopeful of restoring his family to its former glory, arrogant with the members of the States of Brittany, harsh to his retainers at Combourg, taciturn, tyrannous and threatening at home, the only emotion he inspired was fear.' His mother, on the other hand, was a naturally cheerful person, downtrodden by the Vicomte. Chateaubriand has an entertaining description of the family's nightly winter ritual, when the Vicomte would pace the hall for two hours and go to bed sharp at ten, after offering his wrinkled cheek to be kissed in silence. Relieved of his suffocating presence, mother, son and daughter would pour out the torrent of words they had been too frightened to utter in the course of the evening.

The château was originally built by the Bishop of Dol in the eleventh century; but the existing tight cluster of walls and pointed towers dates mainly from the fifteenth century. The castle dominates the little town at its foot and the lake that spreads beyond; its most attractive aspect is the park in which it stands, which is far less formal than most French parks, and is in fact more English than French in feeling, with fine large trees, and cows grazing on the wide stretches of grass between the plantings. If the *Mémoires* give a depressing picture of life in the château, the surroundings were painted in pure vitriol by the waspish agriculturalist Arthur Young, who visited Combourg in September 1788, not long before the outbreak of the Revolution.

> The country has a savage aspect; husbandry not much further advanced, at least in skill, than among the Hurons, which appears incredible amidst inclosures; the people almost as wild as their country, and their town of Combourg one of the most brutal filthy places that can be seen; mud houses, no windows, and a pavement so broken, as to impede all passengers, but ease none—yet here is a chateau, and inhabited; who is this Mons. de Chateaubriant [*sic*], the owner, that has nerves strung for a residence amidst such filth and poverty? Below this hideous heap of wretchedness is a fine lake, surrounded by well wooded inclosures.

The old Vicomte had died in 1786, and presumably young Chateaubriand had little or none of his father's arrogantly feudal concern for the upkeep of Combourg.

The bedroom in an isolated turret, where Chateaubriand spent his childhood nights, is shown to visitors. It contains little except an iron bedstead, a wardrobe—and the skeleton of a cat, from which the tower takes its name of 'Tour du Chat'. A ghost story told in the *Mémoires* concerns one of the Counts of Combourg, who had a wooden leg, and could be met sometimes on dark nights accompanied by a black cat at his heels; or sometimes only the leg and cat would appear. After Chateaubriand's time the skeleton of the cat was discovered under the stairs, and since then—or so they tell you—a disconsolate pegleg can sometimes still be met on the stairs, lonely without its feline companion. Chateaubriand tells us that he was afraid of sleeping alone in his tower, but that 'this harsh way of treating me left me with the courage of a man, without depriving me of that sensitivity of imagination of which they nowadays try to deprive young people'. And so he braved ghosts, owls, the rays of the moon, the wind rattling his door, strange moanings from below—until at four in the morning he heard the Vicomte shouting for his valet, 'like the voice of the last phantom of the night'.

There is no room here to go into Chateaubriand's long and dazzling career as traveller, man of letters, politician, ambassador and foreign minister. But it is worth mentioning his relations with England, as he was a passionate Anglophile and spent seven years in this country as an improverished exile in the 1790s, and a brief spell as French ambassador in London in 1822. He arrived here in 1793 and left in the spring of 1800; as a metropolitan-minded Frenchman he writes that 'all England can be seen in the space of four leagues, from Richmond, above London, to Greenwich, below it'. He saw politicians at Westminster and kangaroos at Kew, met Nelson in Hyde Park, saw Herschel the astronomer at Slough, and witnessed the madness of George III at Windsor. 'The king appeared, white-haired and blind, wandering through his palace like King Lear and feeling with his hands along the walls. He sat down at a piano and played several movements of a Handel sonata. What a fine end to *old England*!' And he found it necessary to change his name to M. de Combourg, as no one he met could pronounce his proper name.

Chateaubriand lies buried in one of the most magnificent situations on the whole coastline of Brittany—beyond Saint-Malo, on the island called the Grand Bé, at the very edge of the sea. The Saint-Malo authorities gave him the site during his lifetime, as a reward for the help he had given them over the construction of a new dock. In 1847, the year before Chateaubriand died, Flaubert visited the Grand Bé one evening at sunset, and mused on the great man's resting-place. 'He will sleep with his head turned towards the sea; in this tomb built upon a reef, his immortality will be like his life, deserted by his fellows and surrounded by storms.' I too made this easy pilgrimage one summer evening, and sitting by Chateaubriand's cross watched the sun sink in a blaze behind the rocky islets off Saint-Malo, while an early moon rose inland in a darkening sky. The tomb bears no name: just an inscription '*un grand écrivain français*', and that is all.

From the Grand Bé you can see the mighty rampart of Cap Fréhel away to the left on the horizon; and no promontory of such impressiveness would be complete without a castle. Fréhel is in fact a double cape, with a lighthouse on one point and the spectacular Fort La Latte on the other. Surrounded on three sides by the sea and on the landward side by a deep gully, Fort La Latte looks virtually impregnable. The castle is basically fourteenth-century, but considerable alterations were made by Louis XIV's military architect Vauban, who added the gun batteries. An oven for heating cannon balls, near the main tower, was constructed in 1795, and the red-hot cannon balls were fired from mortars at enemy ships. During the Second World War the castle was severely damaged by White Russians quartered there during the German Occupation.

On my first visit to Fort La Latte, a good many years ago now, I was mystified by a medieval wheeled battering ram and a number of crude-looking carts round and about the castle. I asked the attendant what they were, and he uttered an incomprehensible word that sounded like '*Layveeking*', with the stress on the first syllable. It was not until I finally saw the film '*The Vikings*' ('*Les Vikings*') that I realised what he meant. For it was at Fort La Latte that a one-eyed Kirk Douglas ordered his men to knock down the outer gate with the balsa-wood battering ram, and then climbed the inner gate by a ladder of axes embedded in it. And it was round the ramparts of the main tower (still with terrifying open holes from parapet to ground level) that he duelled with the intrepid Tony Curtis, before plunging to a well-deserved death on the rocks below.

CHAPTER V

Rennes

THE CAPITAL CITY both of Brittany as a whole and of the Département of Ille-et-Vilaine, Rennes is one of those places that people either like wholeheartedly or detest. It is not a city that inspires lukewarm opinions. Etienne Mignot de Montigny, a scientist and official of the Ponts et Chaussées going round the country on official business in the time of Louis XV, wrote that 'this rich and populous town is one of the prettiest capitals we have in our provinces'; whereas in the opinion of Augustus Hare, the most diligent of Victorian travel writers, 'There is never any life or movement in Rennes, and there is nothing whatever worth seeing.' Such views are still being stated in much the same terms today. I have heard Rennes described as a '*ville morte*', and indeed as far as night life goes it is moribund, if not completely dead; while a businessman complained to me that it is laid out for the stagecoach rather than the car—'*pour la circulation de la diligence, pas pour celle d'aujourd'hui*'. However, both these opinions come from Paris-biased points of view, and it is unfair to judge a provincial city by the standards of the capital. It is true that as the metropolis of French-speaking Haute-Bretagne the Bas-Bretons regard Rennes as something of an anomaly; and whenever I uttered almost my only words of Breton—'*Yermat,*' meaning 'Your health' or '*Kenavo*', meaning 'Goodbye'—in Rennes I tended to be regarded as a fluent Breton-speaker. But as the seat of Brittany's administrative power Rennes has always been the chief pressure-point when the central government has wished to extend its influence over Brittany as a whole; and Rennes has also played as important a role as any Bas-Breton town in resisting, or at least trying to minimise, such influence. In the 1970s it seems to me an attractive and workable place, where I have experienced nothing but kindness and good company.

The city breathes an air of solid, not to say stolid, prosperity. Across its centre runs the Vilaine, which for centuries has been tamed by high stone embankments but is now being driven completely underground by the need to provide more parking space. On either side the *quais* are lined by respectable classical buildings—the Museum, the Palais du Commerce, the former University building. The Vilaine runs due east and west; the north-south axis, equally regular, intersects it at the flowery parterres in front of the Palais du Commerce. Rennes has one of the finest botanic gardens in France, the Jardin du Thabor and its associated Jardin des Plantes; and every open space in the city is ablaze with meticulously laid out flowerbeds, the plantings changing as the year progresses. When I spent some days in Rennes during March, most of the work going on in the streets involved workmen planting out shrubs, with an accuracy that seemed to need constant use of metal rulers to make sure that each one was in the right position. In recent years the plantings have been so outstanding that in 1975 the city was awarded the accolade of French municipal floriculture, the first prize at the Concours National des Villes et Villages Fleuries.

The unhurried speed at which things move in Rennes has its advantages. Traffic actually waits for pedestrians at crossings, more often than not, and the Rennais always seem to have time to help a stranger, as I found one afternoon when I asked the way of a passer-by in the old town. After we had chatted a little, he told me that he was the Deputy Mayor, and asked me back to his ancient stone-walled house for a glass of whisky. He then took me in a slow progress, acknowledging the greetings of friends, to the Hôtel de Ville, where he roused the concierge from his torpor and showed me every detail of that splendid building. Rennes upsets the usual chronological sequence of towns, in which the oldest part is at the centre, and the further you go from the centre the later are the buildings. The heart of Rennes is classical and eighteenth-century, while the narrow cobbled streets and medieval half-timbered houses surround this austere core. This unusual layout is due to a disastrous fire in 1720, which devoured much of the ancient city. It is now like some medieval parchment that has had a hole burnt in it by a candle, and has been repaired by a piece of elegant eighteenth-century printing. To stretch the analogy further, the whole core, medieval and classical, has now been tidied up and mounted on a giant sheet of cartridge paper—the modern dormitory, suburbs, industrial zone, twin university centres and vast Citroen factory, which constitute most of the city's total area.

Rennes (Roazon in Breton) takes its name from the Redones, one of the Celtic tribes of pre-Roman times, whose name survives in even purer form in the nearby town of Redon. By the third century AD it was a strongly fortified town, built at the strategic point where the Ille joins the Vilaine, and standing at the junction of three major Roman roads. To the Celts it was known as Condate, meaning a confluence of rivers. It seems likely that the Redones submitted to Caesar at about the same time as the defeat of Vercingetorix in 52 BC. Not much is known about Rennes under the Romans, apart from the fact that it probably covered much the same area as the oldest part of the medieval town, around the Cathedral. Unlike so many Roman cities, nothing remains to link the Rennes of today with its remotest past. We know little more than that at the time of the decay of the Roman Empire in the fifth century it was the seat of a bishop and was known as the '*Urbs Rubra*', the 'Rose-red City', from the courses of Roman bricks in the stone wall surrounding it.

Any exploration of Rennes should begin in this ancient part. The Cathedral is a dull building, with a ponderous granite baroque façade, built between about 1540 and 1700, and a mid-nineteenth-century interior, all gilding and elephantine polished red-brown columns. About the only object of interest is a tomb with a full-sized reliquary of St Amand, described on a faded label as having been carried through the town '*dans le temps de calamités publiques*', but with no indication of when or what these calamities might have been. Near by are the Porte Mordelaise, a fortified gateway within a stone's throw of the Cathedral, through which the Dukes of Brittany used to pass in solemn procession to be crowned in the Cathedral; and the Ti-Koz (Breton for Old House), now a restaurant, fancifully described as having belonged to Du Guesclin. Of the ancient streets, the Rue de la Monnaie marks the medieval limit of the town. Its name recalls the days when Rennes had its own mint, and there are a good many banks in it still. Du Guesclin's early exploits of arms took place in the Place des Lices, (meaning Lists or Tiltyard), now largely covered by the glass and cast iron of Les Halles, the nineteenth-century meat market.

For the church enthusiast, Rennes can offer quantity but not much quality. The best of them is the Eglise St Germain, down near the river. It is an odd-shaped building, dating mainly from about 1500, with a noble interior and a fine east window, and a spectacular eighteenth-century *baldacchino* over the altar, all white paint and gilding. St Germain and the streets round it escaped the great fire of 1720, and the whole quarter is a smaller reflection of the old town a few hundred yards away.

Though on a far more restricted scale than our own Great Fire a couple of generations earlier, the Rennes conflagration must have been equally traumatic for the inhabitants. It was started by a drunken workman who set fire to his lodgings on the night of December 23, 1720. The fire spread at enormous speed through the old city, where every house had laid in winter stocks of kindling, logs for burning and sides of highly inflammable fatty meat. The situation was not improved by the behaviour of the soldiers called in to help, as they were far more eager to plunder empty buildings than to put out the fire. The local authorities hesitated to demolish any of the houses to form a fire-break, and the Rennais were more concerned about their furniture than anything else. Eventually the fire came to an end with a heavy downpour on December 29; the débris smoked for days afterwards. It is estimated that well over 900 buildings were destroyed, but probably not more than ten or so lives were lost.

This enormous hole burnt in the heart of their city gave the Rennais a tremendous opportunity, and they took full advantage of it. The reconstruction was the work of two architects, the first surnamed Robelin (his Christian name seems to be unknown), who insisted on solid stone buildings, and his successor Jacques-Jules Gabriel, who saw the plans through to their conclusion. The new houses were of standardised design, on a street layout which ignored the old medieval pattern of lanes and narrow alleys. The houses consisted (and still consist) of cellar, arcaded ground floor for shops and craftsmen, three storeys and an attic. The original severity of the design has been hidden for some time by a rash of incongruous shop fascias; but there is now a regulation that any shopkeeper who restores his shopfront has to ensure that the arcading is cleared of nameboards and other clutter.

The grandest building to escape the fire was the Palais de Justice, once the seat of the Parliament of Brittany, and now used for all kinds of local court sessions. Begun in 1618 and more or less completed by 1655, it is a sensible, austere building, facing south across a square full of grass and flowers. The façade, of two storeys and high mansard roof, was designed by Salomon de Brosse, architect of the Palais de Luxembourg in Paris. The most spectacular of the rooms on view is the Grande Chambre du Parlement de la Bretagne, richly painted and gilded and hung with nineteenth-century tapestries. The two loggias jutting high up from the walls were for ladies to see what was going on; the smaller of the two was much used by Madame de Sévigné, who described the Palais as '*le plus beau de France*'. In contrast to the vast barrel-vaulted Salle des Pas Perdus, where deputies and seekers after favour wore out their shoe leather pacing up and down, is the delicate painted panelling of the Chancellerie, where a court still sits six times a week.

Near the Place du Palais is the Place de la Mairie, where the graceful bow front of the theatre and the Hôtel de Ville face each other across yet another of Rennes' fine open spaces. Built by Gabriel in 1734, the Hôtel de Ville (Town Hall) is still the headquarters of the local administration. It is a rather awkward building, which turns its back on the old town and consists of a clock tower between two symmetrical wings. The façade is more remarkable for what you can no longer see there than for any positive qualities. In the tall central niche, now empty except for flagpoles and assorted shrubs, there once stood a large statue symbolising Brittany kneeling at the feet of France, in allusion to the union of the two countries in 1532. The statue was set up in October 1911—the month that saw the establishment of the first of the organised Breton separatist parties, the Parti Nationaliste Breton (Strollad Broadel Breiz), under the leadership of François Jaffrenou and Camille Le Mercier d'Erm. During the unveiling ceremony, Le Mercier d'Erm led a typical *manifestation* against the Monument of National Shame (*Monument de la Honte Nationale*), as the separatists called it; he was later taken to court and fined the derisory sum of two francs plus costs—the equivalent of our farthing damages. For over twenty years the statue stood in its niche, as a constant reminder of Brittany's subservience to France. Then, on the night of August 6, 1932, the secret society Gwenn ha Du (White and Black, the colours of the Breton flag) blew up the statue, and it has never been replaced.

Rennes' main war memorial is inside the Hôtel de Ville. This is the Panthéon, a large room with endless lists of names of the Rennais who died in the First World War. Round the ceiling, in bold lettering, are the names of the great marshals—Joffre, Foch and the others. But one name is hidden under a strip of brown paper, the name of Marshal Pétain, the arch-collaborator, awaiting the forgiveness of history to be revealed once again. Great names abound in the Hôtel de Ville. The cornice of the huge Salle des Fêtes consists of a long succession of famous Bretons, from the corsair Surcouf to the doctor Laennec. Above are the four greatest names of all, at least in the judgment of those who ordered them placed one on each wall: the men of action, Du Guesclin and La Tour d'Auvergne, the men of thought, Abelard and Chateaubriand.

After a surfeit of public buildings and cobbled streets, the Jardin du Thabor, a few minutes' walk from the Place du Palais, comes as a quiet oasis. Unfortunately on the two occasions I have been there it has been raining; but there was some consolation in the form of rain splashing into fish-filled pools and dripping gently off the branches of trees. The Thabor shows the French art of formal gardening to perfection, with flowerbeds tightly planted in abstract patterns, in animal outlines, or in the pattern of the coat-of-arms of Brittany. It stands on the highest plateau in Rennes, and was probably named after the biblical Mount Tabor by the Benedictine monks of St Mélaine, whose garden it originally was. Their church, which hides a medieval interior behind a baroque front, stands by the entrance to the Thabor and is worth looking inside for the fifteenth-century fresco in the south transept.

If you enter the Thabor gardens from the direction of the church, you come first to an enormous rectangular sunken lawn. This is known as the Carré Du Guesclin, from the fact that a statue of the great warrior once stood in the middle of it. The statue suffered the same fate as the one in the niche of the

Hôtel de Ville, being first mutilated and finally destroyed by a Breton secret society in 1946. At the far end of the Carré a column inscribed with the names of Vanneau and Papu commemorates two young Rennais who were killed on the barricades of Paris during the Revolution of 1830. Beyond the Carré the main botanic gardens begin. They are about twenty-five acres in extent, and were largely laid out in the second half of the last century. The Thabor is a place for the serious garden-lover as well as the casual visitor, as it has among its main features an enormous rose garden, with seemingly hundreds of varieties arranged in concentric circles, separated by paths.

In the Rue Gambetta, which leads down to the river from the Thabor, there is an exuberant Art Deco swimming-pool of the 1920s, the Piscine Municipale, with a façade covered in encaustic tiles, a huge blue-streaked triton's head above the door, and a magnificent blue and white interior, like the nave of some chlorine-smelling cathedral. It makes a remarkable contrast with the Palais St Georges next door, a massive arcaded building of 1650, built for Benedictine nuns and still bearing the name 'Magdelaine de Lafayette' (the abbess who ordered it to be built) in huge iron letters above the arcading.

Most of the town's active centre is north of the river. However, the Museum is on the south bank, in a sober stone mid-nineteenth-century building. It is in fact two museums rather than one: the Beaux-Arts, on the first floor, with plenty of Dutch and Italian paintings; and the Musée de Bretagne, on the ground floor, which is in itself a miniature history of the country. For those whose main interest is in things Breton, the Beaux-Arts has a fine collection of pottery of all shapes and sizes from Rennes itself, and from Quimper, Le Croisic and Dinan. Also worth hunting for are the paintings of Jean-Julien Lemordant, not so much for their quality as works of art but for their subject-matter. Lemordant was born in Saint-Malo in 1878 and died in Paris as recently as 1968. In the early years of the century he painted harbour and street scenes, like *La Procession*, which shows coiffed women sitting down to a feast in the street.

The Musée de Bretagne falls neatly into three sections. First, a historical survey, from the geological structure of the land, through Celtic and medieval history, with special emphasis on documents relating to the Duchess Anne, and on episodes of Breton history such as the revolt of 1675 against excessive taxation (the 'Révolte du Papier Timbré'). Second, an enormous room, with one side devoted to the great variety of nineteenth-century Breton costume, and the rest given over to traditional chests, box-beds and other furniture. Whether the puritan-looking clothes of Saint-Malo and the cheerful garments from Cornouaille are some reflection of the local character, who can say?

The third and final section is an outstanding example of the modern museum in practice. The brainchild of the Curator, M. Jean-Yves Veillard, it is an audio-visual room where the history is kept constantly up to date by the latest techniques of presentation. For anyone with a reasonable command of French and half an hour to spare, the main slide-cum-commentary display conveys better than anything else I have come across what has been happening in Brittany since the beginning of the century. Industry, agriculture, the impact of tourism, rural depopulation and unemployment, the revival of a sense of Breton identity—everything, in other words, that the ordinary tourist does not see. Besides this main presentation, which takes place at fixed times of day, there are work-it-yourself films, like an elegant little documentary I watched on seaweed collecting.

Of all the historical events with which Rennes has been connected, the most significant from the point of view both of Brittany and of France as a whole was the Révolte du Papier Timbré mentioned above. Historians see it as both the final despairing protest against the inroads of central government and as the first rumblings of the French Revolution. The revolt takes its name from the stamped paper on which official documents were written, the money from which was a means of raising revenue devised by Colbert, Louis XIV's finance minister. Colbert, says Joseph Chardronnet, 'was both the instigator and the executant of Louis XIV's economic and financial policies; and those policies were a disaster for Brittany. Because he was unable to be master in Brittany as he was everywhere else, Louis XIV swore to tame the Bretons; furious at their resistance, he used savage police methods and brought the country to economic disaster. For him, Brittany was never anything but a country to be exploited, a colony from which it suited him to drain the resources without taking any thought for the well-being and the future of that territory.'

This 'draining of the resources' had been begun by Richelieu earlier in the century, when he established the naval dockyard at Brest, which led to the virtual denudation of the Breton forest to build new ships for the French navy. Colbert's tax-raising policies were a further drain and brought Brittany to the verge of bankruptcy. Not only was a tax imposed on stamped paper, but there was also a tax on tobacco and on pewter ware; and these burdens, added to the enormous sum already raised to purchase Breton immunity from some of Louis XIV's earlier edicts, were seen as the last straw. The revolt against the new taxes began outside Brittany, in Bordeaux, which was held by insurgents for three days in March 1675. In April the inhabitants of Rennes followed suit. The centre for tobacco distribution was sacked, as were the offices concerned with stamped paper and excise dues. The rebels were subdued while they were in the process of attacking the office where duty on drink was administered, and Rennes became quiet again for the moment. Meanwhile the rebellion spread to Nantes and to Saint-Malo, where the authorities prudently bought off crews due to sail for Newfoundland by allowing them to buy tobacco at pre-tax prices.

The King determined to make an example of the insurgents, and the Breton parliament was ordered to discover and arrest the mutineers. The Duc de Chaulnes, who had been the king's Governor in the province since 1669, returned to Brittany at the head of an armed force, first to Nantes, where one of the ringleaders was hanged, and then to Rennes. Throughout June and early July there was an uneasy truce, which was threatened by a proposal to impose a salt-tax (*gabelle*) in Brittany, together with a duty on grain. In July the Rennes *papier timbré* office was again attacked. A contemporary refers to 'loyal inhabitants in such fear of the rioters that they did not dare leave their homes, such were the threats of roaming and licentious elements of the population'.

In Basse-Bretagne fury against the taxes of central government was compounded by hatred of the feudal exactions levied by local overlords. Riots broke out in Guingamp, Quimper and Châteaulin, and were followed by executions in reprisal. Infuriated peasants, known as '*Bonnets Rouges*', sacked the châteaux and the wine in drank their cellars, one group even compelling the local priests to march at their head. Forty parishes took up arms as the church bells rang out for revolt. It was class war with a vengeance; and it was not long before the peasants produced their own '*Code Paysan*', in which they attempted to set right the worst of the disabilities under which they suffered. Under this *Code* they would be free of statute labour for the *seigneurs*; justice would be exercised by authorities chosen from among the local inhabitants; *recteurs* would be paid for their services and would no longer receive tithes or similar gifts in kind; and anyone who administered the *gabelle* would be shot 'like a mad dog'. The money raised from the hearth-tax (*fouage*) would be used to buy tobacco, which would be handed out at Mass together with the sanctified wafers. Finally, social distinction between gentry and peasants would be abolished by intermarriage between the classes. In future, the peasants themselves would be known as *nobles habitants*, to make such marriages less controversial.

Such revolutionary proposals had their counterparts in the beliefs of groups like the Levellers on this side of the Channel. For their implementation the *Bonnets Rouges* needed a leader, and they found one in the person of Sébastien Le Balp, a lawyer from Cléden-Poher, near Carhaix. Throughout July, Le Balp and his rebels ruled Carhaix and the villages round about, attacking tax offices and châteaux, and draining dry the cellars of anyone who stood against them. Similar events took place at Pontivy, where the peasants even threatened to attack the château at Josselin. Meanwhile the Duc de Chaulnes moved from Rennes to Basse-Bretagne, where he tried to divide the peasants by promising a free pardon to those who surrendered. In this manœuvring he was greatly helped by Jesuits from the college at Quimper.

Le Balp was by now ready to proceed from insurrection to active collaboration with the enemies of France. He planned to occupy Morlaix and to hand it over to De Ruyter, the Dutch admiral, whose fleet was cruising in the Channel, but was dissuaded from marching on Morlaix by a false rumour that it was guarded by six thousand troops. The rumour was spread by the Marquis de Montgaillard, who together with his brother was finally responsible for Le Balp's downfall. The Montgaillards were popular among the peasants in the neighbourhood of Carhaix, and Le Balp hoped to enlist their military experience on his side by appointing them commanding officers in a general uprising. On September 3 the tocsin sounded in every parish. Thirty thousand peasants under arms sacked and burnt Carhaix, planning to head for Quimper where the Duc de Chaulnes had his headquarters. Le Balp revealed his plans to the Montgaillards, offering them the choice of joining him or being hewn in pieces. In a last desperate act of defiance, the Marquis drew his sword and ran Le Balp through. Deprived of their leader, the peasants melted away, and the rebellion in Basse-Bretagne was at an end.

The Duc's reprisals were swift and terrible. The *Bonnets Rouges* were hanged by the dozen without even the pretence of a trial. Mme de Sévigné wrote in a letter to her daughter how 'our poor Bas-Bretons flock together in the fields in groups of forty or fifty, and as soon as they see the soldiers they throw themselves on their knees and say *mea culpa*, that's the only French word they know. . . . There's no end to the hangings of these poor Bas-Bretons; they ask for a drink and for it to be over and done with.' As many ringleaders' rebels as could escape fled to the Channel Islands or took refuge with the Dutch.

The Duc next turned his attention to Rennes. He entered the city on October 12 and quartered his troops on the unwilling inhabitants; then, accusing the Breton Parliament of being responsible for the revolt, he summarily transferred the seat of power to Vannes, where it was to remain until 1690. He gave the inhabitants of one of the prosperous suburbs a fortnight to move out and then destroyed their houses. Mme de Sévigné wrote that 'you could see all these wretched people, women in childbirth, old men, children, wandering about in tears not knowing where to go, without food or anywhere to sleep'. Like Butcher Cumberland in the Highlands, the Duc de Chaulnes is still remembered in Brittany centuries later. Finally, the ringleaders were rounded up and condemned. One was banished and two were sent to the galleys; of those condemned to death, two were hanged and four were broken on the wheel. The province was fined the enormous sum of three million *livres*. Ten thousand troops were posted to Brittany for the winter, where they behaved like an army of occupation, looting and raping, and throwing householders from their own windows. Early in 1676 an amnesty was declared, and Brittany slowly returned to normal.

Unfortunately, the seventeenth century had no newspapers to record its dramatic events. Had Brittany's chief daily, *Ouest France*, existed then, it would no doubt have done full justice to the Révolte du Papier Timbré. Founded in August 1944, just after the Liberation, it now has no fewer than thirty-six different local editions, and claims that its circulation of 700,000 is the biggest of any daily in France. The entrance vestibule of its central office, in the Rue de Pré-Botté, behind the Museum, is a soothing place, containing an aquarium as an antidote to the worries of the world. In addition, the main news of the day goes up on large handwritten screens above the main entrance, which is useful if you have run out of money and want to know what is going on. The paper has outgrown these attractive premises and is now out on the industrial estate at Chantepie, in a new building full of electronically controlled doors and humming computers. *Ouest-France* has even evolved its own street cry: at least, on several camping holidays in recent years, my family has been roused by the melancholy cry '*Demandez Ouest(er) France*', in a plaintively minor key, and with the extra syllable tacked on to 'Ouest' to make the rhythm three-in-a-bar.

Like all major French cities, Rennes has its new Maison de la Culture, where everything from plays to exhibitions of local arts and crafts is assembled under one roof. But modern Rennes is most obviously embodied in the graceful twin blocks of flats, each thirty storeys high, known as Les Jumelles (The Twins) or Les Horizons. Vastly superior in their design to the average run of slab tower blocks, they can be seen from most parts of the city; unlike most such blocks, their general effect is cheerful rather than deadening. Some way out of the town, but well worth the visit, is the new university complex, claimed to be one of the most up-to-date centres of electronic teaching in the world.

The country round Rennes still has plenty of trees, notably in the Forêt de Rennes a few miles to the north-east. A trip to the forest can be enlivened even on a dull day by a meal in Liffré, at a country-club-cum-restaurant where enormous joints of lamb are cooked over charcoal in a massive granite Breton fireplace.

CHAPTER VI

Death of a Prince

As YOU DRIVE along Brittany's Emerald Coast between Ploubalay and Matignon, you cross the peaceful estuary of the Arguenon (the name means in Breton White River, from the silt carried down in its upper reaches). Looking downstream from the bridge you can make out the ruined towers of a medieval castle, buried among the trees. This is the castle of Le Guildo, once owned by a prince who began life with the promise of a glorious career before him, yet only twenty-six years later was murdered in circumstances still surrounded by mystery and terror.

The prince, Gilles de Bretagne, was one of those unfortunates who find themselves caught up in the ramifications of power politics, to which they are by temperament utterly unsuited. Born in 1424, he was the youngest of the three sons of Duke Jean V of Brittany, who has come down through history as John the Good (Jean le Sage). 'John the Astute' would perhaps have been a better name for him, as during his long reign, which lasted from 1399 to 1442, he managed to walk the dangerous tightrope of non-alignment with either France or England, preserving Brittany from the worst ravages of the final phases of the Hundred Years War. The ruling families of all three countries were closely inter-related, and the high diplomacy of the time was little more than the getting-together of different members of the same family—a kind of Forsyte Saga, whose prizes were not some minor inheritance but whole kingdoms, to be bought with the blood and suffering of their inhabitants.

Through his wife, Jeanne de France, Duke Jean was connected with the French royal family, as she was the daughter of the mad Charles VI, King of France from 1380 to 1422, and the sister of Charles VII, who succeeded him. Jean's brother, Arthur de Richemont, was Constable of France, the medieval equivalent of commander-in-chief of the armed forces. The

English connection was also through Jeanne de France, as it was her sister, Catherine de France (Shakespeare's Kate), who had married Henry V of England in 1420. Gilles was thus first cousin to Henry VI, who succeeded to the English throne at the age of one on the sudden death of his father in 1422. Throughout the early years of Henry VI's reign England was under the regency of Richard of Beauchamp, Earl of Warwick (1382–1439), to whom Henry V had bequeathed the care and education of his heir. Typical of Jean's flair, or perhaps good fortune, was the Breton involvement at Agincourt in 1415. Jean was marching to join up with the French at the head of 10,000 men, but the battle was over and done with by the time the Bretons reached the scene of action. After Agincourt the tide of fortune seemed to be with the English and against the French, so Jean the opportunist threw in his lot with Henry V, while managing to keep his options open.

It was into this atmosphere of near-incestuous international relations that Gilles was born. He was the Duke's youngest and favourite son; his elder brothers, François, heir to the dukedom, and Pierre, were born in 1410 and 1418 respectively. Both became Dukes in their turn, and both died prematurely; if only Gilles had had more of the circumspection of his father, he would certainly have succeeded while still a young man. In March 1432, as a pledge of his goodwill towards the English, John sent the eight-year-old Gilles as ambassador to London, under the guidance of Jean de Malestroit, Bishop of Nantes and the Duke's chief adviser, and accompanied by 140 knights. The object of the embassy was to strengthen the links between the two countries, and to work for more peaceful relations between Brittany, England, Burgundy and France. Whatever the diplomatic outcome may have been, the personal one was decisive as far as Gilles was concerned. The splendour of London as opposed to the drab cities of Brittany, and the overwhelming reception the embassy received, turned him into an inveterate Anglophile and thus sowed the seeds of his destruction.

In July, Malestroit returned to France, leaving Gilles to the charge of the Earl of Warwick, to be brought up with the eleven-year-old Henry VI. The two could not have been less alike in temperament. Gilles, though the younger, was a natural extrovert leader, while Henry was timid, retiring, a scholar and the future founder of Eton and King's College, Cambridge. Emile Gabory, author of the only book on Gilles, *Le Meurtre de Gilles de Bretagne*, thinks that both cousins were tainted to some degree by the madness of Charles VI, leading in Gilles's case to an unnatural rashness and lack of calculation, in Henry's to excess of caution and introspection. However that may be, their characters were largely complementary, and their friendship was to last until death separated them. The years around 1430 were crucial ones in the reduction of English influence in France, largely due to the inspiration of Joan of Arc, who in 1429 had raised the siege of Orléans and crowned Charles VII King of France at Rheims. It seems strange that Jean had not seen the way the wind was blowing at this time and continued to look to the English, especially since his own brother, Richemont, was Constable of France. No doubt he was used to hedging his bets; and anyway, it is easy to be wise with hindsight.

After two years spent in England in the company of Henry, in 1434 Gilles was summoned back to Brittany by Duke Jean, after being granted an annual pension of 1,000 gold marks (£666) by the English royal treasury. Six years later, as part of his inheritance, Jean gave him the domains of Ingrandes and Chantocé, confiscated from the infamous Gilles de Raiz (or de Retz), Marshal of France, executed for mass murder in 1440. These lands were in Anjou, not Brittany, and here was another cause of Gilles's downfall—the constant desire to carve out for himself a rich inheritance in his own country. As a mark of favour, and also to make use of his son as a link in the chain of friendship with England, in 1440 Jean made Gilles governor of Saint-Malo, then, as now, the usual port of embarkation between Brittany and England. The last journey of Duke Jean's reign was made soon afterwards, to Calais, where he was welcomed with great pomp by the English. In August 1442 he died, leaving behind the memory of a man who combined piety with an eye to the main chance, generosity with a shrewdly calculating mind. François inherited the dukedom, and on December 8 was crowned at Rennes.

Gilles was now in the classic position of the youngest son forced to watch his elder brothers in the enjoyment of their possessions. François had Brittany; Pierre had the magnificent apanage of Penthièvre round the Bay of Saint-Brieuc, with his capital at Guingamp; but he himself had only the lands confiscated from Gilles de Raiz. No doubt sensing this resentment, one of the first acts of François's reign was to send Gilles to England, in June 1443, to ask for the title of Earl of Richmond (Comte de Richemont)—an odd proceeding, as the title was already held by their uncle, the Constable of France. Perhaps François was trying to buy off Gilles's hostility by a move that would obviously be fruitless. Certainly he was right to think that a change of scene in his beloved England would cheer Gilles up, for the time being, at least.

Richmond was traditionally a Breton domain, as it had originally formed part of the Yorkshire lands of the Saxon Edwin, and had been granted by William the Conqueror to a Breton, Brient de Penthièvre. The great castle that still dominates the town on its hill (the 'Riche Mont') was built by Brient's brother, Alan the Red, and eventually passed by inheritance to the Breton Duke Conan IV. However, by the middle of the fifteenth century the dream of the earldom in the far north was faint, if not entirely vanished—'a secular mirage of the Breton princes', Gabory calls it. Out of friendship to Gilles, Henry VI ordered researches to be made into the archives to find out whether the claim to the lands had any foundation, but predictably the results were negative. A more subtle reason for the refusal was that to grant lands to a Breton—who was, after all, more French than English—might lead to a Trojan Horse situation in England. And Gilles landless and eager for the throne of Brittany was a more useful pawn in the power game than Gilles satisfied with broad acres in the North of England.

So Gilles, fêted, laden with gifts and honours, enjoyed the life of London for a while with his cousin. A '*moult beau chevalier*', an old chronicler called him, who foolishly but typically went on record as promising to serve Henry 'in peace and in war'. That promise was worth, in hard cash, another 2,000 gold nobles (1,000 marks) a year from the English exchequer.

As far as the French King Charles VII was concerned, Gilles's overtures to the English had a predictable result. Furious that

Gilles was consorting with the enemies of France, Charles confiscated his lands in Anjou, thus leaving him bereft of all possessions. An international incident that worked to Gilles's disadvantage in the summer of 1443 was a landing by the Duke of Somerset at Cherbourg, at the head of 8,000 men. Striking down through the Cherbourg peninsula, Somerset invaded Brittany and captured the little town of La Guerche, south-east of Rennes. This action seems extraordinary at a time when Gilles was actually on an embassy in London; perhaps it was a move to make Duke François show his hand. If that was the motive, the action succeeded. François reckoned that he now had more to fear from the English than from the French, and from that moment threw in his lot with Charles. As a further sign of his new allegiance to the French, François summoned Gilles back to France. He returned to Saint-Malo in the autumn, frustrated in his hopes, a landless man in a society where only lands meant anything.

Apart from conquest or inheritance, the surest way to acquire lands was to marry a rich heiress. And one was conveniently to hand. Françoise de Dinan, born in 1436, at the age of eight had just come into an enormous fortune on the death of her father and uncle within a few months of each other. Among the domains she inherited was the barony of Châteaubriant in south-east Brittany, and a number of estates in the north, including Le Guildo. At the age of only five she had been officially betrothed to the son of Count Guy de Laval; but this was no just cause or impediment to Gilles. At the head of an armed band he kidnapped the little girl from her home and went through the wedding ceremony with her, finally placing his foot in her bed as a symbolic gesture of possession. This act of brigandage counted as a full marriage, and Gilles came into Françoise's inheritance.

He had made a dangerous enemy of Laval; but he had made another enemy who was to prove mortal. Arthur de Montauban, Duke François's closest adviser, also had designs on Françoise de Dinan. He was as ambitious as Gilles, but far more patient and implacable. Half Italian by birth, he combined, says Gabory, 'the headstrong nature of the Breton with the wiles and deceit of the Italian'. Handsome and immoral, he was rumoured to have been the lover of the Duchess herself.

The ducal court was full of Montauban relatives, headed by Arthur's brother Jean, the Duke's Chamberlain and Marshal of Brittany, and of hangers-on who owed their positions to the support of the powerful Montauban family. The Montaubans were directly related to the ducal house through their niece Françoise d'Amboise, wife of Duke François's brother and future successor Pierre.

The Duke himself, however, was not displeased with the turn of events, which he hoped would turn Gilles from a discontented Anglophile into a landed prince content with the prize he had won. But this was to disregard Gilles's restless nature, which could never stay satisfied for long. For the time being, all the same, he was happy with the beauty and peace of Le Guildo. Here, disregarding the growing rapprochement between Brittany and France—when peace was signed between France and England in 1444 the Duke's ambassadors had openly ranged themselves with the French—Gilles became more Anglophile than ever. He hired an English garrison, surrounded himself with young English nobles, and continued to correspond with Henry VI, who appears to have sent him a letter promising him the earldom of Richmond. Apart from its beauty, Le Guildo was a convenient place for boats with secret messages to slip in and out. And Gilles had time for other intrigues, apart from the political. The Dukes of Brittany were renowned for their celibacy, and Gilles is known to have fathered at least three bastards during his brief time at Le Guildo. The French expression '*courir le guilledou*', whose dictionary meaning is 'to frequent places of ill fame', is said to derive from the uproarious life led by Gilles and his friends. Whether the derivation is correct or not, an expression taken from the back streets is not an unsuitable memorial for that unlucky prince.

Today it is hard to envisage the castle as it was in the days of its glory. To reach it, you take the little road along the east side of the river and branch left, down a steep track where the trees meet overhead. Suddenly a tower appears, still massive and virtually untouched, with ivy clinging to it and great trees rooted among its stones. At the end of the track the ground suddenly opens out into a little inlet, rush-grown and muddy, which must once have been the landing-place for Gilles and his furtive messengers from England. From the far side of the creek you get the best view of the castle, struggling out of its coating of undergrowth. Inside the walls it is surprisingly small and has been put to practical use as a cornfield; little enough is left of the interior, except for a record number of medieval lavatories, still quite usable, and obviously still being used. Indeed, the sanitary arrangements at Le Guildo have only been overtaken in most French houses in the last decade or so. It is the kind of ruin where an owl flies into your face as you fight your way through the brambles and elder trees along what remains of the walls. A Walter Scott, romantic ruin of a castle, not tidied up and tended by officialdom, with no entrance fee and no guide reciting its history by rote: in short, the kind of ruin our great-grandparents knew, where you can still muse on past glories undisturbed, or climb to a window embrasure without a notice to warn you that you are risking your neck.

Some time in 1445 Gilles signed his own death warrant. He sent a letter to Henry VI, which was intercepted by the Duke's spies. In it, he declared that he had always adhered to the English cause and would always continue to do so. François summoned Gilles to appear before the Ducal Council; this was treasonable correspondence, and the penalty for treason was death, even for the brother of the reigning Duke. Gilles's uncle, the good Arthur de Richemont, persuaded Gilles to throw himself on the Duke's mercy. Richemont used his own authority as Constable of France to plead Gilles's case. The plea was successful. Gilles agreed to surrender the governorship of Saint-Malo (presumably François was far from convinced of his change of heart) and to put an end to his correspondence with the King of England. Then came a stroke of bad luck for Gilles. Immediately after the reconciliation, Henry sent an embassy to Brittany to plead for Gilles. That was damaging enough; but the ambassadors also brought a personal letter for Gilles with vague promises of favours to come from Henry. The brothers' uneasy truce was once more broken.

Gilles retired to Le Guildo, where English emissaries continued to fill his head with promises, including a renewed attempt to lure him with the fabulous earldom of Richmond. Meanwhile the Duke was moving more strongly than ever in the direction of France. He spent a considerable time early in 1446 at the court of Charles at Chinon, culminating on March 14 in the act of homage before the King, yet another stage along the road of Breton subjection to France. This had the desired effect from the Duke's point of view. The King confirmed the Bretons in their ancient liberties and, at the Duke's request, stationed a body of 400 armed men on the borders of Brittany, to forestall any English coup under the possible leadership of Gilles.

In June, Duke François left Chinon and returned to Brittany, to his château of Kerango, near Vannes. Here Gilles came to see him, with a final demand for lands in Brittany; but the Duke emphatically refused him, fearing perhaps that to give him more castles might be inviting trouble in the future. For Gilles this was the final humiliation, the ultimate rift. No doubt wild words passed between the brothers; and the Duke gave the order for Gilles's arrest. Once more Richemont pleaded for Gilles before Charles VII, stressing the importance of keeping the peace with England; and François was compelled by the King to countermand the order of arrest. He sent his chamberlain, Jean Hingant, to Le Guildo, with letters of pardon—letters which Hingant told Gilles would guarantee him forgiveness for past misunderstandings, and held out the possibility of lands in Brittany after all.

Then followed an episode which can be interpreted in two different ways. Gilles read the documents; but far from being convinced, swore that he would never go to the Duke, that he had lost his faith in the Constable of France, and that he intended to sail with his wife to England. He threatened Hingant's life, and told his half-brother that with five or six thousand English soldiers he could take the whole country. These were the words either of a man who had become dangerously paranoid, or of an enemy to both France and Brittany who could no longer be safely left at liberty. The probability is that Gilles was suffering from intense mental strain brought on by his divided loyalties and the uncertainty of his position from one month to the next. Further proof of instability came the next day, when Gilles broke down and wept, and wrote a letter to his brother asking to be forgiven. This letter may be apocryphal; or there may be truth in the story that the letter was intercepted by the English faction and destroyed before it could reach the Duke. At any rate, the account François heard was that given by Hingant. Once more he gave the order for Gilles's arrest, and sent the four hundred troops on loan from Charles VII to make sure that his commands were carried out.

Gilles was arrested while playing tennis with his English squires. The French ransacked Le Guildo, carrying off the jewels of Françoise de Dinan, and, more important, getting hold of compromising letters between Gilles and the English. He was taken under guard to Dinan, and dragged before the Duke. Once again Arthur de Richemont was on hand to plead for his nephew; and this time he was supported by the third brother, Pierre. But François was adamant. Gilles must go before the States (Etats) of Brittany to be tried for his life. The Duke would be bound by the decision of the States, which was in effect the Supreme Court of Brittany, convened from time to time when the most vital national affairs had to be decided, and consisting of noblemen, high clergy and leading lawyers.

The States met at Redon on August 5, 1446. The chief prosecutor was the Seneschal Jean Loaisel, who accused Gilles of wishing to hand over both Brittany and France to the English. As was to be expected, Richemont pleaded in his favour, as did a leading member of the clergy, the Abbot of the Cistercian monastery of Buzay, on the Loire. Two French assessors also attended the proceedings. Unwilling to wash Brittany's dirty linen in front of the whole of Europe, the States declared themselves incapable of reaching a verdict. But this was no help to Gilles. The Duke immediately demanded an audience with Charles VII, in company with Montauban and other enemies of Gilles. For the last time Richemont lent his support to the prince, but without avail. Charles ordered a retrial, a fresh dossier was compiled, and in June 1447 Gilles was condemned to an indefinite term of imprisonment—a living death which did not go as far as the Duke had intended, but which meant that Gilles was now his to dispose of as he thought fit.

At the start of his imprisonment, Gilles was comparatively well treated. He was confined first of all at Châteaubriant, where he continued to receive pensions from the treasuries of both Brittany and England. Henry VI had also been concerning himself in the case. He sent ambassadors from London on Gilles's behalf to Duke François and the French King, both during and after the two trials, but the results were inconclusive. Believing finally that only force would achieve anything, he decided to capture a Breton town as bargaining counter for Gilles. He entrusted the mission to François de Surienne, a Franco-Spanish adventurer known as 'l'Aragonais', from his Spanish origin. Surienne spent a year studying possible targets; then in March 1449 he struck. His choice had fallen on the prosperous little border town of Fougères. On March 24, at the head of six hundred men, he stormed and sacked it, handing it over to his men to loot and pillage. Terrified for his safety, the Duke fled from Rennes, within easy striking distance of Fougères, to the remoter security of Vannes. He appealed for help to the French King, who sent four hundred men to the assistance of Fougères. The commander of the French forces, Admiral de Coëtivy, was also empowered to discuss with the Duke the possibility of bargaining for Fougères against the liberty of Gilles.

In the discussions that followed, the English gave evasive replies, which indicated to both François and Charles that Gilles was merely the pretext for taking Fougères and that they were unlikely to recover the town so simply. Matters were brought to a head when an English messenger declared that the Duke of Brittany was a vassal of the King of England and had no right to arrest Gilles in the first place. This was too much for Duke François and King Charles. In June 1449 they signed a solemn agreement that Fougères would be taken by force, and that Gilles would never be freed. The Duke raised an army to liberate the town, and Fougères was put in a state of siege. Surienne held out for three months. By the beginning of November the besieging army was seriously weakened by disease; this meant that, although the town was ready to fall, the Duke could not press his advantage. Surienne was allowed to leave Fougères with what remained of his troops and take refuge in Normandy. The result of Henry VI's intervention was the same as always: far from helping Gilles, the capture of Fougères had changed the status of Brittany and France from that of vassal and sovereign to that of allies fighting in the same cause. The final episode of the Hundred Years War had begun with a helpless prisoner as its unwitting originator.

Meanwhile Arthur de Montauban had not forgotten Gilles. The sentence of imprisonment without term meant that he still had no chance of marrying Françoise de Dinan, which he would certainly have done had Gilles been executed. Before the liberation of Fougères, Gilles had already been moved from Châteaubriant to the Château of Moncontour, about fifteen miles south of Saint-Brieuc, well away from any attempt at rescue and into territory under the control of the Montauban family. In command of the château was Olivier de Méel, a loyal follower of the Marshal Jean de Montauban; as his second-in-command he had Jean Hingant, whom Gilles had threatened earlier at Le Guildo. Gilles had now fallen among implacable enemies, and in spite of his relationship to the Duke he was ill treated and beaten. Henry VI kept up his appeals to both the Duke and King Charles VII, but the two were now firmly allied against England, and he was ignored. Gilles himself appealed to the King, but with the same result. However, it is possible that at the time of the capture of Fougères by Surienne, in March 1449, there was a chance of release for Gilles. Admiral de Coëtivy is said by some sources to have actually been empowered by the King to order Duke François to free Gilles, but this outcome was frustrated by Montauban. Montauban, the story goes, employed one of the Duke's entourage called Pierre Roze to forge a letter purporting to come from Henry VI. Roze had been the English King's secretary, and knew how to counterfeit his handwriting and seal. The letter, addressed to the Duke, threatened to send an army of 30,000 men into Brittany if Gilles was not released. The Duke was furious; and when the French King learned the contents of the letter he saw no reason to doubt its authenticity, and revoked the order of release for Gilles.

Whatever the truth of the story, there could now be no further hope for the prince. He was moved first to a château near Nantes, along with Méel and Hingant; then back north, to the Château de la Hardouinais, a grim place buried in thick woodland near the little town of Merdrignac, not far from Moncontour and so once again in Montauban country. Here he was out of sight and out of mind of both King and Duke.

Méel had been ordered by the Duke to make sure that his brother was confined in a dungeon below water level, and he carried out his orders. Yet Gilles was a man of great tenacity and will to live, and the worst hardships did not break his spirit. In the solitude of his dungeon he would play sadly on a flute; and the gentle notes, floating through the window-slit and across the moat, would prove to the local farmers and foresters that 'their' Messire Gilles was still clinging to life. As the weeks went by and Gilles showed no sign of succumbing, the Duke lost patience. In an outburst reminiscent of Henry II's 'Will no one free me of this pestilent priest?' which led to the murder of Becket, the Duke said to Méel and Hingant, 'I could wish my brother in paradise' ('*Je voudrais mon frère en paradis*'). His words were reported back to Arthur de Montauban; and at a secret meeting outside Rennes—again reminiscent of the four knights at Saltwood Castle plotting Becket's murder—Montauban, his brother Jean, Méel and Hingant worked out the final details of how Gilles was to die. It was decided to poison him, with Montauban's chief steward, Jehan Rajart, as intermediary.

The flute-playing may be only a legend; and during the last months of his life Gilles seems to have generated legends. One tells how an old woman would cross the moat (it must have been a dry ditch if the story is true) and pass water and coarse bread to the prisoner through the window-slit. Knowing he was soon to die, Gilles asked the old woman to bring a priest to hear his confession; this duty was carried out by an old Franciscan friar, who heard the prince's words through that same narrow opening. All the same, Gilles had still not completely lost hope. He sent a final appeal to the Duke, via Méel, threatening to kill himself if he was not handed over to a proper court for judgment, or else set free. But François remained adamant, and Méel returned to the château with no ray of comfort for Gilles.

Meanwhile Montauban had been finalising the details of Gilles's murder. As his accomplices he had not only his steward Rajart but two villains, evilly named Maletouche (presumably so called because his touch meant death) and Oreille Pelue (Hairy Ear); in addition, there was a group of corrupt nobles ready to carry out his plans. With his Italian connections,

Montauban was in touch with the 'academy' in Italy that investigated the properties of poisons and sold them to the Borgias. He had been given three packets by an Italian called Marco, the 'Bastard from Milan', marked according to their effects 'strong', 'stronger' and the third 'even stronger'. The poisons were tried out on a dog and a chicken, which died as soon as they had swallowed them.

The task of administering the poison was given to one of Montauban's hangers-on, Jehan de la Chaize. He told Gilles that his food would be improved from now on, and gave him a stew with the poison mixed into it. Gilles, half starved after weeks on bread and water, fell on the food; but his weakened stomach could not take it, and he vomited up the meal. Several more times the accomplices tried to kill him with poison, but on each occasion Gilles rejected it. Méel concluded that it was ineffective, and ordered it to be thrown in the moat. Poison had failed, but Gilles's killers were not to be deterred. On the night of April 24, 1450, La Chaize, Maletouche, Oreille Pelue and a fourth assassin, Robert Roussel, entered his cell, wound a cloth round his neck and tried to strangle him by hauling on both ends. Summoning up the last of his strength, Gilles seized a wooden bar and felled one of his attackers. The other three picked up a mattress and suffocated Gilles beneath its weight. When they were sure that he was dead, they cleared up all signs of a struggle, cleaned the blood off the body and laid it out on the bed to make it look as though Gilles had died in his sleep. Then they went off on an early-morning hunt, as if nothing had happened.

However, their guilt was not to be so easily covered up. That afternoon a servant from La Hardouinais told the four murderers that Gilles was dead. First they pretended to be surprised, and then said that of course Gilles had been ill for a week or so. They asked their hunting companions to confirm their alibi; after all, they had been out in the field at the moment when Gilles died. But their companions were evasive, saying merely that they would not report anything they had seen or heard. Méel gave as his considered opinion the unlikely story that Gilles had died of grief after hearing the news of the Battle of Formigny, in which the French under the Constable Richemont had decisively beaten the English and which had taken place a few days previously, on April 15. But popular opinion was not deceived, and within days rumours were circulating that Gilles had been murdered, and murdered at the instigation of his brother the Duke.

As with all medieval martyrs, there were miracles associated with the prince almost as soon as he was dead. The Abbot of the near-by Cistercian monastery of Boquen insisted on burying the body in his church. At the head of his monks he went to La Hardouinais, blessed the body of the prince, and, with a cart drawn by four oxen as a hearse, led the funeral procession across the countryside alive with spring. The cortège had reached a certain point in the road when one of the oxen stopped and pawed the ground. It refused to go on until the Abbot vowed to build a chapel to St Gilles, the prince's patron saint, at the spot where they had halted. The body was entombed below the high altar in the abbey church. It is said that no other cart has ever been able to retrace the exact route of Gilles's cortège, and that, somewhere beside the road, a stone still bears the imprint of an ox's hoof.

Yet another legend has it that before Gilles died he called on the soul of the man responsible for his murder to appear before God's throne for judgment within fifty days (or forty days, accounts differ) of his death. Duke François heard that Gilles was dead at the beginning of May, while he was besieging Avranches, held by an English garrison. There was a rumour that the Duke himself was suffering from the effects of poison, administered by the wife of the English commander, who had slept with him in exchange for a safe-conduct out of Avranches for her husband and his troops. He was certainly a sick man at the time, and quarrelled violently with Richemont, who virtually accused him of Gilles's murder. In spite of his military successes, François was tormented by guilt. He had a mass said for the soul of the dead man in Boquen Abbey, and on May 31 held a solemn memorial service in the abbey church of Mont Saint-Michel. On the shores of that desolate bay François was riding at the head of his troops when the Franciscan who had heard Gilles's last confession laid his hand on the Duke's bridle and passed on Gilles's summons to judgment within fifty days. Full of forebodings, the Duke returned to the Château de l'Hermine at Vannes.

Here he set his affairs in order, naming his brother Pierre as his heir, with Arthur de Richemont, their uncle, as next in line to the throne. He said his last farewells to his wife, Isabella of Scotland, made his confession, and died on the night of July 17, not fifty days after Gilles but some eighty-odd. He lies buried before the high altar in the abbey church at Redon (now the Eglise Saint-Sauveur). Whatever his faults may have been as regards his treatment of Gilles, François was remembered by a chronicler as 'the greatest knight who ever wore a sword' (*'le plus grand chevalier qui oncques ceignit l'espée'*); and from the point of view of Brittany in general he was one of the best of the line of dukes. But it is for the death of Gilles, not for his military prowess and political astuteness, that Duke François has his place in popular history.

During the three months that had passed since Gilles's death, the young prince had almost reached the status of a martyr, and Duke François was being openly accused of bringing about his death. One of Duke Pierre's first acts was to bring the killers to justice. In August, less than a month after his accession, he ordered the arrest of Hingant, Méel and the rest. Hingant had disappeared without trace; but Méel was captured across the French border and brought back to Brittany, much to the anger of Charles VII at this violation of his territory by the new Duke. In May 1451 the States met at Vannes to try the murderers. Méel, Rajart, Oreille Pelue and the others were decapitated, and their bodies were quartered and displayed on scaffolds.

Amazingly, at the trial no mention was made of Arthur de Montauban, the real perpetrator of the crime. In such cases it is often the powerful who escape, while the smaller fry are punished; and so it was with Montauban. Apart from his high place in the councils of the late Duke François, he was also the uncle of Duke Pierre's wife, Françoise d'Amboise; and his brother, the Marshal Jean de Montauban, was also implicated to some extent in Gilles's death. Even more extraordinary than Arthur's non-appearance at the trial was his subsequent career. From being courtier, rake and murderer, Arthur turned, with typically medieval change of outward show, if not necessarily of heart, to the life of religion. He became a novice in the Benedictine order of the Célestins; then, finding himself hunted by the Duke's secret police, he took to the road, spending four years wandering the pilgrim routes of France, Italy and Spain. At the end of this time Françoise d'Amboise persuaded Pierre to grant Arthur an amnesty for his crime, and the pursuit was called off.

In Paris, Arthur taught Breton students, as a simple monk. His reputation became known to Louis XI, who had succeeded Charles VII in 1461; and Louis, with remarkable lack of tact, appointed him Abbot of Saint-Sauveur at Redon (in whose abbey church Duke François was buried). This was too much for the Bretons, with their long memories, and at the threat of armed rebellion the appointment was revoked. Not to be beaten, Louis then made Montauban Archbishop of Bordeaux; but he found the position not to his liking and soon returned to the cloister of the Célestin monastery in Paris, where he died in 1478, leaving a reputation for sanctity and learning behind him.

Gilles's widow, Françoise de Dinan ('widow' is scarcely an apt description, as she was only thirteen at the time of the murder, and had never associated with Gilles, let alone slept with him) lived on until the end of the fifteenth century. There seemed no reason why she should not now marry the son of Guy de Laval, to whom she had been originally betrothed at the age of five; but this was forbidden for reasons of state, and in 1451 she married instead her fiancé's father, Count Guy himself. In spite of his comparative age, Guy lived until 1486. On his death, Françoise spent a brief and difficult period as governess to the headstrong girl who was to become the great Duchess Anne de Bretagne (see Chapter XV); and towards the end of her life, at sixty, she at last reached some kind of peace with a third marriage to a nobleman from Picardy. She died in 1500, and was buried in the Dominican church at Nantes.

One cold March day, I set out to try to find the ruins of the Château de la Hardouinais, where Gilles was murdered. They are marked clearly enough on the Michelin map, and I started down the track that I thought must lead to them. As I went on, the path grew more and more soggy, the brambles and bushes became thicker and more entangling, and I finally ended up in a dense pine wood where the thin spring daylight hardly penetrated through the branches overhead. If the remains of La Hardouinais are there, they have kept their grim mystery as far as I am concerned. When I emerged once more into the open, a hailstorm was whipping the surface of the lake by the road; and I thought of Gilles's strange death in that same bleak place and unwelcoming season, more than five and a quarter centuries ago.

CHAPTER VII

Saint-Malo and the Corsairs

ALL OVER SAINT-MALO they sell postcards of peculiarly hideous aspect, in a series called '*Les Corsaires d'Etienne Blandin*'. These disembodied heads, scarred, one-eyed, pipe-smoking, ear-ringed, with red handkerchiefs knotted behind at the neck, claim to be portraits of typical corsairs, with names like 'Adolphe Lancien, known as Vercingetorix' or 'Thomas Le Gueult, known as Bite-his-Eyeball'. In the tourist season small boys piratically dressed hand out leaflets for the waxworks display of corsairs and their deeds in the fortified tower known as the Quic-en-Groigne; while Quic-en-Groigne minivans, crowned by slowly rotating towers, trundle round the outskirts of the town. This aspect of Saint-Malo, the Cité Corsaire as it proudly calls itself, has been exaggerated to such a degree that the other personalities of the place have tended to be overshadowed, if not forgotten—the literary figures like Chateaubriand and Lamennais, the scientists like Maupertuis, even the explorer Jacques Cartier, not to mention the hosts of non-corsair captains and crews who traded with the Indian Ocean and opened up the South American sea route round Cape Horn.

Nevertheless, Saint-Malo's chief fascination lies in its outward-turning seafaring aspect rather than in its contribution to more peaceable or literary activities. And not just in past seafaring, either. If you turn your back on the walled city (Saint-Malo Intra Muros) and walk round the inner harbour, you will pass first of all the yacht marina crowded with pleasure craft of all shapes and sizes and will then come to the Bassin Duguay-Trouin and the Bassin Intérieur, lined with warehouses and stacked high with timber, and smelling of fish, pinewood and diesel fuel, with a whiff of sewage. Apart from the cargo boats there are often more spectacular craft as well. In the summer of 1976 Alain Colas's giant technological marvel, the computer-controlled four-masted yacht *Club*

Méditerranée, was moored at Saint-Malo, after coming third in the single-handed race across the Atlantic; while next door was a huge blue *thonier* (tunny boat) from Concarneau, occupied by fishermen as an organised protest and covered with posters drawing attention to unemployment in the fishing industry, besides the inevitable rash of Communist and anarchist propaganda.

As far as the corsairs are concerned, Saint-Malo needs 'demythologising'. This is the expression of Dan Lailler, who runs the museum and library, and who has made a start with his own excellent museum, quiet and factual in contrast to the flamboyant Quic-en-Groigne, just across the Castle courtyard, and with his guide to the town published by *Ouest-France*. A stroll round the ramparts, which takes about half an hour, takes you past statues of two famous corsairs, the dandified figure of Duguay-Trouin in the full-bottomed wig of Louis XIV's time, and the more traditionally swashbuckling Surcouf, the scourge of the Channel during the Napoleonic Wars. The best time to do this walk is at dusk on a fine summer's evening, as you can then enjoy the splendid sunsets out to sea, or look from rampart height into the dining-rooms of the granite houses, built by the wealthy *armateurs* (shipowners) of the early 1700s, where their descendants (or perhaps Parisians who have rented apartments for the season) sit unselfconsciously at dinner, disdaining curtains between them and the staring crowds a stone's throw away.

Who then were the corsairs, and to what extent did they correspond to the Captain Hook pirate image foisted on the visitor to Saint-Malo? The answer is, very little. The main point is that they were not pirates at all, but legitimate agents of the French Crown, acting under official licence. At least as far back as the thirteenth century, ships from Saint-Malo formed an important part of the French navy, and as the wars with the English grew in length and ferocity their significance increased. But their activities were not regularised until the reorganisation of the French navy by Colbert in the 1660s and the years following. Merchants and captains who wished to fit out ships to *faire la course*, as the activity of privateering was called, had to follow a number of stringent rules, including obtaining the sanction of the Ministry of Marine and depositing a large sum as caution money. The corsair was then issued with Letters of Marque, signed by the King, which entitled him to capture four classes of vessel. These were, first, vessels that refused to lower their flags, whether belonging to a hostile or friendly power after a warning shot had been fired; second, vessels whose papers proved that they belonged to a hostile state; third, vessels that carried no papers and tried to conceal their nationality; and fourth, neutral vessels carrying the goods of an enemy power.

There were definite rules of attack laid down. Though a corsair vessel could approach within firing range of a potential prize under false colours, or without showing any colours at all, she had to hoist her proper colours before opening fire. If she fired on the prize without showing her own colours, she was considered a pirate and hence a criminal. Once the prize was captured, the corsair was bound by further rules. He was not allowed to pillage or sink her but had to close and seal her hatches, take her captain and crew on board his own vessel, and then sail the prize back to port with members of his own crew. Once the prize was back in harbour, officialdom took over. The ship, her captain and crew and her papers were handed over to the naval authorities; and the ship and cargo were then sold, according to a fixed division of the proceeds. One-tenth went to the Lord High Admiral of France, as representative of the Crown; and the remaining sum was divided into three: two-thirds going to the *armateur* and his backers, while the remaining third was divided between the captain, his officers and crew. It is not surprising that the *armateurs* grew fat and built themselves splendid houses, both Intra Muros and in the countryside round Saint-Malo, where their grand '*Malouinières*', as their country houses were called, can be seen to this day, many of them now come down in the world with broken garden walls and smashed gazebos. On the other hand, though the leading corsairs did well enough from their third of the spoils, the average junior officer or crew member had little to show for weeks or months of discomfort and danger at sea.

In spite of the specious legality of *la course*, many *armateurs* were worried about its religious and legal justification, and took care to guarantee themselves against possible sanctions in both this world and the next. The corsairs had their detractors; one eighteenth-century definition was 'men who roam the sea without authority to rob and plunder all that they can get hold of' ('*Les corsaires sont des gens qui courent les mers sans commission pour voler et piller tout ce qu'ils peuvent prendre*'). To prevent any such implication of piracy, the Malouins went to amazing lengths. They gave extensive gifts to the Church, on the basis that alms can redeem sin (in Latin, *Eleemosyna redimit peccatum*); this naturally got the clergy on to their side. Though proper scriptural authority was not forthcoming, a leading Saint-Malo cleric, the Abbé Porée, found the justification of *la course* in the pages of St Thomas Aquinas, where it was stated that 'everything taken for the service of the state and in accordance with the laws is legal'. And the *armateurs* kept their captains under control by classing as serious theft any withholding of their lion's share of the prize money. The lawyers put the matter more simply: anyone who disapproved of the *guerre de course* must be a disloyal citizen, and the *armateurs* were a positive good to the community, since they saved the government the expense of arming a large number of vessels.

The common-sense attitude of the Church to the facts of corsair life was well shown by its attitude to the privateer's marriage vow. As long as a corsair was on the Saint-Malo side of Cap Fréhel, he was supposed to remain faithful; but once he had rounded that tremendous cape, which dominates the westward view from the town, he was absolved from any strict observance of monogamy.

The corsair crews were a good deal more unruly and independent-minded than the regular sailors in the navy. In the first place, they were volunteers for gain, not pressed into the service against their will; and secondly, they nearly all came from Saint-Malo and often knew the captains personally, which meant that discipline could not be over-harsh. On the other hand, there were brutal captains, like the one mentioned in Etienne Dupont's entertaining *Les Corsaires Chez Eux*, which is a mine of information on everything connected with the corsairs (and which incidentally is sold in Saint-Malo bookshops as a paperback). A leading shipowner wrote to one of his captains that there was a constant stream of complaints about his treatment of the crew. The captain was advised simply to keep them frightened but not to harm them (*'Faites-leur peur, mais point de mal'*). Another captain was excused his brutality on the grounds that he was used to voyaging to West Africa, where men were valued against their weight in metal. Ships' boys were recruited from foundlings at the hospital, provided they were fit and twelve years old.

Food was as poor as it was on all vessels in the seventeenth century. The crew ate five meat meals a week, bacon and beef alternately, with cod on Fridays and Saturdays. Apart from brackish water, they had wine to drink, sometimes cider and mead. Brandy was doled out before an attack on a prize, to give Dutch courage; one wonders how many corsairs were cut down drunk in the scuppers, or fell into the sea from the boarding-plank before setting foot on the enemy vessel. If they were wounded, there was always a surgeon on hand to deal with them, though he was not necessarily competent. Ships' surgeons were often young doctors after making a little money so that they could set up practice on land. When not tending the sick and wounded, they were expected to help with the shipboard tasks, to the extent of lending a hand behind a gun; while on the Newfoundland cod vessels they might be asked to use their professional expertise in cutting up fish. If the surgeon's knife or drugs failed, every large corsair vessel was obliged by law to have a chaplain on board, to administer the last rites. Like the surgeons, they were not necessarily the leading lights of their calling, but were often priests who would have been unfrocked if they had not chosen to take their chance on shipboard.

Once back in Saint-Malo with their share of the takings, the corsairs would drink, whore and gamble until the money ran out. The prostitutes lived mainly in the ironically named Rue des Moeurs, the Street of Morals. The police kept an eye on them, and any suffering from venereal disease were sent to hospital, as were those who became pregnant. No doubt a good many of the ships' boys who grew up to be corsairs were the sons of prostitutes, fathered by corsairs home on shore for a spell. Gambling was endemic, and vast sums were wagered and lost. At Nantes the son of a Saint-Malo shipowner lost 40,000 *livres* over a single Christmas holiday. Dupont lists the Malouins' favourite games as *hocca* and *florentini* (both unknown to my dictionary), *bassette* (basset), *pharaon* (faro), *biribi* (some kind of roulette), *toton* (a teetotum or top, with four sides each marked with a different letter; the gambler betted which letter would be uppermost when the top fell on its side).

The greatest of the corsairs, René Duguay-Trouin, describes in his autobiography how easy it was to slide down the slippery slope in the great days of Saint-Malo. When he was a youth in about 1690 he was taken up by an inveterate gambler, who was constantly broke and gambled to pay off his creditors. 'He was brave and handsome, witty and engaging; and also had a passion for wine and the fair sex, which went as far as outright debauchery (an excellent schooling for a young man of my age). He wanted me to share all his pleasures, and made me his confidant and the companion of many of his adventures; he even taught me some tricks with cards and dice, which', says Duguay-Trouin self-righteously, 'I never made use of.'

To guard their treasures the Malouins made use of a special police force—the *dogues*, mastiffs of English stock, which roamed outside the walls of the town from curfew until sunrise. Before daybreak the dog-keeper called them back to their kennels by blowing on a copper trumpet. The first use of the dogs is said to date back to the twelfth century; in 1575 a traveller wrote that 'they are the most savage and furious dogs a man could see anywhere' ('*chiens les plus cruels et furieux que hommes ne sauraient voir*'). At that date there were probably about fifty of them, though in the seventeenth century they were reduced progressively to twelve. By the end of the eighteenth century the *Chiens de Guet* were no longer in existence; but they are still recalled in the Venelle aux Chiens (Dog Lane) near the Castle, and one of them is portrayed in the corner of Saint-Malo's flag.

Their final disappearance is said to be due to the fact that in 1770 they savaged to death a young naval officer, who was returning after curfew from a visit to his fiancée at Saint-Servan. Like so many other Saint-Malo traditions, this story is firmly scotched by Etienne Dupont; though he does admit that a good many '*accidents*' were caused by the mastiffs.

The manner in which the Malouins lived has vanished into history; but their noble houses still remain. Those, that is, that were spared in the terrible bombardments of August 1944, when the Americans occupied Paramé and shelled the Germans, who were hanging on to their fortifications in Saint-Servan. Saint-Malo was in the direct line of fire, and to this day there is no agreement as to who caused the destruction. If you talk to two people in Saint-Malo, one will tell you that the Germans evacuated the city and then set fire to it, while the other will say that the Americans had the chance to put out the fires caused by the shelling, but just let the town burn. Whatever the truth may be, the fact remains that at the end of the war most of Saint-Malo was little more than a shell, and its superb reconstruction is one of the architectural triumphs of the postwar period. Fortunately the great houses of the *armateurs*, which form an unbroken line above the Quai de Dinan and are best seen across the bay from Saint-Servan, were largely untouched, though their stone façades are still pock-marked with holes made by shell fragments and bullets. This section of the town, known as the Quartier de Dinan and later as Californie, was conceived by Vauban, and carried out about 1720. Fittingly enough, the statue of Duguay-Trouin stands outside the houses his exploits made possible.

The older houses had far more timber in their construction than the *hôtels* of the Quartier de Dinan, and they burnt like tinder during the shelling of 1944. However, a certain number of them survive, especially round the Cathedral. There is a fine example in the narrow Rue Pélicot, where No. 5 houses the Société d'Histoire et d'Archéologie de Saint-Malo, a gathering of savants who meet every Wednesday afternoon to burrow among the archives of the town. The room used by the Society has a magnificent stone fireplace, and is reached by a wooden spiral staircase with a rope 'handrail', typical of these ancient buildings.

Before the holocaust of 1944 Saint-Malo had only once faced a real threat of destruction since it was first fortified in the twelfth century. This was in November 1693, when the English launched an 'infernal machine' against its walls—the forerunner of the bouncing bombs and Great Panjandrums of later war technology. It was a ship specially built as a floating bomb, with a shallow draught so that it could sail in close to the walls of Saint-Malo. This is how Lord Russell of Liverpool describes it, in *The French Corsairs*: 'It was fitted out with black sails so that it would be less visible in the dark and was filled with chopped straw, twenty-five tons of gunpowder, 600 bombs and 600 pounds weight of fire-balls. The explosives were placed at the bottom of the ship's hull and covered with the chopped straw, which was sprinkled with oil, camphor, sulphur, ammonia, alcohol and resin.' Enough, presumably, to blow even the strongest walls wide apart; but such was the incompetence of those controlling it that it grounded and was holed on a rock fifty metres off the town, and much of the gunpowder was soaked and made useless. All the same, what was left exploded with a tremendous roar and sheets of flame, though apart from some damage to the wall the only fatality in Saint-Malo was a cat.

By this date Duguay-Trouin, though still only twenty, was an experienced corsair commander. At the start of his autobiography he tells us: 'You will find in these memoirs only military engagements, battles and boarding parties.' That is unduly modest, as he also tells of his capture by the English and his escape from Plymouth; of his gambling and his love-life; and of his greatest exploit, the capture of Rio de Janeiro from the Portuguese and the rescue of a French expeditionary force held prisoner there. This took place in 1711 and was the high point of Duguay-Trouin's career; but an earlier episode, dating from the year of the 'infernal machine', gives the true flavour of corsair life. Duguay-Trouin's account is full of his magical opportunism and flair, which made him an intuitive genius among the more mundane corsairs.

> At that time I obtained command of the King's frigate *Hercules*, 28 guns, fitted out in the port of Brest. I put to sea, and in the course of this cruise took five or six English and Dutch prizes, among them two powerful and well laden vessels coming from Jamaica. The circumstances of this action were too extraordinary for me to leave them untold.
>
> I had cruised for more than two months, and had only a fortnight's provisions left. I was also inconvenienced by the prisoners and by having sixty men sick. My officers and crew, seeing that I was not yet thinking about putting into harbour, stated strongly that I ought to do so, and also that the King's

command was positive on the matter. I was well aware of this, but I was gripped by a secret presentiment of some stroke of good fortune, which made me put things off from day to day. When I realised that I was up against it, I called the crew together, harangued them, and managed to persuade them by a combination of soft words and authority to grant me an extra week's cruising time, assuring them that we would make our fortune and that I would give them permission to plunder. Basically this decision was unreasonable, and I do not understand what made me speak to them so positively; but I was compelled by an inner voice, which I could not fight against.

Chance had it that at the end of this week I dreamt that I saw two large vessels approaching us under full sail. This vision alerted all my senses, and I woke up with a start. I ran on deck, and as day was beginning to break I scanned the horizon. The first thing that struck me was two actual vessels in the same position and with the same sails as those I had seen while I slept. I thought at first that they were warships, because they were bearing down on us under full sail, and they gave that impression. In this belief I sailed as fast as I could away from them; but when I realised that I was outdistancing them easily, I put about and went in to the attack. I made myself their master after about three hours of lively resistance. These vessels had their sides pierced for 46 guns and were carrying 28 guns each; they were laden with sugar, indigo and quantities of gold and silver. The plunder was great, and I was willing to be lax about it because I had given the men my word; all the same, that did not prevent my *armateurs* from making a great deal of money. I took these two prizes to Nantes, where I had my frigate careened, and then renewed my cruise. I took three more prizes, and returned to Brest for a refit.

For all his phenomenal good luck and abilities, Duguay-Trouin was not entirely immune from defeat. In 1694 his ship the *Diligence* was forced to surrender to superior English numbers and fire-power, and he was taken prisoner to Plymouth. His captivity seems to have been remarkably free-and-easy, to begin with at least, as he was given the run of the town and struck up a liaison with the pretty French wife of a local merchant. After a year as a prisoner, he escaped with the connivance of his *fort jolie marchande* and a Swedish skipper, from whom he managed to buy a long-boat 'fitted with a sail, six oars, six muskets and six sabres, biscuits, beer, a compass and other necessary provisions'. Disguised as a Swede, he made his way through Plymouth to the long-boat and put to sea, together with his first lieutenant, bosun, surgeon and valet, who had all been captured with him. After a hard crossing they landed near Tréguier, hired horses and made their way back to Saint-Malo. The amount of freedom given to Duguay-Trouin in England seems extraordinary. Perhaps there was a certain amount of collusion from the authorities; at any rate, the brief account in his autobiography surely cannot tell the whole story.

C. B. Norman, in *The Corsairs of France*, itemises the enormous number of ships captured or sunk by Duguay-Trouin in his active career as a corsair commander, which lasted only twenty years, from 1692 to 1712. The total consisted of '10 English men-of-war, 2 privateers, 7 heavily armed merchantmen, and 66 traders, all flying the English flag; in addition to these we have 4 Portuguese and 3 Dutch men-of-war, 2 powerful Dutch corsairs, and 94 merchantmen of other nationalities'. In spite of—or perhaps because of—the swathe he cut through enemy shipping, Duguay-Trouin aroused the jealousy of the traditionally aristocratic caste of naval officers, and he never reached the rank to which his genius entitled him. But his capture of Rio de Janeiro in 1711 put him beyond the reach of petty envy; though he was so enfeebled by the privations of his life that after his return to France early in 1712 he hardly ever put to sea again. He lived on for another quarter of a century, suffering from gout, headaches and bouts of fever, perhaps malaria; and died in 1736, aged sixty-three, with the rank of Lieutenant-General of the King's Navies.

His character was summed up by Norman as a combination of 'indomitable gallantry, fertility of resource, generosity to his subordinates, courtesy to his prisoners, and an abiding faith in his own star'—adulatory words, but justified by Duguay-Trouin's actions. When he captured Rio, instead of turning over the town to pillage, as most commanders of his day would have done, he arrested any Frenchman caught plundering houses or shops and executed eighteen men who had looted a local church. Indeed, his concern for the defeated Portuguese was so exemplary that the two sides fraternised, largely because the French looked after the wounded and—again far from typical—respected the local women. Similar kindness to the neglected and unfortunate was shown by the respect he paid to Jacques Cassard, the greatest corsair of Nantes, who had fallen on hard times. Seeing the shabby old man drifting aimlessly among the courtiers at Versailles, Duguay-Trouin went over to him in front of the assembly, gave him his purse, and when someone asked who the old man was, replied that he was the best sailor in the service of the King of France. In his memoirs he makes a point of praising his subordinates, especially those involved in the Rio venture, singling out four officers 'who were of infinite assistance to me during the whole course of this expedition, and I confess with pleasure that it was by their activity, their high courage and their good advice that I overcame an infinite number of obstacles that appeared to be far beyond our strength'. How many commanding officers would acknowledge their subordinates in such generous and unforced terms?

Shortly before his death Duguay-Trouin moved to Paris. His will, dated September 7, 1736, mentions legacies to his housekeeper, his *valet de chambre*, his three lackeys, his porter and his cook. There was also a bequest to 'Francillon whom he recognises as his son and who at present lives with him, aged about four years'. One wonders what became of this offspring of the corsair's last years; perhaps he followed his father's footsteps, or joined the Church—the quite unsuitable career for which Duguay-Trouin was educated. Three weeks later Duguay-Trouin died and was buried in the fashionable church of St Roch, in the Rue Saint-Honoré. His memory has been kept alive ever since by a succession of ships of the French navy named after him. The most famous of all was the English training vessel *Implacable*, a man-of-war launched in 1796 as the *Duguay-Trouin*, captured after Trafalgar, taken back to England and renamed. When she sank off Portsmouth in 1949, she was the oldest vessel in the world still in commission. Latest of all is a guided-missile frigate, launched at Lorient in

June 1973, exactly three hundred years after Duguay-Trouin's birth.

In the same month the old corsair's remains finally returned to his beloved Saint-Malo. On June 9 the body was solemnly reburied in the Cathedral, where a slab on the north side of the choir commemorates him. He was laid to rest to the tolling of the bell called Noguette, which he had brought back from Rio in 1712. The name is a corruption of '*Nox Quieta*', and the bell originally sounded the hour of curfew, when the *dogues* were unleashed to roam outside the town. Today's Noguette, recast from the original metal, still rings out at ten o'clock each night, reminding the Malouins of their great past, and of the corsair who was its most illustrious ornament.

Saint-Malo's other corsair hero was born in 1773, a hundred years after Duguay-Trouin. Robert Surcouf was a member of one of the prominent *armateur* families of the town, and, like Duguay-Trouin, was most unsuitably intended for the priesthood. At the age of ten he was sent off to a religious college in Dinan, but his formal education came to a sudden end when he was threatened with a whipping, bit the teacher who was holding him so hard on the thigh that he let go, jumped out of the window, shinned over the wall, and was off in the depths of winter without hat or shoes on. He collapsed on the snow-covered ground, and would undoubtedly have died if some fish merchants from Cancale had not found him lying there and taken him home, more dead than alive. From then on it was the sea or nothing.

Surcouf's career lay much further afield than Duguay-Trouin's, in the Indian Ocean and the Bay of Bengal. France's two island possessions off the coast of Madagascar, Mauritius (then called the Ile de France) and Réunion (then the Ile de Bourbon) lay on the strategic route to India and the Far East; and though France and England were not at war in 1789, when Surcouf made his first major voyage, anyone could see that hostilities were not far off. His earliest experiences at sea had nothing to do with the glories of a naval or corsair career, but with the squalid business of slave-running. After about a year away from Saint-Malo, Surcouf's ship, the *Aurore*, was taking a cargo of slaves from Mozambique to

Mauritius when she was caught in a hurricane and driven ashore on the coast of Africa. The crew managed to escape, but all the negroes shackled below the hatches were drowned. For the next fortnight the crew, Surcouf among them, had to salvage clothing and provisions from between decks, where the stench from the rotting bodies of the slaves was so unbearable that each man could only spend a few minutes at a time there, with a cloth soaked in vinegar over his mouth and nose, and a safety rope round him to drag him out in case he fainted.

This revolting job could hardly be described as a baptism of fire; but in January 1793 France and England were at war once more. The following year, still only twenty, Surcouf was given his first command, the brig *Créole;* and for the next fifteen years he was the scourge of the East India Company's ships. The endless accounts of boarding parties, gundecks raked with grapeshot, and fights with cutlass and boarding axe in the biographies of Surcouf make repetitive reading; as Lord Russell of Liverpool remarks, much of it could have come straight out of the adventures of Captain Hornblower. As a young man, his greatest triumph was the capture of the East Indiaman *Triton* off Calcutta—a David and Goliath affair, in which Surcouf, with a combination of courage and sheer cheek, took a prize that carried twenty-six guns and a crew of 150 with only eighteen men. His official biographer, a descendant confusingly called Robert Surcouf, writes that 'the *Triton* was the first English ship ever taken in the Bay of Bengal. . . . The capture of an English ship at the mouth of the Ganges was a feat of arms as exceptionally bold as an attack at the mouth of the Thames, and the insurance companies were greatly alarmed.'

The climax of Surcouf's career—his taking of Rio, one might call it, comparing him with Duguay-Trouin—was the capture of the *Kent* in 1800. The main facts of the action are clear enough; but the interpretations put on those facts by both sides, and the theatrical nature of the combat, make it a dramatic event as much as a feat of arms. In October 1800 Surcouf was cruising in the Bay of Bengal in the *Confiance*, a privateer vessel designed to his own specifications, with which he had already taken fourteen prizes in a few weeks. At dawn on October 7 one of the men on watch saw a ship on the horizon, and as the

Confiance closed with her it soon became clear that she was a very large and well-armed East Indiaman. Trusting in his unfailing luck, Surcouf decided to attack; and as the odds against him would be great he fortified his men with rum and promised them 'an hour of plunder' if they were successful. Robert Surcouf gives a meticulous account of the preparations for attack. Each crew member had a boarding-axe, a cutlass, a pistol and a dagger in his belt, and carried either a blunderbuss, a lance or a cudgel. Marksmen were posted in the yards and long-boat, to pick off the English officers. The non-combatants were issued with pikes, to use on the enemy, or on any corsair who felt like retreating. Topmen were placed in the rigging, with grenades to rain down on the enemy's deck. Surcouf himself had a cutlass, a dagger and a pair of pistols in his belt and carried a megaphone for giving orders; behind him stood his negro attendant, with two loaded muskets to hand to the captain. Below decks the guns were made ready, and the surgeons prepared a reception point for the wounded, with their boxes of instruments open beside them, and buckets of water, sponges and dressings ready to hand.

The atmosphere on the *Kent*, on the other hand, was quite different from this scene of predatory wariness. A ship of 1,200 tons carrying thirty-eight guns, her own crew had been swollen to a total of 437 by soldiers from another ship who had been taken on board at San Salvador, in Brazil. There were also a number of women passengers on board. It was near the end of their long voyage, and a holiday mood prevailed. The commander of the *Kent*, Captain Rivington, was confident of an easy victory, and suggested that the soldiers and ladies should come up on deck and watch the capture or sinking of a corsair vessel. Robert Surcouf describes the 'tinkling laughter' (*rires perlés*) of the ladies and the exclamations of the men, transcribed as 'Aoh! indeed! all right!' Seeing the number of troops on deck, Surcouf thought at first that the *Kent* might be a *vaisseau-trompeur* or heavily armed decoy, until one of his officers pointed out the women 'twirling their parasols with a mocking air'. Then the *Kent* fired a warning shot over the *Confiance*, and the action began.

The opening moves were like a sinister game of cat-and-mouse, where the mouse was stalking the cat. In a series of skilful manœuvres, countered by increasingly heavy fire from the *Kent*, Surcouf worked the *Confiance* ever closer until he was ready to grapple and board. After one broadside during the manœuvring, the English were astonished to see the *Confiance* still afloat. 'Where they had expected to see enemies crushed and beaten, stretching imploring hands before them and asking for assistance that they were ready to refuse, they saw sailors full of enthusiasm ready to hurl themselves like tigers upon them, their lips drawn back in rage, their faces pale, their eyes bloodshot.' Allowing for Robert Surcouf's love of animal similes—Surcouf is like a lion, while the *Kent* is like a furious bull at bay—a frenzied corsair crew must have been a terrifying sight, especially to civilian onlookers.

Once the corsairs had succeeded in boarding, the result was a foregone conclusion. The English fought hand to hand with great courage, being gradually forced back along the ship. As they were unprepared for such an attack, their superiority in numbers was of little use to them; and when Captain Rivington was killed by a grenade hurled from the mainyard of the *Confiance* the battle was virtually over. Robert Surcouf, after relishing the blood spilt and the bodies hacked to death with axe and cutlass, says that Surcouf called off the carnage after an English midshipman died in his arms, run through by the lance of a negro called Bamboo. 'The blow was so violent that the point of the lance was only stopped by a metal button on Surcouf's waistcoat, which prevented him from sharing the poor midshipman's fate.'

Meanwhile the corsairs were acting on Surcouf's promise of 'an hour of plunder' and were rifling the effects of captain, crew and passengers. Hearing screams from the women rising above the shouts of his men, Surcouf was in time to prevent any acts of rape by locking the women into their cabins and placing an armed guard outside. When the general commotion had died down, the *Kent* and the *Confiance* were separated, and the English passengers and crew were transferred to an Arab dhow, which landed them at Calcutta. All those on board the *Kent* were unanimous as to Surcouf's correct behaviour throughout. However, in the account of the engagement in the *Annual Register* for 1801 it was stated that the corsairs 'shewed no quarter to any who came in their way, whether with or without arms, and such was their savage cruelty, that they even stabbed some of the sick in bed'. Robert Surcouf puts the *Annual Register*'s sour account down to wounded English *amour-propre*, which is probably correct, though his own version tends to turn Surcouf and his men into something approaching corsair Boy Scouts.

During the action the English lost seventy killed or wounded, the French about twenty. The English wounds were more severe than those inflicted on the corsairs, and hardly any wounded survived. 'Implacable tetanus, so dangerous in tropical regions, set in after a few days, and most of the wounded died in terrible agony that froze with terror even the bronze-hearted corsairs who witnessed their sufferings.' Such was the final cruel reality that ended the swashbuckling melodrama. The final act in the saga of the *Kent* belongs in the realm of comedy, however. Surcouf put a prize crew on board the *Kent* and sailed her back to Mauritius, where she was visited by the authorities, wanting their share of the cargo. This included a number of barrels of gold dust, which Surcouf claimed as a proper reward for the dangers his men had been through. The Admiralty officials insisted on their share; whereupon the enraged Surcouf rowed back to the *Confiance* and lined the barrels up on deck. As the Admiralty boat drew near, he ordered his sailors to push the barrels into the sea in full view, shouting to the officials to go and look for the gold themselves. Somewhere in the harbour of Port-Louis the sand must still glint with the golden grains that Surcouf took from the *Kent* and then consigned to the sea-bed—a gesture that was certainly flamboyant, but which deprived many of the corsairs of the chance of buying their longed-for plots of land on the outskirts of Saint-Malo.

Surcouf retired from active seafaring in 1809 and became an *armateur*, growing wealthy and corpulent in the slave trade. But though shorebound, he had lost nothing of his appetite for action, as he proved in 1817 when he took on in succession twelve Prussian officers who had insulted the honour of France in a Saint-Malo restaurant. Challenging all twelve, he fought them with sabres on the beach, killing or maiming eleven and letting the final Prussian go 'to tell the tale'. Surcouf died in the summer of 1827, after months of a painful illness that was probably cancer of the stomach, and was buried with military honours in the cemetery of Saint-Malo. Thousands of miles away, for years to come, English mothers in Calcutta and Madras would threaten their naughty children with a visit from the terrible Surcouf if they did not behave themselves.

Duguay-Trouin and Surcouf were the resplendent tip of a vast iceberg of corsairs, most of whom attained neither fame nor fortune. The effects of one drowned sailor have been recorded, and could have been carried in a small bag: all he had accumulated after years of dangers and privations was 'one sack, one pair of slippers, one badly worn pair of breeches, two headbands, two old vests, two pairs of woollen stockings, three old shirts, one pair of drawers, one knife, one spoon and one blanket'. If captured, the corsairs were usually taken to one of the dreaded prison hulks (*pontons*) at Plymouth, Portsmouth or Chatham, where they mouldered away, not worth ransoming and hardly worth feeding. C. B. Norman gives some revealing statistics on the French losses during the Napoleonic Wars. Between 1793 and 1814 the Royal Navy captured 1,031 French privateers and 69,147 men; but to keep the record straight he admits that 'in the same period the Board of Admiralty issued 10,605 Letters of Marque to British vessels; that is to say, that we had ten privateers scouring the seas for every privateer of the enemy that we succeeded in capturing'. Though Norman wrote his book in the late 1880s, about eighty years after Surcouf's exploits and thirty after *la course* was finally abolished by the Declaration of Paris in 1856, he was obsessed by fears of a revival of privateering. 'Gigantic as the damage was that these sea-rovers inflicted on us in days gone by, would it not be tenfold greater in the wars to come?' In Norman's eyes, France was still England's natural enemy, though in the previous decade the French had been brought to their knees in the Franco-Prussian War. The shadows cast by the corsairs were long indeed. No wonder that they blotted out the outline of the looming menace that lay beyond the Rhine.

To see the corsair myth embodied in its most grotesquely misleading form, you need to follow the coast a few miles east from Saint-Malo, past the bathing beaches of Rochebonne and Le Minihic, to Rothéneuf. Signs in the village point to the Rochers Sculptés—a phantasmagoria of rock carvings above the sea, which every year become more and more blurred through the action of wind and wave, and even more of footwear. Carved over a period of twenty-five years by a clerical recluse, the Abbé Fouré, they portray members of the Rothéneuf family of corsairs, together with an assorted cast of saints, devils, sailors, peasants and sea monsters. The surrealist flavour of the place is best conveyed not by a detailed description, but by a couple of extracts from the English-language brochure, which reaches the heights of inspired nonsense. Here is one pair: 'Crésus, a lank old fallen gentleman, with vulture eyes in his stunted face. Having lost his fortune in debauchery he had become attached to Marie-Jeanne de la Mare, a short pot-bellied woman, gifted with a spongy conk, in the shape of a strawberry always oozing watery snuff.' As for the final fate of the corsairs, it was no doubt well deserved. 'All those monsters with sinister mouths, armed with strong jaws and covered with scales ate their fill of panting bodies torn strips [*sic*]. And so disappeared into their huge bellies the coat-of-arms of the Rothéneufs.'

CHAPTER VIII

The Oysters of Cancale

ONCE A FORTNIGHT or so, for two or three days of exceptionally low tides, the oyster boats chug out from Cancale to the oyster beds of the Bay of Mont Saint-Michel. 'Boat' is perhaps too dignified a term: these are the *chalands*, little more than wooden working platforms, powered by antiquated engines, which can just about manage the couple of miles to the oyster *parcs* and back again. No longer do the fleets of red-sailed oyster smacks (*bisquines*) sail from Cancale to dredge the offshore beds; though you can get some idea of what they looked like from the postcard reproductions of old photographs for sale in the tourist shops. But the *chalands* have a homely kind of attractiveness, and they are all painted up in ways that reflect their owner's pride of possession, or lack of it. To see twenty or thirty of them crawling across the dead flat waters of the bay on a fine summer's morning, or better still to go out on one yourself, is as enjoyable an experience as the Brittany coast has to offer.

Cancale, if anywhere, is the home of the oyster. There are two Cancales: the upper town, with its commanding modern church and general stores; and the lower port, where everything is geared to selling oysters, from the expensive restaurants, where you can pay up to seventy-five francs for a basic meal, to the old ladies down by the jetty, protected by umbrellas from the sun, who will sell you small wizened bivalves for as little as three francs fifty a dozen. In between come the bars for *dégustation*, probably the best compromise, where you can have a few oysters and half a bottle of Muscadet for ten francs or so. If you buy your own oysters, there is always the problem of opening them. A special skill is needed, even with an oyster knife that consists of a handle, a short triangular blade and a small hand guard, like a miniature sword hilt, to protect against cuts from the shell if the blade slips. Opening oysters is not a skill I have mastered; perhaps they have to be caught unawares, before they can bring their powerful closing mechanism into play. At any rate, I have to admit to a rate of only about a dozen in half an hour, which is pathetically sluggish when contrasted with the deftness of anyone who works behind a counter in Cancale.

Without actually going out to the beds it is impossible to get any idea of how much sheer slog is involved, how much hard repetitious work until the oyster is finally ready for sale. You need to be literally thick-skinned as well: by the end of a single day my finger ends were crisscrossed with scratches and cuts of all descriptions, mainly from the tiny barnacles with which the shells are covered. No one works more than an hour without losing a certain amount of blood. And no one works more than a couple of minutes without appreciating the glutinous, boot-sucking qualities of the mud in the bay.

There are three types of oyster grown in the bay. Rarest, and most expensive, are the giant oysters, of 'Walrus and Carpenter' type, called *pieds de cheval* because they are shaped like a horse's hoof, and also known as *véritables Cancales*. These may weigh half a kilo or more, and can cost a pound each, even direct from the grower's counter. Louis XIV, we are told, had convoys of such oysters sent to him at Versailles; though the *ostréiculteurs* no longer have to go so far afield to sell their produce, as their customers now come to them. Next in quality are the *plates*, or flat oysters, also known as *Bélons*, after the Bélon estuary in Finistère, near Quimperlé, from which the finest specimens used to come in former days. Lowest in the ostreicultural scale are the *creuses* (the 'hollow' oysters as opposed to the *plates*), also known as *Portugaises*—though here again, as with the *Bélons*, few if any originate from the place they are named after. The oystermen do not like to admit it, but *Japonaises* is what they should be called, if you are being pedantic. The *creuses* are far more irregular in shape than the *plates*, to such an extent that it is sometimes almost impossible—at least to an inexpert eye—to see where the shell divides.

'Flat' and 'hollow' are gross over-simplifications of what are in fact shells of infinite variety of striation and undulation, of warty excrescence and incrustation; yet if you hold one of each type it is obvious which is which.

In fact, they are quite different animals. The *plate* is the original edible oyster of the Romans, *Ostrea edulis*; while the *creuse* is of two kinds—the Portuguese, *Gryphaea angulata* or *Ostrea angulata*, and the so-called *Portugaise* from Japan and elsewhere, which is *Crassostrea gigas*. (You will never find a pearl in any of them, no matter how many you open, as the pearl oyster, *Meleagrina margaritifera*, is a different genus altogether.) A gruesome pair of coloured photographs in an official monograph called *Les Huîtres et Moules de France* shows the *plate* and the *creuse* in full anatomical detail. Fortunately they bear little relation to the actual thing. The oyster shares with the human race a heart, a liver, a stomach, a mouth, an intestine and an anus; but its specialised evolution has given it an adductor muscle to pull its two halves together, a hinge to enable it to open and close, gills, palps for feeding, and a mantle.

Though they look so different, I must confess that if you gave me a *plate* and a *creuse* to taste I would not be able to tell them apart, and with the oyster now a luxury food it is a branch of gastronomy I am unlikely ever to master. Yet even to my unlearned palate the oyster is still the taste of the sea *par excellence*. As the American author Eleanor Clark puts it, in her prosc poem to the oyster, *The Oysters of Locmariaquer*:

> Intimations of the ages of man, some piercing intuition of the sea and all its weeds and breezes shiver you a split second from that little stimulus on the palate. You are eating the sea, that's it, only the sensation of a gulp of sea water has been wafted out of it by some sorcery, and are on the verge of remembering you don't know what, mermaids or the sudden smell of kelp on the ebb tide or a poem you read once, something connected with the flavour of life itself.

Such flights are far from the day-to-day business of the *ostréiculteur* and his crew, on their way to a day of tending their *parcs*. To them the oyster is hardly a thing of beauty; rather a matter of hard cash. So hard, in fact, that I worked for an afternoon on the oyster beds and then had to pay for a dozen specimens at the end of the day. The *ostréiculteur* who took me out with his crew was M. Jean Clousier, who has named his establishment after the finest of the oysters, 'Au Pied d'Cheval'. He runs what is very much a family affair: the day I went he left his wife in charge of the selling side and took with him his daughter and a strapping twenty-year-old girl helper; a Spanish psychology student from Seville working in Cancale during his summer vacation; a fifteen-year-old boy just out of school, starting his first job; and the *patron's* right-hand man, who seemed to do at least half the work himself.

At about twelve-fifteen we clambered down the rusty ladder at the end of the jetty on to the *chaland.* Some ancient waders were thrown down for me, but as they consisted of two left feet and were too small anyway, I could not really take advantage of them. The *parcs* that were being worked that day were a couple of miles to the south, in the general direction of Saint-Benoît-des-Ondes; fortunately the sea was like a millpond, and St Benedict was plainly keeping his waves to himself. About two dozen other battered craft chugged along in company, through shoals of mullet leaping from the sea like flying fish, towards the tall weed-covered sticks that jut at all angles out of the water and mark the limits of each oysterman's *parcs* (not owned, incidentally, but rented from the Ministère de la Marine Marchande). To me one stick looked exactly like another; but the oystermen knew their own, and with a good deal of manœuvring and shouts of *arrière* and *avance* the boat was jockeyed into position to wait for low tide.

The fall, of about twelve feet or so, lasts about ninety minutes. During that time the water level falls visibly, as more and more of the weed-festooned sticks are revealed. Also revealed are the illegally set fishing nets strung between the sticks; these can foul a *chaland*'s propeller and immobilise it, and the oystermen regard any fish caught in these nets as theirs to take by right. As the sea sinks lower, the final position of the boat becomes critical. The oysters are cultivated in rows, with wide passages between every six rows or so. If the *chaland* is in the wrong place, it can settle on to the oysters, crushing them into the mud and making them useless. Fortunately the position of our boat had been judged exactly, and as the sea finally ran back out of the bay the *chaland* settled down in the mud right in the middle of the passage.

The oyster beds at low tide are an extraordinary sight. Like all the best cultivation, they combine man-made symmetry with the unpredictability of the natural scene. One's first impression is that there are no oysters at all, only rows of what appear to be large overlapping wafers stretching away into the distance on metal frames. These are the plastic *poches*—mesh sacks in which the oysters are kept for the first year or two of their growth period, before being transferred to the cleaning *parcs* below Cancale harbour. The day's task consisted of turning the *poches* and shaking out the oysters, to make sure they were evenly spread. It does not sound much like hard work, but the combination of the lowness of the metal frames (about eighteen inches above the mud), the razor-sharp barnacles with which many of the oysters are covered and which manage to poke through the mesh of the *poches*, and the sheer number of the sacks that need turning over, make it a back-breaking job. The two girls romped through their work; but the boy apprentice, on his first day in the *parcs*, had a hard time of it. When I remarked that at least the weather was grand and the view was marvellous, he said he agreed, but wished he were somewhere else. Would he still be there in thirty years' time, I wondered, perhaps an *ostréiculteur* in his own right, or still working for another *patron*, with millions of turned-over oyster sacks behind him, and millions still to come?

The most exhausting part of the business has nothing to do with the oysters themselves but concerns the mud that forms their natural element. This mud is like nothing I have encountered anywhere else. Strangely enough, you can skate across it in waders, or even in bare feet, but once you have stood in the same place for more than a few seconds it takes charge. It does not engulf you, certainly not much beyond the ankle; but it has a peculiarly retentive quality that delights in absorbing your feet. After my ancient plimsolls had been sucked off at almost every step, I abandoned them altogether and went barefooted, after being assured that there was no danger of treading on broken bottles or any man-made rubbish. Fortunately this turned out to be correct, and I did not meet a single barnacle-covered shell either. This mud is 'ooze' in the *Oxford Dictionary* sense, where it is defined as 'wet mud or slime; esp. that in the bed of a river or estuary'. The French do not call it *boue*, which is ordinary mud, but *vase*, which is this special tidal variety. Pure grey in colour, it is of a single oozy consistency, with no lumps in it at all. If ever the oyster trade collapses, the *ostréiculteurs* could become mud exporters, as it is just the kind of stuff for women wrestlers in Hamburg to wallow in, or for the French themselves to use in their mud cures in the institutions devoted to *Thalassothérapie* (seawater cures).

The first set of *poches* were full of young *plates*. When these had all been turned, we went on to the next series of rows, which contained *creuses*. Here it was not a matter of shaking them in the sacks but of hitting them with bits of wood. This is because of the shape of the *creuse*, which does not grow regularly like the *plate* but tends to worm its way through the plastic mesh of the *poche*, leading to cut sacks (plastic is expensive), and, more important, to deformed oysters. If bits get broken off the shell in the process, it is better than a written-off oyster, which is the alternative. As the young oysters grow inside the *poches*, so do the green crabs that prey on them; in fact, they grow to such a size that they are trapped inside the mesh by their own greed. The crabs are the main enemies on these particular beds, and they have to be hit too, wherever possible. Though they are solid-seeming, they collapse into a sad-looking slime, little more than greenish mud among the grey mud that coats the oysters, adding their own pathetic addition to the *vase* underfoot.

By the time the last of the *creuses* had been turned and hit back into their sacks the sea was starting to fill the runnels. In the Bay of Mont Saint-Michel the tide is reputed to come in as fast as a galloping horse. That may or may not be true, but it certainly comes in to knee-depth in the time it takes to skate and lurch over twenty yards of mud. Like a film being played backwards the morning's sequence was reversed. The *chaland* floated off the mud; the oysters disappeared back under the water, then the illegal fishnets, then most of the length of the marker sticks. Back we chugged to Cancale, less confidently than we had set out, as water in the petrol made the engine splutter, and a swell was getting up.

The *parcs* below Cancale jetty are accessible any day at low tide, and this is the place to watch the other activities of the oyster-growers. Here, a few hundred yards out, the massive *pieds de cheval* are grown direct on the sea bed, not in *poches*, and are picked up direct for sale to the customer. The mud here is comparatively shallow and non-glutinous, and could hardly be dignified by the name of *vase*. By the shore are small enclosures surrounded by low concrete walls, where oysters of all shapes and sizes are spread about to clean themselves internally, disgorging their impurities in mud-free water. The heavy preliminary work of freeing the shells of their coating of mud has been made far easier since the advent of a cleaning machine. Oysters are tipped by the basketful into a hopper at one end of the machine, travel on a conveyor-belt through a strong jet of water, and emerge at the other end clean enough for the shop counter.

The never-ending work done at Cancale represents only the final stages of a long period of growth and cultivation. In their early life, the larval oysters, known as spat, are grown on special tiles (*tuiles*), shaped like curved pantiles and dipped in lime, in the warmer waters of southern Brittany, especially in the Gulf of Morbihan. Stacks of the white tiles can be seen piled up by the waterside at any of the little Morbihan fishing villages, such as Le Bono; they are left on the shore high and dry until they are needed for the next batch of oysters. The spat normally begins to grow on the tiles in about July. By the following January the baby oysters (*naissains*) are ready to be removed (the word used is *décoller*, unstick), and shifted by lorry to the chillier waters of north Brittany, where they are put into *poches* and taken out to the oyster beds. The turning and cleaning process goes on for three years or so, and the oysters are eaten at about four years old. This applies to the *plates*; the faster-growing *creuses* are normally eaten younger, at about three. Their whole career is somewhat different from that of the *plates*. In the first place, they are imported as spat from Japan and British Columbia, as opposed to being home-bred in Brittany. Secondly, in their early stages the *creuses* are not grown on tiles but on plastic tubes, which are set vertically in the mud of the *parcs*, in contrast to the bigger oysters in their horizontal *poches*.

It is these early stages that have been described so superbly in Eleanor Clark's book, from which I have quoted above. She ranges in space and time all over Brittany, through mythology, history, literature, tourism, and loving description of the people of the Morbihan fishing village of Locmariquer; always returning to the oyster, growing obstinately on its tile in defiance of all that the sea and natural enemies can do to it. Her book ends with a near-disaster for the oyster, as well as for wild life throughout Europe: the terrible winter of 1962–63. On January 17 and 18, 'the upper stretches of all the estuaries, of Crach, Auray, La Trinité, were frozen over; the parks and basins froze solid; a band of ice eight or nine inches thick formed around the whole Bay of Quiberon'. At La Trinité millions of tiles covered with *naissains* were caught in the ice. 'Ten days later, although the air was not much warmer, the region echoed with the crash and boom of ice breaking in the spring tide. Oysters trapped in the chunks were swept out to sea; others were driven under the *vase* by the weight of the ice, or by storms.'

This was a devastating blow, from which the *naissain* trade of the Morbihan recovered with difficulty. Far more insidious and even more destructive has been the parasitic sickness known as the Aber Disease, which was first recorded in 1970. Appearing in two estuaries, Aber Wrac'h and Aber Benoît, in the extreme north-west of Brittany, it spread southward to Brest and Arcachon, and as far afield as Galicia in Northern Spain; and eastward along the coast of Finistère and the Côtes-du-Nord as far as the Bay of Saint-Brieuc. By 1975 it was firmly entrenched in every oyster-growing area along the whole south coast of Brittany. The most productive research into the disease is not being done in France, as one might expect (there is after all the Institut Scientifique et Technique des Pêches Maritimes at Nantes, which exists to look into such things), but in England, at the Portsmouth Polytechnic. The research is being undertaken by Dr David Alderman, who thinks that there is little likelihood of a antidote. In an article in the *New Scientist* of July 18, 1974, he gave an outline of the disease: 'The organism which is believed to be responsible . . . grows mainly in, and disrupts the lining of, the oyster's digestive gland. This organ is the main nutrient-absorbing organism of the animal and its eventual destruction by the pathogen seems to be the major cause of death.' In other words, the oyster is slowly starved by a single-cell equivalent to the tapeworm in the human being. Seen under the microscope, the parasite shows up as a gently glowing reddish circle—quite an attractive little object, belying its lethal capabilities.

Official concern at the possibility of the disease spreading to this country is shown by a Ministry of Agriculture press notice, dated May 7, 1974. 'Anyone considering the importation of oysters, oyster seed and other molluscs from France and certain other countries for deposit (relaying) in tidal waters and adjoining foreshore of England and Wales is reminded that, to prevent the introduction and spread of diseases, this movement is allowed only under licence issued by the Minister of Agriculture, Fisheries and Food. The French flat oyster industry has been severely damaged by disease in recent years, and no licences have been granted for the importation of French flat oyster seed since 1972; none will be issued until the risk of the introduction of disease into British oyster beds is removed.' Behind the deadpan prose lies a very real fear of infection at places like Whistable and Colchester, infection compounded by the irresponsible way in which many French growers have carted infected *naissains* from one *parc* to another, with no particular effort at screening for Aber Disease. Dr Alderman refers to yet another example of irresponsibility: trays of living French flat oysters have been allowed to drift across to the English coast, and no doubt many of them have the disease. Finally, some of the young *creuses* imported into Brittany from Japan are not altogether above suspicion. As Captain Cook's sailors killed the non-resistant Tahitians with measles and the common cold, so a disease that would not affect the tough Japanese oyster might well be lethal to the susceptible European variety.

Not only are the *plate* and the *creuse* different in appearance, but their sexual cycles are quite distinct. The *plate* is what is known as an 'alternating hermaphrodite'—that is to say, it changes sex regularly, the frequency depending on the warmth of the season. The adult oyster usually begins as a male; after ejection of the sperm it gradually changes to female; then after breeding it becomes male again, and so on. The female takes in the sperm together with the minute planktonic organisms that form her food, and fertilisation takes place inside the shell cavity. After fertilisation the oyster becomes 'white-sick', and has a milky appearance when opened. The fertilised eggs or larva (known as spat) grow for a fortnight or so inside the mother, gradually becoming darker; at this stage the oyster is known as black-sick. The familiar belief that oysters should only be eaten when there is an 'R' in the month no doubt stems from the unappetising appearance of a good many opened oysters during the breeding season, which occurs during the warm weather from May until August. At Cancale they sell them all the summer, and I have not found that milkiness makes any difference to the taste.

When the black-sick stage has been reached, the spat is ejected and floats around for a week or so, before settling on an available hard surface. In the case of oysters in the wild state—that is, breeding in large banks that build up over the years—this would normally be on other oyster shells. The oysterman has to lay down his own equivalent, known in this country as 'cultch'. It may in fact be cleaned oyster shell, or a firm gravelly surface; and in the Morbihan it is the stacks of limed tiles. Once the spat is anchored, it is there for good, or at any rate until it is removed from the tiles to be transferred to other *parcs*. Any oyster that has begun life on the tiles will always have a fragment of lime adhering to its 'foot'—one way of identifying the genuine article.

In contrast to the hermaphroditic *plate*, which is larviparous, the *creuse* keeps to the same sex throughout its life, and is oviparous. As with fish, its sperm and ova are shed into the sea before fertilisation. Perhaps this is why the *creuse* is that much tougher than the *plate*: it has been exposed to potential enemies from the very beginning, with no brief fortnight of protection within the maternal shell. The enemies of the spat are virtually all creatures that scour the sea looking for easy pickings, especially small crabs. The mature oyster has three main enemies: the starfish, which wraps itself round the oyster's shell and inexorably pulls on the two halves until the adductor muscle is exhausted and the oyster opens; the slipper limpet, which feeds on the same plankton as the oyster and thus deprives it of its food supply; and the oyster drill, which pierces the shell to get at the flesh within.

When it comes to eating oysters, man is as cruel as their other predators, as he also eats them while they are still alive. The only passages in which *Les Huîtres et Moules de France* becomes anything like lyrical is when its author, or panel of authors, turns from the *parc* to the table. They begin by the test for edibility. To make sure that an oyster is alive, it is only necessary to touch lightly the dark-coloured edge of the flesh with the point of a knife or to let fall a drop of lemon juice on it; the oyster's ciliary fringe will retract. Moreover, the shell should contain water when it is opened. The bigger the oyster, the less water there will be in the shell, and the more fragile the shell. There is an art in setting out a plate of oysters, which 'should be very carefully opened several minutes before they are served. The "fish" should be intact, and any fragments of shell should be carefully removed. As they are opened, they should be laid out on a dish or plate, on top of a layer of powdered ice. This contact with the ice brings them to the table in better condition. Oysters and other shellfish should always be served chilled but *never frozen*. At the last minute, before serving, they can be put briefly in the refrigerator.'

Purists may be surprised at finding not only lemon juice recommended to go with raw oysters, but also vinegar with chopped shallots, and even tomato sauce. Recommended wines to be drunk with oysters should be 'light, not too strong or too old', chosen from among the following: Graves, Entre-Deux-Mers, Chablis, Pouilly-Fuissé, Meursault, Riesling, Sylvaner, Muscadet, Champagne, Moselle and Rhine wines. In the oyster's homeland, at least, there is no need to go beyond the Muscadet.

The oyster is recommended 'as an aid to convalescence, for states of depression, for anaemia and pregnancy disorders'—no mention, however, of its supposedly aphrodisiac qualities, for which Casanova is said to have eaten fifty oysters every evening, to keep his strength up. Its nutritive value is compared with that of milk, slightly to the oyster's advantage, as it is richer in albumen than milk, and so 'restores the wear on the human organism'. However, it consists of 86 per cent water (milk is 87 per cent), which makes it a highly expensive way in which to ingest a few necessary salts and other nutrients. At the very end the booklet can no longer contain its feelings and breaks into rhyme: '*Fruits de mer, Santé de fer*.' But whether the iron constitutions of the Cancale oystermen and women come from eating the creatures or working among them, who can say?

The oyster features, though in a very minor way, in one account of the genesis of the greatest of all the French hymns to the sea, Claude Debussy's three orchestral sketches *La Mer*.

According to Debussy's friend René Peter, writing his reminiscences of the composer in 1931, the party with which Debussy was staying at the time sailed over from Saint-Lunaire in a storm, and replaced what they had lost through seasickness at one of Cancale's oyster restaurants. Forty years or so after the event Peter remembered the oysters (though he also remembered that he did not like them)—'Oh! those beautiful oysters, grey-beige in colour with glistening reflections' ('*d'un ton gris-beige au reflets gras*'). During the voyage to Cancale, Debussy had revelled in the violence of the weather, although even the boat-owner and his mate were alarmed for their safety. The boatman got furious and accused him of risking their lives for the sake of '*sensations fortes*'. To which Debussy replied: 'There is one powerful sensation I have never experienced, the sensation of danger! It is not unpleasant. You are alive!' 'What if you die?' asked the practical boatman. 'Better like this than from pneumonia or cancer,' answered Debussy.

By a lucky stroke of serendipity I came across quite a different account of this episode while delving in the library of the Société d'Historie et d'Archéologie at Saint-Malo. Among the academic subjects listed in the index of the *Annales* of that erudite and most helpful Society one incongruous entry caught my eye—*Claude Debussy sur la Côte d'Eméraude*, written in 1959 by Dr Petit de la Villéon. By dint of questioning those who remembered Debussy's visit, notably 'old people with long memories', Dr Petit worked out a sequence of events that had Debussy sailing back to Saint-Enogat from Cancale after lunch, which makes a good deal more sense than René Peter's account. As a storm was brewing, none of his friends would sail with him, so he boarded a *bisquine* without them. When he got back, his head was full of themes for the work, which he jotted down. But as there was no piano in the house, he had to try them out on the harmonium in the local church. 'And that was how the masterpiece made its entry into the world on the old harmonium of Monsieur le Curé of Saint-Enogat.' Though a good oyster lunch was not mentioned, the epicurean Debussy would surely have not let such an opportunity pass. And perhaps *La Mer* owes something of its magical sparkle and sonority to the mental vigour imparted by a dozen *pieds de cheval* washed down by a bottle of Muscadet.

CHAPTER IX

Quimper

SOME TOWNS ARE a perpetual delight. Quimper is one of these, a light-hearted place, especially when compared with the administrative sobriety of Rennes. The centre of Rennes is dominated by the Hôtel de Ville, all classical symmetry; that of Quimper by the fretted pinnacles of the Cathedral, gothically exuberant and crowned by the statue of Gradlon, the legendary King of Cornouaille. If you want to enjoy both places in a short space of time, you should abandon the car and take to the train, which will not only give you a much better idea of the scenery but will throw you among all sorts and conditions of Bretons. In the course of a single journey I met an old lady of eighty who had left school at ten to herd her parents' cattle, and who was a fanatical devotee of all the doings of our royal family; a very proper mother and daughter on their way home to Douarnenez; and a man who swore that only Bretons were charged the excess fare on express trains, while those born outside Brittany were let off. The road will take you through the Brittany of new white-painted Monopoly houses, enormous out-of-town hypermarkets, and heavy lorries grinding through village streets. The train, on the other hand, crosses country where hardly a house is to be seen. Water-meadows and salt-pans, pine-covered moorland, small orchards, neglected-looking or ruined farmsteads, upland streams and anglers—this is the rail-traveller's view. Perhaps it is more the Breton's own view than the tourist company's; but it is there.

Between Vitré and Rennes, the railway runs through meadows along the meanders of the Vilaine. South-west to Redon it follows the Vilaine's lower course, and in fact the train is the only means of seeing this particular landscape, as the roads keep to the high ground on either side of the valley. From the train you can see the massively squat Romanesque tower of the Eglise Saint-Sauveur at Redon, which lies off the tourist routes; and can appreciate the extent to which the development of southern Brittany has been controlled by the course of its rivers. This is especially true at Auray, where the railway strides across the river on a viaduct; and even more so at Lorient, where from the train you have a magnificent view up and down the Scorff, an enormously wide riverscape of cranes, barges and small grey-painted naval craft. The railway brings you to Quimper along the gentle little valley of the Jet, the best approach of all.

Compared with Rennes, Quimper is still very much a small country town, with a population of only 60,000, as opposed to the quarter-million or so of Rennes, and Quimper is certainly much more immediately attractive to look at. Whereas the Vilaine in Rennes is made to run as man commands it, the Odet that flows through Quimper is still a bubbling stream, flowing fast over stones on the river bed, and is incredibly clean, at least to the eye. I was walking beside it one morning and thought there was something strange about it. Then I suddenly realised what it was: whereas in England the average town river is full of old prams, car tyres and miscellaneous rubbish, the Odet was perfectly clean. Perhaps it has not yet struck the Quimpérois that a river makes an ideal dumping ground. Or perhaps they just like a clean river.

The Odet divides Quimper's town centre neatly into two halves. On the north side, the Cathedral, many of the public buildings and the ancient cobbled streets; on the south, the hanging woodlands of Mont Frugy, hardly a mountain, but a beech-covered slope a hundred feet or so high that brings the illusion of an endless forest right into the heart of the town. Below Mont Frugy the rows of parked cars on the river bank are largely hidden by rows of London-looking plane trees. Quimper's name, like Rennes' Celtic name Condate, means a confluence of rivers, Kemper in Breton (the Cornish equivalent is Gamper). The rivers that meet there are the Odet, the Jet, and a third little stream, the Steir, which cuts through the old town from north to south. It was this abundant water supply, together with rich deposits of white clay and plenty of wood for firing, that led to the establishment of Quimper's famous potteries as far back as Roman or even Gaulish times.

For centuries Quimper had a reputation for out-of-the-way provincialism, at least since La Fontaine's rude words about it at the start of his fable *Le Chartier Embourbé* (*The Carter Stuck in the Mud*).

> The driver of a haywain
> Found his cart stuck in the mud. The poor man
> Was far from any human aid.
> It was deep in the countryside,
> Near a small town in Lower Brittany
> Called Quimper-Corentin. We know that Destiny
> Sends people there when she wants to drive them mad.
> God keep us from that road!

Writers on Quimper normally leave the carter there, well and truly stuck. Fortunately he gets out in the end, with the verbal encouragement of Hercules, though without the hero's physical assistance, which would have been much more use to him.

As Henri Regnier pointed out in his edition of the *Fables*, there is more to La Fontaine's words than meets the eye. For Quimper was used by Louis XIII as a place of exile, the Siberia of seventeenth-century France. He sent his own confessor, Père Caussin, to Quimper, after Caussin had been caught intriguing against Richelieu. However, Caussin finally came to love the place, though at first he complained bitterly to the Pope about his solitary life, battered by the waves (though they hardly come up the Odet as far as Quimper), and surrounded by a flock who uttered 'barbarous grating noises' (*grincements barbares*) instead of a recognisable language.

Quimper is more than the capital of modern Finistère: it is the chief town of that imprecise and myth-filled corner of south-west Brittany known as Cornouaille, a name derived from our own Cornwall. It is hardly surprising that Quimper's main square is named after Corentin, the patron saint of the town, that the Cathedral is dedicated to him, or that the street that leads from the river to the square is named after Gradlon, the legendary king of the lost city of Ys. As La Fontaine's verses show, the saint's name was formerly coupled with that of the town. In later years the amalgamation became shortened to Quimpertin, then to Quimper alone; though during and after the Revolution the town was known briefly and prosaically as 'Montagne-sur-Odet', from its two main topographical features.

St Corentin, for all his legendary characteristics, is a far from mythical figure. Born about 375, he spent much of his early life as a hermit in the forest near Plomodiern, a village at the foot of Menez Hom, the mountain that guards the Crozon peninsula. Here, as Albert Le Grand tells us, he was kept alive by a constantly recurring miracle. 'Though he was content with a few lumps of coarse bread, which he begged from time to time in the nearby villages, and with wild herbs and roots, which the earth produced by itself, without human labour or toil, nevertheless God sent him a small fish to swim in his spring. Each morning the fish swam up to the saint, who took it and cut off a piece for his food, and then threw it back in the water. At once it became whole again, without scar or wound, and every day without fail it swam to St Corentin, who dealt with it in the same manner.'

This miracle was witnessed by King Gradlon, who was out hunting in the forest and asked the saint for something to eat. Corentin cut a small piece off the back of his fish and gave it to the Master of the Household to share with the King and his court; the official roared with laughter, but changed his tune when he found that the fish was enough for everybody. Naturally impressed, Gradlon first of all endowed Corentin with a monastery, and then offered him the bishopric of his new town of Kemper-Odetz, later called Kemper-Corentin.

The story of the fish is the best known of the culinary miracles associated with St Corentin; but even more delightful is the way in which he entertained two of his fellow saints, who came to visit him at his woodland hermitage. St Corentin, as a good Breton, made *crêpes* for them, which he sprinkled with flour. 'But God, who never abandons those who have placed all their trust in Him, made a miraculous provision for the nourishment of his servants: for when St Corentin went to draw water from the spring, he found it full of fine large eels, from which he took enough to satisfy the appetites of his guests.'

Gradlon too must have had some basis in fact. Like King Arthur, he may have been a post-Roman warlord who fought off the Norse invaders and then ruled over Quimper. But he is best known as the unhappy ruler of the sunken city of Ys, whose church bells can still be heard ringing below the waters of the Bay of Douarnenez, and which the music-lover can recapture through Debussy's piano prelude *La Cathédrale Engloutie*. The legend tells how Gradlon was betrayed through the wiles of his daughter Dahut, or Ahès. The city of Ys was protected from the waves by a series of sluice gates which could only be opened by a key that the King kept round his neck. But Dahut fell in love with the Devil, who had come to Ys disguised as a young prince to bring the city to its doom. The Devil persuaded Dahut to take the key from her father's neck while he lay asleep. The sluice gates were opened, the sea flooded in, and the city of Ys was drowned—all except King Gradlon, who escaped on his horse, the noble Morvarc'h (meaning 'Horse of the Sea' in Breton). In desperation Dahut clung to the horse behind her father, but as the waves threatened to overwhelm them, Gradlon thrust her into the waters and came safe to land.

Gradlon, mounted on Morvarc'h, still surveys his city from the parapet between the towers of the Cathedral. The original statue is said to have been put there in the fifteenth century, but it was smashed in the Revolution, and this is a modern copy. Until the Revolution the Quimpérois kept up an ancient custom which no doubt originates in the prehistoric cult of dead kings. On the eve of St Cecilia's Day (November 22) the Cathedral choir would stand on the balcony beside the statue and sing an anthem, while one of the town officials (*valet de ville*) climbed up on to the horse behind the stone King, holding a bottle, a glass and a napkin. He tied the napkin round Gradlon's neck, filled a glass and held it to the King's lips. Then he drank it himself and hurled the glass into the square below, where the crowd fought to catch it before it smashed on the ground. No one ever caught it; and so no one ever won the prize of a hundred *écus* offered to the successful catcher. The ceremony ended with a laurel branch placed, like a sceptre, in the King's hand. Thus Gradlon was honoured as lover of music and good cheer, and as ruler of his people.

The graceful twin spires of the Cathedral dominate Quimper from every direction. Yet though they look entirely right and seem as though they must have been there for centuries, in fact they date from comparatively recent times, as they were only built in 1854. Before that, the towers were capped by low pyramidal roofs covered in slates, which were known somewhat disparagingly as the *éteignoirs* (candle snuffers) of St Corentin. Quimper Cathedral is a splendid building in its own right, and doubly so in Brittany, where elaborate Gothic buildings are the exception rather than the rule. Its most remarkable feature is the considerable angle between the axes of the choir, which dates from the mid-thirteenth century, and of the nave, built two centuries later. The usual explanation is that the angle symbolises the angle of Christ's drooping head on the cross; but this does not appear to be the case at Quimper. The probable reason is that the choir is on the alignment of the Chapel of Victory built for the tomb of Alain Cainhart, Count of Cornouaille, in 1058, while the nave is on the different alignment of the Romanesque church it superseded.

The interior is sombre, darkened by heavily coloured stained glass. The finest of the furnishings is the organ, which rises above a stone screen. The brief announcement that it was reconstructed in 1643 by Robert Dallam, '*fraîchement émigré d'Angleterre*', conceals a fascinating story of Anglo-Breton understanding which I ran to earth in the library of the Royal College of Organists. Robert Dallam (1602–1665) was a member of a famous family of organ-builders, which flourished throughout the seventeenth century. His father, Thomas Dallam, emerged into the light of international history in 1599, when he was sent by Queen Elizabeth to construct an organ in Constantinople for the Sultan, the 'Grand Turk'. For some reason, in 1642 Robert left England and settled in Quimper with his wife. The organ historian Huskison Stubbington, who goes into great detail in two articles, *The Dallams in Brittany* (published in *The Organ*, Vol XIX, October 1939 and January 1940), suggests that Robert emigrated after judging how the Civil War was likely to turn out, in view of the Puritans' hostile attitude to organ-playing and building.

Calling himself 'Organist to the Queen of England' (possibly he held an official appointment to Henrietta-Maria, or possibly he just wanted to impress the Quimpérois), Dallam immediately obtained the post of Cathedral organist, and by 1643 had entirely reconstructed the Quimper organ. After a short time, probably about 1645, he left Quimper and settled near Plougastel-Daoulas, in north Finistère. Operating from this centre, he spent the next fifteen years rebuilding the organs in some of the finest churches in Basse-Bretagne, and ended up as organist of the Cathedral of Saint-Pol-de-Léon, near Roscoff. In 1660, the year of the Restoration, he sold his share of the business for the large sum of 2,400 *livres* and returned to England, where he worked on the organ of New College, Oxford. He is buried in New College Chapel.

Robert Dallam left his sons Thomas and Toussaint in Brittany to carry on the family tradition, which they did with great success for the remainder of the seventeenth century. The startling organ at Sizun, with its odd *trompe l'oeil* balustrading, was rebuilt by one of the Dallams in 1688; in the same year a doubtless completely Frenchified 'Messire Thomas d'Allam' was working on the noble organ at Pleyben; and the final piece of Dallam work known was at Rumengol, in 1699. Much of what they did has been destroyed by later builders; but in their day they must have had a tremendous reputation to win so many important contracts against native Breton and French opposition.

Between the Cathedral close and the river runs a stretch of the old town wall, strongly fortified, where the Bishops of Quimper used to stroll and enjoy the view, undistracted by the life of the town swarming outside. The close itself is a delightful spot. It is reached through a little cloister just south of the Cathedral, and this quiet oasis, shaded by a large weeping willow, forms an outdoor anteroom to the Musée Breton. The Museum, currently in the process of reorganisation and expansion, is housed in a splendid stone Renaissance building, once the Bishop's Palace, notable for the magnificently wide spiral staircase which gives access to the various rooms of the collection. The museum is especially rich in local pottery, as you would expect, and also in furniture and carved wood of all kinds. It is worth climbing the staircase to the top, as the highest room contains a complete set of furniture laid out as it would have been when in use—chests, box-bed, table, benches, cupboard. Another room is full of cabinets containing the enormous variety of clothes worn in Cornouaille in the nineteenth century. Costumes, feasting countrymen and townscape are combined together in the lively Brueghel-like painting by Olivier Perrin, *Le Champ de Foire à Quimper*, painted at the beginning of the nineteenth century.

The strangest object in the collection is the conical stone known as the Menhir de Kernuz, which faces you as you enter the museum. Discovered in 1878, it was probably set up at the very end of the Megalithic period, perhaps about 400 BC. It is reputedly carved with four Gallo-Roman deities, and is thus an early example of one religion appropriating the monuments of an older one, as the Christians were to do in subsequent centuries. The gods, if you can make them out, are said to be Mercury, Hercules, Mars and 'the god with the mallet', no doubt Vulcan.

Quimper's superb art collection is in the Musée des Beaux-Arts, across the little Place Laennec north of the Cathedral. This square is the scene of a lively open-air market, and is named after the inventor of the stethoscope, who sits, cast in bronze, surveying the market women on a large and uncomfortable-looking volume entitled *Auscultation*, whose English meaning, according to the *Oxford Dictionary*, is 'the action of listening, with ear or stethoscope, to the sound of the movement of heart, lungs, or other organs'. After a total reconstruction lasting three years, the Musée des Beaux-Arts was reopened in the summer of 1976. Based on the art collection of a nineteenth-century connoisseur, the Comte de Silguy, it includes works by Italian and Dutch masters, as well as such big *genre* pieces as *Le Départ de la Tour d'Auvergne*, which shows the Breton hero of the Napoleonic Wars (see Chapter XVIII) off to fight for his country, with a haversack of books at his side and a cap of liberty on his head. From the great tradition of Impressionist and pre-Impressionist art there is a fine Boudin, *Le Port de Quimper*; and though there is no work by Gauguin there are some fine Sérusiers, notably the powerful *La Vieille de Pouldu*, which shows a grave and ageless peasant figure leaning on the haft of a mattock, with a rocky seascape behind.

A special section in the Beaux-Arts is now given over to the work of Max Jacob, poet and artist, friend of Picasso, Apollinaire and Cocteau, who was born at Quimper in 1876. Jewish by birth and yet profoundly Breton, his life oscillated wildly between the intellectual ferment of Paris and the consolations of Roman Catholicism, to which he became a convert. Though his reputation has been thrown into the shade by his more brilliant and self-advertising contemporaries, he is artistically far and away the most famous Quimpérois of recent years; and his centenary was honoured not only at the Beaux-Arts, but by naming the main bridge across the Odet the Pont Max-Jacob. He has been described as a surrealist—and yet he said that 'obscurity is a sign of weakness of mind' (*esprit*, the word he used, is virtually untranslatable, as it can mean wit or the whole spiritual and mental make-up of a person). Like the composer Erik Satie, whose work he greatly admired, he hid his seriousness of purpose behind a clown's mask, which has meant that even his religious convictions have at times been taken for the mask of a *poseur*.

His parents were small shopkeepers in the Rue du Parc, the main shopping street of Quimper, overlooking the river. As a child Max was brilliant, with talents that could have taken him anywhere, but at the age of twenty or so he decided to become a full-time artist, and went off to Paris to seek his fortune. Between about 1898 and 1900 he eked out a miserable existence doing all sorts of odd jobs, and at the turn of the century fell in with Picasso, equally hard up, with whom he shared a room. As the room was small and had only a single bed, they alternated: Max worked in a shop during the day and slept in the bed at night, while Picasso slept during the day and painted at night. During the early years of the century Max had his earliest written works published, while still continuing to paint. The first, a children's story, appeared in 1904.

In 1907 he moved to Montmartre, to a sordid little room behind some shops in the Rue Ravignan. Here, two years later, he experienced the blinding, Pauline conversion to Christianity that determined the course of the rest of his life. His description of the event has a moving directness, beginning in his little room, then trying to express the inexpressible, and ending with a *fin-de-siècle* aesthete's appreciation of Christ's clothes.

> I had come back from the Bibliothèque Nationale; I had put down my briefcase and found my slippers; and when I looked up, there was someone on the wall! there was someone! there was someone on the red wallpaper! My flesh fell to the ground! I was stripped naked by lightning! Oh

> immortal instant! oh truth, truth! tears of truth! joy of truth! unforgettable truth. The Body of Christ was on the wall of my poor room! Why, Lord? Oh forgive me! He was in a landscape that I myself had painted, the Lord Himself, all beauty, elegance and sweetness! His shoulders and bearing! He wore a robe of yellow silk with blue facings.

His first major work was a novel based on life in Quimper, *Le Terrain Bouchaballe*, on which he was working as early as 1910 but which did not appear until 1922. Among the few pieces of furniture Max possessed was an old Breton chest, into which he used to throw all his fragmentary writings. From this welter of material he produced, in 1916, his key work, *Le Cornet à Dés* (*The Dicebox*), whose chance results lie scattered about the printed page. To call the work 'surrealist' is perhaps misleading, but it is a useful shorthand description. *Le Cornet à Dés* consists of a succession of prose poems, some only a few words long, some half a page or so, in which images are juxtaposed as they are in a Salvador Dali painting, but in which they also develop in a certain direction, as they do in a cartoon film.

The title of *Le Cornet à Dés* comes from one of these brief utterances, which have to be given in full to convey their flavour. '*Vous êtes comme une écumante soupe au lait sous l'aérostat, montagnes, et, de là, sort bientôt, comme d'un gigantesque cornet à dés, le bonhomme globe, le front du Père Double Sphère.*' 'O mountains, you are like a frothy milk soup below an air-balloon, and from it will soon emerge, as from a giant dicebox, Mister World, the forehead of Father Double Sphere.' Is this a hymn to God's majesty expressed in facetious form, a consideration of the role of chance in life, or a schoolboy love of assembling words with little attempt at coherence of content or meaning? Perhaps all three elements are involved. Max's poems reveal certain obsessions: the hot-air balloon is one, Napoleon is another, a small moonlit room a third. Sometimes he seems to be describing a work by Picasso, with Picasso's own early monomanias: 'I am bringing you my two sons, said the old acrobat to the Virgin of the Rocks playing on her mandoline. The younger son knelt down in his pretty little suit; the other carried a fish on the end of a line.'

In 1915 Max Jacob had been baptised into the Roman

Catholic Church, with Picasso standing godfather. Then, in June 1921, he made the first of his sudden and complete changes of direction. He moved to the monastery of Saint-Benoît-sur-Loire, near Orléans, where he gave himself up to religious practices of the most rigorous and ritualistic nature, cutting himself off almost entirely from his old friends, and completely from the hectic artistic life of Paris. He described his new existence in a letter to his friend André Salmon—a hermit's idyll for the former wit and *raconteur*.

> Did I tell you that I was living in a secularised monastery whose curator is a Benedictine? I look out over an orchard where I water the lettuces from time to time, draw water from the well and pick baskets of cherries or raspberries—quite on my own. And there is a basilica, the oldest and most Romanesque in France. I'm writing its history, anonymously. . . . I lunch and dine with the local priest and often with the priests from round about, who are becoming my friends. . . . The priest is a world on his own (*un monde à lui seul*), and the curate is a Hercules who will make his mark in the world.

As the priest was a republican and the curate a royalist, Max found himself embroiled in their quarrels. His chief confidant was Jules, the local sabot-maker, with whom he had long religious discussions.

From these peaceful years of the mid-1920s date the *Poèmes de Morven le Gaëlique*. It would be hard to imagine poems more different from those of *Le Cornet à Dés*. Whereas *Le Cornet* is elliptical, full of jokes and allusions to Max Jacob's private world of symbols and memories, the *Poèmes* are crystal-clear and simple in language, harking back to Max's childhood in Quimper. Julien Lanoë rightly remarks in his Preface to the poems, 'You would think yourself at the beginning of the sixteenth century'—in other words, at the period of the great parish enclosures, when sculptors of a naïve genius blended the human, the divine and the grotesque in the sculptured processions of the calvaries (see Chapter XII). Many of the poems deal with Christmas and the Holy Family. The innkeeper tells his wife to prepare hotwater bottles for Mary's lying-in. The local band has practised its pieces of music to celebrate the birth. The Virgin says she must buy another sponge and an enamel bath for the baby.

There are poems about the life of the sabot-maker, the travelling huckster, the girl who gets married and finds that after a month or two of wedded bliss she is drudging from morning to night. But Max's sharp eye is never blinded by nostalgia. Here he is on 'Modern Girls of Douarnenez' who want to keep up with the times.

> With their diplomas and certificates, every fisher-girl now wants to be a lady. Goodbye, tight little *coiffes* and pink aprons. I will be like the mayor's wife, I will be like the doctor's wife, I will be like the ladies of the factory owners. I will also have a beach robe, a tennis racket and a lover or two in tow; if they are rich, I'll ride in their cars. Meanwhile I'll be a postmistress, a registered nurse, a teacher in the depths of the country. On the farm I had company in the evening as I did my spinning after supper. Now I am all alone with my hat and my mirror! Alas, my heart has not changed. It still jumps when a boy passes by, and I'm afraid when the wind blows.

In stern contrast is the 'Burial in Brittany' (*Enterrement en Bretagne*), where the poet's eye turns to the woman who has just lost her husband, but has no time to mourn, what with keeping all the visitors supplied with coffee, and constant attendance at Mass. 'Now you can cry as much as you like, but you won't have the time, because you will have to earn the black bread to feed your children by working at the factory from morning till evening. Try to find another husband who can help you.'

After seven years, monastic life at Saint-Benoît suddenly palled, and in 1928 Max Jacob moved back to Paris. Here he set himself up in luxury, surrounding himself with a court of young acolytes and living on the sale of his gouaches. In 1932 he was made a Chevalier of the Légion d'Honneur; but he found his Parisian existence increasingly distasteful, and in 1936 returned finally to Saint-Benoît. Roger Toulouse, whose haunting portrait of Max hangs in the Beaux-Arts at Quimper, met him for the first time during that year and described him in terms that read like an artist's notes for a painting.

> Max was small, dressed like a clerk or someone in retirement: waistcoat, watch and chain, trousers creased like concertinas falling over his slippers, low shoes, big feet. I noticed that he had sloping shoulders, his fingers were short, broad and square, his head was heavy but with a great refinement in the shape of the lips, bushy eyebrows which he constantly played with, as one twirls a moustache. Beautiful eyes with enormous and slightly flecked eyeballs. Wrinkles as though a hurricane had carved his forehead. Very white hair that stuck out on either side of his face like will-o'-the-wisps.

Once established again in his religious routine, he haunted the Basilica, in an agony of remorse for his eight years in Paris—'the most criminal period of my life', he called it. It is hard to know what could have justified such self-abasement, unless it was intense mortification at having indulged in the homosexuality of Cocteau and his friends. The outward manifestations of his inner torment were noted by observers. He would spend six hours a day kneeling on the cold flagstones of the Basilica, and would slowly follow the Stations of the Cross around the walls, sometimes sobbing, or striking himself on the breast and crying: 'Forgive me, Lord, I am the good thief (*le bon larron*) of the Crucifixion.' Max gradually adopted the role of unofficial guide to the Basilica. But with the fall of France in 1940, followed by the Occupation, his activities were more and more circumscribed. He was forced by the Gestapo to wear the yellow Star of David that denoted him a Jew, and the members of his family disappeared into the concentration camps; his brother and sister died at Auschwitz in 1944. Max's own time finally came on February 24 of that year. Arrested by the Gestapo, he was taken to Drancy—a north-east suburb of Paris that had been turned into a transit camp for French Jews being taken to the gas chambers. From the Gare d'Austerlitz he scribbled a last note to his friend the Curé of Saint-Benoît: 'Excuse this letter written by a shipwrecked man with the co-operation of the police. Just to let you know that I will soon be at Drancy. I have some conversions in hand. I trust in

God and my friends. I give thanks for my martyrdom which is now beginning. In respect and friendship, Max Jacob. (I leave no one out of my daily prayers.)' But he was spared the worst martyrdom of millions of his race. Exhausted and weak from privations, he had an attack of bronchial pneumonia and died at Drancy at the beginning of March. In 1949 his body was recovered, and now lies buried in his beloved Saint-Benoît.

Towards the end of his life Max Jacob ruminated upon his forthcoming death in a religious meditation. 'My ancient flesh,' he wrote, 'my soul is leaving you. They will put you where you belong, in the manure heap that is a cemetery. They will engrave a name soon obliterated by the dancing hours of the sun. A generation or two will read this name offhandedly, with a vague memory of a rather grotesque old man. Another old man will say "I knew him". That's all. Your works will soon be old-fashioned and forgotten, and the photograph of your face will not be kept by anybody, since you didn't even have a son. This is death! This is death the inescapable, death the inescapable (*la mort inéluctable*).' If Max Jacob's reputation has been saved at the eleventh hour, so to speak, by his fellow-citizens of Quimper, it is by no means too late. His gouaches are there for all to see in the Beaux-Arts; his poems are there to be read; and the odd and touching facts of his life speak more strongly as he moves further from us in time. Just off the Rue du Parc is the small courtyard surrounded by half-timbered houses where Max spent his childhood. Renamed the Cour Jacob in 1976, it still gives the view of the Cathedral spires soaring above the roof-tops that he knew a century ago, and that stayed with him through all the vicissitudes of his tormented existence.

A short way from the river, and parallel to the Rue du Parc, is the Rue Kéréon, the most celebrated of Quimper's ancient streets. I first got to know it under disagreeable circumstances, driving down it in the rush hour on a wet October evening. The street is not a particularly long one, yet it took me about half an hour to negotiate it, as all the traffic was caught up in the aftermath of a teachers' demonstration for more pay. Thus I spent more time in the Rue Kéréon than it perhaps warrants —though of course it is full of those superb houses, stone on the ground floor and half-timbered above, that are Quimper's pride. Worth looking out for in the Rue Guéodet nearby is an ancient house with four grotesque groups of carved stone figures holding up the main beam of the façade. A little way up the hill is the prettiest square in Quimper, the Place au Beurre, which used to be called by the even more delightful name of Place au Beurre en Pot.

These old streets lay within the domain of the Bishop, in the walled town or Ville Close, whose western limit was defined by the little River Steir. On the other side of the river was secular Quimper, the Duke's Domain or Terre au Duc, perpetuated in a square of the same name. As in the Ville Close, the Middle Ages live on in the street names of the Terre au Duc—the Venelle du Pain Cuit (Bread Lane), situated naturally below the Duke's Mill (Venelle du Moulin-du-Duc), the Venelle du Poivre (Pepper Lane), the Venelle de la Glacière (Ice-house Lane).

Yet all this—Cathedral, Ville Close, Terre au Duc—is not the oldest part of Quimper at all. This lies on the other side of the Odet, ten minutes' walk away, in the little backwater of Locmaria. In Roman times Locmaria was called Aquilonia, and it seems probable that this was the original seat of the bishopric, before it was transferred to the other side of the river in the time of St Corentin. At any rate, Locmaria has one of the most beautiful Romanesque churches in the whole of Brittany, a massively austere building, with a superb west door and sturdy cruciform nave columns, dating from the early eleventh century. Worth looking out for is the grave-slab of the Abbess Marie de Bourgneuf; at first glance the carving seems primitively medieval, but in fact she died in 1656. South of the church is a quiet little flower-filled cloister, again medieval-seeming but in reality seventeenth-century.

A few steps from the church is the famous Quimper Pottery, which you can visit on conducted tours. Once you have seen one pottery you have more or less seen them all; though Quimper is bigger than most. What is remarkable about it is the intense traditionalism that frowns on any departure from time-hallowed designs. Each artist works with a pattern in front of him or her, and I was greeted with a mixture of pity and surprise when I suggested that they might occasionally try out their own originality. The result can be seen in the museum that forms part of the Pottery: the crude vigour of the early designs has been softened and sentimentalised. Only the splendid Quimper colours—red, orange, blue, green—form an abiding link with the older ware.

Pottery was certainly made at Aquilonia; and small potteries came and went at Quimper in the Middle Ages. But the modern ware dates only from 1685, when Jean-Baptiste Bousquet took over the '*poterie*' run by the Priory of Locmaria and turned it into a *faiencerie*, *faience* being the glazed ware whose manufacture was transmitted by the Arabs to Spain (*majolica* derived from Majorca) and Sicily, and was then spread by Italian craftsmen all over Europe. Bousquet, a good businessman from Marseilles, bought up neighbouring properties and left a flourishing factory when he died in 1708. During the eighteenth century the pottery was inherited from father to son, or son-in-law. The greatest name was that of Pierre Clément Caussy, trained at Rouen, who in 1747 published a *Traité de la Faience*, which not only gives the secrets of the potter's craft, but is also a handbook on running a factory in an eighteenth-century paternalistic way.

The typical Quimper ware, on which the modern products are based, is that of the nineteenth century, the period of the so-called 'Grande Maison', distinguished by the maker's mark HB. This stands for Hubaudière-Bousquet, which unites the names of the founder of the pottery and of Caussy's daughter, who married Antoine de la Hubaudière and carried on under her married name (with an interlude as 'Citoyenne Caussy') after her husband was guillotined. The last member of the family was killed in action in 1915.

Two other nineteenth-century Quimper potteries, of lesser importance but still significant, were those of Eloury-Porquier-Beau, and Dumaine-Tanquerey-Henriot, each named after successive owners. Henriot and Porquier amalgamated in 1913; and the final merger took place in 1968, when the HB and Henriot factories united under the title of 'Les Faienceries de Quimper'.

CHAPTER X

Bombarde, Biniou and Gavotte

EVERY YEAR, DURING the last week in July, Quimper is given over to the skirls of *biniou* and *bombarde* (Brittany's bagpipe and oboe) and the rattle of drums; to an endless parade of *coiffes* and aprons for the women, and knee-breeches and beribboned hats for the men; and of course to a vast influx of tourists who have come to see the biggest folk festival in Brittany. This is the week of the Fêtes de Cornouaille (in Breton, Goueliou Kerne), where the Bretonism of Brittany can be seen at its most concentrated. But the show is far more than a tourist attraction. Apart from the colourful displays, the festival includes a great deal of what ardent Breton patriots prize most highly; thus when I attended the festival in 1976 there were plays in Breton, a Celtic folk evening with groups from Scotland and Ireland, and a day devoted to the celebration of the work of Max Jacob. Each year too there is a chance to compare Breton folk culture with those of quite distinct origins (in 1976 the countries were Romania and Tahiti).

The enormous number of people taking part make the festival very much a matter of general involvement. You cannot get away from a school choir practising in the streets, a *biniou* player droning away to himself in the shade of an ancient wall, a couple of coiffed girls eating candyfloss, toddlers trying out the steps of the gavotte. Some idea of the numbers involved can be got from the fact that in the grand procession through the streets of the town on the final Sunday there are three thousand men and women in costume and a thousand musicians, at a conservative estimate. I can think of no better way to appreciate the variety within the apparent near-sameness of Breton costume and dance than to spend the whole of the final Sunday of the Fêtes de Cornouaille watching the show. This is a fairly daunting prospect, as to do it properly you will have to spend the best part of nine hours concentrating, often under not particularly comfortable conditions. But by the end of the day you will either have become a *bombarde, biniou* and gavotte addict, or swear you will never go to another folk festival as long as you live.

Throughout the morning the grand procession (*Grand Défilé à Travers la Ville*) unfolds a circular tour of Brittany in sound and costume, beginning at Quimper, working clockwise through the central mountains to Brest, along the northern coast to Saint-Malo, inland through Rennes to Nantes, then along the southern coast through Vannes and Lorient, and back once again to Quimper. In the main stadium of the Place de la Résistance you can watch the spectacle with an accompanying commentary; or you can try to see the show as it winds through the streets of the town—though to see much you really have to stake out a claim on the pavement well in advance. For the seeker after precise knowledge the stadium is the place, but for the general atmosphere it is better to take your chance along the flag-bedecked streets.

All the participants, whether singers or dancers, wear costume. The dancers (*cercles*) alternate with the bands (*bagadou*, plural of *bagad*), in the proportion of about sixty *cercles* to twenty *bagadou*. The *bagad* is normally made up of *binious*, *bombardes* and drums (the *batterie*), though there are regional variations. In Basse-Bretagne the normal pattern is kept; but as you get towards the more cosmopolitan Haute-Bretagne you will find hurdy-gurdies, accordions and violins. In general, the more mountainous and remote the region, the simpler the music, and the more dour the costume, tending towards an unrelieved black. Conversely, the easier the living, the brighter the colours, such as the brilliant green of the strawberry-growing region of Plougastel, or the stylish black waistcoats and orange ties of Locoal-Meudon on the Gulf of Morbihan. Fittingly enough, Quimper has the greatest number of *cercles* and the widest variety of costume, ranging from white baggy Russian-type breeches to the traditional Quimper blue. This is supposedly because after the Napoleonic Wars the canny Quimper tailors bought up unused army surplus cloth, which happened to be blue. Hence the popular Breton name *glazik* ('little blue') for someone who comes from Quimper.

As one *bagad* and the *cercles* that march behind it give way to the next in succession, there comes a curious moment when you can hear the two bands simultaneously, one retreating, the other coming towards you, which produces a strangely disorientating effect, made even stranger by the underlying similarity of the music played. Not the least splendid part of the spectacle comes from the banners carried by the leading man in each *bagad*, enormous flags straining in the wind, which must be a tremendous burden in the numerous halts that interrupt the regular flow of the *Défilé*. While the procession winds through the town, often all that can be seen over the heads of the crowd are a few *coiffes* and these dominant banners, inscribed with the name of the band, or with heraldic devices like the red dragon (similar to that of Wales) carried by Quimper's popular Bagad Kemper. Some of the groups bear articles that emphasise their locality or chief industry: the girls of Cancale, in their mauve aprons and black dresses, carry oyster baskets, the marshmen of Guérande hold salt rakes, a group from the rich farmland near Rennes carry hay-rakes, flails and winnowing baskets. And the men of Saint-Malo have as their mascot a boxer—today's rather tame substitute for the *dogues* that once patrolled outside the walls of the town from curfew until sunrise.

The morning wears on, and the earliest groups fall out after completing the course of the *Défilé*. The few men and women wearing wooden sabots adjust the bedroom slippers (no longer straw linings, as in the old days) worn inside them. Others push back hats, or loosen *coiffes* and light up cigarettes; and by lunchtime all the cafés and bars are packed. The participants need to keep their strength up, because the afternoon's proceedings are as long as those of the morning, and a good deal more strenuous, as the dancers go through their taxing routines, and the musicians stand still in the baking three o'clock sun, no longer shaded by the tree-covered bulk of Mont Frugy to the south.

The afternoon's occasion is known as the *Abadenn Veur*, or Great Assembly. It is divided into two sections: first, the presentation of the Reine de Cornouaille for the coming year; and second, a display designed to show off the vast scope of the Breton dance. In 1976 this took an unusual form: a quadruple sequence of dances, each illustrating one of the seasons of the year. As far as the presentation is concerned, the Queen of

Cornouaille is no simpering Miss World contender, mouthing platitudes about her ambitions for the future and her desire to use her prize money for the general good of mankind. In the first place, the prize is nothing extraordinary—about £250; and secondly the qualifications are fairly austere, though the Queen must be a girl worth looking at as well. She needs to be Breton-speaking (not as common an attribute as might at first be thought, even in Basse-Bretagne), to be knowledgeable in the steps of the dance, in Breton music and in all aspects of Breton history and culture. Throughout the Assembly she sits at the back of the stadium, with a good view of the proceedings but not actually taking part, between her maids of honour. The Queen has her own march, played at her presentation—the *Marche des Reines de Cornouaille* (in Breton, *Bale Rouanezed Kerne*).

Most of the dances are described as gavottes, but not the classical gavotte made familiar by the works of Bach and other eighteenth-century composers. The gavotte, according to the *Oxford Companion to Music*, is 'a dance form coming originally from the Pays de Gap, in France, where the inhabitants are called Gavots. It was taken up at the court of Louis XIV . . . its court and Paris popularity lasting until the French Revolution.' But it underwent extensive transfusions of vitality when it left the court for the backwoods of Brittany. From being a 'slow and stately dance', as the same source describes it, in two or four time, it has taken on a great variety of forms. It may be in triple time, fast or slow, decorous or riotous; though it still retains the characteristic lifting of the feet, as opposed to the minuet, where 'the feet were shuffled along the floor'. The *Oxford Companion* mentions a delightful feature of the early gavotte: 'In its first aristocratic use kissing was a part of the ritual of this dance, but this was superseded by the presentation of bouquets or chaplets.' Kissing has certainly not died out among all gavotte dancers, even in the public arena of the *Abadenn Veur*, and many of the girl dancers carry flowers, perhaps a relic of the alternative tradition. Like other ancient dances, the gavotte may well be far older than it appears, dating back to Breton prehistory. Henry Blackburn, in his book *Breton Folk*, refers to this tradition in his description of a gavotte danced in the streets of Châteauneuf-du-Faou in 1874. 'The gravity of manner and the downward look of the women in certain figures, as they advance and retire with hands down, give a peculiar quaintness to the gavotte, which, apparently rollicking and unrestrained, is, in fact, orderly and regular in every movement. The circular motion of the dancers, now revolving in several circles, now in one *grande ronde*, is traced by M. Emile Souvestre, and other writers, to Druidic origin and the movement of the stars.'

Before each group of dancers walks, trots or runs—depending on the ultimate speed of the dance—on to the stage, they go through a curious warming-up ritual in the tunnel leading to the arena, swinging their linked hands backwards and forwards to get themselves into the rhythm of the music, which has already started up. The music tends to be an endlessly reiterated strophic tune, played on *biniou* and *bombarde*, the *biniou* providing a constant stream of sound, plus bagpipe drone, while the *bombarde* is used as the main melodic instrument, usually playing in unison with the *biniou*. Harmony in the classical sense is rudimentary, or non-existent.

The four seasons are preceded by an introductory section, culminating in a carnival gavotte before the austerities of Lent. Here one of the dances is performed face to face, as at the time of its origin the clergy had forbidden couples to dance closely together. The spring section begins with an Easter Passion song and ends at Whitsun, with a hobbyhorse dance reminiscent of morris dancers, though without the bells round the knees. The summer dances cover the period from Midsummer Night (*La Saint-Jean*), and takes in the harvest (normally in July), and then the dances of the *pardon* month of August and early September, when a breathing-space in the agricultural round allowed country people to take time off for the annual religious processions to small chapel, parish church or major centre of pilgrimage. The *pardon* dances are among the most spectacular of the whole *Abadenn*—the Ribbon Gavotte (*Gavotte avec Rubans*), where the men kick their feet in the air as high as possible behind their partners' head; the Tobacco and Handkerchief Gavotte (*Gavotte avec Tabac et Mouchoirs*), in which these articles are presented respectively to the best of the male and female dancers. The final *Dérobée* (Pilfering Dance) is a dance-cum-game, in which a surplus man tries to 'steal' one of the girls from another male dancer—a kind of musical chairs, in fact.

Autumn in Brittany was formerly the time of leisure, and hence of marriages—marriages perhaps finally arranged at one of the *pardons* a month or two before. So most of the songs and dances have marriage as their theme; though the longest dance of the whole afternoon celebrates the prime autumn concern of the Loire valley, the Muscadet grape harvest. Here, in the *Chants et Danses des Vendanges*, is what amounts to an extract from a folk opera. The dancers begin slowly enough, but towards the end the men swing the girl dancers uninhibitedly over wine barrels, while the master of the harvest offers silver bowls of last year's vintage to those within arm's reach of the platform. The winter dances include a stamping dance (*Danse du Loup*), without instrumental accompaniment, to warn the wolves from the shepherd's flock (the last wolf in Brittany was killed about 1870), and a *Pastorale*, in which eight shepherds lead on the dancers, sumptuously adorned in brilliantly embroidered costumes and carrying staffs crowned with moons and stars. There were until recently twelve such costumes; but even the Fêtes de Cornouaille are not immune from the criminal malaise of the times, and a few years ago four costumes were stolen from the small festival office.

The 1976 *Abadenn* was marred by a far more serious crime, or attempted crime—a bomb exploded in an uncompleted bank, showering the streets with débris. After a certain amount of surging around in the stadium, mainly to see what was going on, the audience returned to its places. Meanwhile the dancers, players and commentator continued imperturbably, with true Breton concentration on the task in hand. This was, said the local paper, the eighth such *attentat* in Quimper in the past year. Presumably one of the more extreme of the Breton liberation movements was responsible.

The *Abadenn* ends with the exhilarating Dance of a Thousand (*Danse des Mille*), which should perhaps be more properly called the Dance of Three Thousand. To the music of the Sonerien Du—a group of musicians who combine the traditions of *biniou* and *bombarde* with elements of pop music, such as guitar, electric piano and high amplification—all the dancers join hands, and for twenty minutes or so snake backwards and forwards on and around the platform in the cheerful *Gavotte des Montagnes*. Those of the audience who know the steps join in, and everyone spills back across the river into the old town.

But this is far from being the end of the day. At nine-thirty in the evening the tireless Quimpérois are back in the stadium again for the *Soirée des Lauréats*, in which all those who have been judged the best in the various events of the previous week make their final appearance before the crowd. The Queen of Cornouaille appears once more, demure in *coiffe*, kerchief and apron. The leading *couple* (duo of *biniou* and *bombarde*) are given small keepsakes in the form of peacock feathers, in place of the real feathers worn by the *sonneurs* of South Cornouaille, in the days when peacocks were no doubt more common in Brittany than they are today. Then the leading *cercles* dance into the dusk, and then into the dark—until midnight, in fact.

For two more hours the alleyways of Locmaria are full of dancers, with the gavotte now well and truly in their bones, drinking cider and beer and lurching more and more unsteadily as the *fest-noz* (night festival) proceeds. The Sonerien Du, gathering fresh reserves of energy from somewhere, are playing their hearts out under the plane trees. Children, grandmothers and visitors of all ages join hands with complete strangers to form a chain along the dusty paths, leaving the dance after a minute or two, or continuing until they feel they are dry enough for another drink. At two in the morning the last dancers reel home, leaving nothing but piles of rubbish and an empty stadium, soon to be dismantled, in the Place de la Résistance.

'Praise the Lord! We are a musical nation!' exclaimed the Rev. Eli Jenkins in Dylan Thomas's *Under Milk Wood*, as he listened to a Welsh voice uplifted in song. He could equally well have applied his outburst to the Bretons; though their music does not take the form of the massed choirs, singing heartfelt choral harmony at Eisteddfods and rugby matches, in which every Welsh man or woman worthy of the name participates. As festivals like the Fêtes de Cornouaille show, Breton music is mainly instrumental. The *biniou* relates it to Scotland, the *bombarde* to Catalonia and the Arab countries, the harp to Wales and Ireland. Yet it is something different, unique. As René Abjean says in his excellent little monograph, *La Musique*

Bretonne: 'What is there in common between the Scottish pibroch and the way in which the *biniou koz* is played? Between the songs of the streets of Belfast and the *kan ha diskan*? Between the Lutheran chorales of the Welsh and the *kantik ar Baradoz*? There is not a single Celtic music, there are a number of Celtic musics.'

All folk music stems from the way in which its particular language is sung, as song always antedates instrumental music. Solo Breton singers use a harshly nasal tone, '*voix calleuses et nasillardes*' Abjean calls these voices. The tunes are often familiar from other sources: even the Breton national hymn is the Welsh anthem *Land of My Fathers*; and its Breton title, *Bro Goz Ma Tadou*, means precisely the same thing. The specifically Breton tunes are more often than not taken from such collections as those of Hersart de la Villemarqué, who at the end of the *Barzaz-Breiz* noted down the tunes to which he had heard the poems sung in the 1830s; or those taken down by François-Marie Luzel, in the second half of the nineteenth century. The *couple* of *biniou* and *bombarde*, rather than the human voice, is now the natural means of Breton musical expression. The *biniou* takes two forms: the *biniou braz*, or great *biniou*, in other words, the ordinary Scottish bagpipe with three drones; and the *biniou koz* (old *biniou*), which as its name suggests was in use in Brittany before the *biniou braz* came south across the Channel. The *biniou koz* is a good deal smaller, and has only a single drone; it sounds an octave higher than the *biniou braz*, and produces a peculiarly sharp and piercing tonal quality. The *bombarde* is a double-reed instrument, looking like an oboe that has been sat on vertically. Its loud, commanding tone is that of the medieval shawm and has little in common with the pastoral gentleness of the modern oboe. It can be used as a solo melody instrument; in a *couple* it normally plays in unison with the *biniou* (or, in the case of the *biniou koz*, an octave lower). The Second World War almost saw the extinction of the *biniou*; Abjean says that by 1943 only a handful of players were left in Brittany, but ten years later there were hundreds and now there are thousands of players.

The near-miraculous effect of the *biniou* on Bretons far from home is described by La Villemarqué in his commentary on the poem *Le Mal du Pays* ('Homesickness'). The Compagnie des

Indes found that the Breton crews of their vessels were literally dying of grief and homesickness when they were sent abroad to the Far East. So the Company authorities had the excellent idea of including a *biniou*-player with each crew; and the familiar skirling notes, turning the hot and dusty plains of India into the damp and stony fields of home, 'sweetened the weariness of the Breton's exile and lessened the bitterness of his regrets'.

For better or for worse, the *couple* is a Breton symbol. *Bombarde* and *biniou* have formed the image of Brittany, 'an image which,' says Abjean, 'has brought with it elements of nationalism with all the advantages and disadvantages that result from this kind of situation. Thanks to it many young Bretons have learnt music and discovered Breton culture. The one disadvantage is that the *biniou* and *bombarde* have sometimes taken too exclusive a role in this music.' To form a *bagad*, they join forces with a variety of drums, thus approximating to the Scottish pipe band. The average *bagad* has twenty-five players, though this is not universal: eight *binious*, ten *bombardes* and seven drums—four *tambours de fond* (snare drums), with a powerful, brittle tone, two tenor drums and one bass drum. The repertory of the *bagadou* is a mixed one, consisting of traditional Breton tunes and also of specifically composed *bagad* music.

Biniou and *bombarde*, with their pungent and far-carrying sounds, are essentially outdoor instruments for accompanying the march or the dance. An indoor instrument that the younger generation of Breton musicians has made very much its own is the Celtic harp, that magical instrument with which the bards of Ireland, Wales and Brittany have, since the days of Merlin, accompanied their prophetic utterances. A much smaller instrument than the big harp of the classical orchestra, its current revival is mainly associated with the name of Alan Stivell, who is as popular in Ireland as he is in Brittany. Stivell sings his own words and music, as well as playing the Celtic harp, *bombarde*, Irish flute and Scottish bagpipes. Sometimes his settings are simple, perhaps just a song with harp accompaniment; or he may take a traditional Breton tune and put it through its paces, ending with the full drum and electric guitar treatment; or he may bring forward an Irish jig in some amazing instrumental guise, arranged perhaps for dulcimer, flute and organ. Stivell is in the true tradition of the ancient bards. In his poem *Delivérance* he looks forward to some future condition of pan-Celtic unity, to the day when

We, whose name is known by the birds of Brittany,
Which has been banished from all the human languages,
From all the libraries and all the maps of the world,
We, the peasants and fishermen, shall open our hearts
To all the peoples of the planet Earth.

Stivell and the other leaders in the establishment of a new Breton folk music have grafted on to their ancient inheritance a good deal of the elements of pop music, as I have mentioned in the case of the Sonerien Du, whom I heard playing at Quimper. Such musicians are permanently in demand; a few nights later I heard the Sonerien Du once more, at the other end of the country, playing at a dance at Saint-Servan just outside Saint-Malo. Though this was primarily a teenage occasion, it was quite free of the surly elements of the generation gap. In the first place, there was a fair sprinkling of young children and their parents; and when my wife and I came to collect our own teenagers at about midnight we stayed for an exhilarating half hour, drawn into the chain of the gavotte by an overwhelmingly friendly crowd.

Of the remaining instruments found in Breton music, the medieval hurdy-gurdy (*vielle*) is nowadays played only by groups from the Saint-Malo region. Scholes in his *Oxford Companion* says that it is 'probably still alive in parts of France'; obviously he had not been to Brittany. At the *Abadenn Veur* I heard a pair of hurdy-gurdies being played very professionally by two identical-looking small girls. The hurdy-gurdy is a semi-automated form of the violin; with the right hand the player turns a handle attached to a rosined wheel, which makes the strings sound, while the left hand operates the keys of a small piano-type fingerboard to give the correct note. The violin, descended from the medieval rebeck (*rebed* in Breton), has come back into popularity with the growing interest in Irish folk music. Proof of this interest can be seen in any Brittany record shop with a stock of Breton records: Alan Stivell, Gilles Servat and the Tri Yann group rub shoulders, or rather sleeves, with Irish records, from innocuous folksongs to the most rabid liberation songs of the IRA. The accordion seems to have been brought back to Brittany by troops returning from the trenches after the First World War.

A more academic strain in Breton music is represented by composers such as Jean L'Helgouac'h, whose arrangements of traditional tunes can be found on many records. His Suite for bombarde, trumpet, horn, trombone and tuba, inspired by Brittany's megalithic monuments, was played at the Fêtes de Cornouaille. Erwan Ropars has composed works for the full *bagad* of *bombarde*, *biniou* and percussion.

In an extract quoted above, René Abjean writes of the *kan ha diskan*. This means literally 'song and descant', but the descant bears little or no relation to the type of high vocal accompaniment sung to our Christmas carols. The *kan ha diskan* is a song of the mountain regions, sung by two singers, in a kind of relay race or leapfrog. The first singer sings a phrase, the second chimes in with the last three notes or so and sings his phrase, the first singer takes over again and so on. It is sung to be danced to, at a steadily accelerating pace. As Abjean describes it: 'Gradually the rhythm speeds up, the words break in on the first couplet which is followed by many more, and the whole thing is linked together like a perfect mechanism of clockwork precision. The rhythm must be kept exactly, because the dancers will not accept any errors in the timing. With a final *tra la la la* after the last couplet the two singers come to a halt, often as exhausted as the dancers, though they have not themselves joined in the dance.'

More than the traditional costumes, which are really museum pieces, and more than the dances, which are revivals incapable of further evolution, music is Brittany's living and growing link with her cultural past. A young Breton nationalist I spoke to in Quimper said that he disapproved of events like the Fêtes de Cornouaille because they encourage tourists, and tourists rot a country (*'la tourisme pourrit la Bretagne'*). This could hardly be said of the country's music, which in its various forms holds the country's aspirations far more than any firebrand political action or newspaper article. It is an art that can be shared by all ages, unlike most Western music, which is divided firmly along generational lines, and it has the adaptability

Above, The oyster *parcs* of Cancale, as the tide begins to uncover the plastic *poches* (sacks) in which the oysters are grown

Centre left, The glutinous mud, for which waders are needed

Left, Close-up of a *poche*

Centre right, Oysters of the largest type (*pieds de cheval*) in a cleaning tank at Cancale

The Fêtes de Cornouaille, held every July at Quimper. *Above*, A lively dance from the Nantes region, celebrating the new vintage

Below left, Pairs of dancers in the gavotte, and players of the *bombarde* (Breton oboe) relaxing from their exertions

ove, Nineteenth-
ntury
graving of a
pical peasant
erior

ght, The front
a *lit-clos* (box-
d) similar to the
e in the
graving

Breton life in the 1870s, as drawn
Randolph Caldecott. *Above*, Horse f
at Le Folgoët. *Centre left*, Peasa
praying at a roadside *calvaire*. *L*
Children playing among the cabba
at Saint-Pol-de-Léon. *Centre right*, T
artist 'sketching under difficulties'

Above left, Belfry gable of the chapel of Trémalo, near Pont-Aven

Above right, Gauguin's *Christ Jaune*

Below, The medieval wooden statue in Trémalo chapel, which inspired Gauguin to paint his picture

Contrast in seascapes: the beach at La Baule in summer, and the lagoon at Saint-Cado on an autumn evening

Above left, Spring-cleaning the statue of St Yves at Ploumilliau

Above right, Medieval statues outside the chapel of Sainte-Anne-la-Palud

Below left, A Breton graveyard in the 1830s

Below right, Today's graveyard: at Argol, in the Crozon peninsula

Above, Statues on the great *calvaire* at Saint-Thégonnec, probably carved about 1600: Christ bound and scourged, and Pilate washing his hands

Below left, Elaborate Baroque reredos in the church at Sizun

Below right, The twisted spire of Saint-Gonéry chapel, near Tréguier to absorb all manner of outside influences. Brittany still awaits her Bartók, Sibelius or Vaughan Willians, to bring her folk music into the mainstream of the European tradition. But there is surely nowhere else in the Western world where popular music is more genuinely popular, or draws its strength from a deeper well of tradition and passionate commitment.

CHAPTER XI

Poets among the Peasants

HIGH ABOVE THE little seaside resort of Saint-Cast, commanding a splendid view of the Channel, stands a monument to one of the obscurer engagements of the Seven Years War. This was the Battle of Saint-Cast, which took place on September 11, 1758; the commemorative column is surmounted by a rusty cast-iron sculpture group portraying the Breton greyhound trampling on the British lion. On June 5 that year an army of 14,000 men under the Duke of Marlborough (grandson of the great First Duke) had landed at Cancale, with the aim of capturing Saint-Malo. They failed in their objective, and after ravaging the countryside as far as Saint-Servan, they returned to England. A second landing, this time under General Bligh, was made in September, on the other side of Saint-Malo at Saint-Briac. Owing to strong winds the British fleet had to leave this anchorage for the greater safety of Saint-Cast, across the bay. Bligh reckoned that he would be unable to capture Saint-Malo without naval support, and decided to march round the coast to rejoin the ships. He was delayed for a day by a small French force which successfully held the crossing of the Arguenon at Le Guildo; this delay gave the French commander-in-chief, the Duc d'Aiguillon, the chance to regroup his forces to such effect that the British were defeated at Saint-Cast, and once more had to retreat from Brittany. The monument, which was put up in 1858 to mark the centenary of the battle, mentions both the Duke and the bravery of his troops ('*ab Aiguillonio Duce et Militum Virtute*').

Bare facts are one thing; but legend is quite another, and the Battle of Saint-Cast gave rise to its own legend. The story goes that a company of Breton troops from the regions round Tréguier and Saint-Pol-de-Léon were marching into battle against a detachment of infantry from the Welsh mountains, who were singing one of their national songs. Suddenly the Bretons halted. They had recognised the tune as one of their own country songs, and began to bellow out the chorus. The Welsh halted in their turn; then, throwing down their arms in defiance of their officers, Welsh and Bretons fell on one another's necks.

The source for this story is that classic of Breton literature, the *Barzaz-Breiz* (*Songs of Brittany*), by the Vicomte Hersart de la Villemarqué. Published in 1838, the *Barzaz-Breiz* was the first book that made the world at large conscious of the fact that the Bretons had their own literature, and, more important, that their literature had nothing to be ashamed of when put alongside the corpus of the world's great writings. Even the sophisticated Parisians were astonished, George Sand going so far as to call one of the poems 'greater than the Iliad, more complete, more beautiful, more perfect than any masterpiece that has issued from the human brain'. La Villemarqué reaped the benefit of the pioneering work done by earlier writers such as Le Gonidec, who in 1807 codified the rules of Breton grammar and in 1821 produced his *Dictionnaire Celto-Breton*. The *Barzaz-Breiz* was in the tradition of bardic writings like those ascribed to Ossian, of the Border Ballads which had such an influence on Scott, and of the medievalising poems of Chatterton. It consists of about eighty poems of varying lengths. The Breton verse originals appear in small type at the foot of the page, with La Villemarqué's prose translations above, and each poem has an explanatory introduction and postscript. Most of them are in four-line rhyming stanzas, with eight syllables a line.

Here is a rendering of two verses of *The Battle of Saint-Cast*, at the moment when the opposing Celts recognise each other.

> The Saxon archers, when they heard
> These songs, stood still without a word,
> For verse and tune were both so fair
> They stood and listened spellbound there.
> 'Archers of England, tell us this,
> 'Do you stand still from cowardice?'
> 'We are not cowards, but we know
> 'We all are Bretons, friend not foe.'

The kind of archaising that makes redcoats into archers is common in the *Barzaz-Breiz*, as indeed it is in all folk poetry.

The English are always called Saxons (Zaozon, the Scottish Sassenach), and England is the Land of the Saxons (Bro-Zaoz). The poem's hero is not the Duc d'Aiguillon, but Morel d'Aubigny, who commanded the forces in the field. The Duke sensibly watched the proceedings from the safe vantage-point of a windmill, which gave rise to the remark: 'The French army was covered in glory, and the Duc d'Aiguillon in flour.' Courage apart, the Duke was a highly practical man, who from about 1755 laid out the road network of Brittany along its present lines—a strategic operation comparable to General Wade's road-building in the Scottish Highlands after the '45 Rebellion.

Before leaving *The Battle of Saint-Cast*, it is worth mentioning an extraordinary parallel to the meeting of the Bretons and the Welsh, which is described in Gerhard Herm's *The Celts*. At the battle of Aquae Sextiae (Aix-en-Provence), fought in 102 BC between the Gauls and the Romans under Marius, Celtic auxiliaries were fighting on both sides, the Ligurians with Marius and the Ambrones with the Gauls. Quoting Plutarch's account of the battle, Herm tells us that 'the Ambrones, attacking Marius's army, used their own tribal names as war-cries. When the Ligurians "heard and understood the cries, they too shouted out their own names, for the Ligurians are known after their origins as Ambrones" '. But unlike their fighting successors at Saint-Cast, these warriors do not seem to have let the ties of common ancestry suppress their desire to kill one another.

The bulk of the poems take as their starting-point some historical event or personality. Naturally battles and heroic deeds take a high place, like *The Battle of the Thirties* (*La Bataille des Trente*, now usually called *Le Combat des Trente*), which celebrates one of the most dramatic episodes of the Hundred Years War. On March 26, 1351, thirty Bretons under Robert de Beaumanoir, commander of Josselin on the French side, met thirty English knights, and fought them hand to hand for the best part of the day. The battle took place at the Half-Way Oak (Chêne de Mi-Voie), at the point mid-way between Josselin and Ploërmel where the monument known as the Colonne des Trente now stands. The English commander is called by La Villemarqué Bembro or Bembrough, and this name has been faithfully followed in subsequent accounts of the Combat des Trente. La Villemarqué leads his poem up to the quotation that has become a proverb. At the height of the fray Beaumanoir called out for a drink, and was answered by one of his men with the words: 'Drink your blood, Beaumanoir, your thirst will pass' (*'Bois ton sang, Beaumanoir, ta soif se passera'*—in itself a line from a poem supposed to be contemporary with the battle). Here is how La Villemarqué puts it:

> Then Robert, Lord of Beaumanoir,
> Shouted 'I thirst! My throat's on fire!'
> Du Bois rebuked him where he stood:
> 'Friend, if you're thirsty, drink your blood!'
> When Robert heard Du Bois exclaim,
> He turned his head away in shame,
> Fell on the Saxons instantly,
> And slew five of their company.

However, the chronicler Froissart makes no mention of the famous rebuke to Beaumanoir. He describes, in medieval French that clanks like a suit of armour, how 'there took place a very wonderful feat of arms in Brittany' (*'avint en Bretaingne ung moult mervilleux fait d'armes'*). Froissart makes the battle a matter of honour between knights fighting for their ladies—unlikely on the face of it, though in the Middle Ages motives for battles were often mixed. Beaumanoir came before the walls of Ploërmel, and challenged the English commander to a fight with lances between two or three picked knights on either side. Froissart calls the commander either Blandebourch, Blancquebourcq or Branquebourch in the course of a couple of pages; but nowhere does the name remotely resemble Bembro. And he was not an Englishman at all, but a German soldier of fortune (*ung saudoyers alleman*), in command of a motley band of Germans, English, Bretons and other nationalities—a typical collection of mercenaries, in fact. The name is also spelt Brambourc in the old poem that contains the classic line about Beaumanoir quoted above; and the various spellings, together with the fact that the commander was a German, make it almost certain that he was either called Brandenburg or came from there.

Brandenburg, as it is easier to call him, took up Beaumanoir's challenge but said he would prefer twenty or thirty knights, so that the deed would be spoken of throughout the world in times to come 'in halls, in palaces, in squares and other places' ('*en sales, en palais, en plaches et en aultres lieus par le monde*'). Beaumanoir and he agreed that there should be thirty on each side, twenty-five on foot and five on horseback. The account of the battle reads like a particularly bloodthirsty football match, everyone fighting 'like Roland and Oliver' (the heroes of Roncesvalles). There was even a half-time, after four French and two English had been killed, during which both sides drank wine, adjusted their armour and cleaned up their wounds. Then, doubtless sore and slightly tipsy, they set to again. In the second half the English had the worst of it and were finally routed by one of the French knights on horseback. At the end of the day Brandenburg and eight of his men had been killed, and all the survivors on both sides were wounded more or less severely. Beaumanoir took the defeated English back to Josselin, and they were subsequently ransomed. Froissart tells us that some years later at a banquet he met one of the Bretons who had taken part, a knight called Yewains (Gawain) Charuels, who still bore the scars of the battle. 'His face was so chopped and cut about that he showed that the battle was hard fought' ('*Il avait le viaire si détaillet et décopet qu'il monstroit bien que la besongne fu bien combatue*'). No doubt Charuels dined out on the Combat des Trente for the rest of his life.

The Colonne des Trente now stands on an 'island', isolated between the two halves of a dual carriageway. You can only get to it if you are coming from the direction of Ploërmel; coming from Josselin you have to make your way on to the westbound carriageway, doubling back on your tracks. It is a tall granite obelisk, with an unreadable plaque dated 1893 on the north face. Behind it, under the pine trees, is a far older memorial: a stone plinth with a cross on top. In lettering that looks seventeenth-century the words 'MARECHAL DE BEAUMANOIR' can just be made out, cut in tribute to the leader of the thirty Breton heroes.

La Villemarqué did not only concern himself with battles long ago. For example, *The Song of the Pilot* concerns the engagement in 1780 between the French frigate *La Surveillante* and the English frigate *Quebec*, which only ended when the *Quebec* was set on fire and *La Surveillante* was holed. Heroically, the English rescued the French crew in their lifeboat; as a tribute to their courage, when they reached shore they were not treated as prisoners-of-war but were given the rights due to shipwrecked mariners. A poem called *Le Prêtre Exilé* deals with a tragedy all too frequent at the time of the Revolution. An exiled priest from Vannes sees himself like one of the Jews in their Babylonian captivity; his flock is scattered, and brambles grow over the stones of his church. The *Barzaz-Breiz* has gentler and more personal themes, apart from the descriptions of heads knocked in and general mayhem. There is the song of the leper, who is rejected by his girl at the first signs of the disease; the duet for the King and Queen of the June Festival; the story of beautiful Jeffik who falls ill and dies, in *The Flowers of May*:

As I fetched water in my pail
I heard the gentle nightingale:
'The hedgerow flowers fall one by one,
'The month of May has nearly gone,
'And that is why I always sing:
'Happy the girls who die in spring.'

One or two of the poems have political overtones, like *The Husbandmen* (*Les Laboureurs*), which according to La Villemarqué dates from the seventeenth century. It echoes the countryman's everlasting complaint about the raw deal he gets from landlord, priest, king, lawyer and townsman alike.

The husbandman is made to pay, he pays out everything.
Three or four taxes every year he has to pay the king.
He has to pay the landlord, the money isn't there.
His goods are seized and sold off cheap, he's driven to despair.

The nostalgia for the great days of old that runs through the *Barzaz-Breiz* is crystallised in the poem *Le Temps Passé*, a hymn to times past, which La Villemarqué places significantly at the end of the first and main section of the book. It takes the form of a discussion between two millers, three travelling hucksters (*pillaouers*), and seven farm-workers (*laboureurs*), each in turn lamenting some aspect of the past that has vanished. Thus the Second Miller says that in the old days the green uniform of the tax officials was nowhere to be seen; the First Farm-worker that the lady of the manor used to fill the poor man's haversack with oatmeal, but he now has to slink away in fear of the dog; the First Huckster that young Bretons are now sent to die in foreign lands. The First Miller sums up the mood of the piece:

> The good old days are past and dead,
> To misery we are betrayed.
> We are betrayed on every hand.
> The grain rots in the rotten land.

This poem has one of the longest introductions of any, and in it La Villemarqué sets down his philosophy about the possible future of his country, a philosophy that can be matched today among the moderate Breton nationalists. 'The yearnings still felt by the most enterprising of modern Bretons, principally among the mountain-dwellers, are nowadays translated into little more than rustic outpourings (*rustiques effusions*). The national spirit that drove the fathers to revolt no longer drives the sons to rebellion, but keeps them in a kind of opposition to the present (*dans une sorte d'opposition contre le présent*).' This opposition is still a living force 140 years later.

In the same introduction La Villemarqué gives an account of how he came across the original of *Le Temps Passé*, on a farm in the Montagnes Noires, where pilgrims to a local festival were spending the night. After supper they climbed the hill to the chapel that was the goal of their pilgrimage, and danced and sang until night fell. 'Behind them was the chapel with its whitewashed walls, its gloomy graveyard, its tombs buried in the grass, its thousand little crosses of black wood, the mysterious shade of its tall elms, its separate ossuary with arches festooned in ivy, whose green curtain, gently lifted by the wind, afforded glimpses of the hallowed bones of their ancestors.' On the bridge in the valley stood the beggars displaying their sores to the pilgrims for charity, while at the horizon's edge the rounded hills of the Montagnes Noires were outlined against the setting sun. This was the background against which the millers, the farm-workers and the hucksters launched into *Le Temps Passé*, where Brittany is personified as a dead baby in an ivory cradle, whose death has driven the whole population mad with grief.

> The baby died, died long ago.
> They sing and rock it to and fro.
> They rock the cradle night and day,
> Since sorrow took their wits away.

La Villemarqué was a young man of only twenty-three when the *Barzaz-Breiz* was published in 1838, and he sprang to literary fame overnight. That year he was awarded the bardic crown at the Abergavenny Eisteddfod; and the rest of his long life was devoted to spreading the gospel of Breton language and literature, as author of books on mythology and legend, and as editor of Le Gonidec's Breton grammar and dictionary. He died in 1895, having lived for nearly all his life on the family estates at Kéransker, near Quimperlé.

The *Barzaz-Breiz* had not been out for many years when the first attacks began on its authenticity. La Villemarqué has been criticised on two counts: first, for passing off as genuine many poems that he had tidied up and made presentable; and, a much graver charge, that a large number were mainly if not entirely written by him. However, recent study of the original manuscripts by Donatien Laurent, of Brest University, appears to have largely vindicated La Villemarqué; though no doubt, as with all scholarly disputes of this nature, complete agreement one way or the other will never be reached. Not only did La Villemarqué collect, adapt or concoct the words of the *Barzaz-Breiz*, he also noted down the music to which they were sung. Like the words, the tunes have been tidied up, to make them consistent with the rules of classical harmony. Thus the flattened seventh of the modal folksong scale becomes a natural, which deprives the tunes of their authentic flavour, and makes them sound like Anglican hymns. Nevertheless, in his realisation that the words of a folk ballad cannot be divorced from the tune to which they are sung, La Villemarqué was a true pioneer. And the poems of the *Barzaz-Breiz* are still sung to the tunes he noted down: I have a fairly recent record of Breton music on which *The Swan* (*Ann Alarc'h*) is sung to the constantly changing rhythm of the melody that La Villemarqué collected.

The *Barzaz-Breiz* had an incalculable influence and an immense literary progeny. A collection of poems called *Les Bardes et Poètes Nationaux de la Bretagne Armoricaine*, published in 1918, contains hundreds of poems by dozens of poets, in both French and Breton. The reworkings of La Villemarqué vary from direct translations into French verse to adaptations of his more social and political themes; it is noticeable that as the nineteenth century turns to the twentieth, the poems advocating Breton independence and separatism get louder and more insistent. The Preface is by Anatole Le Braz, who, like La Villemarqué, was a collector of his country's legends; but who, unlike him, has never been accused of trying to pull poetic wool over his compatriots' eyes.

Le Braz did for Brittany's wealth of prose legends what La Villemarqué had done for its poetry. But, coming on to the scene some half-century later, he was working in a field in which the guidelines had already been clearly laid down, and where the traps were no doubt more obvious. Born at Saint-Servais, south-west of Guingamp, in 1859, Le Braz became a teacher at the Lycée in Quimper, where he collaborated with the folklore enthusiast François-Marie Luzel in collecting Breton popular songs. He was a fluent Breton-speaker, which was a tremendous advantage to him when he began to gather material for his masterpiece *La Légende de la Mort* (1893). In this collection, set down in a matter-of-fact way with no attempt at fine writing, Le Braz got to the heart of a country where life and death were without any clearcut distinction.

The nearest parallels I can think of to these stories are the carvings in a medieval cathedral, where on the capitals and misericords men and women go about their daily tasks cheek by jowl with devils, angels, saints, animals, spirits, and all the multifarious inhabitants of the other world. In *La Légende de la Mort* irreverence and intense belief mix to the same degree. For example, when you die and go to heaven, there are ninety-nine bars on the way. You have to have a drink in all of them, and if you can't pay, you're swept off to hell. The Lord does the rounds once a week, and takes up to paradise any souls that are not too drunk to accompany him. Or there are the stories of the good priest Tadik-Coz, who is adept at cheating devils of their prey of souls.

But the Bretons lived too closely with death to make light of it much of the time. Some of the stories refer to the *intersignes* or omens which foretell that a death will soon take place. In Breton these were called *traou spont*, meaning terrifying events, and like the omens of any superstitious people they could be anything from the sight of an animal to an incident of the working day. The Bretons' chief contribution to the mythology of the graveyard is the Ankou, the harvester and coachman of death, and also death's personification. He is a tall thin figure, with a cadaverous face hidden under a wide hat, and he may appear as a skeleton dressed in a shroud. He sits on a heavy creaking cart, piled high with corpses and drawn either by a single skinny horse, or by two horses, one fat and one thin. As death's harvester, the Ankou carries a scythe, but the blade is attached the opposite way to a normal scythe, and he swings it from left to right instead of from right to left. One story concerns the blacksmith of Ploumilliau, who mended the Ankou's scythe when he should have been at Midnight Mass, and died the next morning for his pains. Indeed, you are as likely to die if you do the Ankou a good turn as you are if you cross him in some way; which is perhaps only another way of saying that the Ankou stands for the arbitrary nature of death.

The spirits of the dead are known collectively as the Anaon, a singular noun with a plural meaning. More often than not souls in Purgatory, they are half way between the living and the souls in Paradise, and are fond of returning to their familiar haunts on earth. Sometimes all they want to do is to come and warm themselves by the fire, since the Bretons believe that the other world is as cold as ice. The souls of those drowned at sea who have not been given Christian burial are known in general as Iannic-ann-ôd (John-of-the-Shore), and they go howling along the beach. If you answer one of them howl for howl, it may cost you your life. 'The first time you answer, Iannic-ann-ôd will cross with one bound half the distance between you. If you answer a second time, he will cross half the remaining distance. If you answer a third time, he will break your neck'. Some of the Anaon are souls that have never made the rounds of the important Breton shrines during their lifetime. After death they have to repair the omission, advancing one coffin's length a day, and carrying their coffin on their back.

Anatole Le Braz's own life was haunted by death. His father, his brothers and his sisters were all drowned in a boating accident at the mouth of the Jaudy river below Tréguier; he outlived two wives; and his only son was killed in the First World War. In spite of these personal tragedies, his ardour for the Breton cause stayed with him until his death in 1926; and he was especially successful as organiser of conferences in the United States, where he was active from 1914 to 1919. He died not in his beloved Brittany, but away in the south of France, at Menton.

Here is a very short Le Braz story, which typifies the dead-pan way in which he sets the mundane side by side with the supernatural. As in all the tales of the Lost City of Ys, the theme is that the souls of the inhabitants would be saved, if only some mortal would do one of them a good deed.

> Two young men from Buguélès used to go every night to cut seaweed at Gueltraz, which is against the law, as everyone knows. They were busy about their task when an old woman, bent under a load of firewood, approached them. 'My lads,' she said, appealing to them, 'please could you carry this load to my house? It's not far, and you'd be doing a great favour to a poor old woman.' 'Too bad,' said one of them, 'we've better things to do.' 'And,' said the other young man, 'you might report us to the customs men.' 'Curse you!' the old woman shouted. 'If you had answered yes, you would have saved the city of Ys.' And with these words she disappeared.

CHAPTER XII

Chapels and Calvaries

ON A HILL above Pont-Aven, tucked away between farm buildings and a long avenue of beech trees, stands the little chapel of Trémalo. There are hundreds like it all over Brittany: a simple stone building, with a low-pitched shingled roof sweeping to within six feet of the ground, and a tiny open belfry, reached by steps cut in the gable end. Inside it is better preserved than most of these remote chapels; its frieze of grotesque carved faces at beam level has been freshly painted, as have the grinning monsters whose jaws grip the ends of each beam. What singles it out is the treasure that makes it unique in Brittany: the painted wooden figure of Christ on the cross, with arms stretched stiffly out and head downcast, which inspired Gauguin to paint one of the greatest of all his pictures, the *Christ Jaune* (now in the Albright-Knox Art Gallery, Buffalo). I came to Trémalo one hot summer lunchtime, with a postcard of the Yellow Christ for comparison, and felt a shock of astonished recognition at seeing the original set high on the wall. Gauguin has captured the sinewy strength of the carving, bringing it out of the chapel and into the undulating folds of the autumnal Breton countryside. Behind the emaciated yellow figure a handful of slate-roofed cottages nestle among the red-brown of the autumn trees; while the three Marys at the foot of the cross are three Breton peasant women, with eyes downcast, wearing the *coiffes* and aprons that Gauguin would have seen every day in the fields round Pont-Aven.

The Yellow Christ represents the austere, mystical aspect of Breton religious art. But most of the figures found in Brittany's chapels are rooted in the everyday world—statues of saints, each of whom looks after one or other of the ailments to which we are heirs, and who will intercede on our behalf if we approach them in a proper frame of mind. The finest group I have come across is in the chapel of Notre-Dame du Haut, in the countryside outside Moncontour—itself a most attractive little medieval town, cosy in fact, if granite can ever be cosy. Inside the chapel are the brightly painted statues of no fewer than seven saints concerned with healing—the *Sept Saints Guérisseurs*. There is hardly an illness that does not come into the domain of one or the other of them. St Yvertin holds his head, to show that he is concerned with migraines. St Houarniaule, otherwise known as St Hervé, cures irrational terrors and nervous depression. In former times such fears were put down to catching sight of the *loup-garou*, or werewolf, and so Hervé holds a wolf on the end of a leash. St Hubert, with billhook, cures wounds; St Méen wards off madness; St Lubin takes care of eye disorders and rheumatism; while St Mamert holds open his intestines, to show that he is concerned with digestive complaints. The only woman in the group, St Eugénie, strikes a more optimistic note, as she ensures an easy delivery in childbirth; though there is another school of thought that associates her, like Yvertin, with headaches. Such medieval-seeming naïveté of faith may make the outsider smile; but the number of votive plaques with '*Merci*' on them, and an up-to-date register where today's visitors record their complaints, show that it may be the sceptic's ideas that need revising.

The centre of the cult of St Hervé is another chapel on a hill, or rather a mountain, in so far as Brittany has any mountains. This is the Ménez-Bré, the highest point in north Brittany, visible soon after you leave Guingamp on the Morlaix road. At its summit is a neat little stone chapel dedicated to St Hervé, with tremendous views, especially westwards towards the Monts d'Arrée. However, any religious atmosphere the place may once have had is now largely dissipated, as the whole summit plateau is used for motor-cycle scrambling. Hervé himself is one of those half-legendary saints whose life stories are more symbolism than fact. Not only was he a bard and a monk, but he was blind from birth as well, his mother having prayed that her child should never be deceived by the outward appearances of things but confine himself to the inner light within—a prayer that was answered all too literally as far as Hervé himself was concerned. The wolf that accompanies him may be the *loup-garou*, as at Notre-Dame du Haut; another explanation is that Hervé commanded the wolf to serve him after it had eaten the donkey that fetched and carried for him. Hervé also had an equivocal reputation as a horse thief:

Sant Herve Mene Bre,
Laer an noz, laer an de

—'St Hervé of Ménez-Bré,' begins an old Breton rhyme, 'thief by night and thief by day. . . . Horse-thief by night and day.' There may be some connection here with the horse cult of Penmarc'h, away in south-west Finistère.

Hervé the Christian monk shared both his blindness and his bardic powers with Gwenc'hlan, one of the last of the Druids, blinded by a Frankish prince for his patriotism. He is said to have prophesied the future history of Brittany; and a haunting poem called *The Prophecy of Gwenc'hlan* has been handed down in the *Barzaz-Breiz* of La Villemarqué. The bard sings that he has lived long enough and is ready to die, going on to describe a mythical fight between the wild boar and the horse of the sea, and ending with a private and gloating vision of revenge.

'The general's head it is my prize,
And I must have his two red eyes.
I will tear out his eyeballs two
Because he cruelly blinded you.'

The speaker is an 'old sea-raven', one of Gwenc'hlan's animal familiars.

Saints and bards were at home on Ménez-Bré, and so was the Devil; though his wiles were continually foiled by the priest who served the chapel, known as Tadik-Coz (Little Old Father). In past centuries—Anatole Le Braz tells us in *La Légende de la Mort*—a funeral service known as the *Ofern Drantel* or Thirtieth Mass was held at the chapel on Ménez-Bré —the last of the '*trentaine*', the thirty masses said for a dead man's soul. The peculiarity of the *Ofern Drantel* was that the Mass was said backwards, and the congregation consisted of the souls of all those who had died in the region during the previous year, together with any number of devils eager to get their claws on the latest soul. 'The priest who held the service,' says Le Braz, 'had to be both clever and brave. At the foot of the mountain he would take off his shoes and climb barefoot, as he had to be a priest "right down to the ground". He climbed the hill with a holy-water stoup in one hand and a sprinkler in the other, sprinkling the water all round him as he went. Often he could hardly go forward for the crush of dead souls, eager to catch a few drops of holy water which might ease their sufferings for a moment.'

After the service the priest would give each devil a flax-seed, 'since devils never agree to leave empty-handed'. On this occasion, as they filed past Tadik-Coz to allow him to inspect their claws, he saw that one of them was clutching the soul of the dead man. So he struck a bargain. 'Well, my friend,' said Tadik-Coz, 'you're looking very pleased with what you've got in your claws. I can't see anything to be proud about myself. I knew the dead man while he was alive. A miserable bloke. His life was so wretched that your hell will seem like paradise to him. When you've led the kind of life he led on earth, you've nothing much to be afraid of, even an eternity of torment.' The devil agreed that the soul was not really worth keeping, but asked for Tadik-Coz's own soul in exchange. The priest agreed, provided that the devil could ask him a question he was unable to answer. The devil scratched his head, thought for a while, and finally asked Tadik-Coz to show him something he had never seen before. Whereupon the wily priest took a knife and an apple out of his cassock, cut the fruit in two and showed the core, which no one had ever seen. The devil admitted defeat, and Tadik-Coz went back to his rectory in the village of Bégard, 'rubbing his hands with delight'. Tadik-Coz seems to have been modelled on a medieval *recteur*, the Abbé Guillermic of Bégard, who won a great reputation as exorcist and sorcerer. After his death—so Le Braz was told by the informant from whom he took down the story—there was no one able to perform the *Ofern Drantel* with the same effectiveness.

The highest point of the Monts d'Arrée likewise has its own chapel, dedicated more conventionally to St Michel, who fought with the Devil on most of the high places of northern Europe. The views from the Montagne Saint-Michel are even more spectacular than those from Ménez-Bré, as the country is wilder—though the vast panorama takes in that symbol of technology the Brennilis atomic reactor, not to mention a tall television mast. But the chapel is in a disgraceful state: when I went there in 1977, the doors were banging in a furious March wind, slates were missing from the roof, and there was human excrement on the floor. It must be hard to keep an eye on so isolated a spot, and vandals will be vandals the world over; but surely the authorities should do something to prevent this little chapel, in one of the grandest places in Brittany, from falling into complete dereliction.

Indeed, decay of a more or less serious nature is common to half the Breton chapels I have seen. Not as bad as Montagne Saint-Michel, but typical all the same in its general air of neglect, is the Chapelle du Temple, a tiny building a mile or two west of Matignon, on the Emerald Coast. It lies beside a country lane in an overgrown churchyard, and to visit it you have to borrow the enormous key from the farmhouse on the other side of the road. The chapel takes its name from the Knights Templars, who owned the land round about, and is said to date from the fourteenth century. Inside, it can hardly have changed since the Middle Ages. The floor is of beaten earth, there are holes in the roof, and the banner of the Templars still hangs on the wall. What is unusual in so minute a chapel is the number of images of the Virgin—four of them altogether, two large and two small. The large ones are of Notre-Dame du Temple and Notre-Dame de Bon Secours; of the small images, one is a tiny jewel-like effigy kept behind glass, while the other, in a niche on the south side of the altar, is known as the *Vierge Miraculeuse*. The miracle commemorated by her name took place in 1758, after British soldiers had landed in Brittany—the soldiers later defeated at the Battle of Saint-Cast. When the troops entered to plunder the chapel, the statue of the Virgin wept, and shamed them into leaving without taking anything.

It would be easy to pass the Chapelle du Temple without noticing it; but this cannot be said of the chapel in the village of Saint-Gonéry, on the road to the Pointe du Château beyond Tréguier. Externally it is distinguished by a twisting spire, almost corkscrew-like. It took this shape when the original wooden framework decayed, allowing the lead roof covering to twist as it settled. When the framework was rebuilt the locals were so attached to the spire's odd appearance that they insisted it should be preserved. Though it is extraordinary enough on the outside, the chapel of Saint-Gonéry is even more extraordinary inside. The wooden nave roof is painted from one end to the other with scenes from the Old and New Testaments, curiously Byzantine-looking, though they were painted in the sixteenth century. On one typical roof panel Adam and Eve sit guiltily terrified, clad from head to foot in tiny leaves. Directly below is a Last Supper, with Judas stealing away from the table at the promptings of a horned devil. I first saw these marvellous paintings nearly twenty years ago; and on my most recent visit I found that in the interim they had decayed badly, and that holes in the panelling had been botched up with planks and rusty nails. However, the old lady who acts as guide said that the chapel was about to be refurbished by the Beaux-Arts, so this may by now have been done.

The chapels so far described have all been inland; but there is an equal number built by the sea—on clifftops, by lonely beaches, on promontories and islets cut off at high tide, on sea-walls lashed by the waves. Typical of these is Notre-Dame de la Joie, near Penmarc'h (see page 327); and just as exquisite is the chapel of Saint-Cado in the Morbihan, which is built on an island linked to the mainland by a narrow causeway. It stands in the lagoon known as the Rivière d'Etel, which cuts deeply into the coast between Auray and Hennebont. When I went there one calm autumn afternoon the lagoon was like a millpond, and reflected the strange light that fades into the distance on those few days when summer and winter are in equipoise. Behind the chapel is a stone crucifix approached by a triple flight of stairs, used by the local fishermen to stretch their nets over for mending. St Cado came from Wales, and the cross-Channel links are proclaimed by a picture of the Glamorgan church of St Catwg's, Gellygaer, inside the chapel, and an old rhyme high up on the walls that tells how the saint

Anglois de nation, prince de Clamorgant [sic]
Puis abbé, vient, débarque et réside céans.

('English by race, prince of Glamorgan, then priest, he came, landed and lived here.') The poem goes on to say that he was attacked by pirates and finally moved elsewhere. Cado had his own encounter with the Devil, who agreed to build a bridge from the island to the mainland, provided that he could carry off the soul of the first creature to cross it. So in a single night the Devil built a bridge of enormous stones, confident of getting a soul—preferably Cado's—the next morning. But the wily saint sent a cat across the bridge, and the Devil was foiled once again.

A few miles from Saint-Cado, near La Trinité, is the chapel of Saint-Philibert, a much humbler building in a workaday setting of jetties and ancient oyster barges. It was getting dark when I saw it, and the blue-painted ceiling covered in stars, which would probably have looked tawdry by daylight, glowed mysteriously in the dimly lit interior. Outside, as at so many chapels, is a holy well with a stone canopy over the top, a spring that was no doubt venerated long before the chapel was built.

Another chapel that surveys the hulks of superannuated boats is Notre-Dame de Rocamadour at Camaret, a busy port on the seaward end of the Presqu'Ile de Crozon. The chapel is built on the Sillon de Camaret—a natural breakwater formed of large pebbles, which gives its name to the town, *kam* in Breton meaning curved, and *ero* meaning furrow, or the ridge of earth turned up by the plough. Though it seems strange to find a Breton chapel bearing the name of a town in the Dordogne, there is a logical explanation. In the Middle Ages Rocamadour was a halting-place on the pilgrim route to St James (Santiago) of Compostela, in north-west Spain, and was itself also a centre of pilgrimage. Travellers from northern and central Europe usually made the whole outward journey by land, as it was harder than going by sea and thus more meritorious. But on the return journey the same conditions did not apply; so they tended to go overland from Rocamadour to Bordeaux or La Rochelle, and from there sailed north round Brittany, often calling at Camaret *en route*. The chapel was built early in the sixteenth century, and became a shrine for pilgrims and sailors who might be held there for weeks during unfavourable weather. Our Lady of Rocamadour was the protectress of sailors in danger of shipwreck: hence the many *ex voto* ship models that hang in the chapel, placed there by sailors saved from drowning. The chapel's belfry had its top knocked off by an English cannon ball in 1694, when an Anglo-Dutch invasion fleet anchored off Camaret, landing a force of 1,300 men on the Sillon. They were beaten off by a combined force of French regulars and Breton militia from Camaret; and the belfry has been left unrepaired as a constant reminder of that famous victory.

An impressive relic of a modern shipwreck that cost a good deal in terms of money, if not of lives, can be seen in Camaret's Tour Vauban, the fortified tower that once guarded the mouth of the harbour and is now a museum. This is the nameboard of the *Torrey Canyon*, which was found in a filthy condition by local fishermen after the tanker broke up between Land's End and the Scillies in 1967, spilling thousands of tons of oil into the sea and polluting huge stretches of the Breton coast. It was the *Torrey Canyon* disaster that first highlighted the modern problem of oil spillage from supertankers, and produced a dramatic impact on the consciousness of all those concerned with the sea, from fishermen to holidaymakers. The *Torrey Canyon*'s nameboard has now been cleaned, and occupies a prominent position among old maps and charts, diving gear and other reminders of nautical matters.

Appalling though it was, the *Torrey Canyon* disaster was dwarfed into insignificance by the wreck of the *Amoco Cadiz*, which in March 1978 broke up on the north-west coast of Finistère, disgorging a quarter of a million tons of oil into the sea. All along that coastline, from the Rade de Brest round to the Bay of Saint-Brieuc, the *marée noire* (black tide) soaked into the sand of the holiday beaches, blackened the rocks, filled every little pool and crevice, and left an oily froth marking the limit of each succeeding wave. I explored the area in early April, only three weeks after the catastrophe, and found a coast that stank like a petrol station and was almost totally without seabirds, apart from a few sick-looking gulls with oil-fouled wings and bellies. The water of the estuaries glistened with oily iridescence, and every individual reed was coated from base to tip with its own dark brown covering. Before the disaster some plant species had only just recovered from the *Torrey Canyon* spillage, so it is hard to see how this second monstrous dose of pollution can be eliminated much before 1990. Far more than the wild life suffered: it was an unmitigated disaster for the fishermen of Portsall, where the tanker broke up offshore, of Aber-Wrac'h, Lilia, and all the other little fishing ports of that wild and jagged coast.

Like all such tragedies, it brought out the best in those involved in clearing up the mess. Each town and village had its own 'black tide' headquarters, which co-ordinated the activities of local inhabitants and volunteers from outside, allocated different *secteurs* of the coast to the cleaning parties, and kept records of the amount of oil (*mazout*) collected into polythene-lined pits behind the tideline. National Servicemen were drafted in from all over France, and everywhere I saw working parties shovelling oily sand into plastic sacks and dustbins, and hosing down the rocks with jets of water, powered mainly by antiquated municipal fire engines. By the end of each day the workers were exhausted, their yellow oilskins covered with filth and their eyes reddened by fatigue and oil fumes. Yet they had the energy to break into song every now and then before returning to their exhausting task. Looking at mile after mile of oil-glistening rock, from the Pointe du Château, past the once-pink boulders of Ploumanac'h, by Roscoff, Brignogan and Aber-Wrac'h to Portsall, I could only marvel at their high spirits and optimism. Of course, the disaster should never have occurred in the first place; and every day the local papers had columns full of recriminations for official incompetence and lack of preparedness. Most worrying are the fears for the future: what happens if in the years to come—in spite of new regulations to keep tankers clear of the Brittany coast—one of the new breed of super-giant tanker three times the size of the *Amoco Cadiz* cuts too close inshore and runs aground? No tug on earth could tow it off, and a third major spillage could be the death-blow for North Finistère's fishing fleet and holiday trade.

Sea and shipwreck both seem equally remote at a very Welsh-looking chapel only a little way from Camaret, near Lannulien south of the town. It is surrounded by trees and has a spring near by. As a local guidebook says, 'If one feels like forgetting sea air and splendid scenery for a moment, one should sit down in the cool shade of Lannulien's elms, on the grass of the meadows, to savour true silence and peace.'

This random choice of ten chapels, scattered all over the country, has hardly scratched the surface of the discoveries that are to be made. A large number of them are kept locked —Notre-Dame du Haut, Le Temple and Saint-Gonéry for a start; but it is always worth finding out which cottage or farmhouse looks after the large and usually rusty chapel key. Far more than the often dismal larger churches, the Breton chapels are a constant challenge to the inquisitive noser-out of treasures, and almost without exception repay any effort involved in getting into them.

Outside every chapel and parish church, at nearly all crossroads and at frequent intervals beside main roads and country lanes, you will find stone calvaries, ranging from simple crosses, through naïve crucifixion scenes, to the elaboration of the great *calvaires* at Pleyben or Saint-Thégonnec, which are dominated by realistic representations of the Passion, and teem with dozens of small carvings showing episodes in the life of Christ. In their variety and sheer number these calvaries are the distinguishing mark of Breton religious art. Other Celtic and Catholic countries have roadside shrines and crucifixes, but nowhere else do they pervade the landscape as they do in Brittany. Though the oldest of them date back to the late Middle Ages, most of them, in spite of their apparent antiquity, were set up in the last century. During the Revolution, hundreds if not thousands were destroyed, and their replacement was still going on when Thomas Adolphus Trollope visited Brittany in the late 1830s. 'During the Restoration', he writes, 'there was an idea of replacing all, which had been destroyed in that terrible year, 1793. But the notion was abandoned, when it was found, from accurate returns, that it would cost 1,500,000 francs to accomplish this in the single department of Finistère alone. They are rapidly being replaced, however, by the crucifixes and virgins, raised daily almost by the devotion of the richer peasants. A Bas-Breton farmer's highest ambition is to place an enormous granite crucifix by the roadside, with his name, and that of his wife, cut on the pedestal, together with a request to the passengers to pray for the repose of their souls. Frequently, the hard and careful savings of many parsimonious years are devoted to this purpose by men, who literally have barely food to eat.' And he quotes from Emile Souvestre, who remarked in *Les Derniers Bretons*: 'One could say without exaggeration that in certain places our cross-country roads are paved with saints: there is a complete *macadamisage* of heads, bodies and limbs of Christian statues.'

I came across a collection of such statues, which looked as though they had been taken down from a major *calvaire* in some upheaval and never replaced. This was in the big chapel of Lambader, near Landivisiau, whose gloomy interior contains shelves of granite statues—the Wise Men bearing gifts, Mary riding sidesaddle into Egypt, shepherds playing the bagpipes. Perhaps they were taken down and hidden at the start of the Revolution and have been waiting ever since to be replaced on some long-vanished calvary. The chapel also has a wonderfully carved and fretted rood screen (*jubé*).

The *calvaires* reached their culmination in the great *enclos paroissiaux* (parish enclosures), centred on the valley of the Elorn river, which runs east-west across Léon and flows into the Rade de Brest. Slightly later in date than the Cotswold wool churches, they were built like those churches from the profits of agriculture, by farmers and merchants who had grown rich from flax and hemp. Like a stone symphony in four movements, the *enclos* always takes the same basic form, though the emphasis and the details may differ. It consists of a parish church surrounded by a wall; a triumphal arch forming a grand entry; an ossuary, where the bones of the dead were stored; and a *calvaire*, on which all the resources of the sculptor's skill were lavished.

Three of the finest of the enclosures—Lampaul-Guimiliau, Guimiliau and Saint-Thégonnec—are signposted as the '*Circuit des Trois Enclos*'. Taken together they form an open-air museum of the Breton Renaissance and give an excellent idea of its originality and power. But to experience that Renaissance at its source, so to speak, you should seek out the *enclos* at La Martyre, an isolated village near Landerneau. La Martyre has not got a spectacular calvary—as is often the case, the *calvaire* forms part of the triumphal arch—but it is the oldest of all the *enclos*, dating from the mid-fifteenth century, if not earlier, and its time-ravaged beauty is far more moving than the spruce appearance of later and better-maintained examples. In addition, the unravelling of the story of La Martyre is a fascinating piece of architectural detective work. The man who unravelled it still lives in an ancient house in La Martyre, and reckons that he will never come to the end of its revelations and its mysteries. The presiding spirit of La Martyre, Fons de Kort, is a Dutchman, and how he came to be there at all makes an intriguing story. One day he was sketching a medieval house in the village when its elderly owner came out and asked him if he would like to live there. He said he would; terms were agreed; and now M. de Kort lives in what is reputed to be the oldest inhabited house (outside ancient towns like Morlaix) in the whole of Brittany, under the shadow of the church he has made his life's work.

The riddles of La Martyre begin with its name, which means 'The Martyrdom'. By tradition it derives from the martyred King Salomon or Salaün, King of Brittany in the middle of the ninth century. The nephew of King Nominoë, he came to the throne in the bloodthirsty fashion of the times by murdering his cousin Erispoë at the altar. He was an active and successful ruler from his *coup d'état* in 857 until 872, when he gave up the throne and retired to a hermitage in the Forest of Brocéliande. But he was not allowed to sink quietly into a devout old age: two years later the partisans of the murdered Erispoë burst into the church where Salomon was praying, stabbed his young son to death before his eyes, then blinded him and cut off his head. Though his life had hardly been exemplary, even by ninth-century standards, he was canonised as early as 910, and he was revered as one of the greatest of Breton rulers. The dedication of the church at La Martyre to St Salomon is further confused by the fact that there was an earlier Salomon who was also murdered in about 420, during the upheavals at the end of the Roman Empire. This Salomon is said to have been the predecessor of Gradlon, King of the lost city of Ys, and to have been killed at La Martyre itself.

Whichever Salaün is commemorated, La Martyre was certainly a well-established shrine by the early Middle Ages. The oldest section of the church (the massive base of the west tower) is dated by M. de Kort as early as the eleventh century, because of the fourteen apostles carved on its columns—the original Twelve less Judas, together with Paul, Barnabas and

Matthew, to bring the number up to fourteen. This was the number currently accepted in the eleventh century, but not later. The tower is sturdy enough to have been used as a fortification, and in origin the *enclos* was as much military as religious: the wall could be patrolled, and in later centuries, when the annual fair that grew up at La Martyre was famous throughout Europe, the seneschal and his men could make sure that the huge crowds were kept under effective control. But what strikes the eye at La Martyre is not so much the overall appearance of the church and its surroundings, which are close-knit and not easy to appreciate as a whole, as the detail, and in particular the porch and ossuary that stand side by side at the main entrance.

The south porch of La Martyre is one of the marvels of Brittany. Carved with angels, peasants and coats-of-arms, it is crowned by a tender Nativity, which even in its present mutilated state is a touching and beautiful work of art. On the evidence of its carvings, the porch has been dated to about 1460, and it is here that M. de Kort has deployed his detective work to the full. For example, he has identified ten of the carved shields round the porch, and suggests that the bearded and mitred figure of Herod, carved in the outer row of stones behind the Virgin, may be a portrait of the reigning Duke, John V of Brittany. Directly behind the Virgin's head an attendant holds the shield of the De Kersauzon family, and M. de Kort makes the not too far-fetched suggestion that the young mother may be the wife of Guillaume de Kersauzon, the chief donor of the porch, and seneschal (military and civilian controller) of the fair.

If Mary is the seneschal's wife, is the rather humble-looking Joseph, wearing an odd pudding-basin hat, De Kersauzon himself? It seems unlikely at first sight, as the figure is so obviously subordinated to the Virgin; but who knows whether the seneschal may not have placed himself there as almost a figure of fun, in a medieval gesture of humility? The Virgin was originally carved suckling her child, with her breasts bare; but at some stage child and breast were hacked away, and the Virgin's arms now cradle a flat expanse of stone. What the complete figure originally looked like can still be seen on the old *calvaire* at Tronoen (see page 327). At La Martyre the

Virgin may have been mutilated by the Revolutionaries; or, following M. de Kort's theory, by some *recteur* whose prudish parishoners decided that bare breasts and religion did not go together.

The scenes on either side of the porch are full of down-to-earth sketches of Breton life, like the hooded peasant unconcernedly playing *crosse* (a kind of primitive hockey or golf), while an angel announces the Nativity directly overhead. Here and there on the stonework M. de Kort has found traces of paint, which show that the whole porch must once have been coloured as brilliantly as an illuminated manuscript—a glorious frame for the sumptuously dressed nobles, headed by Guillaume de Kersauzon, who would deliberate on the long benches inside the porch, while the locals stood outside in the churchyard following the debate. And as always in Brittany, death was close at hand in the shape of the skeletal figure of the Ankou, carved holding a severed head above the holy-water stoup.

At La Martyre life is in literal fact next door to death. Jammed against the porch, and echoing its general shape in the Renaissance style of the early seventeenth century, is the ossuary, where the bones of the dead were stored. For all its grim function, it is a cheerful, almost light-hearted little building, and was originally painted gold and blue, in contrast to the rainbow colouring of the porch. Over the door are angels holding scrolls, on which the message of the ossuary is spelt out in Breton for all to read. 'AN MARO HAN BARN HAN IFERN IEN . . .'—'Death, judgment, cold hell, when a man thinks upon it he must tremble. Foolish is he whose spirit does not meditate upon these things, knowing that he must die.' The Breton hell, like Dante's lowest circle, was a cold place, where even the doubtful comfort of fire was denied to the souls of the damned. A curious feature of the ossuary is the Egyptian-looking caryatid at the far corner, who appears to be supporting half the weight of the building on her head.

Such ossuaries are now either locked and empty, as at La Martyre, or turned into shops for selling guidebooks and postcards, as has happened at some of the other major *enclos*. In their heyday they were ghoulishly terrifying places, covered outside with little boxes showing the skulls grinning through, and piled high inside with the other bones unearthed when the graveyard was dug up to make room for fresh corpses. According to Flaubert, who visited the ossuary at Quiberon in the 1840s, the skull (*chef*) was only kept in its box for twenty-five years, after which it was added to the general jumble of bones.

Inside, the church at La Martyre has some good grotesque capitals, and a painted frieze (*sablière*) at beam level, whose charming little carvings include *biniou* players and a plough pulled by two pairs of oxen and a pair of horses. The crucifixion scene in the east window has been identified by M. de Kort as the work of Jost de Negker, a Fleming born at Antwerp about 1485. Dated 1535, the glass was no doubt imported into Brittany via La Martyre's annual trade fair.

In spite of M. de Kort's devotion to the church, and a certain amount of repair work going on (to the roof at least), the general impression at La Martyre is one of somnolent decay. Such a medieval treasurehouse deserves to have money poured into it before it is too late; unfortunately, as elsewhere in Brittany, one has the feeling that not only cash but general interest is sadly lacking. On the other hand, if it were tidied up and smartened, as has been done at the three famous *enclos* and at Pleyben, it might lose its magic and become just another beautiful tourist trap. Such is the paradox of conservation, and it is a problem without any real solution.

The circuit of Lampaul-Guimiliau, Guimiliau and Saint-Thégonnec is best begun from the little market town of Landivisiau, rather than from Morlaix, as in this direction the *enclos* fall in chronological order. Landivisiau is worth seeing anyway, for its holy well dedicated to St Thivisiau. This has sculptures built into it, including one of John the Baptist encouraging a shivering Christ to enter the water. With French practicality the spring is fed straight to a communal washing-place. It is not much used nowadays, and I saw only one solitary housewife scrubbing away, the lone survivor of the gossiping women who once exchanged scandal over the shirts and bed-linen, but now sit at home disconsolately watching the tumbler-drier.

The most obvious feature of Lampaul-Guimiliau's church is its curious sawn-off spire. Built in the 1570s, it was originally seventy metres high, thus rivalling Saint-Pol-de-Léon's

Kreisker, at seventy-seven metres. But early in the last century it was struck by lightning, and has never been rebuilt. Though the name 'Lampaul' bears no obvious affinities to 'Saint-Pol', it is in fact named after the same saint, 'Lam-' being merely the prefix meaning 'religious settlement'. A painted statue shows St Pol leading a dragon by his stole tied round his neck—a feat elsewhere ascribed to the Saint on the Ile de Batz, near Roscoff. It is a very small dragon, and is certainly not the grim monster of Batz. A nearby wood is still called the Coat-ar-Serpent, or Wood of the Dragon. St Miliau, from whom the other half of the village's name is derived, is also depicted in a delightfully naïve relief panel, which judging by the clothes is eighteenth-century in date. Miliau or Miliaw was a sixth-century prince of Cornouaille, heir to his father's throne. In the course of a quarrel over the succession, Miliau's brother cut off his head, whereupon the prince picked it up and held it against him, while the severed neck gushed with blood. On the strength of this grisly miracle, he was canonised. The unknown carver has portrayed Miliau in proper princely robes, with a crown round the decapitated head. The wicked brother is a Dick Turpin highwayman in a cocked hat, booted, spurred and topcoated, sheathing his sword as he prepares for his getaway on a white horse, while Miliau's son is a little Breton boy, wearing clogs and holding his wide-brimmed hat. St Miliau appears again at Ploumilliau, away to the north-east, near Lannion. When I went there in March, the image of the saint was being given his annual spring-clean in the church porch, together with St Yves from the same interior.

The *calvaire* at Lampaul-Guimiliau is not much more elaborate than a good many wayside examples. But Guimiliau's *calvaire* is of astonishing richness, covered with carvings in which the Renaissance spirit has hardly begun to break through the wild fantasy of the Middle Ages. Built to an X-shaped ground plan, it writhes with a double row of figures taken both from the Bible and from Breton legend; and though it is now almost four centuries old, the hard granite has scarcely been affected by those hundreds of winters and thousands of rainstorms, apart from taking on the blotches and lichens of age. Incongruous among the figures of the Disciples and the Holy Family is the carving of the Three Holy Women, who watch over the burial at the foot of the Cross. The right-hand figure is dressed in detail as a sixteenth-century court lady, and is said to be a portrait of Mary Queen of Scots, as naturalistically carved as the sculptor could make her. Mary was executed in 1587, which must have been about the date of the *calvaire*. If it is indeed a memorial to her, it would be hard to imagine a more graceful tribute. One of Brittany's legendary unfortunates is also portrayed in a sinister tableau: Katell-Gollet (Catherine the Damned), renowned for her immorality, is being dragged and goaded down to hell, represented as a gaping mouth of stone.

The final flowering of the *enclos* was at Saint-Thégonnec, where the superb ossuary, with its broken pediment and twin rows of columns, was not built until the end of the 1670s. (The village came into brief prominence three hundred years later, when Miss Brittany 1975 was a Saint-Thégonnec girl.) The saint himself is rather obscure, apart from the fact that he tamed wild animals to drag the stone from which he built his church; and he is often portrayed driving a wolf in harness, like St Hervé. The *calvaire* has only a single row of carvings at the foot of the Cross. The faces are often grotesque to the point of caricature and look like three-dimensional Tenniel drawings. One of Christ's tormentors is said to represent Henri IV, whose conversion to Catholicism in 1593 with the words 'Paris is worth a Mass' was regarded as sheer hypocrisy by the fervently religious Bretons. I assume that Henri is the grinning figure with an upswept handlebar moustache, dressed in knee-breeches, crumpled boots and zigzag fringed jerkin, pulling on one end of a cord passed round Christ's wrists. At any rate, this is the only figure that fits the written descriptions; and it makes an interesting comparison with Mary Queen of Scots at Guimiliau. As Henri IV died in 1610 and the *calvaire* is known to date from that year, the figure may be a symbolic declaration of loyalty to his successor, Louis XIII.

This part of Brittany has other notable calvaries—at Plougastel-Daoulas, for example, in the heart of the strawberry-growing country, where the *calvaire* is famous for its carving of Katell-Gollet, and at Pleyben, the most monumental of all the *enclos*. Pleyben's church has a magnificently painted baroque interior and, unlike La Martyre, is magnificently maintained.

The figures on the grand *calvaire* are in mint condition. Even the food at the Last Supper can be made out—a sucking-pig, fruit, some kind of crusty pie. The calvary is signed along the lower stretcher of the table 'FAIST A BREST PAR M: IV: OZANNE: ARCHETECTE', with justifiable pride for a noble work.

I have scarcely mentioned, let alone done justice to, the other aspects of the major *enclos* apart from their calvaries. At Sizun, one of the finest of them all, it is the *porte triomphale* at the entrance that first catches the eye—a unique three-arched structure, with a gallery running the whole way along the top. Sizun's church has a riotous interior of painted and gilded altars and reredoses, in lively contrast to the austere granite façade; its fanciful elaboration is paralleled at Saint-Thégonnec and elsewhere.

The *enclos* with their calvaries are the granite embodiments of the religious fervour of the Bretons. Their religion took on flesh and blood in the processions known as *pardons*, similar to such gatherings in other Catholic countries, but distinguished in Brittany by the fact that almost every village and every shrine once had its own *pardon*, and an enormous number are still held to this day. The mixture of piety and human misery, of devotion and the grotesque that marked the old *pardons*, needed a poet to describe them; and those who want to recapture the atmosphere of those vanished processions should turn to Tristan Corbière's long and sombre poem on the *pardon* of Sainte-Anne la Palud (see page 206). The church that forms the hub of this *pardon* is in a meadow only a few hundred yards from the Bay of Douarnenez—a peaceful setting of cows and green turf, ideal for the crowds of pilgrims who flock to Sainte-Anne on the last Sunday in August. During 1977 there was an exhibition of photographs of modern *pardon*-goers inside the church, the purpose of which was to question how much, if any, religious feeling still survived at Sainte-Anne—a question to which there would presumably be a different answer given by everyone who went there.

Apart from the covered altar behind the church, at which Mass is celebrated during the *pardons*, Sainte-Anne la Palud could be any country church anywhere in Brittany. But this is not true of the two greatest *pardon* centres of all, Sainte-Anne d'Auray, near Vannes, and Le Folgoët, north of Brest, whose entire *raison d'être* is the annual concourse and procession. Sainte-Anne d'Auray, where the *pardon* is held at the end of July, is intimidatingly huge in scale, with a vast basilica, an enormous open space for the crowds to gather, and a gigantic war memorial to the quarter-million Bretons who were killed in the First World War, consisting largely of a great flight of steps leading to an open-air altar. Below it are echoing vaults which years ago I explored at dusk by matchlight; but what was there I can no longer remember. Sainte-Anne owes its fame to a miraculous statue of the mother of the Virgin, which a local farmer called Yves Nicolazic discovered in 1623, buried in the earth. After the usual scepticism from the priesthood, Nicolazic was vindicated, and St Anne has been revered here ever since. Not only is she honoured as the mother of the Virgin: she is also the patroness of Brittany—'*Mamm Goz ar Vretoned*', 'Ancient Mother of the Bretons'. According to one story, Anne was a Breton who made her way to Palestine, gave birth to Mary and in the course of years returned to Brittany. There is probably confusion here with Ana, the mother goddess of the Celts. But whether Ana or Anne, she is greatly venerated.

Le Folgoët is a good deal older than Sainte-Anne d'Auray. Its basilica is largely fifteenth-century, whereas that of Saint-Anne is nineteenth-century; while the legend behind its foundation is correspondingly more ancient and imaginative. Folgoët means in Breton 'the Fool in the Wood', and the place takes its name from Salaün or Salomon, a simpleton who lived in the region in the mid-fourteenth century. According to Albert Le Grand, he made his home in a wood outside Lesneven, 'near a fountain, having no other bed than the cold earth, on which he slept, in the shade of a knotted tree, which served him as sky and as roof'. Every morning he would attend Mass in Lesneven, continually intoning the words '*O Itroun Gwerhez Mari*' ('Lady Virgin Mary'), and living on the charity of the inhabitants. Back in his wood, he would dip his bread in the fountain to soften it; and in the depths of winter he would jump into the water up to his armpits before climbing his tree and shaking one of the branches, shouting '*O Maria!*' continually. Not surprisingly, the neighbours called him Salaün-ar-Foll, Salomon the Mad. He died in about 1358, and after his death a white lily grew from his grave, with the words 'AVE MARIA' inscribed in letters of gold on its petals. Curious to discover where the miraculous flower came from, the clergy dug down to its roots, and found that it was growing from the mouth of Salaün.

Then politics took over. In 1364 the Montfort Duke Jean IV, fresh from his victory over the House of Blois at the Battle of Auray, saw in the story of Salaün the means of strengthening his influence over the Bretons of Finistère. He ordained that a chapel should be built on the spot and laid the first stone himself in January 1365. The shrine of Le Folgoët was specially favoured by successive Dukes of Brittany and grew rich as a result, culminating in the visit by the Duchess Anne during her Breton pilgrimage of 1506 (see page 232). The story of Salaün is told in the windows at the east end of the basilica; and later miracles are commemorated in other ways, such as the carved relief showing a rail crash in 1882, from which Bretons on their way to Lourdes escaped unharmed. International solidarity is maintained at Le Folgoët by a small urn, containing earth from Scotland, Picardy and Brittany, and offered by the Black Watch in memory of 'the brotherhood in arms of the Celtic peoples' during the First World War. Le Folgoët's *pardon* takes place at the beginning of September.

The pilgrimage centre of Saint-Jean du Doigt is well to the east of Le Folgoët, beyond Morlaix. Thomas Adolphus Trollope went to the *pardon* there and wrote a macabre account of its horrors, ignoring its function as an integral part of Breton life of the time (see page 241). The account of the shrine's origins, as told by Albert Le Grand, is as lyrical and fresh as that of Le Folgoët is odd—a springtime legend, set likewise in the Brittany of the medieval dukes. After John the Baptist's execution by Herod at the instigation of Salome, his remains suffered the usual dispersal into relics scattered around the Christian world. His right forefinger passed into the keeping of the Patriarch of Jerusalem; and from there it was removed by a Norman girl called Thecla, who took it with her to Normandy, where a church was built to house it near Saint-Lô.

The finger's miraculous arrival in Brittany took place during the Hundred Years War, in about 1437. A young Breton from the village of Plougasnou was working in Normandy, and at the end of his period of service wanted to take a part of the relic home to Brittany. 'Before setting out on his journey,' says Le Grand, 'he went as was his custom into the church of St John, where he offered up a prayer with extraordinary fervour and devotion. He suddenly felt full of inner joy and lightness of spirit, and without really knowing the source of his happiness began the journey. As he passed through a village, the bells of the church began to ring of their own accord, and the trees bent and bowed down as he passed by—to the great astonishment of the people, who suspected him of being a sorcerer, arrested him and locked him up in prison.' After praying to St John, the young man was miraculously whisked from jail to his own parish, and woke up by a fountain that has ever since had healing powers. Back in Plougasnou the bells once more rang and the trees bowed down. The young man went into the village chapel, where the parishioners found him on his knees in front of the altar. 'Before their eyes, the church candles lit of themselves, and the holy relic—which, without his knowing it, he had been carrying at the junction of his right hand and arm, between flesh and skin—leapt on to the altar. When our young man saw this, he thought he would die of joy, and remained for a long time without uttering a word. Then, recovering his senses, he rose and proclaimed to the people what had happened to him, assuring them that it was the finger of St John the Baptist.' A sceptic might see in the account an early example of subcutaneous concealment of a precious object, as carried out by diamond smugglers today. At any rate, the young man convinced everybody, right up to Duke Jean V, who laid the first stone of the new church near Plougasnou on August 1, 1440.

I went to Saint-Jean du Doigt hoping to see the finger, which according to a lady in the village shop was kept by the *recteur* in a box. But alas, it was a Monday, the *recteur's* day for being away from the village, so I never managed to see it. The church is entirely surrounded—submerged might be a better word—by hideous polished gravestones. The best thing about it is a pretty Renaissance fountain outside, with a little figure of God the Father on top, and water splashing down on to the Baptist's shell and from there to Christ's head. Inside, it is a dank and chilly building, tall and narrow; admittedly I went in March, at a damp time of the year, but that seems little excuse for green mould on the walls and owl droppings on the floor. On the other hand, the church has had bad luck during this century—in 1925 the belfry and steeple were struck by lightning, and in 1955 there was a fire that destroyed much of the interior—and no doubt the parish is a poor one, in spite of those who flock to the *pardon* at the end of June.

Bretons will tell you that the true spirit of the *pardon* survives not so much at these pan-Breton centres as at the smaller inland places, where the *pardon* is still closely linked to the lives of the local people. I have myself been to only one—at Châteauneuf-du-Faou, an unpretentious little town in the hilly heartland of Brittany. Châteauneuf is built on a ridge above the Aulne, which here forms part of the Nantes-Brest canal and flows wide and deep. The tree-clad slopes that fall away to the river below the town are said to be haunted by the ghostly mounted squadrons of King Arthur, patrolling the Montagnes Noires whenever Brittany is threatened by war. The *pardon* takes place on the last weekend but one in August, and we came upon it quite by chance, as always seems to happen with the most memorable occasions in Brittany. We were camped down by the Aulne, and about 9.30 on the Saturday evening, as it was growing dark, we heard amplified bidding prayers echoing down from the spiky chapel of Notre-Dame des Portes, set high among the trees. We climbed the steep zigzag pilgrims' path to the summit, and came on the procession just as it was emerging from the chapel door—hundreds of flickering candles lightening the gloom, followed by white-robed clerics and choir, and then the gold-crowned effigies of the Virgin and Child, carried by six men of the parish aged over fifty.

We joined the candlelit procession as it wound up through the town, past the blaring loudspeakers and cracking rifle shots of a fair, which fell silent for a minute or two as the Virgin was carried by, up by the parish church with its memorial to the forty-three men of Châteauneuf shot by the Nazis, past shops and the town fountain, and down again to the chapel. Throughout the procession, which lasted half an hour or so, prayers and hymns were electronically relayed from the chapel—a whole town wired for religion, but not done in a brash or over-insistent way, as the atmosphere was one of extraordinary gentleness and peace on that warm summer night. The prayers were relevant to every Breton in the procession—prayers to the Virgin for the family, and for the unemployed, since *chômage* (unemployment) is one of the curses of Brittany. They were punctuated by the invocation to the Virgin, '*Je vous salue Marie, pleine de grâce, le seigneur est avec vous*', and at the end the whole procession chanted the solemn three-in-a-bar of the Breton hymn to Notre-Dame des Portes: '*Itron Varia ar Porziou, Klevit mouez ho pugale*' ('Our Lady of the Gates, hear the voices of your children'). Back once more at the chapel, we were all, unbelievers included, promised absolution for taking part in the procession; and the Virgin was returned to the brilliantly lit interior until the following day.

On Sunday morning there was a *grande messe*; and in the afternoon an open-air service, with the congregation sitting on rows of seats up by the altar, or else spreadeagled on the grass—the whole of Châteauneuf-du-Faou out in force, from the smallest babies to old ladies in the tight local *coiffe*, wearing thick black furs for respectability, and holding umbrellas to keep off the heat of the sun. Then the procession was repeated, this time with ten women of the parish carrying the Virgin and Child; the priest thanked the Bishop and blessed the congregation; the Mother and Child were placed by the chapel altar for another year; and the bells clanged out across the Aulne.

Though we were tourists, we were not treated as outsiders but were welcomed to the grave calm of the occasion, which had no trace of folklore about it. What struck me most was the informality of the *pardon*: when the Virgin's crown got entangled in the branches of an overhanging tree, it was as though some member of the congregation's *coiffe* was in danger of being dislodged. For that weekend at least, the white-robed '*Mam da Jesuz*' became a real mother, and we were all her children together.

CHAPTER XIII

The Stone Guns of Roscoff

JUTTING FROM THE church tower of the little harbour town of Roscoff are two stone cannon, which bring a warlike note to that peaceable and intricate structure of grey stone. The church was built at the height of Breton prosperity and defiance of the outside world in the sixteenth century, and these stone guns were reputedly set into the tower to warn off the English in the two directions from which their ships might be expected to attack: north towards the open sea, and west along the narrow channel between the mainland and the Ile de Batz. Stone guns are subject to decay like everything else, and one at least is a replica; I was shown the original, worn to a stump, in the garden of the Abbé Feutren, Recteur of Roscoff and the leading authority on the history of the town. The rest of old Roscoff is built in the same grey stone as the church, which gives the town centre a dour, northern look, an impression heightened by the fact that on the various occasions I have been there almost everything was shut. Admittedly my longest visit was just before All Souls Day (November 1), when the inhabitants were out polishing the granite tombs of their relatives and decorating them with flowers in preparation for the annual procession of Toussaints through the streets of the town. Like Dieppe and Boulogne, now that Roscoff is a cross-Channel shipping terminal, it has become a place to be hurried through on the way to distant destinations rather than visited for itself.

To judge from external appearances, Roscoff has not really shared in the prosperity brought to the area round about by the opening of the new deep-water harbour. Built for the export of vegetables—mainly artichokes and cauliflowers from the rich belt of agricultural land known as the Ceinture Dorée—across the Channel to the West Country and Ireland, the harbour now disgorges boatloads of passengers, who rush through Roscoff and Finistère on their way to the holiday resorts further south. But even the least observant driver cannot fail to notice the agricultural wealth of the country for the first dozen miles or so: everything during the growing season is green or blue-green, with the curly leaves of cauliflowers and the thistly heads of artichokes pushing right up to the doors of the white-painted farm cottages, and invading the back gardens of Roscoff itself. The area has always been agriculturally rich. Flaubert noted it when he passed that way in 1847, adding, with the true Parisian's condescension for things rural, 'but what is that to me?' Never one to let a good opportunity for a witticism pass, he writes: 'I have noticed that the richest country areas are generally the most ugly. They are like virtuous women: you admire them, but you pass by them on the way to find others.' A little unfair on the Ceinture Dorée, perhaps; but no one would award it the highest marks for scenic beauty.

The growth of the region's prosperity has been of a far more overtly political nature than anything we are accustomed to in this country. It mixes together organisation, marketing and even tourism in what might seem an illogical way, but is certainly an effective one. The controlling body is known as the SICA (Société d'Intérêt Collectif Agricole), which was established in 1961 and has its luxurious headquarters at Kérisnel outside the market town of Saint-Pol-de-Léon. Before the SICA came into being, the local farmers were disorganised and at the mercy of entrepreneurs who rigged the market as they thought fit. This situation was brought to an end by a group of young farmers know as the JAC (Jeunesse Agricole Catholique), led by Alexis Gourvennec. In the late 1950s Gourvennec and his friends, still in their twenties, set up a village-by-village organisation among the growers. After being continually stalled both by the central Ministry of Agriculture in Paris and by the Sous-Préfecture in Morlaix, in June 1961 they decided on typically Breton direct action. Three thousand growers gathered in Morlaix, and Gourvennec and a few colleagues occupied the Sous-Préfecture building—a symbolic gesture which led to his being jailed for three weeks, but which showed that the growers had at last been welded into a political force to be reckoned with.

Early morning at Kérisnel makes a dramatic picture. Shortly after first light the roads from Saint-Pol-de-Léon and the surrounding villages are jammed with laden lorries and trailers. On arrival at the market each grower is given an order number, while the buyers take a look at the loads. According to the order of sale, the grower drives his trailer right through the market building, in front of the buyers, who watch the loads from steeply raked rows of desks through a large plate-glass window. On the opposite wall large clock-face indicators record the bids, one dial for cauliflowers (measured in heads) and one for artichokes (measured in kilos). The produce is sold by Dutch auction, beginning at an agreed maximum price and working down. The steadily falling price is shown by a pointer on the clockface, which has 100 divisions, each representing the fall of a centime. When a dealer sees a load that meets his requirements, he presses a button on the desk in front of him. The pointer stops immediately at the price so far reached; and the dealer's code number appears on the indicator. The electronics of the system are highly sophisticated, and it is impossible for two code numbers to appear simultaneously. Each grower is allowed two passes in front of the dealers; if his produce remains unsold after the second pass, he has to return the following day.

In recent years the SICA has expanded into wider fields, notably the building of the deep-water harbour at Roscoff, and the setting-up of a shipping company to carry produce (and now tourists) between Roscoff and Plymouth, Roscoff and Saint-Malo, and—most recently—Portsmouth and Saint-Malo. The company's name, BAI (Bretagne-Angleterre-Irlande), indicates its commercial origin in the vegetable trade—an origin masked by the modern title of Brittany Ferries. Here again the political power of the SICA was revealed in the spring of 1975, when the German TT Line reopened the Saint-Malo/Southampton route. Gourvennec engineered an alliance between the farmers of the Ceinture Dorée and the Communist seamen's union at Saint-Malo, and made sure that the TT Line's enterprise was stillborn. In 1975 the words 'TT Line Go Home' were to be seen sprayed on the walls of Roscoff, and no doubt they are still there.

As a town, Saint-Pol-de-Léon has obviously benefited from the presence of Kérisnel; it is no longer the dead-and-alive place it used to be. I shall always have a friendly feeling towards it, since one misty Sunday morning in October when I succeeded in locking my keys in the car in the main square of the town, among the church-goers. I wandered around until I met a gendarme who was testing car headlamps for angle of beam, which is a Sunday-morning activity in that part of the world. Leaving his post, he strode with me to the car, armed with screwdriver and pliers. When these were no good, we adjourned to a café, where we drank beer and telephoned around until we found a garage proprietor who would come out on a Sunday. Ten minutes later he arrived, with a formidable collection of bent pieces of wire, which he inserted into the inner workings of the door, opening it in about forty-five seconds. An episode which restored my belief in the rightness of the world.

All this took place below the splendid twin-towered Cathedral, magnificent on the outside but austere within, apart from a fine rose window in the south transept. There are some good sixteenth-century choir stalls, and a succession of tombs of the Bishops of Léon, including that of Mgr de la Marche, the last of the line, who died in exile in London in 1806. He was known to the Breton farmers as the 'Potato Bishop' (Eskob ar Patates), as his efforts on their behalf succeeded in lowering the taxes levied on potato crops. An earlier Bishop, Mgr de Rieux, who died in 1651, has eternity lightened for him by the little figure of his Vicar-General who sits beside him and reads to him; so comfortable is the Bishop that he is nicknamed the '*Bien-assis*', or well-seated. More macabre are the four shelves of reliquaries containing the skulls of Saint-Pol's notabilities down the years—three centuries of them, from the 1550s to the 1850s.

A reliquary on the choir's north side contains the head, finger and armbone of St Pol. Also preserved is the saint's bell, which, according to the notice beside it, 'was miraculously landed at the foot of the saint by a huge fish'. St Pol (St Paul-Aurelian) was born in England in 492, was educated in Wales with St Samson, became a hermit and founded his first monastery at the precocious age of fifteen. In 517 he took to the sea, crossed the Channel and landed on Ushant, from where he made his way to the Ile de Batz (pronounced Ba, with the -tz silent). Here he tamed a dragon which was terrifying the neighbourhood, and, tying his stole round its neck, 'led it like a dog on the leash, hitting it with his staff' to the end of the island, where he made it jump into the sea. The nineteenth-century church on Batz still preserves his stole, or what passes for it, together with a reliquary containing fragments of his bones. After this miracle honours were showered on St Pol. He became Bishop of Léon in the town that was later named after him, and in 566 retired from the world to Batz, where he died at the enormous age of 104 in 596, so emaciated from his austerities that he was nothing but skin and bone, and if he held up his hands the light shone through them.

Apart from the Cathedral, Saint-Pol-de-Léon's chief claim to architectural fame is the tower of the chapel known as the Kreisker. Built in the fifteenth century, its tall spire (77 metres, 246 feet) dominates the artichoke and cauliflower fields for miles around. I must confess that I do not find it in the least beautiful; but it makes an extraordinary Gothic exclamation-mark in a countryside that has few vertical features.

Roscoff's living counterpart to Saint-Pol's stone Kreisker is a giant fig-tree, prominently marked in the town as 'Le Grand Figuier', growing in the garden of the old Capuchin convent. It was planted about 1620, when the convent itself was founded, and is like no other tree I have ever seen. The main trunk is hidden behind the straitjacket of an irregular stone wall, while the branches are supported by a forest of granite columns. I paced it out, and made it about twenty-six yards square.

A strong historical tradition links Mary Queen of Scots with Roscoff. In August 1548 she is said to have landed there, at the age of five, to be engaged to the Dauphin; a tradition maintained by the name 'La Tour Stuart' for one of the seaward turrets of the town's ancient fortifications. Near the tower are inscribed stones commemorating the connection: one says that Mary landed 'on the shore at the site of the slipway' ('*sur la grève à l'emplacement de la rampe d'accés*'); while another identifies a medieval doorway as the 'door of the Chapel of St Ninian, called the Chapel of Mary Stuart' ('*Porte de la Chapelle de St Ninian, dite de Marie Stuart*'). A dilapidated stone house near by bears the inscription 'Mary Stuart House', but this is patently wrong. The Abbé Feutren has discovered from the archives that the house was not built before 1585, and that the site was a piece of vacant ground in 1548.

However, the Roscovites' belief that Mary landed in their town seems to have a firm basis in fact, despite claims that have been made for Pempoul (the harbour of Saint-Pol-de-Léon), and even for Brest. Mary's arrival in France was a high affair of state. In 1548 Scotland was still an independent kingdom, but was coming under increasing threat from England; and an alliance by marriage was in the obvious interests of France. Mary was born on December 9, 1542. Five days later, on December 14, her father James V was defeated and killed by the English at the Battle of Solway Moss, and Mary became Queen of Scots at less than a week old. James V had been married first to Madeleine, daughter of François I; his second wife, and the mother of Mary, was Mary of Guise. François died in 1547 and was succeeded by Henri II; and it was Henri's son François, two years younger than Mary, who was the Dauphin she had come to France to meet. The agreement for the betrothal was the result of lengthy diplomatic negotiations between France and Scotland, with Protector Somerset declaring his strong disapproval on behalf of England—a disapproval that the two countries concerned chose to ignore. Mary set sail from Dumbarton at the end of July 1548, with an entourage that included the French poet Joachim du Bellay, and four little girls of her own age. In charge of the expedition was the Sieur de Brèze, whose letters to Marie de Lorraine and Henri II chart the progress of the voyage.

The journey was appalling. It took the ships about a week to get beyond the Firth of Clyde, and once in the open Channel past Land's End they were caught in a violent storm. De Brèze wrote in a despatch that 'the fury of the sea was unleashed, with the tallest waves I have ever seen in my life, and to our consternation the rudder of our galley was broken'. However, they managed to replace it and eventually landed at Roscoff after a crossing of eighteen days. On August 18 De Brèze wrote from Saint-Pol-de-Léon how the young Queen had been less seasick than anyone else, and had laughed at those who had been sick—a phenomenon still to be seen on cross-Channel boats when the going gets rough, and the passengers sort themselves into green-faced adults and children demanding egg and chips. From Brittany the royal party proceeded in the leisurely manner of the time to Paris; and about the middle of October Mary finally met her future husband. Fortunately they liked each other. Mary spent the next thirteen years in France—the happiest period of her tragic life. In April 1558 the young couple were married. François succeeded his father as François II in September 1559, but the following December he died, and Mary was left a widow for the first time. He was sixteen and she was nearly eighteen. Mary returned to Scotland early in 1561, to the glories and miseries of her much-chronicled career.

As befits a place that has always looked towards the sea for its livelihood—it was, like Saint-Malo, a 'nest of corsairs' ('*nid de corsaires*')—Roscoff has one of the most famous centres of marine biology in the whole of France. The main square of the town is the Place Lacaze-Duthiers, named after the zoology professor at the Sorbonne who established the Station Biologique in 1872, as his contribution to setting France to rights again after the humiliations of the Franco-Prussian War. For twenty years previously Henri Lacaze-Duthiers had explored the coastline of France for a possible site, and he finally settled on Roscoff because of the unique richness of its offshore marine life. The Station fulfils two main functions: as an international teaching centre, with over a thousand students, a quarter of them from foreign universities; and as an institute devoted to the study of 'zoology, algology, bacteriology, marine biology, genetics, biochemistry, physiology, geology, physical geography, biological oceanography, and oceanography as applied to fishing'. Such at least are the subjects listed in the Station's centenary leaflet. M. Louis Cabioch, the Sous-Directeur, told me that 700 species of seaweed alone are studied there, while the investigation of plants and animals on the seabed is important for understanding the ocean-wide effects of pollution. A fortress-like aquarium, open from May to September, forms part of the Station.

The house in the square that was the first home of the Station Biologique was occupied for a time by Tristan Corbière, one of the strangest figures in French nineteenth-century literature. Bearded, hook-nosed and long-haired, his profile is carved on a plaque near the window of the *poste météorologique* that tells you such things as the temperature and barometric pressure of the moment. Born in Morlaix on July

18, 1845, Corbière was only twenty-nine when he died, and he left only a single book of poems behind him. Yet *Les Amours Jaunes*, as the book was called, had a tremendous impact when it was published in 1873, and the discovery of these astonishing and often difficult poems has been not the least of the many pleasures I have had while writing this book. His father, Edouard-Jean-Antoine Corbière, came from Brest and was a captain of the *long-cours*—the long-distance voyages round Cape Horn and up the coast of South America. More important, perhaps, from the point of view of heredity, Corbière *père* wrote a number of novels about the sea, of which the best known was *Le Négrier* (*The Slave-Dealer*), published in 1832. When his son wanted a dedicatee for *Les Amours Jaunes*, he inscribed it simply 'A l'Auteur du *Négrier*'. Until the age of sixteen, young Corbière—christened Edouard-Joachim—went to school in Morlaix and Saint-Brieuc, and during boyhood already showed traces of the tuberculosis that was to kill him.

For most of his adult life he alternated between Paris, where he took the name Tristan to sign his poems, and Roscoff, where he came to restore his health. He was an extraordinary mixture of bravado and sensibility, of conceit and self-disgust; after his death a friend described him as '*menfoutiste*'—untranslatable in English, but meaning roughly someone who doesn't give a damn for anything or anybody. His poems convey a powerful sense of self-deprecation: in one he calls himself '*Bâtard de Créole et Breton*', in another he complains '*Je suis si laid!*' This reference to his ugliness comes in a poem called *Guitare*; and if Corbière had been alive today he would surely have been a prophet of the pop culture, or perhaps a follower of the 1950s generation of American hippie poets. Occasionally he even went as far as self-disfigurement, as a friend described in a memoir written after Corbière's death. 'One day he appeared with his head, face and eyebrows shaved. He looked horrible. On another occasion he disappeared for several weeks, and then returned with a pointed beard, looking quite devilish.'

This same friend, Vincent Huet, gave an account of Corbière's life at Roscoff, where with characteristic wildness he became a sailing fanatic. 'Blasé from early youth, he was subject to fits of spleen'—that favourite affliction of the French Symbolist poets.

To distract him, his father had a sailing-boat built for him. From that moment, he was always at sea, slept only in a hammock, and was always dressed like a sailor, in sou'wester, heavy cape and sea-boots. He was weighed down to the ground by all this gear. One day a friend looked him up at Roscoff and they went for a sail. Between Roscoff and the Ile de Batz there is a powerful current and the passage is extremely dangerous. His friend said to him casually: 'I would like to be shipwrecked once in my life, to know what it feels like and to be able to talk about it from inside knowledge.'

Corbière took note of this rash confession. On the way back to Roscoff he headed the boat to where the current was fastest, deliberately steered in the wrong direction, and drove the craft on to the rocks. They both ended up in the water, but managed somehow to escape drowning. As his friend set foot on the rocks he asked Corbière: 'Don't you know your own channel better than that?' 'Of course I do,' said Corbière. 'But as you wanted to be shipwrecked and I am your host, my duty was to satisfy your curiosity and carry out your wishes to the full.'

When in Paris, Tristan Corbière lived in a single room. His only furniture was a wooden chest, on which he slept fully clothed. Whenever he had any money, which was not often, he would leave it on the mantelpiece for his friends to help themselves. His death was the outcome of another piece of *menfoutisme*. In the cold winter at the beginning of 1875, he had a bad attack of pneumonia. which he thought he could cure by going out into the street and getting thoroughly chilled. Dying, he was taken to the house of some friends at Vincennes called Dubois, and wrote home an untranslatable pun: '*Je suis à Dubois dont on fait les cerceuils*' ('I am staying with the Wood used for making coffins' is an approximation). His mother brought him back to Morlaix, where he died on March 1; his father died only a few months later.

Shortly after Corbière's death, he was hailed by Verlaine as 'a Breton, a sailor, and the scorner *par excellence*. A Breton with hardly any Catholic observance, though a believer in the Devil; a sailor neither naval nor merchant, but a furious lover of the sea which he would only ride during the storm, fiery beyond belief on that most fiery of steeds; so contemptuous of Success and of Glory that he seemed to challenge those two imbeciles to make him feel sorry for them.'

Corbière's poems divide themselves, like his life, into two alternating themes: the Villon-like verses celebrating the night-life of Paris, with hymns to his mistresses, real or imagined, to his guitar, to his pipe, and to the insomnia that plagued his life; and the poems in the sets he called *Armor* and *Gens de Mer*, which as their titles imply deal with Brittany and Corbière's beloved sea. Typical is the poem he addressed to his adopted town, *Au Vieux Roscoff*, which he punningly subtitles 'Berceuse in North-West Minor'. The poet begins by invoking the town as 'Pirates' refuge, old nest of corsairs, in the storm sleep your good granite sleep above cellars where the sea laps.'

Trou de flibustiers, vieux nid
A corsaire!—dans la tourmente
Dors ton bon somme de granit
Sur tes caves que le flot hante.

He tells Roscoff to snore on. 'You can shut your single seaward eye, which has been watching the English for three hundred years.' He calls the town affectionately an old ship at anchor (*vieille coque bien ancrée*) and an old sailors' tart (*vieille fille à matelots*), addressing the last verse to the iron cannon half sunk in the mud, which 'sleeps its heavy sleep of rust'. 'Go on: snore into the wind, old snorer, keep your furious throat levelled at the English, and loaded with spindly gorse in flower.'

Va: ronfle au vent, vieux ronfleur,
Tiens toujours ta gueule enragée
Braquée à l'Anglais! . . . et chargée
De maigre jonc-marin en fleur.

On the opposite page the sonnet called *Le Mousse* (*The Ship's Boy*) reveals Corbière at his simplest and most direct. It takes the form of a brief dialogue between the poet and the boy, whose father has been lost at sea, just one of hundreds on that wild coast in the days of small boats and scant respect for sailors' lives. '*Mousse*: so he's a sailor, your father', says the poet. The boy answers: 'A fisherman. Lost a long time ago. He spent a night away from my mother and slept among the breakers. Mother keeps a grave for him in the cemetery—with nothing inside it. I'm now her husband on this earth, breadwinner for two little children.' 'Was nothing washed up on the beach from the shipwreck?' 'His pipe-holder and his sabots. . . . Mother weeps, on Sundays, for his soul's repose. . . . I'll get my own back when I'm a grown-up—sailor!'

La mère pleure, le dimanche,
Pour repos . . . Moi: j'ai ma revanche
Quand je serai grand—matelot!—

Both *Au Vieux Roscoff* and *Le Mousse* are miniatures; but Corbière is capable of a far more extended range and a far more savage tone. The longest of all his poems is based on the *pardon* of Sainte-Anne la Palud, still held on the last Sunday in August. Called *La Rapsode Foraine*—'the itinerant ballad-monger'—the poem is in some ways reminiscent of Thomas Augustus Trollope's description of the *pardon* of Saint-Jean du Doigt (see page 241). But whereas Trollope was writing as a horrified and fascinated observer from the outside world, Corbière is full of the rage and irony of the insider who sees the hypocrisy of the scene yet feels pity for it, and recognises himself in the figure of the *rapsode*, 'the baying human figure against the *calvaire*; she's like half a blind woman: she is one-eyed, and has no dog'.

Une forme humaine qui beugle
Contre le calvaire se tient;
C'est comme une moitié d'aveugle:
Elle est borgne, et n'a pas de chien . . .

Corbière's artistry is shown by the fact that he does not introduce his chief character until the last verses of the poem. He begins with a tongue-in-cheek dedication to St Anne ('*De la Bonne Femme Sainte Anne, Grand'tante du petit Jésus*'), Christ's 'great-aunt' whose image forms the focus of the *pardon*. The ironic prayer to the carved oak statue is punctuated by asides about Joseph, who is portrayed as the concierge sweeping the steps up to the crib where Jesus lies, or about the lost souls who are 'lost' through drink; and ends with a verse of deadpan sarcasm. 'Until next year, then! Here's your candle; it cost me two pounds.... Give my regards to the Virgin, and don't forget the Trinity.'

—A l'an prochain!—Voici ton cierge:
(C'est deux livres qu'il a coûté)
... Respects à Madame la Vierge,
Sans oublier la Trinité.

After the prayer, Corbière brings on his parade of the faithful, drinking from the water where 'scrofulous Jobs' have bathed their infected bodies, and going round the church three times on their knees; the maimed with their wounds like 'living rubies under the sun', the consumptives, the epileptics; the man with a cancerous growth leaning against a tree that grows mistletoe, the mother and daughter with St Vitus' Dance:

Là, ce tronc d'homme où croît l'ulcère,
Contre un tronc d'arbre ou croît le gui.
Ici, c'est la fille et la mère
Dansant la danse de Saint-Guy.

It is only now that the *rapsode* appears, bawling out for a copper or two the ballad of Magdalene, the Wandering Jew or Abelard. 'Her name is Misery. She was born by chance; and by chance she will die—somewhere.' The poet recognises her as his sister. If you give some tobacco for her pipe, 'her hollow cheeks will wrinkle into a smile, and her scabby hand will make the true sign of the cross.'

Tu verras dans sa face creuse
Se creuser, comme dans du bois,
Un sourire; et sa main galeuse
Te faire un vrai signe de croix.

In this last stanza Corbière draws the threads together: the old woman whose sunken cheeks are the flesh of which St Anne's wooden features are a feeble copy, and the unwashed body which can make the 'true sign', as against the falsities of organised religion. It is worth comparing the poem with Charles Cottet's painting of the same *pardon* in the Musée des Beaux-Arts at Rennes. True, Cottet was painting a generation later, when the most harrowing aspects of the *pardon* had been tidied away out of sight, or been got rid of by medical and social services; but all the same it is hard to believe that poem and painting reflect the same event. Five monumental women in Breton costume are picnicking in the foreground, in an atmosphere of calm contentment. Behind them are several large groups of people, who appear to be standing about talking; while in the background a file of tiny figures is queuing up decorously to enter the door of the church. Times have changed, and the *pardon* is no longer a time to reflect upon human splendours and miseries but merely a good excuse for a blow-out.

It would be a pity to leave Corbière on a note as grimly elevated as that of *La Rapsode Foraine*. Quite a different side of his character is shown by the poem he wrote in memory of his dog Pope, who died after being shot, presumably accidentally, and was of a breed unknown to Cruft's but delightfully called by Corbière 'Gentleman-dog from New-land'. Pope no longer needs to follow like a servant or lick like a whore; he doesn't need to recognise his bowl or his master, or walk on his hands, like a human being. He can remain himself.

Toi! rester toi; ne pas connaître
Ton écuelle ni ton maître,
Ne jamais marcher sur les mains,
Chien!—c'est bon pour les humains.

The poem to Pope was written on the Ile de Batz, and the little island is a good place to spend a fine afternoon. It is an islet of miniature stonewalled fields manured with seaweed, of narrow paths leading down to saltings facing the mainland, of yuccas in flower and cacti. There is a lighthouse that can be climbed at the far end from the landing-point; and, as I mentioned earlier, the church has some relics of St Pol. I found it one of the most peaceful places in the whole of Brittany. Little wonder that St Pol chose to die in the remote calm of his monastery of Batz.

CHAPTER XIV

Nantes

By rights, Nantes should have no place in an up-to-date book on Brittany. Nor for that matter should La Baule, the Grande Brière or Saint-Nazaire. For by the kind of local government reshuffle with which we are ourselves all too familiar, in the 1960s a new region was created from the five Départements on either side of the Loire. Known as the Pays de la Loire, it links Nantes and Loire-Atlantique with the Vendée to the south, and with Mayenne, Sarthe and Maine-et-Loire upstream—convenient no doubt from the point of view of Paris-based administrators, but traumatic for the Nantais, who are now no longer inhabitants of Brittany, at least officially. Yet for centuries Nantes was the spiritual and intellectual dynamo of the country, disputing the primacy with Rennes, and the chosen home of the Dukes of Brittany, whose great castle still dominates the centre of the town. Shorn of Loire-Atlantique, Brittany now has four Départements only. Not only has this been a blow to the Bretons' self-esteem, but it has added another dimension to the desire for independence from Paris. All over the walls of Nantes, and even more so in left-wing Saint-Nazaire, you will see posters announcing meetings for the return of Loire-Atlantique to the Breton fold.

The city has always been ambivalent with regard both to Brittany and to France as a whole. It has a totally un-Breton elegance and style, while the great sweep of the Loire that runs through its centre gives it a feeling of consequence and grandeur you will not find in Rennes. Nantes looks outward to the sea, from which its prosperity came, rather than inland to the heart of the country. The road system tells the same story. Whereas Rennes is at the centre of a spider's web of routes, radiating to all the corners of Brittany, the two main arteries from Nantes are the Loire Valley route to Angers and beyond, and the Brittany south coastal road. As a Breton city, Nantes has other anomalies. It is the centre of wine production in a cider country, and it is built of *tuffeau*, the limestone of the Loire Valley, rather than of the Breton granite. Yet here again Nantes compromises, as the lower storeys of the old houses were built of granite, the lower courses of the Cathedral are granite, and so is the outer wall of the Château, though the inner, more elegant sections are of the softer stone.

Nantes is a baffling town to get to grips with, at least when you first arrive there. I came by car from the south, crossed various branches of the Loire, was carried in a swirl of traffic below the walls of the castle and then back across the river again in the merciless one-way system, coming to rest in desperation by means of a sudden lurch into a factory yard. Even the Nantais find their town difficult, and it has probably always been so. Seventy years ago Baedeker remarked that 'Nantes is nowadays a handsome modern town, but the absence of main thoroughfares makes it difficult for the stranger to find his way'. There are now plenty of main thoroughfares, but their logic only becomes clear when you realise that several of them are built on what were once branches of the river. Thus the main shopping street, the Cours des Cinquante Otages, swings round what was once the bed of the Erdre (now demoted to an underground pipe); while the elegant streets that make up the Ile Feydeau once stood on a proper island, with quaysides instead of streets to north and south. Most surprising of all, in view of the Château's landlocked appearance, the Loire once flowed directly beneath its walls, as the little water-gate in the south wall bears witness.

Like nearly every major town, Nantes owed its growth to its commanding situation on a river. In pre-Roman times it was an important centre, named after the Namnetes, one of the Gaulish tribes who allied themselves with the Veneti and were conquered by Julius Caesar in 56 BC. During the centuries of Roman rule it grew to be the commercial and administrative centre of Armorica; but with the collapse of Roman power in the fifth century its easy access from the sea meant that it was under constant attack from pirates, first the Saxons and then the Norsemen. In their *drakkars* or dragon-headed longboats they swept up the Loire, pillaging and slaughtering, until they were finally checked and routed in 937 by Alain Barbe-Torte, only twenty years old, who made Nantes his capital. The ancient town of the Gauls, the Romans and the dukes was centred on the Château; and this is where any exploration of Nantes naturally begins. The castle is a magnificent place, so impressive that it prompted a startled exclamation from Henri IV, who had gone there in 1598 to sign the Edict of Nantes guaranteeing freedom of worship for Catholic and Protestant. '*Ventre Saint Gris,*' exclaimed the overawed King, '*les ducs de Bretagne n'étaient pas des petits compagnons!*' Untranslatable, but the sentiments shine through. Certainly the two Dukes, Jean V and François II, who were responsible for the massive fifteenth-century fortifications, were anything but lightweights, if that is what Henri IV meant. But the character who permeates the castle is François's daughter, Duchess Anne (see Chapter XV), who has eclipsed all the Dukes who went before her. She commissioned the fanciful Renaissance façade of the Grand Logis, and the Tour de la Couronne d'Or, with its lofty double balcony from which the court ladies could watch the tournaments in the courtyard below; while the 'Golden Crown' from which the tower takes its name—the wrought-iron well canopy, originally gilded, at its foot—bears the twisted cord (*Cordelière*) of the Franciscans, one of Anne's devices, and the royal fleur-de-lys.

Traces of an older castle are marked out in stone in the middle of the courtyard, and a single tower (the Vieux Donjon) still remains from the thirteenth and fourteenth centuries. The Duchess Anne built the most powerful of all the fortifications, the Tour du Fer à Cheval, whose horseshoe-shaped rooms, superbly vaulted, now house the Musée des Arts Décoratifs—examples of craftsmanship from statues of the saints to pistols. There are two other museums in the Château: a regional collection of clothes, furniture, ironwork and musical instruments; and the Musée des Salorges, a specifically Nantes collection devoted to 'seafaring, gastronomy and ancient trades'. This is a treasurehouse for those who like to potter around acquiring useless information. There are figureheads, model ships and naval uniforms, relics of the whaling trade, iron-bound sea-chests, and a scale model of an 1837 invention for distilling sea-water. There are some of the first preserve jars containing asparagus and spinach, bottled about 150 years ago, and ancient sardines which must be of almost the same vintage. Best of all is a large model of the Petit-Beurre factory (which still survives within easy walking distance of the Château), together with a collection of superb presentation biscuit boxes. I had never known the meaning of the mysterious letters 'LU' associated with Petit-Beurre, until I came to the Salorges Museum and learnt that they were the initials of Lefèvre-Utile, the founder of the concern.

The Cathedral is directly behind the Château, only a couple of minutes' walk away. It has an exceedingly high nave; but unfortunately that is all that I was able to see in 1977, as the remainder had been closed off after a disastrous fire gutted the east end in 1972. Like the castle, it was built mainly by Dukes Jean V and François II. The magnificent Renaissance tomb of François and his wife was in the closed part of the building, which was disappointing, as by all accounts it is one of the finest monuments of its date in France. Over an arch on the Cathedral's north wall is a shield, with the Duchess Anne's motto '*A ma vie*', which does not mean very much in French, but makes more sense if it is taken as a pun on the Latin '*Amavi*', 'I have loved', referring to Anne's love for her Breton people. In the north aisle is a most unusual feature to find in a church—a well, said to have been used by pilgrims on their way to St James of Compostela in Spain. What remains of medieval Nantes is west of the Cathedral, round the Place du Change, where one or two of the narrow half-timbered streets have been pedestrianised.

The great commercial days of the eighteenth century, when Nantes, like Bristol, grew rich on the profits of the slave trade, have survived in the houses of the Ile Feydeau, a double row of tall *hôtels* with the Rue Kervégan running between. These were the houses of the wealthy *armateurs*, who fitted out ships for the '*commerce triangulaire*'. The three sides of the triangle consisted of a run to Africa laden with brandy and manufactured goods to exchange for slaves; the slave run to the West Indies; and then the run home to Nantes with spices, cotton and sugar—some of which ended up as brandy for the next voyage. The houses are built round courtyards, with galleried staircases soaring up to the roof. One of them has a negro's head carved over a window arch, as a reminder of where the money to build it had come from. The Place de la Petite Hollande at one end of the Ile is an indication of the importance of the Dutch to the triangular trade. When Mignot de Montigny visited Nantes in 1752 he remarked that the Ile Feydeau was a '*quartier tout neuf*', whose houses were still being built.

The centre of sociability and general activity in Nantes is round the Place Royale, a circle rather than a square, with a fine fountain symbolising the Triumph of the Loire at its centre. Near by is the Place Graslin, dominated by the classical portico of the theatre, dated 1784. When that argumentative agriculturist, Arthur Young, came to Nantes in 1788, on the eve of the Revolution, the theatre was 'new built of white stone', and he set down his views on this temple of luxury in an impoverished land.

> *Mon dieu!* cried I to myself, do all the wastes, the deserts, the heath, ling, furz [*sic*], broom, and bog, that I have passed for 300 miles lead to this spectacle? What a miracle, that all this splendour and wealth of the cities in France should be so unconnected with the country! There are no gentle transitions from ease to comfort, from comfort to wealth: you pass at once from beggary to profusion,—from misery in mud cabins to Mademoiselle St. Huberti, in splendid spectacles at 500 liv. a night (21l. 17s. 6d.). The country deserted, or if a gentleman in it, you find him in some wretched hole, to save that money which is lavished with profusion in the luxuries of a capital.

Near the theatre, just off the Rue Crébillon, is the most attractive place to shop in Nantes—the covered arcade, built on two different levels, called the Passage Pommeraye, a nineteenth-century window-shoppers' paradise of cast-iron pillars, drooping statues and overhead glass, all recently restored.

The finest architectural group in Nantes is undoubtedly the Cours Cambronne, whose two rows of houses face each other across a wide gravel rectangle, closed to traffic. It all looks very Parisian. In the centre of the rectangle is a statue of the Napoleonic hero General Cambronne, grasping a sword in his right hand and a shattered eagle standard in his left. The plinth is carved with his call to the Imperial Guard at Waterloo, 'The Guard dies but does not surrender' ('*La Garde meurt et ne se rend pas*'); however, it is not carved with the single word '*Merde!*', which he is said to have uttered when called upon to surrender, and which has been known ever since as the '*mot de Cambronne*'. A true son of Nantes, Pierre-Jacques-Etienne Cambronne was born near the city in 1770, and died there, full of age and honours, in 1842.

In this general direction, it is well worth going to the Musée Dobrée in the Place Jean V, not just because it houses the heart shrine of the Duchess Anne, but because of its extensive treatment of the early history of Nantes. There are three buildings altogether: the steep-roofed stone manor house of Jean V, where a plaque tells us the Duke died on August 28, 1442; the nineteenth-century pseudo-Romanesque palace, built by Thomas Dobrée for his main collection; and an ultra-modern building opened in 1975, devoted to prehistory and the Gallo-Roman period, and including such curiosities as bricks from the post-Roman Merovingian period, moulded with human and animal figures. The main building is beautifully laid out, and contains some magnificent carved woodwork taken from Nantes buildings demolished in the course of the relentless march of progress, notably corner-posts (*poteau cornier*), carved with figures, of the type still fairly common in places like Quimper and Morlaix. Upstairs there is a set of the terrifying little engravings by Jacques Callot, who lived from 1592 to 1635, and set down in meticulous detail the horrors of the Thirty Years' War. The hangings, firing squads, tortures and robberies of Callot's *Misères de la Guerre* are direct ancestors of Goya's *Disasters of War*. They also form a prelude to the displays on the floor above, which deal with the Revolution and the post-Revolutionary period, when Brittany and the Vendée were racked by warfare between those who supported the new order, and the Chouans, or counter-Revolutionaries, who were against it.

The day after Arthur Young fulminated against the Nantes theatre, he made some perceptive remarks about the general state of mind among the local people (September 22, 1788):

> Nantes is as *enflamme* in the cause of liberty, as any town in France can be; the conversations I witnessed here, prove how great a change is effected in the minds of the French, nor do

I believe it will be possible for the present government to last half a century longer, unless the clearest and most decided talents are at the helm. The American revolution has laid the foundation of another in France, if government does not take care of itself.

In the event, the volcano was on the point of erupting. During the final days of 1788 the States of Brittany met for the last time, before the Revolution overwhelmed them. Their chief concern, as always, was for a guarantee of Brittany's special privileges as agreed with France at the Act of Union of 1532; but events were moving too fast for them, and such considerations were irrelevant to the French as a whole. In June 1789 the Assemblée Nationale was set up; on July 14 the Bastille was stormed; in August feudalism was liquidated by decree; and during the autumn all Church endowments were confiscated. And finally Brittany itself disappeared as an officially recognised entity. As Chardronnet puts it in his *Histoire de Bretagne*: 'On January 15, 1790, the division of France into Départements suppressed once and for all the name of Brittany from every map and every official document. As far as the government was concerned, henceforward it was just five Départements like all the others. Life, which is stronger than paper, had made them five Breton Départements, but that was all!'

It was obvious that the Revolution had no intention of recognising Brittany, and the attacks on the Church further infuriated the Bretons. The execution of Louis XVI in January 1793 was another shock to a deeply traditional people; and all these causes united to drive many Bretons to become counter-Revolutionaries, or Chouans. (The name is said to derive from *chat-huant*, the screech owl, whose cry they imitated.) Further cause was given by the excesses of the Reign of Terror in Nantes, associated with the sinister figure of Jean-Baptiste Carrier. He instituted the notorious *noyades* (drownings), whereby aristocrats, priests, or anybody who was considered an anti-Revolutionary, were loaded on to barges which were then scuttled in the Loire. The Musée Dobrée has a section devoted to Carrier, illustrating among other things the '*mariages républicaines*' he instituted: couples would be stripped naked, tied together and thrown into the river to drown. A pamphlet issued after Carrier himself received his just deserts in 1794 called him 'worse than Nero', and described how 'with his lecherous and savage eyes, he would devour the nakedness of his victims, whom he dared to couple together in death'. The Revolutionary Tribunal, which was responsible for the Terror, was set up in March 1793; and the same month saw the outbreak of revolt in the Vendée and the start of Chouannerie among the peasants in Brittany. Significantly, their slogan was '*Vive le roi, vive la bonne réligion.*'

Chardronnet draws an illuminating parallel between the Chouans of 1793 and the men of the anti-German Resistance 150 years later. 'In 1793 the French officials, coming to a Brittany that had lost its autonomy and its ancient liberties, were intruders and foreign oppressors, especially in the countryside. These foreigners had come to plunder the countryside by their requisitions, in the same way as the Germans sent produce to Germany; conscription made a worse impact on the population than the S.T.O. (compulsory labour service in Germany) was to do: defaulters from conscription were the main recruits to the Chouans, as they were to the *maquis*. The blind and merciless guillotine terrorised the people and decimated it far more than the deportations and executions of hostages by the Germans would succeed in doing. Among the population, the Chouans were the Resistance fighters, while the townsmen and the bourgeois officials, concerned for their peace and quiet and ready to sell themselves to grow rich, figured as the collaborators. . . . But there was one difference: the cause for which the Resistance of 1941–44 fought was on the winning side; whereas the cause for which the Chouans fought was crushed.'

Though Chouannerie was in many respects a spontaneous movement occurring among the peasants, its first hero was an aristocrat, the Marquis de la Rouërie. Born at Fougères in 1750, he fought for George Washington in the War of Independence, and in 1783 returned to Brittany from America. In 1788 he was one of the twelve Breton nobles sent by the States to Versailles to put their case before Louis XVI—a move which landed them all for a short time in the Bastille. Though he had suffered in this way from the Ancien Régime, La Rouërie reckoned that it was better than the Revolution; and in the hope of re-establishing the ancient rights of Brittany, he founded a counter-Revolutionary organisation called the Association Bretonne. Throughout 1791 he scoured Brittany, winning supporters for a general uprising planned for the following year. But his plans suffered a setback; and the uprising was put off until March 1793. Meanwhile La Rouërie continued to canvass support, so energetically that in January 1793 he fell ill with exhaustion and went to recuperate to a château near Lamballe. Realising his physical state, his colleagues tried to keep from him the news that the King had been guillotined; but he happened to see a paper giving the news, and the shock killed him. He was buried in the garden of the château.

The Association Bretonne had already been betrayed to Danton by a certain Dr Chévetel, who was in La Rouërie's confidence. A band of revolutionaries came to the château, dug up La Rouërie's body and cut off his head. All his papers were discovered, and as a result twenty-seven of his followers were arrested and taken to Paris to be judged before the Revolutionary Tribunal. Twelve of them were condemned to death and guillotined in June 1793.

The second key figure of the Chouan movement was Georges Cadoudal. His career sums up the whole of Chouannerie, in its combination of unswerving principle with ultimate failure. Born near Auray in 1771, he first came into prominence in March 1793, when he was placed in command of the Chouans in the Morbihan. The campaign had some initial success; but it was doomed when General Hoche, one of the ablest of the young commanders thrown up by the Revolution, was appointed commander in the West in the summer of 1794. The following April a treaty was signed, granting amnesty to all the Chouans who laid down their arms; but meanwhile exiled French royalists had been drumming up support in England, and on June 27 an expeditionary force from England landed on the coast near Carnac. The command was fatally split between two French aristocrats, the Comte de Puisaye and the Comte d'Hervilly. Not only were they incapable of agreeing on an effective plan of campaign, but they were at odds with the Chouans, who joined them under Cadoudal. They had no interest in re-establishing the rights of Brittany, but were fighting to restore the monarchy and recover their old privileges. While the royalists and Chouans argued, Hoche acted. He forced the Chouans and *émigrés*—numbering altogether about 20,000, including women and children—back on to the Quiberon peninsula, writing contemptuously to his chief-of-staff that 'the Anglo-Emigré-Chouans are trapped like rats on Quiberon, where the army has them hemmed in. I hope that we will be rid of them in a few days.' Many of the Chouans saw how things were going and slipped off home by sea. On July 20 Hoche attacked and drove the remaining troops to the end of the peninsula. Some managed to reach the English fleet, which was anchored offshore; but over nine hundred surrendered. In spite of protests from Hoche, the prisoners were summarily tried and shot outside Auray, in a field now called the Champ des Martyrs.

Cadoudal himself escaped; but the Quiberon fiasco was a disaster from which the cause of Chouannerie never really recovered. In the months that followed, the Chouans were encouraged to lay down their arms by various measures instigated by Hoche, including pardons for defaulters from conscription and the restoration of religious freedom. But at the end of 1797 renewed religious persecution led to a Chouan revival. In August 1799, in what was almost a repeat performance of 1793, Cadoudal was appointed commander-in-chief of the royalist troops in the Côtes-du-Nord, Finistère and Morbihan. As in the earlier campaign, the Chouans had some successes to begin with, especially round Nantes, Saint-Brieuc (renamed Port-Brieuc by the Revolutionaries) and Rennes; but circumstances had been completely changed by the advent of Napoleon. Late in 1799 he was appointed First Consul, and France was on her way to internal stability for the first time since the Revolution.

Cadoudal was as implacably opposed to Bonapartism as he was to Republicanism in general; and when in March 1800 yet another amnesty was proclaimed, he refused to accept the rank of General offered him by Napoleon and fled to England on a fishing boat. Like de Gaulle in a later war, he was made commander-in-chief in exile; but unlike de Gaulle he never returned in triumph. In 1800 the French armies won resounding victories, at Marengo and Hohenlinden, and Chouannerie was swept away on the tide of patriotism. For a year in 1802–03 there was peace between France and England, and when war broke out again in the spring of 1803 Cadoudal tried his last desperate gamble. He landed in France with a crazy scheme to kidnap Napoleon. The plot failed; Cadoudal was arrested and shot by firing squad in Paris in June 1804, a month after Napoleon had proclaimed himself Emperor. His body was handed over to medical students for dissection, and what was left is now in a mausoleum on the outskirts of Auray. Georges Cadoudal was a failure in terms of results achieved; but to the Bretons he remains a powerful symbol.

A few minutes down the hill from the Musée Dobrée and you are on the banks of the Loire. Opposite are the cranes and warehouses of the Nantes dockland, and a little upstream the white slab blocks of the University—modernity on a large scale, though not as prominent as the enormous office block known as the Tour de Bretagne, which looms like a tall brown pillar above the heart of the city. If you follow the old course of the river, by the Ile Feydeau, below the Château and on to the station, you come to the Jardin des Plantes, the prettiest open space in Nantes. As a park should be, it is full of old men snoozing in the sun and children playing; it also has a monument to Jules Verne (born in Nantes in 1828), some splendid trees, its own nursery gardens and a magnificent conservatory almost up to Kew Gardens standards. But the biggest playground of Nantes is some way to the north, beside the Erdre. This is the Parc de la Beaujoire, on the outskirts of the city. You can get to it either by bus or by taking a boat up the Erdre from the yacht basin, below the tall copper monument to the forty-eight hostages shot by the Germans in 1941.

Beaujoire makes a superb setting for France's greatest flower show, the Floralies Internationales, held every few years at different centres, but now seemingly settled at Nantes. It is ordered very differently from Chelsea. True, there are new plant varieties on display, but the emphasis is on the national rather than the individual, with stands from countries as far afield as Peru and Thailand; and the police are more in evidence than the French equivalent of Chelsea Pensioners, if such personages exist. I went to the Floralies on the opening day in 1977, on a wild and blustery May afternoon. The overall view of Beaujoire was exhilarating, with the flags of the nations flapping in the wind, the double row of fountains leading the eye down to the Erdre, and an army of sailing dinghies scudding about on the sparkling river. When I got there, Mme Giscard d'Estaing was due to arrive to open the Floralies in three hours or so. Security police were everywhere, workmen cleared away piles of rubbish and made frantic last-minute alterations to the outdoor displays, and bulldozers and lorries tended to meet head-on on the narrow paths. Above the main gates the flag of Nantes outflapped and outpatterned all the Union Jacks and Tricolours, with Brittany's black ermines on a white background, and the city's own galleon under sail in one corner.

At about four-fifteen the naval cadets, who were to form the guard-of-honour, began to gather in a desultory way on the tarmac inside the main gates. The flags were lowered, and two shivering children in gym shorts stood by each flagpole, ready to haul away when Mme Giscard arrived. Half an hour later the band of the Garde Républicaine formed up, resplendent in dark blue and gold, with red cockades and white belts and bandoliers; then sharp on the dot of five '*la première dame de la France*' arrived, dark and elegant, heralded by the flashguns of dozens of press cameras and frantic shoving by the police. The band twirled their trumpets and blew a fanfare, the drums banged, the children hauled up the flags, and the Floralies was on. The local enthusiasm for flowers spills over into the streets of the city, where it is often difficult to squeeze past the pavement displays outside the flower shops.

The Nantes climate is not only good for flowers: it is also good for vines, which grow mainly south of the Loire and can even be found in the outer suburbs of the city. The Nantais are proud of their wines, and are concerned to make their virtues known to the outside world. For this reason they have set up the Comité Interprofessionel des Vins d'Origine du Pays Nantais, which has premises opposite the Château entrance. Here you can sample Muscadet (the only Loire wine that is at all well-known), Gros Plant (a white wine slightly drier than Muscadet), and Coteau d'Ancenis-Gamay (a rosé produced upstream round Ancenis, as its name suggests). I was instructed in the mysteries of Nantes wines by M. Germain, the Directeur of the Comité, who—understandably enough—interpreted the whole history of Nantes in wine-growing terms. During the early years of the Roman Empire, the Gauls were forbidden to grow vines; but this prohibition was lifted when they were given full citizenship in the third century. From then on vineyards have been a constant feature of the Loire Valley. The Norsemen plundered the ripe grapes in their *drakkars*, while the early Dukes of Brittany were as much vineyard cultivators as warriors. The type of grape has improved down the years. The Gauls had a fairly crude vine known as Lambrusque, which gave way in about the tenth century to the Berligou, grown by the Dukes. The Gros Plant was introduced in the sixteenth century, or thereabouts; while the Melon de Bourgogne, from which the Muscadet vine derives, was imported in quantity from Burgundy after a disastrous succession of frosts in 1709.

Muscadet should be drunk slightly chilled but not frozen: about an hour and a half in the refrigerator is recommended, but it should never be put in the icebox. It goes ideally with seafood; though as a leaflet issued by the Comité says, 'one drinks it when one is thirsty, no matter when'. It is best drunk young, the year after the vintage, and never more than four years old. The same leaflet mentions what food should be eaten with each of the three Nantes wines: with Muscadet, all crustaceans and fish; with Gros Plant, shellfish and crustaceans; and with Gamay, meat and cheese. And the wines of Nantes are as full of life and sparkle as is the whole of that delightful city, sprawling at its ease along the banks of the Loire.

CHAPTER XV

The Great Duchess

FOR MORE THAN a week at the beginning of February 1514, a long and mournful procession made its way across the chilly countryside between Blois and Paris. The procession was escorting the mortal remains of Brittany's Duchess Anne, twice Queen of France, from the Château of Blois, where she had died at the age of not quite thirty-seven, to the basilica of Saint-Denis, north of Paris, the last resting-place of the monarchs of France. The sombre cavalcade first followed the south bank of the Loire to Orléans, then took the route of today's N20 through Artenay, Janville, Angerville, Etampes and Montlhéry to Notre-Dame des Champs, outside Paris.

Among the escort was Brittany Herald-of-Arms, who wrote a description of the panoply that attended on the dead Queen. The advance party consisted of a master of the household (*maître d'hôtel*) and his officers, who organised the meals along the way. Then followed four hundred torch-bearers carrying torches emblazoned with Anne's device, and fifty torch-bearers from the town of Blois; the other *maîtres d'hôtel* and the gentlemen of the royal household; the keeper of the purse (*escuyer de la despense*), preceded by all the pages clad in velvet, six of them mounted on horses (*hobins*) which were caparisoned in black velvet cloths down to the ground with a white satin cross on their backs, so that only the eyes could be seen; the *cheval de croppe* (pillion horse) led by a groom, and the Duchess's ceremonial steed, the *haquenée d'honneur*, led by another groom. Then came the funeral carriage, drawn by six fine cobs likewise covered in black velvet with a white satin cross, and a similar covering was laid over the coffin. At front and back of the carriage walked all the heralds and pursuivants of France, led by Brittany Herald-of-Arms, he tells us proudly, bearing Anne's crown.

At each town the body was placed for the night in the most important church, where services were held and vigils kept under the watchful eye of the archers of the Swiss Guard. Once Paris was reached the cortège was swollen by monks and cross-bowmen, the musicians, clergy and lawyers of the city, the university dons, and such privileged individuals as the twenty-four salt-carriers of Paris. For two days the body lay in state in Notre-Dame, where the populace was exhorted to pray for the soul of the '*très haulte, très puissante, très excellente, magnanime et très débonnaire princesse, madame Anne*'; then it was taken on the final stage of its long journey to Saint-Denis. Here it was lowered into the ground, with a space left beside it for the burial of the King. Earth was thrown on the coffin; and Brittany King-of-Arms cried in a loud voice: 'The most Christian Queen and Duchess, our sovereign lady and mistress, is dead. The Queen is dead. The Queen is dead.' Then three court officials, weeping, laid on the coffin the hand of justice, the sceptre and the crown; and all the *maîtres d'hôtel* broke their staves of mourning and cast them into the grave. Finally, clasping their hands together and uttering prayers and lamentations, the princes, princesses and the States of the Realm went from the church to the funeral feast, 'whose final course was the fruit of sorrow' ('*le dernier fruict fut d'angoisse*').

It is not out of place to begin the Duchess Anne's life with an account of her obsequies, because with her died for more than three centuries the dream of a Brittany independent of control from the central government of France. This struggle was the recurrent theme of Breton history throughout the Middle Ages, as was shown by the life and murder of Gilles de Bretagne (see Chapter VI); and though seen as part of this struggle Anne's career must ultimately be counted a failure, her constant efforts to keep Brittany independent, and her ferocious love for her own people, have made her into a symbol that is still potent today.

Anne was born on January 25, 1477, the elder daughter of Duke François II by his second wife, Marguerite de Foix. It was Duke François's misfortune to have reigned when Louis XI was on the throne of France; for Louis was one of the greatest of the French kings, unswerving in his goal of winning the dukedoms of Burgundy and Brittany to the central power, and with a combination of patience, cunning and ruthlessness that made him the match of any ruler in Europe. Sir Walter Scott painted a sinister portrait of him in *Quentin Durward.* In opposition to Louis's strategy, which consisted of winning leading Bretons to his side and outright attacks on Brittany, François opposed a policy of alliance with the enemies of France, principally England and Austria.

Louis died in 1483. His son, the future Charles VIII, was still only thirteen, and the country was governed as regent by his elder daughter, Anne of Beaujeu, who had been well trained in Louis's centralist ideals. As in any regency, powerful factions formed, among them one led by Louis, Duc d'Orléans, who in 1476, aged only fourteen, had been forced against his will to marry Louis XI's saintly but physically unattractive younger daughter, Jeanne de France. Amid the political ups-and-downs, in 1487 Louis d'Orléans had to flee from the French court and took refuge in Brittany, where he formed the nucleus of a group of dissatisfied expatriate Frenchmen, upsetting in turn the Breton advisers of Duke François II. The previous year the Duke had betrothed his daughter Anne to the Austrian emperor Maximilian, which considerably strengthened his hand against the French. It was at this stage that Anne of Beaujeu decided on an all-out campaign to bring Brittany to heel. In May 1487 a French army of 15,000 men invaded Brittany, but after some initial disasters the Bretons rallied. The next year the French sent a still more powerful force, under their great general Louis de la Trémoille. The final battle took place on July 28, 1488, at Saint-Aubin du Cormier between Rennes and Fougères; the Bretons were routed, Louis d'Orléans was taken prisoner, and many of the survivors were massacred. Three weeks later, Duke François signed a humiliating treaty with Charles VIII at the Château du Verger, near Angers, of which the chief clause was that he would not marry off his daughters without the consent of the King of France. On September 9 François died, physically worn out and mentally beaten; and Anne his daughter was Duchess of Brittany.

Nothing is more astonishing than the way in which children in the Middle Ages were able to exercise supreme authority at an age when modern children are just beginning secondary education. Anne was not twelve when she became Duchess, yet even in extreme youth she showed her future quality. Under

François II's will the Maréchal de Rieux had been appointed her tutor and Françoise de Dinan her personal adviser, but Anne was easily their match. The burning question of state was who was to be her husband. She was already betrothed to the widower Maximilian of Austria (whose own daughter Margaret was betrothed to Charles VIII of France, thus adding a further complexity to the proceedings); but de Rieux and Françoise de Dinan were in favour of a Breton nobleman, Alain d'Albret, who was nearly fifty, with a spotted face and a savage temper. So repelled was Anne at the prospect that in February 1489 she broke with de Rieux and took refuge in Rennes, leaving de Rieux, Françoise de Dinan and d'Albret in control of Nantes. So after only a few months of the new reign Brittany was fatally split.

In February 1489 Anne was crowned in Rennes cathedral, and her position was strengthened somewhat by military help from England and Spain. In November the following year she was married by proxy to Maximilian of Austria. The furious d'Albret, thwarted in his own marriage plans, handed over Nantes to the French. Early in 1491 Charles VIII invaded Brittany once more, on the pretext that Anne's proxy marriage to Maximilian was a breach of the Traité du Verger. Soon all that was left to Anne was her city of Rennes, where she was besieged with a small army under the Maréchal de Rieux once again loyal to her cause. She was reduced to selling her jewellery to pay for troops and supplies. The whole country was in chaos, ravaged by the French army, by Anne's mercenaries, and by armed and masked brigands of neither persuasion. A document of the time guarantees indemnity to Anne's supporters 'who have taken food and other things from the subjects of the Duchess, except in cases involving murder, burning down of houses, rape of women, and acting as guides to the French, their enemies'. Not surprisingly, Brittany was sick of war, and there must have been a general sigh of relief when Anne and Charles signed a peace treaty at Rennes on November 15.

Then occurred one of those episodes that make the Middle Ages such a wildly unpredictable period. Within four days of signing the treaty with the man who had been devastating her country, Anne had agreed to marry him. Theologians were found to declare the proxy marriage to Maximilian null and void, and on December 6, 1491, Anne married Charles VIII at the Château of Langeais, in Touraine, and was both Duchess of Brittany and Queen of France. She was not yet fifteen. Perhaps she was advised to agree to the marriage by her counsellors for reasons of policy; but it is more likely that her mind was made up by the prospect of becoming Queen of France, and of marriage to a youth much nearer her own age than either d'Albret or Maximilian of Austria. Charles was twenty-one and a great jouster and horseman, with a head full of dreams of knightly prowess. He was not particularly bright; a modern historian has called him 'a ninny', and the chronicler Commynes, contemporary with Charles, was hardly more polite. 'The said king', he wrote, 'was never anything but a puny man with very little sense, but he was so good it was impossible to behold a better creature.'

The terms of the marriage contract, no doubt largely emanating from Anne de Beaujeu, were far from favourable to Anne de Bretagne. Both partners surrendered equally their claim to rights over Brittany, which was little more than a form of words, since the Duchess of Brittany was married to the King of France. More important, Breton separatism was nipped in the bud by the conditions attaching to Anne's remarriage, if Charles predeceased her without leaving an heir. She could marry only the new king, if that were possible, or as second best the heir apparent to the throne. Though the terms were in France's favour, both countries were overjoyed at the marriage. Overseas it was a different story. Maximilian of Austria was furious, as he had lost both an actual wife (even though by proxy) and a potential son-in-law; while Henry VII of England tried to make capital out of the situation by encouraging the powerful Vicomte de Rohan in an abortive rebellion.

Unlike these disgruntled outsiders, Charles and Anne seem to have been remarkably happy with the arrangement and with each other. We have a vivid picture of the young couple—rather an odd-looking pair—in a despatch written by the Venetian ambassador in 1492.

> The King of France is twenty-two years of age, with a small and ill-formed person; he has an ugly face, with large light eyes, with which he sees rather badly than well, an aquiline

> nose much out of proportion to the rest of his face; his lips also are big, and he keeps them constantly open; he has certain nervous movements in his hands which are not pleasant to see, and he is slow of speech. According to my opinion, which may very well be wrong, I feel convinced that in body as well as in mind he is not worth much. However, everyone in Paris praises him for his very great skill in tennis, hunting and jousting, exercises to which for good or ill he devotes much of his time. They praise him also because he has given over the charge and government of his affairs to certain members of the secret council, and will no longer leave to others the task of deliberating. They say that in his decisions he gives proof of high intelligence. The Queen is seventeen. She also is small and thin in person, visibly lame in one foot, although she uses a false heel; very determined for her age, so much so, that if a wish enters her head, by smiles or tears, at any cost she will obtain it.

Their first child—a son and therefore the new Dauphin—was born eleven months after the marriage, in October 1492. The Venetian ambassador's description does not make them sound as though their heredity promised much; and in fact the boy, christened Charles-Orland (an Italianate spelling of Roland) after the hero of Roncesvalles, died three years later. Anne's three other children by Charles (two sons and a daughter) all died in infancy; and not unexpectedly those superstitiously inclined put the deaths down to the fact that Anne had married Charles when she was already married—in the eyes of God at least—to Maximilian of Austria. After the death of the Dauphin, says the gossiping Abbé de Brantôme, Louis d'Orléans tried to cheer her up, but his well-meaning efforts misfired. Both Charles and Anne were grief-stricken, so the court doctors recommended all sorts of new entertainments ('*nouveaux passe-temps, jeux, danses et momeries*'), to take their minds off the blow. 'M. d'Orléans put on at the Château of Amboise a masquerade with dances, at which he fooled about so much and danced so cheerfully—so it has been said and written down—that the Queen thought he was behaving light-heartedly because he saw himself nearer the throne of France, now that M. le Dauphin was dead. She bore a great grudge against him, and looked on him with such disfavour that he was forced to leave Amboise in a hurry and go to his château at Blois.' There was more than a touch of Queen Victoria about the Duchess Anne.

Charles VIII pushed his nostalgia for the great days of medieval romance further than naming his son after Roland, or taking part in tournaments. He dreamed of reviving the days of the Crusades, of recovering Constantinople from the Turks who had taken it in 1453, ultimately even of liberating Jerusalem itself. The wars he waged were in fact much nearer home—in Italy, where he fought several campaigns, culminating in the capture of Naples in 1494. Commynes has left a telling eye-witness picture of Charles keyed up before his victory at Fornova, in the Apennines, the following year. The King was mounted on a fine horse called Savoy, which was 'black and had only one eye; and though it was small, it was a good size for him who rode it. It seemed that this young man was quite different from what nature had made him both in size and bearing; for he was very timid in speech and is so still, and this horse made him look big, and his face was handsome and of a good colour, and his speech bold and wise.'

On April 7, 1498, Charles received a letter from Savonarola, the Florentine monk who was the scourge of Papal corruption, summoning him to Rome to reform the Church by the sword. Preoccupied by the message, he was walking at Amboise with Anne and his courtiers to inspect some new sculpture that was being executed in one of the château's courtyards. To get from the courtyard to a tennis game he was due to watch, he had to pass through a low gallery with the sinister-sounding name of Galérie Hacquelebac. Here Charles struck his head hard against a projecting stone corner; though dazed for a moment, he seemed to recover and watched the tennis, but suddenly collapsed and was carried to a nearby room, where he was placed on an ancient bed. Here he lingered for a few hours, and died at eleven at night. The diagnosis at the time was apoplexy; in modern medical terms, it was presumably a brain haemorrhage.

It may or may not be true that history repeats itself; but it certainly seemed to be doing so in the case of Anne de Bretagne. However, being the widowed Queen of France was quite a different matter from being the orphaned Duchess of Brittany; and Anne had now had nine years' experience of power politics to help her cope with the situation. The heir to the throne was Louis, Duc d'Orléans—that same Louis, now aged thirty-six, who had taken refuge at her father's court, who had fought for the Bretons at Saint-Aubin du Cormier, and who had offended Anne by his levity after the Dauphin's death. As soon as he heard the news of Charles's death, the new Louis XII rode straight from Blois to Amboise, to pay his respects to the dead, and to comfort the Queen. Under the terms of the Traité du Verger, had Louis been free to marry, he would have been obliged to marry Anne. But as has already been mentioned, he had been forced years earlier to marry Jeanne de France; and Louis XI had looked on while the marriage was consummated, to ensure that there could be no grounds for an annulment. The heir apparent was a cousin of Louis, the four-year-old François d'Angoulême, whom Anne could hardly marry for a good many years, even by medieval calculations.

The problem was solved by the brutal solution of declaring that Jeanne was so deformed that consummation had never taken place, and that she could never bear children. Poor Jeanne retired from the world to found a religious order, gave herself up to good works, and after her death left such a reputation for holiness behind her that the Church awarded her the title 'Blessed' (*Bienheureuse*). The Pope who granted the annulment was the infamous Alexander VI, of the Borgia family, who agreed to co-operate with Louis in return for favours to his son, Cesare Borgia. In December 1498 the decree was handed to the King by Cesare, dressed in cloth of gold and festooned with jewellery for the occasion; and the marriage of Louis and Anne took place early in the New Year at the Château of Nantes. Brantôme thought that Louis had been in love with Anne in earlier years, when she was still married to Charles VIII, 'for it is with great difficulty that one can dispose of a great fire when once it has seized upon a soul'.

Whether because of Louis's affection for Anne, or because of her strong political bargaining position, the terms of the new marriage contract were far more favourable to Brittany than those Anne had made with Charles. As far as the succession was concerned, Brittany would go to the second son of the union, or to the daughter if there were no son. If the union resulted in a single son only, the second son of that son would inherit the duchy. If the Queen died before the King, without leaving any children, the duchy would revert to her legitimate heirs. As important to Anne as the succession was the safeguarding of the Bretons' traditional rights and privileges. Louis promised to respect these, and also guaranteed that the government would continue as it had been under the ancient dukes. The officers appointed by the Queen would stay in office, and the Queen would have the right to make appointments when offices fell vacant. The States of Brittany would keep the power to levy hearth tax and other impositions; Bretons would only be tried in courts of their own country; and the Breton nobility would not have to serve outside Brittany except in extreme national emergencies. Finally, currency would be struck jointly in the name of the King and the Queen-Duchess.

Louis let Anne get on with the business of governing Brittany, while he concerned himself with the affairs of France. 'He did not take a single *sou* from the Duchy,' says Brantôme; instead, Anne gave money and gifts to loyal servants of France from her own revenues. Recognising her patriotism, Louis nicknamed her '*ma bretonne*'. She appointed a personal guard of a hundred Breton gentlemen, and made her court into a finishing school for young women ('*une fort belle escole pour les dames*', says Brantôme), who modelled themselves on her austere and dignified behaviour. Brantôme tells us that one of his aunts was brought up by Anne. 'She had a great retinue of ladies and girls; and so far from turning anyone away, she would ask the gentlemen of the court if they had any daughters they would like to entrust to her.' This League of Gentlewomen was known as La Cordelière, from the braided cord, like a dressing-gown cord, that encircled the escutcheon of her coat-of-arms. Her serious-mindedness was unshakeable. One of Brantôme's stories about her concerns M. de Grignaux, a linguist and practical joker. Anne was fond of entertaining ambassadors, and prided herself on throwing into the conversation the occasional foreign word, which she learnt from de Grignaux. One day she asked him for a few Spanish words, as she was due to meet the ambassador.

Without explaining what the words meant, de Grignaux taught her 'a fairly indecent expression' (*quelque petite salauderie*) and then went off to tell the King what he had done. The King was highly amused, but warned Anne against using the expression. Far from seeing the funny side, she was furious, and would have banished de Grignaux from the court if he had not made the most abject apologies.

In October 1499 Anne and Louis had their first child, a daughter who was christened Claude; later to be the queen after whom Reine Claude plums are named. Evil omens accompanied the birth: heavy rains had prevented the vines from ripening, the plague broke out in Paris, and the old bridge of Notre-Dame fell into the Seine. Anne was determined to keep Brittany out of the clutches of France as far as the succession was concerned, and in 1501 she betrothed Claude to Charles of Luxembourg, the grandson of Maximilian of Austria and the future Emperor Charles V. This was too much for Louis, who in 1505 made a will ensuring that Claude should marry the heir to the throne, François d'Angoulême. What made this move even more bitter to Anne than the blow to the independence of Brittany was that, though she was appointed regent in the event of Louis's death, among the inner council decreed for her would have been François d'Angoulême's mother, Louise of Savoy, whom Anne detested. At the time Louis drew up this will he was so ill that he was thought to be dying, in the aftermath of an inconclusive campaign in Italy. Like Charles VIII, he had his frustrated dreams of Italian glory.

As soon as the King had recovered, Anne set out on a pilgrimage of thanksgiving to the shrine of Le Folgoët, north of Brest, in fulfilment of a vow. The journey turned out to be far from a simple pilgrimage; rather, it was a triumphal tour through her duchy that lasted for several months. She made a complete circuit of the country, along the route of today's N165 from Nantes through Vannes and Hennebont to Quimper, then up the coast to Le Folgoët, where she arrived on August 19. Albert Le Grand describes how every year the Duchess would send alms and gifts to Le Folgoët, including jewels and vestments of cloth-of-gold. She financed the completion of the church and its dome, and on this visit, which was to be her last, she provided money for a sacristan's salary and for three children to sing during the services and assist at Mass.

From Le Folgoët she went to Brest, and while there visited the dockyard to see the pride of the French fleet, which she named *La Cordelière*. This mighty vessel (*'ce beau vaisseau et grande masse de bois'*, Brantôme calls her) was part of the universal naval build-up at the beginning of the sixteenth century, and anticipated by almost a decade Henry VIII's thousand-ton *Great Harry*, launched in 1514. Anne lived to see one of the most glorious engagements of French naval history, in which *La Cordelière* played the main role. In August 1512 the English and French fleets went into action off Ushant. Though the French with twenty ships were greatly outnumbered, they had the wind in their favour, and managed to board and sink half the English vessels. A dozen ships at once attacked *La Cordelière*, but she beat them off, sinking some of them and putting the rest to flight. Finally an English ship got close enough to set her on fire. Most of the officers, crew and marines escaped in the lifeboats; but the captain of *La Cordelière*, a Breton called Hervé Porzmoguer, stayed on board and launched a suicide attack against the English flagship. With his own ship ablaze, he grappled the English vessel until she too caught fire. Then both ships exploded and sank to the bottom.

From Brest, Anne continued her circuit through northern Brittany, passing through Saint-Pol-de-Léon, Morlaix, Tréguier, Guingamp, Saint-Brieuc, Lamballe and Dinan. Apart from Rennes, there was thus hardly a Breton town of consequence she had not visited, and her welcome had been tumultuous in all of them.

In May the following year, by a cunning piece of diplomacy, Louis XII prevailed on the States-General to make a solemn plea that Claude would marry the heir to the throne, and not a foreign prince. Among those who made the request were the States of Brittany. The same month Claude and François were formally betrothed; but Anne did not give up so easily. As it was more than likely that she would have a son, she inserted in the betrothal contract a clause to the effect that any such son would inherit the dukedom, irrespective of the terms of her own marriage contract. In fact she had two sons, one born in

1508 and the other in 1512, both stillborn. A second daughter, Renée, was born in 1510, and survived to marry the Duke of Ferrara. But Anne's hopes of a healthy son were never realised.

Her last years were embittered by her disagreement with Louis over his renewed campaigns in Italy, and in particular over his hostility to Pope Julius II. In 1510 the French bishops had agreed that Louis had the right to wage war on the Pope, as Julius had meddled in affairs of state, instead of sticking to religion. It was in the aftermath of this confrontation that the battle between the English fleet and *La Cordelière* took place, as England had joined an anti-French coalition.

At the beginning of 1514 Anne fell seriously ill in the château of Blois. Worn out by her confinements and the childbed fever that followed them, and exhausted by her unavailing efforts to influence the succession as she wished, she had little fight left in her. On Monday, January 9, she died, at six in the morning. An eyewitness recorded the calm beauty of Anne after her death. 'And to speak of the face of the said lady, from the time her face was left uncovered until the following Tuesday, which was nine days, no one within the memory of man had seen so fair a face. For it seemed she had just fainted, or fallen asleep. For in her eyes, mouth and nose everything was so seemly that it was a marvel, and there was no unpleasant smell, so that no prince, lord or lady worthy to kiss or touch the face of this noble lady needed to fear any danger. And several notable persons said it was because she had loved and served God, being so full of virtues, grace and goodness, that Our Lord had kept and preserved her said beauty.'

The Brittany Herald-of-Arms described Anne's cortège, as we have seen; he also described the ceremonies when her heart was buried in the Cathedral at Nantes, 'of which heart she had made a gift to her Bretons, as her good friends and loyal subjects'. With the somewhat ghoulish anatomical interest of the day, the courtiers inspected the heart when it was removed from the body, and were amazed at its large size (*comme la noble royne avoit si grant cueur*). It was enclosed for burial in a golden heart-shaped casket, inscribed with an eight-line poem telling how the greatest heart of any woman who ever lived lay within, which opens with the lines:

En ce petit vaisseau de fin or, pur et munde,
Repose ung plus grant cueur que oncque dame eut au munde.

The casket is now the chief treasure of the Musée Dobrée, in Nantes, though it is now empty. The heart itself, or its ashes (accounts differ), was thrown away at the time of the Revolution.

For all our knowledge of the details of the Duchess Anne's life, she remains an enigmatic figure. Brantôme gives her the usual attributes of virtue—'good, honourable, well-spoken, and of an elegant and subtle wit'. But she was also vindictive, as she proved in the case of the Marshal de Gié, a prominent member of the powerful de Rohan family. At the time of Louis XII's serious illness, during the Italian campaigns of the early 1500s, the Marshal ordered the banks of the Loire to be guarded, to prevent any pro-Breton coup in the event of the King's death. Anticipating this, Anne loaded three or four boats with her treasures and sent them down the Loire towards Nantes; but they were stopped on the way by the Marshal's men and turned back. Furious at this rebuff, Anne had De Gié arrested for peculation and high treason; he was first of all condemned to be beheaded, but the sentence was commuted to suspension from office for five years and banishment to a distance of ten leagues from any place where the Court might be. He retired to his château of Le Verger—the same château where the Traité du Verger had been signed in 1488. The university students of Paris, politically minded then as now, produced a lampoon on the incident full of untranslatable puns, which prompted Louis to order them to leave the Queen alone or he would hang those responsible. 'There was a marshal who wanted to shoe an ass (pun on Anne and *âne*), but she gave him such a kick that she threw him out of the court over the wall into the orchard (the literal meaning of Le Verger).' Brantôme says that the Queen decided to commute de Gié's death sentence, not out of any spirit of forgiveness, but 'because death is the true cure for all ills and griefs, and being dead he would be too happy'. In disgrace, however, he would die a new death every day.

How can one reconcile this unpleasant side of her character with the love in which most people seem to have held her?

Perhaps she was better worshipped at a distance, embittered as she was by frequent disappointments in both her public and her private life. There was no doubt of her courage and mental toughness, in the dispassionate way in which she put the child-bearing abilities of her body at risk to secure the succession. The formidable tower known as the Quic-en-Groigne at Saint-Malo is always said to owe its name to a contemptuous remark by the Duchess Anne. When the Malouins objected to having this fortification built outside their walls, not for their defence but to keep them in check, she said disdainfully: '*Qui qu'en groigne, ainsi sera: c'est mon plaisir*' ('Complain who will, so it will be: I will have it so'). From the great stone 'A's' carved over the fireplaces at the Château de Josselin to street names in half the towns of Brittany, the Duchess Anne has left her mark.

After her death it seemed as though all her efforts had gone for nothing. In May 1514 Claude was married to François d'Angoulême, and the following New Year's Eve, Louis XII himself died, aged fifty-two, shortly after making a third marriage to Mary, the eighteen-year-old sister of Henry VIII. As Brantôme says sardonically, 'a most beautiful princess, young, and too much so for him, which was bad luck on him' ('*dont mal luy en prit*'). François d'Angoulême was now François I, and lost no time in confounding Anne's wishes. Queen Claude died in 1524, after bequeathing Brittany to the Dauphin François. This linked the duchy to the French crown for the foreseeable future; but successions are not always reliable, and François I went further. Tactfully he persuaded the Bretons that their own best interests were the same as those of France, at the same time warning them what would happen if they persisted in their desire for independence. In the face of an offer they could not refuse, the States of Brittany were gradually won round to asking the King for union with France. In August 1532 they met at Vannes, and sent François a unanimous request for union. The King was graciously pleased to grant their request; and on August 13 the final Act of Union was published at Nantes.

In his edict François guaranteed to respect the ancient rights and privileges of Brittany, covering all aspects of civil and ecclesiastical administration. There can be no doubt that the union of the two countries was a matter for rejoicing in Brittany;

the historian Durtelle de Saint-Sauveur refers to the 'days of joy' (*journées d'allégresse*) that followed. It was left to the twentieth century to erect a symbolic statue in Rennes showing Brittany on her knees before France pleading for the union to take place, and for the separatists to christen it the 'Monument of National Shame' and finally blow it up.

CHAPTER XVI

Victorian Viewpoints

THROUGHOUT THE SUMMER months of 1839 an observant and fluent young writer, accompanied by an artist with an eye for the sombre and the grotesque, toured the length and breadth of Brittany. The book that resulted from their wanderings is unequalled as a source of information on the Bretons before tourism became big business. The railways had not yet arrived in Brittany, roads were still under construction, inns and hotels were primitive, and the only way in which the country could be properly visited was 'by discarding all other equipage than the staff and knapsack'. Thus prepared, author and artist set off for the unknown, rather in the spirit of those visiting the Atlas Mountains or Nepal at the present day. The *terra* was not altogether *incognita*, but it was obviously with a certain amount of trepidation that they left the resort country round Dinan and pressed on into the badlands beyond.

The writer was Thomas Adolphus Trollope, elder brother of the great Anthony. Born in 1810 (Anthony was born in 1815), Thomas Adolphus does not deserve the oblivion into which he has fallen, overshadowed by his brother's giant reputation. So prolific was he that, in the words of the *Dictionary of National Biography*, 'it is probable, having regard to the prodigious amount of his periodical and journalistic work, that he emitted more printed matter than any of his family'. His Brittany tour gave him the subject for his first book, *A Summer in Brittany*, published in two volumes in 1840 by Henry Colburn, of Great Marlborough Street. On the title page the words 'by T. Adolphus Trollope, Esq, B.A.' appear in considerably smaller type than the inscription 'edited by Frances Trollope'. This was the family's formidable matriarch. Born in 1780, she married in 1809 Thomas Anthony Trollope, who seems to have been a cantankerous character. He was called to the Bar in 1804; 'but', says the *DNB*, 'his irritable temper frightened away the attorneys, nor was he more successful as a farmer in Harrow

Weald'. He spent ten years trying to farm, and in the late 1820s decided to seek his fortune across the Atlantic. Though aged over fifty, he took Frances and the two boys to the States, 'determined to employ the remains of his fortune in another speculation, still less promising, that of establishing a bazaar for the sale of fancy goods in Cincinnati'. This harebrained scheme was foredoomed, but it had one good effect: it launched Frances on a belated but highly successful career as an author.

On her return home in 1830 she wrote *Domestic Manners of the Americans*, which was published in 1832, and was well in advance of its time in having a strong anti-slavery bias. Thomas Anthony's melancholy career ended soon after. Back in London, he failed as a property speculator, left the country, and in 1835 died near Bruges, 'from premature decay, partly induced by an injudicious course of medicine'. That same year Frances wrote the first of her novels, at the age of fifty-five—surely the latest starter of any successful novelist. From then on, until her death almost thirty years later, she poured out a stream of novels, unread today but marked, says the disapproving entry in the *DNB*, 'by the vigour of her portraits of vulgar persons'.

This, then, was the tough and able mother who edited *A Summer in Brittany*; and she was connected too with the artist whose engravings illustrate the book. His name was August Hervieu; one of the legion of nineteenth-century artists of the second rank, he exhibited at the Royal Academy and other London galleries between 1819 and 1858. His pictures seem to have been mythological/historical, to judge by two shown at the RA—*Sappho Imploring Venus from the Leucadian Rock* (1824) and a sketch for *The Battle of Thermopylae* (1825). More relevant is his *Portrait of Mrs Trollope*, shown in 1833. I have not been able to find any record of his dates of birth and death, or even of his nationality, though from his name he was obviously French. Frances met him in America, and he travelled round the States with her as illustrator—a situation which made the tongues wag wherever the couple went: the middle-aged bluestocking lady asking awkward questions, and the young French artist.

So Thomas Adolphus and August went off to Brittany, no doubt amid a barrage of advice from Frances. The book is a splendid combination of diverse talents. Though only fourteen of Hervieu's engravings appear—which must represent a very small proportion, as Trollope says that he was drawing and sketching all the time—their claustrophobic atmosphere provides a complete contrast to the breezy style of the writing (See opposite page 64 and between pages 160 and 161). The engraving on the title page of the first volume encapsulates Hervieu's view of the country. A sullen peasant stands, arms crossed, wearing a broadbrimmed hat, wide breeches (*bragou braz*) and sabots. At his feet apples have fallen from a tree, while behind him are a number of woolsacks, and a barrel inscribed '*cidre*'. Half hidden by the branches of the apple tree is a statue with the name 'Duguesclin' carved on the plinth; while sketched in the shadowy background are another peasant in an oxcart, a tall *calvaire* and a hill with a solitary menhir. In other words, the stereotype primitive Brittany, with all the elements of the *mise-en-scène* in their appointed places. By contrast, Thomas Adolphus's writing is altogether lively and light-hearted. (Incidentally, this title page has the modern Anglicised spelling 'Bri*tt*any', whereas Trollope uses throughout the more sensible and etymologically correct 'Brita*nn*y'. It would be interesting to know when general acceptance of the 'wrong' spelling finally took place.)

Like all good nineteenth-century travellers with a summer at their disposal, Trollope and Hervieu took it slowly—so slowly, in fact, that the first 150 or so pages is devoted to Normandy, before we find them losing their luggage on the way to Saint-Malo, and nearly sinking into the quicksands on an abortive trip to Mont Saint-Michel. But it is not the near-disasters and discomforts that make *A Summer in Brittany* so fascinating, as much as the wealth of detail of an almost anthropological nature. If Trollope had been alive today, he would have been the ideal creator of television travelogues. As it is, his book remains by far the best introduction to Brittany I have come across. Over and over again I was struck by the timelessness of his observations on the people and the places, and also by his almost complete lack of prejudice (excluding his loathing of Roman Catholicism, which blinded him to the virtues of such masterpieces as the *calvaires* of Saint-Thégonnec and Pleyben).

This is not the place to give a potted version of Trollope; there are vivid descriptions and pertinent remarks on almost every page. He is a master of a tongue-in-cheek style of writing which can reach the heights of irony, as in his description of the peasants at a cattle fair in Pontivy—the first occasion on which he heard 'the harsh sounds and guttural pronunciation' of Breton in every mouth.

> The stillness of demeanour, the grave, severe manners, and a pathetic silence of the Bas-Breton peasants, is one of their most striking characteristics. Unless when strongly excited by some powerful feeling, there is a degree of stedfast [*sic*] immobility about them, which forms the strongest possible contrast to the habits and temperament of the peasants of the rest of France. I have been assured also that their bodily insensibility is correspondingly remarkable. My own experience of the difficulties of making my way through a Breton crowd, would lead me to think them utterly destitute of the sense of feeling. The most vigorous punches in the ribs, and most determined application of the whole force of the back and shoulders against his person, will fail to make a Breton peasant move out of your way, or even look round.

His Dickensian sense of the grotesque, even of the humour in scenes of horror, is shown by his brilliant description of the *pardon* at Saint-Jean du Doigt, ten miles north of Morlaix. The finger that has given rise to the *pardon* is reputedly that of St John the Baptist, miraculously brought to Brittany by a young Breton in the fifteenth century (see page 192). The finger, if touched, was reputed to restore sight to the blind, hearing to the deaf and health to those with all sorts of diseases, who came to the *pardon* in force. Trollope describes the healthy pilgrims walking round the outside of the church telling their beads, sometimes making the circuit on their hands and knees.

> Just outside the moving circle thus formed, and constituting a sort of division between it and the rest of the crowd, were a row of mendicants, whose united appearance was something far more horrible than I have any hope of conveying any idea of to the reader. Let him combine every image that his imagination can conceive of hideous deformity and frightful mutilation; of loathsome filth, and squalid, vermin-breeding corruption; of festering wounds, and leprous, putrifying [*sic*]

sores; and let him suppose all this exposed in the broad light of day, and arranged carefully and skilfully by the wretched creatures whose stock in trade this mass of horror constitutes, so as to produce the utmost possible amount of loathsomeness and sickening disgust; and when he has done this to the extent of his imagination, I feel convinced that he will have but an imperfect idea of what met my eyes at St Jean du Doigt.

Inside the church, however, the horror of the scene gives way to pure farce.

The crowding, pushing, struggling, and jostling, at the entrance to the passage in front of the altar, was tremendous. Here, high above the heads of the undulating crowd, mounted on a level with the top of the altar-rails, was a beadle, with a good stout cane in his hand, with which he was laying about him vigorously; wacking [*sic*] the most violent and impatient of the crowds over their heads and shoulders; much in the same manner that a Smithfield drover regulates the motions of an irritated and over-driven herd of bullocks.

Though *pardons* are now much tamer and less unsettling affairs, there are quite different aspects of Breton life and character that are unchanging. One of these is the Breton's homesickness when he is forced to leave his country against his will. Trollope visited a farm near Trégastel, where one of the sons had been conscripted two years earlier, and the family was without recent news.

However great a hardship the conscription may be in other parts of France, its effects are elsewhere light and trifling in comparison with the affliction it produces in Britanny. The affection of the Breton peasant for his native country, as is the case in other similar instances, is strong in proportion to the smallness of the benefits for which he has to thank her. Transport him to a land smiling with rich corn lands and a glowing vintage, place him beneath the bright sun and serene sky of earth's most favoured clime, and he will pine and sicken for the love of his own gorse-grown hill, and the rude breezes of his own tempestuous coasts.

I myself came across the same sentiments in a Breton family, whose son was in his last few weeks of two years' national service. Though he had only a month to go, and was being exiled no further from home than the other side of France, his parents saw him off from the station with as much concern as though he were off for a couple of years to join the Foreign Legion.

Another observation with a contemporary ring concerns the shattering effect of a military short-back-and-sides on the Breton's self-esteem. 'I have been assured', says Trollope, 'that when the young conscripts are obliged to submit the long streaming locks, of which a Breton peasant is so proud, to the unpitying regimental scissors, the operation produces an agony of grief and not unfrequently abundant showers of tears.' It is only in the last few years, with the onset of shoulder-length hair for young men and a generally shaggier look for their fathers, that the Breton costume has begun to look right again. Nothing seems more absurd today than a photograph of twenty years ago, showing a Breton with short-back-and-sides wearing the traditional broad hat and abundantly decorated costume. The two simply do not mix.

It is hard to judge what influence *A Summer in Brittany* had on its readers, but I suspect that it must have done more than any other book to boost the popularity of Brittany as a tourist country. There were already plenty of English people who had chosen to live there, presumably as a kind of tax haven. Dinan was a centre of English settlement—a Jersey or Malta of the 1830s, at a time when the English were still the financial lords of Europe. In 1839 Dinan was

> one of those towns which have become colonies of English emigrants. It is very pretty and conveniently situated, and was very cheap; and so a tribe of our wandering countrymen 'marked it for their own'. No Egyptian ever dreaded the approach of a swarm of locusts more than the native residents of the little towns of France do the settling down of a flight of English. For the result in both cases is the same—scarcity and dearness of every article of consumption. . . . I met, in the remoter parts of Britanny, three or four old Englishmen, many years resident in the country, who constantly retreat

before the advancing flood of their countrymen like the squatters, those pioneers of civilisation in the western forests of America; well knowing that to live cheaply they must find some part of the country where English gold has not yet penetrated. At Dinan the English have a place of worship and a resident clergyman. . . . Notwithstanding the English, you may live very comfortably at a tolerable hotel for £3 a month.

No doubt Dinan's tree-shaded Jardin Anglais, with its splendid view, across the valley of the Rance, dates from this period of English colonisation. Nowadays, instead of paying £3 a month, you would be lucky to find anywhere at less than £6 a day.

As to the 'remoter parts' where the discriminating settled, Trollope does not specify, though no doubt a number of them were around Huelgoat in the Monts d'Arrée, a little Devon for the self-exiled. This area had everything for the sketcher and the sportsman, categories into which most nineteenth-century gentlemen of leisure fell, no matter how bad the draughtsmanship or how imprecise the aim of the gun. 'For the first,' says Trollope, 'there is an infinite variety of combinations of rocks, wood, and water, with an abundant supply of picturesque figures, of both sexes and all ages. For the second, there are partridges, and hares, and trout, in any quantity he pleases to kill, wolves frequently to be met with, stags sometimes, and boars occasionally.'

Trollope must have spent a busy winter writing up his travels, which show not only intense personal observation but wide reading in the classics of literature on Breton history. His subsequent career is worth a brief outline. In 1843 he and Frances Trollope left England and settled in Florence, where she wrote her novels and he began to specialise in Tuscan history. In 1848 he married Theodosia Garrow (herself a writer), and built a house in Florence, the Villino Trollope, where the Trollopes played host to the Dickenses, the Brownings, George Eliot and other literary lions. Frances died in 1863 and Theodosia soon after, in 1865. The following year Thomas Adolphus married again and embarked on a career as a journalist, acting as Italian correspondent for the *Daily News*.

In 1873 he moved house to Rome and employment to the *Standard*, working for them until he finally retired to England in 1886, where he died six years later. The *Dictionary of National Biography* shows us the old man at his literary work in Rome, where he would write from eight in the morning until two in the afternoon, 'standing at a high desk near the window, and after lunch smoking a cigar among his friends to the strange accompaniment of a glass of milk.' As he sipped and inhaled and looked out across the city, perhaps his mind roved back across forty years, to that summer when as young men he and Hervieu walked their fifteen miles before breakfast, scratched their fleabites, fell into streams, drank cider, met savants, priests and cranks, pondered upon the significance of menhirs, and gazed with joy and curiosity upon the strangely-clad, long-haired, wild-speaking backwoodsmen of Pontivy and Trégastel, of Huelgoat, Lannion and Saint-Jean du Doigt.

Forty years after Trollope and Hervieu, a very different author and artist visited Brittany, and produced a book in their turn. They came to the country with entirely different preconceptions, for Brittany was by now well on the tourist map; the railways had been built; there were roads everywhere; and the modern concept of the brief summer holiday for all, rather than the extended tour for the few, had become established. By the 1870s the Victorian cast of thought had every Englishman under control. Whereas Trollope looked on the Bretons with a sympathetic eye, and tried to understand what made them the way they were, the late Victorians could not really forgive them for not behaving like subjects of the Queen.

Henry Blackburn, whose *Breton Folk* was published in 1880, was a successful journalist, editor during the 1860s of the topical magazine *London Society*, then in the 1870s art director of the *Pictorial World*. More important than his writings was the fact that in his editorial capacity he was able to encourage the best graphic artists of his day, among them Du Maurier, Walter Crane and Randolph Caldecott. Caldecott is remembered today for his marvellous 'Picture Books', which told the stories of John Gilpin and the Babes in the Wood, of the Queen of Hearts and the Great Panjandrum, with a simplicity of line that looked forward to Beardsley, and a nostalgia for the eighteenth century that turned every scene into a Georgian Never-Never-Land. In his early days, he was patronised by Blackburn, and it was in the capacity of illustrator with a lightning ability to pin down a scene or a face that he accompanied Blackburn on three trips round Brittany, in 1874, '78 and '79.

Caldecott was born in 1846 in Chester. As a young man he worked as a bank clerk, first in Whitchurch, Shropshire, and then in Manchester, where he also studied art at evening classes. While at Manchester he sold drawings to Blackburn's *London Society*, as well as to other magazines; and by 1872 felt enough confidence in his future to come to London and establish himself as a freelance illustrator. He was one of the best of the 'special reporters' of the 1870s, who were sent out on assignments, not to write up stories, but to draw them for instant publication, in competition with one another to get their pictures in first. He made his first foreign tour with Blackburn, to the Harz Mountains, in 1872. Blackburn's *The Harz Mountains: A Tour in the Toy Country* (1873) included about thirty drawings by Caldecott, and other artists also contributed. *Breton Folk* was entirely illustrated by Caldecott; it had no fewer than 170 drawings, which completely eclipsed Blackburn's rather stodgy text.

Blackburn was something of a sentimentalist. He saw Brittany as the west wing of an old country house, 'haunted, and full of mysteries and legends, its furniture is antique, and has seldom been dusted or put in order'. Above all, Brittany was made for the amateur artist, who is constantly being told to draw such-and-such a view from such-and-such a vantage point before moving on. He is everlastingly reminding the reader of the country's 'picturesqueness', seeing it as a superb set of artist's props, but as little else. 'It would be strange indeed if a country sprinkled with white caps, and set thickly in summer with the brightest blossoms of the fields, should not attract artists in search of picturesque costumes and scenes of pastoral life. Rougher and wilder than Normandy, more thinly populated, and less visited by the tourists, Brittany offers better opportunities for outdoor study, and more suggestive scenes for the painter. Nowhere in France are there finer peasantry; nowhere do we see more dignity of aspect in field labour, more nobility of feature amongst men and women; nowhere more picturesque ruins; nowhere such primitive habitations and, it must be added, such dirt.' The words 'it must be added' reveal the true Victorian in a nutshell.

The best idea of how attitudes had changed between 1840 and 1870 is given by Blackburn's reaction to the 'public exhibition of disease and human deformities' that still formed an obtrusive aspect of the *pardons*. Where Trollope put down everything on paper—with a certain ghoulish relish, perhaps—Blackburn skates over the unpleasant side of Saint-Anne d'Auray, to avoid offence to his readers. 'We have purposely said little of the repulsive side of the spectacle; of the terrible-looking men and women who have come out of their hiding-places to kneel at the shrine and to beg from strangers; who wander about like savages, and are propitiated with beads.' To him the crippled and the maimed were unsightly blots on the picturesque horizon, to be tidied away out of view. 'It would seem a consideration of some consequence to the numerous English residents abroad, though we seldom hear it touched upon, that their children must of necessity be brought in contact with so much that is cruel and repulsive. . . . It is a source of wonder to visitors to the principal towns that the residents cannot persuade the authorities to keep more decently their streets and public ways.' He also remarks on the Bretons' cruelty to animals—the 'tortured calves and half suffocated pigs' that Trollope did not appear to notice. Blackburn must have been a thoroughly kind-hearted man, but without much inclination to delve into the underlying reasons for the primitiveness of Breton life. And no doubt, as the writer of a popular travel book, he was quite right not to do so.

If we only had Blackburn's text, *Breton Folk* would probably have fallen into oblivion. But if it is read as an extended commentary on Caldecott's drawings, it becomes much more worth while. To Caldecott, the Breton scene was a source of inexhaustible humour. Whereas Hervieu's storm clouds herald the end of the world, Caldecott's merely send Bretons scurrying for shelter under enormous umbrellas. The subtitle of the book he illustrated on the Harz Mountains was *A Tour in the Toy Country*, and there is something irresistibly Toytown about even the most worked-over of Caldecott's Brittany drawings. This is the kind of thing, of course, that makes modern Bretons writhe—the Bécassine approach that sees every Breton man as a clown in a beribboned broad hat, and every Breton woman as a demure coiffed doll. Every now and then Caldecott draws himself, trim-bearded, wearing a straw hat and with his coat over his arm, looking quizzically at the comic characters with whom he has briefly made contact.

Yet Caldecott aspired to be a serious artist in his own right. For example, his lively drawing of the horse fair at Le Folgoët was turned into a bas-relief shown at the Royal Academy in 1876. Judging by pictures of other Caldecott reliefs I have seen (there are several reproduced in Rodney K. Engen's biography) all the life would have vanished in the translation from pen-and-ink to plaster and bronze. His work was taken seriously both by Van Gogh, who called him 'original and highly interesting', and by Gauguin, who said that Caldecott's drawings of the geese that flap and hiss beneath the hoofs of John Gilpin's runaway horse were 'the true spirit of drawing'.

Might there have been some connection between Gauguin's admiration for Caldecott and his visits to Pont-Aven, which began in 1886, the year of Caldecott's death? Caldecott exhibited at the Paris Salon of 1881, and a French edition of his illustrations for various periodicals was published the following year. Given Gauguin's interest in Caldecott's work, it is not beyond the bounds of possibility that he got hold of a copy of *Breton Folk*—in which case he would certainly have appreciated the drawing of the centre of the town (now called the Place Paul Gauguin). Where today the juggernauts thunder and the tourist traffic belches fumes nose-to-tail, in the 1870s artists played cards and drank in the middle of the road, outside the Pension Gloanec.

Pont-Aven was picturesque, no doubt of it, and Blackburn obviously warmed to the town, where 'the art student, who has spent the winter in the Quartier Latin in Paris, comes when the leaves are green, and settles down for the summer to study undisturbed'. He goes on to describe Pont-Aven's great advantage from the artist's point of view. 'Its inhabitants in their picturesque costume (which remains unaltered) have learned that to sit as a model is a pleasant and lucrative profession, and they do this for a small fee without hesitation or *mauvaise honte*. This is a point of great importance to the artist, and one which some may be glad to learn through these pages. The peasants, both men and women, are glad to sit for a franc for the greater part of a day; it is only at harvest time, when field labourers are scarce, that the demand may be greater than the supply, and recruits have to be found in the neighbouring fishing villages. Once or twice a week in the summer, a beauty comes over from Concarneau in a cart, her face radiant in the sunshine, the white lappets of her cap flying in the wind.' And Caldecott himself amplified this with his own impressions (which make one regret that he did not write the text as well). 'On approaching Pont-Aven the traveller notices a curious noise rising from the ground and from the woods around him. It is the flickering of the paint brushes on the canvases of the hardworking painters who come into view on leafy nooks and shady corners. These artists go not far from the town where is cider, billiards and tobacco.'

Many of Caldecott's illustrations are far more sophisticated than they at first appear to be. Rodney Engen points out that the breezy drawing of barefoot peasants winnowing near Saint-Brieuc is a reworking of a Millet theme; but unlike Millet there is no hint of social commentary. In this drawing the woman with a sack of grain on her back is balanced by three runt-like pigs on the opposite side of the foreground; while behind the adults' semi-serious game of separating the wheat from the chaff two children are fighting over a winnowing sieve. Children are never far away from any of these drawings. At a betrothal meal in Guémené, while the cider flows free and the young couple look demurely downwards, a boy sits fast asleep with his head on the table; at Quimper, while a local busybody reads the news, the greatest attention to what he says is being paid by a little girl, not to mention the dog at her feet; and children sit by the well, look after the animals, or play hide-and-seek among the cabbage stalks of Saint-Pol-de-Léon, as they do to this day.

Conscription was still the same as it had been in Trollope's day; and so too was the general lot of the farm labourer. Elsewhere Blackburn refers to the weary monotony of the peasant's life.

He is just where he was in 1850, and where his father was in 1820. The great Chemin de Fer de l'Ouest, that was to do so much for the owners of the land and the tillers of the fruitful soil of Brittany, which has been driven through the heart of the country, with its enormous viaducts and its trains of cattle trucks; which has thrown up embankments of earth that shut him off from the rest of the world, appear to have done little good. A train rushes past his patch of land every day, and perhaps his priest is in it, on his way to Paris or Rennes; it no longer startles his children or his pigs, for it has passed now for years; but 'Traffic', or what is generally understood by the term, scarcely exists, and passengers, excepting in summer, are few and far between.

Not only were those ostensibly served by the railways little better off: neither were the railway employees themselves. At Saint-Thégonnec, Blackburn listened to a tale of woe from the local station-master, who had expected great things from the coming of the railway but who had been sadly disappointed. 'I live in a vast solitude, the monotony of which is only broken by the passing of five or six trains a day; scarcely anyone comes near me; a stray tourist or two in the summer, and an occasional visit from a wolf in winter, one of which has killed my favourite dog.' To offset the tedium, he kept 'a brood of turkeys' for distraction; but he could never really relax, as he was on duty night and day in case the telegraph bell rang.

If the gloomy station-master is to be believed, wolves were still an occasional menace; and they certainly featured as a sporting quarry. Here again, as in Trollope's time, the hills of Basse-Bretagne were the haunt of enterprising Englishmen, though the centre has shifted from Huelgoat to Callac, between Guingamp and Carhaix.

We cross the purple mountains where the solitary shepherd in goat's-skin coat tends his flocks on poor pastures, and where the almost equally solitary Englishman is busy with a fly-rod. At Callac, where comfortable quarters are to be obtained, many Englishmen stay for the fishing and shooting seasons; the streams are well stocked with fish, and there is little difficulty in getting permission for fishing. The game laws are very strict in France, as is well known; the opening and closing of the shooting season varies every year, the prefect deciding the day in September when shooting may begin. The *chasse courant*, which includes hunting the wolf and the wild-boar, commences about a month later. The seasons close at the end of January, and whenever snow is on the ground.

Caldecott drew the shaggy-coated shepherd, leaning on his staff with his back firmly towards the artist. He did not bother with the lonely fly-fisherman, who was no doubt one of the fellow-countrymen with 'draggled beard and grey knicker-bockers' described by Blackburn, either a tourist or one of the several hundred English people living in Dinan. By the time *Breton Folk* was written the Côte d'Emeraude was an established summer playground. Dinard had been put on the map by an American named Coppinger, who built a château there in the 1850s. Blackburn mentions about 800 'houses and villas in pleasant gardens' let for the summer months, there were a number of hotels, and the Casino was open for business. The smaller seaside places shared in the boom. 'At Dinard you play at croquet on the sands; at St Briac you scramble over granite rocks, and fish in the pools under their shadows; at St Jacut you wander over the sands with a shrimp-net, and in the evenings help the nuns to draw water from the well.'

The bucket-and-spade middle-class summer residents were the potential readers of *Breton Folk*, so it is hardly surprising that Blackburn played down the wilder, Celtic undertones of the country. Perhaps he did not notice them. And it was certainly not in Caldecott's nature to do so. His sunny temperament and feeling for the odd and the comic were hardly the right ingredients for anyone who wanted to delve below the surface. Yet he was far too strong an artist to produce the kind of 'picturesque' dull drawings that Blackburn must have had in mind. Caldecott's view of Brittany tells at least one half of the truth; for poverty has its humorous as well as its squalid and pathetic side, and the gentle eye can often see as deeply as the scathing one. When he is drawing not only children, but a woman proudly putting on her *coiffe* before a mirror, or a pair of young lovers, Caldecott no longer indulges in caricature.

Occasionally he draws an actual portrait, like the nineteen-year-old Augustine, who worked in the hotel in Quimperlé where he and Blackburn stayed, and who inspired Blackburn himself to a lyrical character sketch. 'She did the work of three Parisian *garçons*, and walked upstairs unaided with portmanteaus which it would require two men to lift, anywhere out of Brittany. She slept in a box in the kitchen, and dressed "somehow" in five minutes. She ate what was left, contentedly, at the end of the day, and rose at sunrise to do the laborious work of the house; helping also at harvest-time in the fields. She had the sweetest of smiles (when she liked), an unconquerable habit of taking snuff, and a murderous way of killing fowls in the morning which we shall not easily forget.' Such tough competent girls are still the backbone of many small Breton enterprises, and they grow into still tougher and more competent older women.

In spite of the effortlessness of his drawings, Caldecott obviously found his Brittany trips with Blackburn something of a strain. After his return from their 1878 tour he wrote to a friend: 'I should have written to you—even from Brittany, the land of cider & sardines—before now, but to confess the truth, the sitting on Inn benches under pretense [*sic*] of studying and sketching the forms of the passerby, for a month is somewhat unhinging to a mind dwelling in a body not over robust.' In fact, he was to live only a few years after *Breton Folk* was published; though in those few years he produced nearly all the children's books upon which his reputation rests. He died of heart failure in Florida in the cold winter of 1885–86, a month before his fortieth birthday—having gone out there for the good of his health.

Two of the smaller drawings in *Breton Folk* sum up the man. In one, he shows himself struggling to open a gate for two girls in aprons and *coiffes*. In the other, which he called 'Sketching Under Difficulties', he sits smoking a cheroot, attempting to draw surrounded by children in Breton costume, with his left arm round a little girl, a small boy on either side, and a baby held by an elder sister waving its arms ecstatically towards him.

CHAPTER XVII

A Circuit of Towns

DINAN MUST BE the best-known and most visited little town in the whole of Brittany. And not surprisingly, as it has everything the tourist could wish for: narrow medieval streets, a delightful view of the river Rance, a tree-shaded garden behind the church, curio shops and restaurants, flowers spilling into the streets from window-boxes. In fact, Dinan can stand for the best of ancient Brittany, and those who visit it from Saint-Malo and the resorts of the Côte d'Emeraude need really look no further. Dinan was popular with the English as early as the 1830s, and its tourist popularity has never faltered. Nowadays you approach it at high level, by the spectacular viaduct across the Rance, which brings you to the Place Du Guesclin at the upper end of the town. But to get an idea of the original impact of Dinan, you should forget about cars and take the zigzag path down to the Rance below the Jardin des Anglais, then walk along the river to the medieval bridge and climb the steep slope of the Rue du Petit Fort between the jutting half-timbered houses, and so back to the old town.

The Jardin des Anglais was originally the burial-ground of Dinan's main church, the Basilique Saint-Sauveur, which has a Romanesque west entrance and dates mainly from the fifteenth and sixteenth centuries. Its chief monument is the heart-shrine of Bertrand Du Guesclin, marked by a tall black slab in the north transept. Du Guesclin, Constable of France in the fourteenth century, is one of the heroes of French military history, though his reputation in Brittany itself has always been equivocal. He was born near Dinan, in the Château de la Motte-Broons, about 1320, the eldest son of a minor member of the Breton nobility. As a child he was remarkably plain. The troubadour Cuvelier described him in his long narrative poem on Du Guesclin's life and deeds: 'I believe that there was no child so ugly from Rennes to Dinan. He was snub-nosed and swarthy, scowling and stocky; his father and his mother hated him so much that they often wished him dead or drowned in running water.' No doubt it was parental hostility that made him succeed against all odds: with such an unpromising start in life a child either succumbs or goes on to great things. Young Bertrand first came to general notice at a tournament held in Rennes in 1338, when in schoolboy-hero style he borrowed a horse and armour and proceeded to unseat one knight after another, until his own helmet was knocked off and the crowd saw his surly beetle-browed face. The occasion of the tournament was the wedding of Jeanne de Penthièvre with Charles de Blois. After the death of Duke Jean III in 1341, Charles became one of the claimants to the Duchy of Brittany, supported by the French king, Philip of Valois. The other claimant, Jean de Montfort, owed allegiance to the English king, Edward III; and for over twenty years the rivalry of the Houses of Blois and Montfort made Brittany a battleground, and a pawn in the political manoeuvres of England and France.

However miserable the situation may have been for Brittany as a whole, it suited young fighters like Du Guesclin. Legend relates that he stole money and jewels from his mother—poetic justice for the years of rejection—and hired a band of thugs to harry Montfort's English mercenaries. Throughout the battles, skirmishes and treaties of the 1340s and 1350s he remained loyal to the Blois faction. By 1354 he was well enough known to be sent to England among the Breton nobility to treat for the ransom of Charles de Blois, who had been defeated and captured by the English army in 1347. During one of the truces of the 1350s, when the opposing factions drew breath before returning to their mutual slaughter, Du Guesclin fought a single-handed tournament with Sir Thomas Canterbury; the pretext for this savage encounter was that Canterbury had taken prisoner Bertrand's younger brother Olivier, against the spirit of medieval warfare in time of truce. The duel took place in Dinan's market place, and only ended when Du Guesclin, after fighting with lance and sword, nearly killed Canterbury by smashing him in the face with his mailed fist. At about this time Du Guesclin married a Dinan girl, Typhaine de Raguenel, who was a bluestocking, interested in astrology and gifted with second sight. As the times were so uncertain, he moved her from Dinan to Mont Saint-Michel, where she spent her time studying the stars and the writings of the philosophers.

As far as the War of Succession was concerned, Du Guesclin had backed the losing side by supporting Charles de Blois. At the Battle of Auray in 1364 Blois was killed and Bertrand himself was taken prisoner, and ransomed for the enormous sum of 100,000 crowns. The pro-English Montfort was now Duke of Brittany, as Jean IV, and Du Guesclin, with his loyalties now to France rather than to Brittany, fought for the French king in Spain. Since 1364 Charles V, known as the Wise, had been King of France; and he showed his wisdom by commissioning Du Guesclin to weld an army out of the marauding bands known as the *Grandes Compagnies*, unemployed since the Battle of Auray and the peace that followed it. This unlikely army had the task of dethroning the King of Spain, Pedro the Cruel, and replacing him by his brother, Don Enrique. As M. Coryn puts it in his romanticised life of Du Guesclin, *Black Mastiff*: 'Along the banks of the Rhône went Bertrand, a strange Pied Piper whistling the tune of Spanish gold, and they followed after him, that horde of man-eating rats, fascinated by his piping.' When he reached Avignon Du Guesclin even managed to get the Pope to give his cut-throat troops absolution, by making it clear that he would unleash them on the papal treasures unless the Pope complied.

In 1370 Bertrand was recalled from Spain to fight the English, who had again invaded France. Appointed Constable (commander-in-chief) of France by Charles V, he spent the last decade of his life in almost constant warfare. But though he was as successful as ever as a general, his final campaigns in Brittany have tarnished his reputation among the Bretons ever since. In 1373, on the orders of Charles V, Du Guesclin marched against Brittany and forced Duke Jean IV to flee to England. But at the end of 1378 Charles threatened to annex Brittany, and the Bretons forgot the sufferings that Montfort had brought them. In August 1379 he was welcomed back in triumph, as legitimate Duke and symbol of Brittany's determination to be independent of France at all costs. Once more Du Guesclin was ordered to march against his own people, but as he crossed the borders of Brittany his army melted away. Many of them were Bretons, who had been happy to fight the

English but refused to attack their fellow-Bretons. Unhappy at being considered a traitor in his own country, and furious that his loyalty to the French crown was being suspected at court, Bertrand offered to resign the office of Constable, handing back the great sword that symbolised his authority. But Charles V would not accept his resignation, and sent him off to fight the English in another part of France, to the Massif Central, where he died on July 13, 1380, while besieging the town of Châteauneuf-de-Randon, near Le Puy. The English commander, in a chivalrous gesture of honour to Du Guesclin, pressed the keys of the town into his dying hands. Thus Bertrand triumphed in his final siege, as he had in so many others for the past forty years. His body was carried in solemn funeral procession across France to Paris, where it was buried with full honours in the church of Saint-Denis, the burial-place of the French kings. His heart was placed in a silver casket and taken to Dinan, where it remains to this day. Less than three months later Charles V himself was dead, and followed his loyal general, 'Messire Bertran', to the vaults of Saint-Denis.

To a non-Breton, Du Guesclin hardly seems to deserve the opprobrium that has been heaped on him by the nationalists, and led to their blowing up his statue at Rennes in 1946 (see page 79). His chief defect was that he was too loyal, that he did not slide from one allegiance to another as a more efficient time-server would have done. When the War of Succession began in the early 1340s, both Blois and Montfort had equal support. Du Guesclin's mistake was to back the loser as far as Brittany was concerned; but he would surely have been far more disloyal to his principles if he had come round to Montfort after the Battle of Auray. And once he had taken the oath of allegiance to Charles V as Constable of France, he was caught in a conflict from which only resignation or death could release him. One of the most famous poems in La Villemarqué's *Barzaz-Breiz*, called *The Swan*, celebrates the return of 'good Duke John' to Brittany, and keeps the curse of posterity for Bertrand du Guesclin.

> . . . And where the Frenchmen fall, they'll stay
> Until the final judgment day,
> Until they're judged and punished all,

Above, The seventeenth-century ossuary and fifteenth-century porch at La Martyre, near Landerneau

Below left, Detail of the porch carving. The Virgin was originally carved suckling the infant Christ, but at some period the sculpture was mutilated

Below right, Carving on the door surround. The hooded peasant is playing *crosse*, a forerunner of hockey or golf

Above, The congregation at the *pardon* of Notre-Dame des Portes, at Châteauneuf-du-Faou

Below left, Carried by the women of the town, the Virgin leaves the chapel

Below right, The procession winding up through the streets of Châteauneuf-du-Faou

bove, Artichokes growing right up to
ıe houses in the *Ceinture Dorée* round
aint-Pol-de-Léon

ight, Seaweed gatherer on the
illon de Talbert, a shingle bank
orth of Tréguier

elow, Salt marshes (*marais salants*)
ear Guérande

Above left, The château in the centre of Nantes, the favourite residence of the Duchess Anne of Brittany, who is shown *above right* on a medal of 1499

Below left, The watergate of Nantes château

Below right, Negro's head on the house of a Nantes shipowner who had grown rich in the slave trade

Above, Open-air fish market at Auray

Below, The medieval bridge at Auray, with its small customs house

Vannes: ancient wash-houses, with the medieval fortifications behind

ight, Punts on the
rande Brière.
he 'mast' in the
reground is part
the boat's
shing mechanism

elow, The annual
ater sports held
ear Fédrun, in the
rière

Above right, A sabot-maker of the Grande Brière

Above left, M. Roger Aoustin, a Brière fenman, with eel spear and peat-cutting tools

Right, Out on the open waterway in his punt

But most their traitor general.
Rain dripping from the trees he'll have
As holy water for his grave.

A later writer, Roger Vercel, takes a more charitable view. 'As for his little *patrie*, Brittany, it was not contempt, but a deep love that made him want to link it to France. . . . Should one reproach him with having tried to put forward by two centuries the date of the inevitable union? Because he tried too soon, perhaps, should one forget with what intelligent patience he made ready ready for that union, with what love, unable to distinguish between the two nations, he realised it in himself?'

Twenty-five miles or so west of Dinan is Lamballe, a good deal less interesting for the lover of old buildings than Dinan (though it has a few medieval houses such as the fifteenth-century Maison du Bourreau, now the Syndicat d'Initiative), but much more relaxing to shop or wander about in. It has expanded considerably in recent years, and now suffers from a bewildering one-way system, which means that you are liable to do a couple of circuits of the town before you find a road that leads you to the centre. Lamballe is renowned throughout North France for its stud farm (*haras*), an enormous place, with stables built round a vast sanded yard, the *Cour d'Honneur*. Each stable has rows of stallions in individual stalls, mainly Breton draught-horses (the *Trait Breton*). Some of them, so the guide told us, are used as breeding stock for the horse butchers, whose golden horse-head signs can still be found here and there. One of the most prominent victims of the French Revolution, the Princesse de Lamballe, took her title from the town. A close friend of Marie-Antoinette, she was guillotined in September 1792, and her head was paraded on a pike outside the prison where the Queen was held captive. Equally unfortunate, though in a very different way, was Antoine-Joseph Jobert, a Lamballe doctor who rose to be personal physician to Napoleon III and died insane in 1867. In one of his periods of madness, he went into a Paris post office, grabbed a clerk by the ears and tried to haul him through the counter window, shouting: 'Excellent! The baby's the right way round!' History does not relate whether the clerk was safely delivered.

A motorway now links Lamballe with Saint-Brieuc, the main town of the Côtes-du-Nord. But it is worth leaving the motorway at its halfway point and making for Saint-Brieuc by the old main road, through the villages of Yffiniac and Langueux; for in the summer every house along the road has a display of strings of garlic and sacks of onions and potatoes—among the best bargains of the region. Saint-Brieuc is growing too fast for comfort; but it has a magnificent site, on either side of the dramatic valley of the river Gouédic, which means that a deep cleft filled with greenery cuts the urban sprawl in two. The town centre is a bustling place, with plenty of pedestrianisation going on. At the entrance to the main shopping street, the Rue Saint-Guillaume, the rejection of the car is spelt out loud and clear: 'Pedestrians, this street is yours' (*'Piétons, cette rue est à vous'*). St Guillaume was a battling medieval bishop of Saint-Brieuc, Guillaume Pinchon, who defended the town against one of the Dukes of Brittany in the thirteenth century; while Brieuc or Brioc was one of the original Seven Saints of Brittany and came over from Britain in the sixth century, along with St Malo, St Samson and the rest. Guillaume Pinchon was largely responsible for the frowning, fortress-like cathedral, whose twin towers glower down on the Place Général de Gaulle. Directly opposite is the ultra-modern Mairie, all glass and white concrete, with fountains in front. It is in perfect contrast to the cathedral, and proves that modern buildings do not have to be bogus-ancient to fit in with the most venerable neighbours.

I always associate Guingamp, Lannion and Morlaix together, partly because on the map they stand neatly at the corners of a flattened isosceles triangle of roads, and partly because they are in fact rather similar, with medieval nuclei and the usual white blocks of flats going up in the suburbs. Guingamp is a quiet little town, with one of the most superbly original churches in the whole of Brittany. In Notre-Dame de Bon Secours the Gothic and the Renaissance co-exist side by side: indeed, they do more than co-exist, as the Renaissance has been grafted on to the Gothic and interpenetrates it both outside and inside. The old buildings of the town press so close upon the church that it is hard to take it in as a whole; but the difference between the two epochs of building is summed up by the two west towers. The north-west tower (Tour de l'Horloge) is fourteenth-century Gothic, with a pyramidal roof capped by a little bell turret; while the south-west tower—known for some reason as the Tour Plate, though it is far from flat—is a massively buttressed sixteenth-century structure, with a Latin inscription proclaiming it 'a tower of strength against the face of the enemy', and a battery of stone cannon jutting from the parapet to give teeth to the proclamation. The originality of the Renaissance work is astonishing. A major reconstruction programme became necessary after most of the medieval south-west tower collapsed in 1535, leaving—so says a stone inscription on the tower—'a great ruin, pitiful to behold' ('*la grande ruisne, piteuse à voir*'). Two years later the first stone of the new tower was laid. The name of the architect is known: he was Jean le Moal, a young enthusiast for the new Renaissance style, and it says much for the go-ahead outlook of sixteenth-century Guingamp that he was given a free hand.

If Le Moal's work outside was enterprising enough, his internal rebuilding was spectacular. The triforium gallery on the south side was recast in the most fanciful Renaissance style. It consists of a double arcade surmounted by S-shaped scrolling, and a strange recessed gangway above, with uprights that look like stone chair-legs, and each bay of the arcade topped by a scallop shell below the Gothic vault. The whole interior is tall and narrow, built of a glowing brownish-pink granite; and its irregularities all cohere in a remarkable way, from the triforium gallery to the internal flying buttresses that look like delicate membranes of stone.

Another rare feature of Guingamp church is the north-west porch, the Porche Notre-Dame, which has a black Madonna high on the wall, and on the floor a stone labyrinth, whose windings lead the pilgrim to the words AVE MARIA at its centre. The *pardon* of Notre-Dame de Bon Secours (Itron Varia Gwir Zikour) used to be a wild occasion. In the 1830s, Emile Souvestre tells us in *Les Derniers Bretons*, after the solemn torchlit procession was over, the crowds of pilgrims cast aside their inhibitions. 'Cries of joy, shouted names, bursts of laughter succeed the contemplative dignity of the nocturnal procession. The crowd of penitents gather in the square, where they all have to sleep higgledy-piggledy on the bare ground. So the holy ceremony in honour of the Immaculate Virgin ends more often than not in an orgy; the girls and boys meet and mingle, take one another's arms, excite one another, chase one another through the dark streets; and the next day, when the sun rises, many girls rejoin their mothers, with red faces and downcast eyes, and one sin more to confess to the parish priest.' This pagan aftermath to a Christian *pardon* (which incidentally still takes place on the first Saturday in July) no doubt dates back to the time when a fertility goddess was worshipped at Guingamp. And the elegant fountain in the Place de la Centre, decorated with half-naked nymphs, dolphins, winged horses and other creatures, is a suitably pagan spring for the worship of the Celtic Earth Mother.

Lannion has become something of a boom town in recent years with the growth of the electronics industry, symbolised by the great white radome of the Pleumeur-Bodou satellite telecommunications centre, which sits like a gigantic golfball on the heathland a few miles to the north. Built on either side of a fine wide river, the Léguer, Lannion has some of the best half-timbered houses in North Brittany, notably in the Place Général-Leclerc and the alleys leading off it.

Morlaix shares its half-timbering with Lannion, but its site is completely different. Whereas Lannion is built on and around a hill, Morlaix is down in the steep-sided valley of the Dossen and is dominated by a gigantic railway viaduct, built in the 1860s. Transportation of one sort or another seems to be one of the town's main preoccupations. Owing to its layout, Morlaix is a hard place to get into and out of, and on the two occasions I have been there practically every road in the centre has been undergoing major alterations. The town's Breton name is Montroulez; its French name was used in a punning way for the Morlaix motto '*S'ils te mordent, mord-les*' ('If they bite you, bite them back'). This dates back to an English raid on Morlaix in 1522. The English troops found it undefended, as most of the inhabitants were at an out-of-town festival. They pillaged the houses and then proceeded to drink themselves unconscious in the cellars; when the locals returned they found them helpless and massacred them, so that the town fountain ran red with English blood. Besides the motto, the Morlaix coat-of-arms features the French leopard face to face with the English lion, in mutual hostility.

Brittany would not be Brittany without its saints, and their highly-coloured lives would have been largely unknown, had it not been for Father Albert Le Grand, of Morlaix, from whom I have quoted freely throughout this book. Le Grand's work was part of the seventeenth-century Roman Catholic revival in Brittany, which culminated in the missions of Père Julien Maunoir, a Jesuit who tramped the countryside for over half a century, preaching hell-fire to the Breton peasantry. Born in Morlaix towards the end of the sixteenth century, Le Grand became a Dominican friar at an early age, and his religious vocation combined with an interest in the remote past drew him naturally to studying the ecclesiastical origins of his native land. He completed *Les Vies des Saints de la Bretagne-Armorique* in 1636, dedicating it tactfully to the States of Brittany and thus ensuring the approval of the laity as well as that of his fellow-clergy. He was shrewd enough to anticipate the patronising smiles of the sceptics; indeed, he wanted to stop them reading his book altogether. In the Preface he wrote: 'I forbid absolutely that this book should be read by Atheists, by Freethinkers, by the Uncommitted, by Heretics, and by those conceited persons who, calculating the power of God according to the measure of their ill-tuned brains, laugh at the marvels which He has accomplished through His servants, and believe in nothing that overtops the summit of their feeble understanding, wishing to submit Faith to the Laws of Reason.' After such a warning, it might be thought that Le Grand's *Lives* would be nothing but religious platitudes, whereas in fact they are highly readable, even in a forbidding two-column format. So pleased were Père Albert's contemporaries with his book that a number of poets were inspired to write stanzas about it, making fairly inaccurate anagrams of his name, such as '*La Perle de Bretagne*' taken from most of the letters of '*Père Albert Le Grand*'. Sadly, he did not enjoy his success for very long, as he died early in the 1640s, after revising and adding to his *Lives*.

You can get from Morlaix to Brest along the new motorway; but it is more rewarding to take the N12 along the Elorn valley through Landerneau, yet another attractive old town built on either side of a river. I remember Landerneau not only for its buildings but also for a magnificently ample prostitute of Mother Earth stature, smiling her way across the traffic at a busy intersection like a galleon under full sail. Perhaps she lives in Landerneau and carries on her trade in Brest.

Brest is the Portsmouth of France: for centuries the country's greatest naval centre, but now somewhat run-down with the general decline in Western naval power. Like Portsmouth, Brest sits uneasily in the surrounding region, being no more an integral part of Brittany than Portsmouth is of Hampshire. Brest suffered terribly at the time of the Liberation in 1944 (see page 306). As at Saint-Malo, Lorient and Saint-Nazaire, the Germans hung on grimly until the town was almost obliterated around them; thus it has no counterpart to the narrow streets, pubs and up-and-down houses of old Portsmouth. But in one major respect Brest scores over Portsmouth, and that is in the magnificence and scale of its setting. The open waters of Spithead cannot compare with the virtually land-locked expanse of the Rade (roadstead) de Brest, where in the great days vast fleets could lie safely at anchor, protected from the Atlantic swell by the Crozon peninsula, and from seaward attack by the narrow and easily guarded Goulet de Brest. Not only is the Rade de Brest a splendid natural harbour, but it is also the major confluence of the main rivers into the heart of Finistère—the Aulne, the Elorn and, to a lesser extent, the Penfeld, on whose banks old Brest was built.

Of that old town virtually nothing survives, except the château on the east bank and the sonorously-named Tour de la Motte Tanguy directly opposite. When I went to Brest my first voyage of discovery was along the Rue de Siam, the main shopping street, to see if I could find No. 41. A century ago this was an establishment called Au Prince Eugène, devoted mainly to naval uniforms, and I had found its trade card in a guidebook to Brest dated 1860. It obviously had an international clientèle, as the card announced 'Hollands Spreeken, English Spoken, Deutsch Sprechen'. Apart from naval uniforms, it sold '*Twines, Coachmanns, Sacs*' and any number of other mysterious garments of the 1860s, assuring its clients that all clothes unsold at the end of the season went for export. Alas, No. 41 is no longer Au Prince Eugène but is a Prisunic supermarket instead; however, the Rue de Siam is still a centre of the clothing trade, as Liberty's is next door to No. 41 and Burton of London is nearly opposite. And naval uniforms are still very much in evidence throughout the town; though surprisingly it is full of officers, with ratings nowhere to be seen. Perhaps that reflects the numerical balance of the modern French navy. At the heart of Brest is the Arsenal, upstream from the castle—the naval dockyard which stretches along both sides of the Penfeld and can be visited only by French citizens. However, the foreigner can get a good idea of the place by walking across the mighty Pont de Recouvrance, the biggest vertical-lift bridge in Europe, with its two H-shaped pylons from which the central span is suspended. Looking upstream you can see a vast rusty crane, kept as an industrial monument, I was told, but now a dangerous structure and due to be removed; an enormous naval gun mounted on the quay; and a few small grey warships at anchor.

The Tour Tanguy has one of the best little museums I have come across in Brittany—so well looked after that you are not allowed to walk round it in bare shoe leather, but are supplied with felt pads for skating round the well-polished floor. The tower is itself part of Brest's history, built in the fifteenth century by Tanguy de Chastel, one of the most powerful Bretons of his time. The exhibits include models of old Brest, and a fine collection of nineteenth-century photographs of presidential visits to the harbour, and other bewhiskered and bemedalled state occasions. Most memorable are the nineteenth-century engravings of scenes from convict life, for Brest's harbour was built largely by convict labour, from the mid-eighteenth century on. The great *bagne* or prison stood on the right bank of the Penfeld, looking upstream from the bridge. Built in 1750–51 for the *galériens* (the name derives from the galleys to which earlier criminals were condemned), it was described in almost lyrical terms by the civil servant Mignot de Montigny, who visited Brest when the *bagne* had just been built.

> The prison building where the convicts are confined is the most beautiful, the biggest, the cleanest and the best arranged building of its type ever built. The height of its long galleries and the convenient placing of a large number of water cisterns make the place cleaner and healthier than most religious houses. It holds 2,400 prisoners, employed turn and turn about at different tasks about the harbour. The convicts work for a week and rest for a week. Nine hundred at a time

are employed, of whom the greatest number work at enlarging the quays along the harbour. Those at work are given one and a half litres of wine a day, which costs the King two *sous* per man. They are taken back to the prison at dinner time. They are fed on thirty ounces of white bread a day and soup made of broad beans. The construction work on the harbour costs the State only 5,000 *livres* a year, for the convicts' wine.

They are commanded in prison by officers (*commis*) and under-officers. They are chained on benches, distributed in four enormous galleries. Those who chain them and unchain them are called *argousins* (warders). Convicts can only be employed outside the prison in groups of five chained couples at a time. They are taken to and from work by an armed guard or halberdier (*pertuisanier*), who answers for the safety of the convicts by being put in the place of any fugitive. If anyone escapes, the country round about is warned by a cannon fired from the ramparts. . . . Sick convicts are taken to hospital, where they are chained to their beds in a locked room. Those who are condemned to the galleys for 101 years can make a will, but those who are condemned in perpetuity are not allowed to do so.

This is the description of a typical man of the Enlightenment, to whom no doubt all was for the best in the best of all possible prisons. Ninety years later Flaubert visited the *bagne*, which had become one of the tourist attractions of Brittany, and left a scathing indictment of its inhuman brutality. 'Unless you are an engineer, a shipwright or a smith,' he wrote, 'Brest is not a particularly interesting place. The harbour is beautiful, I agree; magnificent, if you like; gigantic, if you insist. "It's impressive," as they say, and "it gives the idea of a great nation". But these heaps of cannons, cannonballs and anchors, the infinite distances of these quays that confine a sea without movement or incident, a sea that itself seems to be condemned to hard labour, these huge straight workshops full of screeching machinery, the continuous clank of the chains of the convicts, passing row on row and working in silence—all this sinister, pitiless, unnatural mechanism, this heaping-up of organised mistrust, soon weighs down your spirits with its tedium and wearies the sight. . . . Here nature is absent, proscribed, as nowhere else on earth; it is the negation of nature, a stubborn hatred of it, both in the iron bar that smashes the rocks, and in the sabre of the guard who hounds the convicts.' However, this was France and not the England of Dickens's floating hulks, and the convicts had their consolations in the shape of seven streets of brothels built behind the *bagne*—dark and silent places, in contrast to the roistering whorehouses of the free sailors of the navy and merchant marine. 'When are they open? At unknown hours, at the quietest moments of the darkest nights. At such times the warder who has slipped away from his post enters there, as does the convict who has escaped from his confinement, often warder and convict together, helping each other, protecting each other. Then, when the day returns, the convict shins over the wall and the warder turns his head away; no one has seen anything.'

The engravings in the Tour Tanguy give visual reality to the written accounts of the *bagnards*' existence. We see them asleep in their chains on wooden platforms; at work hauling massive timbers; after death being hurtled down a chute into a deep pit. We see them being flogged by their fellows, and kneeling round the guillotine as the blade falls. Most horrific of all in its implications is the scene of a launching ceremony. The distinguished spectators gather round to watch the vessel slide down the slipway, but attention is on a convict with an axe, whose task is to cut away the last vertical prop below the ship's bow. If he succeeded in jumping back in time, he would be released; but eight times out of ten the convicts were crushed to a pulp by the ship passing over them—a blood sacrifice to the god of the sea, with elements of a gladiatorial show, made even more macabre by the respectable top hats and crinolines of the assembled company. If a convict succeeded in escaping, the countryside round about was alerted by gunfire—the so-called 'Brest thunder' (*Tonnerre de Brest*). Fleeing through a hostile countryside, and easily identifiable from his yellow trousers and letters T.F. (*travaux forcés*, forced labour) branded on his shoulder, he was almost certain to be picked up within a few hours. Instead of tracker dogs, the prison authorities used the local gypsies, who knew every inch of the countryside far better than the convicts, and relied for their income on their success in recapturing prisoners. For the convict, it meant a return to floggings, leg irons and the chain gang. At least in the Brest *bagne* everything was more or less in the public eye; and the public presumably knew and approved of what was done. But in 1864 the brutalities were swept under the carpet, as it were, in response to nineteenth-century humanitarianism, or hypocrisy. The *bagne* was closed, and reopened on Devil's Island off the coast of South America, where the convicts were conveniently out of sight and out of mind.

The postwar white concrete Brest looks forward, rather than back to the melancholy shadows of its past. It is now firmly in the mainstream of Breton culture with its Université de Bretagne Occidentale, which is a thriving centre of Celtic studies; while a drive through the Port de Commerce past big freighters and oil tankers shows that a decline in naval strength need not mean a decline in maritime activity. And somewhere under Brest there may still be fortunes to be made, as in 1944 the Germans are said to have buried quantities of loot before they finally surrendered. Like nearly all such legendary treasures, it probably does not exist at all; but it will no doubt pass into folk memory, along with the gold that is said to lie below the menhirs.

Concarneau away on the other side of Finistère makes its living from the sea, as Brest does; but there the resemblance ends. There are really two Concarneaus: the old walled town (Ville Close), built on a narrow island and surrounded by a complete circuit of fortified walls; and the modern fishing harbour, which hems in the Ville Close on every side. Concarneau is famous for its Fête des Filets Bleus (Festival of the Blue Nets), originally a simple ceremony for blessing the nets in order to guarantee success in the forthcoming fishing season, but now expanded into a week-long folk festival during the second half of August. It is similar to the Fêtes de Cornouaille at Quimper, except that the crowds of visitors are jammed into the narrow main street of the Ville Close instead of having the freedom of a spacious town. The origins of the festival are recalled by the nets that are hung for the occasion all round the narrow causeway that leads from the mainland to the walled town. In Concarneau there is an iniquitous charge for walking on the ramparts; but you can avoid this by following the Rue

Vauban (which incidentally has a museum devoted to Concarneau's fishermen and fishing industry) to the far end, where there is a perfectly good stretch of rampart where you can stroll free of charge.

During one of his stays in the Pont-Aven area, Paul Gauguin took part in a brawl in Concarneau, whose after-effects may well have shortened his life. In May 1894 he organised a trip to the Ville Close with some friends, including his current mistress known as 'Anna the Javanese', who emphasised the exotic nature of her appearance by carrying a tame monkey around on her shoulder. The local children began by taunting her, and finally started to throw stones. One of Gauguin's friends caught a child by the ear, a group of sailors emerged from a café, and a full-scale brawl developed. Gauguin described the incident in a letter. 'My leg is broken level with the ankle, and the bone has pierced right through the skin. As regards Anna, at Concarneau they threw stones at us. I knocked out a ship's pilot who had attacked me, with two blows of my fist, then he went to look for his crew and fifteen men fell on me. I carried on the battle master of the field, and of myself. Then my foot caught in a hole, and I fell over and broke my leg. Once I was down, sabot kicks rained down on me, and finally I got away. I had to be carried to Pont-Aven, but I'm getting better.' Gauguin was laid up for two months and had to take morphine for the pain in his leg. Finally, to add insult to injury, Anna the Javanese rifled his Paris studio while he was away and walked off with the proceeds.

The seafaring picturesqueness of Concarneau did not inspire Gauguin to paint it; but this neglect has been more than made up for since by the hordes of amateur artists who line the quays on a fine summer day. Gauguin spent most of his time in Brittany down the coast, for a few years at Pont-Aven, and later at Le Pouldu. He first came to Pont-Aven in the summer of 1886, three years after throwing up his profitable job on the Paris Stock Exchange to become a full-time painter. By this time his Danish wife Mette had broken with him, but they were still on writing terms, and a letter to her a month or so after his arrival shows him already the acknowledged leader of a cosmopolitan group of artists living at the Pension Gloanec. 'I'm working here a lot, and quite successfully. I'm respected as the ablest painter at Pont-Aven, though it's true I don't get a sou the richer. Perhaps that will come later. In any case, it's gaining me a reasonable reputation, and everyone here (American, English, Swedish, French) fights for my advice, which I'm stupid enough to give them, because they definitely make use of me without due acknowledgment. I'm not getting fat at this job; I now weigh less than you do. I'm becoming as bony as a herring, but on the other hand I feel rejuvenated. The more problems I have the more my strength recovers, but that doesn't encourage me. I don't know where I'm going, and I'm living here on credit. Money worries are a great discouragement, and I'd like to see the end of them.' What Gauguin hoped to find in Brittany was no doubt a simple life removed from the cultural infighting of Paris; what he in fact found was an established group of indifferent painters (already remarked on by Henry Blackburn in the 1870s, see page 248), to whom he inevitably became an artistic father-confessor, by reason of his greater age and authority.

However, the scenery and people of Brittany provided the inspiration for his best work for almost five years—a period broken by two expeditions that seemed abortive but were crucial for his art. The first was his journey to Panama and Martinique which lasted for most of 1887, and rekindled the love of tropical scenery and savage surroundings that had lain dormant since his voyages as a merchant seaman during his youth. The second was his melodramatic few months spent with Van Gogh in Arles at the end of 1888, which culminated in the notorious scandal when Van Gogh cut off his own ear with a razor. More important for the development of both artists was the liberating effect each had on the other. In later years, Gauguin would proudly describe how it was due to his influence that Van Gogh had begun to paint with 'yellow on yellow on yellow'.

At Pont-Aven, Gauguin's leading disciples—though he always disclaimed the term—were Paul Sérusier and Emile Bernard. Sérusier's picture, *The Talisman*, painted under the trees of the Bois d'Amour beside the Aven river, juxtaposed violently contrasting colours in a way that was quite foreign to Impressionism's gentle intermingling of tones, but which pointed the way to Gauguin's own Tahitian pictures. Sérusier coined the name 'the Nabis' (from a Hebrew word meaning 'prophet') to describe the group that adopted the new ideas of 'Synthetism', in opposition to Impressionism. Bernard, twenty years younger than Gauguin, was a key figure in the group, and it was after seeing one of Bernard's paintings that Gauguin painted his great *The Vision after the Sermon* (now in the National Gallery of Scotland, Edinburgh.) In this work Gauguin abandoned conventional perspective altogether, contrasting the coiffed audience of peasant women with the small figures of Jacob and the Angel, wrestling on a brilliant red field. Gauguin offered this masterpiece free to the priest of Nizon, a village outside Pont-Aven, but the gift was turned down on the grounds that the parishioners could not possibly understand it. Yet it has far more in common with the ancient stone *calvaires* than any of the conventionally 'religious' paintings that abound in Breton churches.

In the autumn of 1889 Gauguin moved from the bustle of Pont-Aven to the remote village of Le Pouldu, on the Finistère coast some twenty miles away. Le Pouldu has grown a certain amount since then, but it is still little more than a seaside village with a few large hotels. Gauguin is said to have stayed in a cottage where the Hôtel de la Plage now stands; but the tobacconist who runs the shop on the exact site did not seem too sure when I asked him. In a letter written to Emile Bernard from Le Pouldu the following summer, Gauguin portrays himself as a cross between a Noble Savage and a 1960s-style hippie, doing little or nothing down by the seashore. 'I don't know who's been telling you that I go walking on the beach with my disciples. As far as disciples are concerned, there's De Haan who works away by himself, and Filiger who works in the house. I walk about like a savage with long hair and do nothing at all; I've not even got my paints or palette. I've made some arrows and I practise shooting them on the sand as though it was Buffalo Bill country (*comme chez Buffalo Bill*). So. There's your self-styled Jesus Christ.' He also practised more usual arts of self-defence: in the autobiographical jumble of fact and anecdote he called *Avant et Après*, Gauguin describes how he took up fencing at Pont-Aven with a retired sailor turned fencing-master, and learnt to box (*la boxe anglaise* as opposed to *la boxe française*) from a painter called Bouffard.

In the spring of 1891 he sailed on the first of his journeys to Tahiti; and the rest of his life belongs almost entirely to the South Seas and the wider history of art. Yet this first journey was something in the nature of an experiment, as he was back in the summer of 1893, and spent most of the following year once more at Pont-Aven and Le Pouldu. It was during this period that the tragi-comedy of the brawl at Concarneau took place. In 1895 Gauguin left Europe for the last time. He lived for six years on Tahiti, and then, as his finances worsened, moved to the remote Marquesas Islands away to the north-east—a long-drawn-out parallel to his Brittany move from Pont-Aven to Le Pouldu. In May 1903 he died of a heart attack, in extreme poverty, under threat of a lawsuit, ravaged by syphilis, and mourned by all the Marquesans among whom he lived. On his easel was the painting *A Breton Village Under Snow* (now in the Louvre). Sometimes said to be his last work, it seems more likely that he had brought it from Europe as a reminder of his years in Brittany. As a final irony, when Gauguin's few effects were auctioned off, it was displayed upside down and sold as a picture of Niagara Falls.

Though Gauguin is remembered today by the Place Paul Gauguin in the centre of Pont-Aven, you will not find any of his paintings on display in the town. However, a small gallery behind the Mairie holds exhibitions relating to the artist every summer, from mid-June to mid-September; in 1977 it showed the work of Gauguin's contemporary Henri Rivière, who specialised in scenes of Breton peasant life. And you can still walk as the Nabis did beside the rocks and trees of the Bois d'Amour—a walk that nowadays has a bonus in the shape of a fish-farm twenty minutes upstream, where you can buy trout netted fresh from the waters of the Aven.

Gauguin was well acquainted with Quimperlé, one of the prettiest towns in Brittany. It is linked with Quimper in a local saying, which runs 'If Quimper is the smile of Cornouaille, then Quimperlé is its kiss'—the exaggeration of local patriotism perhaps, but not unjustified. The names of both towns derive from Kemper, meaning 'confluence of rivers'; but whereas Quimper means 'confluence' pure and simple, Quimperlé means 'confluence of the Ellé river', which joins the Isole and flows south to the sea, renamed the Laïta. Quimperlé consists of the old town, the Ville Basse, built where the rivers meet, and the more recent Ville Haute, on the hill towards Pont-Aven and reached by steep flights of steps from river level. The town's chief glory is its circular church, the Eglise Sainte-Croix, built originally in the eleventh century and modelled on the Church of the Holy Sepulchre in Jerusalem. In contrast to the angular severity of later Gothic churches, everything about Sainte-Croix is gently rounded—round overall plan, round central tower, rounded apses at east, north and south, rounded roofs over the different sections. The only right-angles are at the main west entrance, inside which is a spectacular stone Renaissance screen depicting Christ in Majesty and the four Evangelists, surrounded by a riot of carved figures and filigree decoration. Behind the church are several massively timbered medieval houses, notably the so-called Maison des Archers.

Another town built where two rivers join is Lorient, one of Brittany's chief harbours, which stands on the wide estuary of the Scorff just below its junction with the Blavet. It was founded in 1666 as L'Orient, to be the home port of the Compagnie des Indes Orientales, the French equivalent of the East India Company. Lorient was virtually destroyed at the end of the war; but like Brest it has been entirely rebuilt in the same white nondescript concrete style. Arthur Young visited Lorient in September 1788 and was as uncomplimentary about it as he was about almost everywhere else in Brittany. 'I found l'Orient so full of fools, gaping to see a man of war launched, that I could get no bed for myself, nor stable for my horse, at the Epee Royale. . . . But what makes l'Orient more known is being the appropriated port for the commerce of India, containing all the shipping and magazines of the company. The latter are truly great, and speak the royal munificence from which they arose.' Lorient owed its prosperity to Louis XIV; his predecessor, Louis XIII, gave his name to Port-Louis, which was Lorient's forerunner as the headquarters of the Compagnie des Indes. It lies on the other side of the estuary, and you have to drive almost a full circle to get there. However, it is worth seeing for the enormous scale of its fortifications, and the strange feeling of strength combined with weariness that pervades it. Port-Louis is little more than a great granite wall frowning across the estuary. Built in the mid-seventeenth century, it has remained virtually unchanged ever since. Life has passed it by and moved across the estuary to Lorient.

Auray has had a warlike past for so sleepy and peaceful a town. In 1364 the War of Succession ended with the Battle of Auray which took place outside the town; and more recent bloodshed is commemorated at the Champ des Martyrs a little way to the north. In this quiet tree-surrounded rectangle 952 Royalist prisoners were shot at the end of the Quiberon campaign of 1795 (see page 219). They are commemorated by a small Doric temple, in the sorry state of most monuments of this sort in Brittany. The market bustle of Auray is up at the top of the hill, by the church (yet another church built with defiant stone guns jutting from the walls). An ancient cobbled street leads steeply down to the river and the medieval bridge across it to Saint-Goustan, where a plaque on one of the quay-side houses commemorates the landing of Benjamin Franklin in Auray in December 1776, on his way to Paris to negotiate an alliance between France and the newborn United States. Auray is the centre of a group of artists who call themselves the 'Peintres de Bretagne'. Founded by the painter Annick Eschermann, their aim is to bring Brittany into the mainstream of European art without either cutting their Breton roots or relapsing into provincial folksiness, and their annual summer exhibitions in Auray show that this goal can be achieved by artists of widely different styles, from the abstract to the representational.

When Franklin went from Auray to Vannes he did not have a particularly pleasant journey. He wrote in his journal: 'The carriage was a miserable one, with tired horses, the evening dark, scarce a traveller but ourselves on the road; and to make it more comfortable, the driver stopped near a wood we were to pass through, to tell us that a gang of eighteen robbers infested that wood, who but two weeks ago had robbed and murdered some travellers on that very spot.' Today the same journey takes about twenty minutes. But if the roads have changed beyond recognition since Franklin's day, Vannes itself is not all that different, especially since a major restoration of the old town has got under way. The administrative centre of the Morbihan, Vannes has achieved civic dignity without pomposity. In many ways it is comparable to Quimper, though everything in Vannes

—at least in the medieval part, called 'Intra Muros' (Within the Walls) as at Saint-Malo—is on a much smaller scale. Even the long stretch of medieval wall, complete with towers and machicolations, has been domesticated by a sweep of formal municipal gardening in the drained moat at its foot. There are two surviving gateways of any consequence into the old town, which between them sum up several hundred years of the history of Vannes: at the north end of the walls the sturdy medieval Porte Prison, at present being extensively restored; and at the south end the elegant Renaissance Porte Saint-Vincent, crowned by a statue of the saint with his right hand raised in blessing.

It is strange to find a Spaniard rather than a Breton as the patron saint of one of Brittany's major towns; but St Vincent Ferrier preached at Vannes and died there, and his tomb and reliquary are in the cathedral. The Place Valencia in the heart of old Vannes commemorates the Spanish town where he was born in the 1350s. For decades he preached all over Europe, reuniting the Roman Catholic Church when it was in danger of being torn apart by schism. Père Albert Le Grand lists his apostolic journeys, which covered 'the whole of Spain, the islands of Majorca, Minorca, Sardinia and Sicily, the whole of Italy, most of the German states, the Low Countries, England and France'. St Vincent arrived in Brittany in 1416 and spent some time in Nantes before moving on to Vannes, which he entered 'riding on a bad-tempered donkey' ('*monté sur un meschant asne*'). He refused to lodge with the Duke in the Château d'Hermine, preferring to stay in the house of an ordinary citizen. From Vannes he travelled throughout Brittany, preaching to 'great and small, wise men and fools'. Even though he preached in Spanish, he was understood by the multilingual society of Bretons, French, English, Flemish, Irish, Germans and other nationalities employed by the Dukes of Brittany for their business affairs. Le Grand puts it down to a miracle, but it seems more likely that his travels had made St Vincent an excellent linguist. In April 1419 he became mortally ill at Vannes and died after a short illness, in the presence of the Duchess of Brittany, and mourned by all the people of Vannes and the country round about. Père Albert describes the poetic miracle that accompanied his death. 'All that morning a great number of white butterflies of marvellous beauty were seen to flutter beside the window of his room, and they did not leave until he had rendered up his spirit. The pious believed that it was a flight of angels who, in the guise of these little creatures, waited for the release of his holy soul to escort it to eternal life.'

Vannes Cathedral is a hodgepodge of styles, ranging from the thirteenth-century Romanesque of the north-west tower to the odd circular Tour Renaissance, decorated with pilasters and scallop shells, which was added in the sixteenth century on the north side of the nave. Apart from the tomb and relics of St Vincent, kept in the chapel of the Tour Renaissance, the most remarkable feature of the interior is the Treasury, which is unusually rich in religious objects of all kinds, from an ivory crucifix to a lurid statue of the flayed St Bartholomew, carrying his skin over his arm. The prize rarity is a small wooden marriage casket, decorated with painted scenes of court life in the twelfth century—hawking, jousting, making music, dancing. The colours are still brilliant; and it is thought that the casket came originally from the south, perhaps Aragon or Languedoc. In the thirteenth century it was turned into a reliquary and covered with silver plate, which explains the perfect preservation of the jewel-like scenes.

Opposite the west front of the cathedral is a recently opened covered market, converted from the medieval Salle de Parlement of Vannes. Known as La Cohue ('The Hubbub'), it is full of craftsmen in metal and leather, artists, pancake-sellers and other purveyors to a largely tourist trade. Old Vannes may be in some danger of turning into a mummified tourist trap, since the pedestrianised streets, with cobbles newly relaid, are rapidly filling with trendy boutiques of all sorts. At the moment you can still find nettle-grown stone staircases that will take you on to a forgotten stretch of town wall, and the tumbledown wash-houses by the moat must still look much as they did three centuries ago. But Vannes, like all such picturesque places, is in danger of what in Brittany might be termed 'Locronanisation'—the turning of a working town like Locronan, near Quimper, into a quaint oldeworlde craft centre, with the real life drained out of it.

Meanwhile, the restoration proceeds splendidly, under the guiding eye of the body known as ARIM (Association de

Restauration Immobilière). The Ilot de Restauration covered by the scheme takes in virtually the whole of the old town, from the walls on the east to the wide Rue Thiers on the west. Already the car has been banished from many of the little streets and squares, which are on a toylike scale too small for the internal-combustion engine. The Rue Saint-Salomon, the Rue des Halles, the Rue Noë, the Place Valencia can now be enjoyed in peace and quiet—an object lesson to towns such as Quimper that are doing little about the setting-up of pedestrian areas. In the Rue Noë, not far from the heads of the self-satisfied stone corbel figures of 'Vannes and his Wife', is the museum, an old-fashioned place crammed with relics of the Morbihan's prehistory, and with a huge collection of stuffed birds mouldering away under glass cases.

And so to Redon, the final stop on this lightning circuit of Breton towns. It is worth visiting for one reason alone: for its grand church, all that is left of the medieval monastery of Saint-Sauveur. Above the central crossing rises one of the architectural glories of Brittany—the arcaded Romanesque tower, built in the twelfth century, with dumpy round arches open to the winds. Its unique shape is matched by its stone, which consists of grey granite and dark red sandstone, used at random to give the tower the appearance of a building hewn from natural rock. In complete contrast is the tall Gothic bell tower, which has been isolated from the main church since a disastrous fire in 1780 destroyed most of the nave. Redon has another peculiarity: the railway runs at the very foot of the church, and you may well have to wait for a train to clear the level-crossing before you can walk from car park to church entrance.

CHAPTER XVIII

The First Grenadier

MOST TOWNS IN Brittany of any size and importance have a Place de La Tour d'Auvergne, a Rue de La Tour d'Auvergne, or a Caserne (Barracks) de La Tour d'Auvergne. This sonorous name, typifying French military glory, belonged to a far from typical soldier. An extraordinary blend of the savant, the eccentric and the hero, La Tour d'Auvergne was one of the strangest of the great men produced by Brittany. He was born with the simple surname of Corret in the small town of Carhaix, on December 23, 1743, and christened Théophile-Malo—the second son, and third of the four children who survived to maturity, of Olivier-Louis Corret, a local lawyer. Corret had married a young widow, Jeanne-Lucrèce Salaün, four years previously, and the couple spent most of their family life in a wing of the Château de Kergoat, near Saint-Hernin, a few miles south-west of Carhaix. Théophile-Malo was born in the centre of Carhaix, in a solid stone house just behind the Mairie. He was only five when his father died, and his early upbringing and education were dominated by his single-minded mother, whose sole ambition was for him to become a professional soldier.

The country round Carhaix was not entirely agricultural during the mid-eighteenth century. Two of the villages, Huelgoat and Poullaouen, were centres of lead-mining; and these quiet places, today among the beauty spots of the region, were loud with the noise of pumping engines and glowing at night with the fires of furnaces. A signpost in Poullaouen points down the hill to La Mine, and the workings are still to be seen there, now filled with water. Around them is a wasteland of grey spoil, flattened by the tyres of lorries and surrounded by the cottages of a hamlet called La Vieille Mine. Mignot de Montigny visited the mines in 1752 and remarked on the fact that they were 'almost inaccessible' to vehicles. He also noted that sixty German miners and a German engineer were employed there. Perhaps as young Théophile-Malo, already speaking French and Breton, wandered the streets of Carhaix, he heard the miners chatting in their outlandishly guttural tongue—one of the many languages he was to master in later years.

In 1753 Théophile-Malo entered the Jesuit college at Quimper, with his head full of ideas of future military glory, and with a powerful sense of the fitness of things instilled by his mother—'each one in his place, each one in his rank, each one in the situation appropriate to his position', says his biographer, F. Taldir Jaffrenou. At the college his chief mentor was his uncle, Père Thomas Corret, one of the band of dedicated Jesuits who for the best part of a century had been missionaries in the backlands of Brittany. Thomas instilled in Théophile-Malo a strong religious sense, on top of the powerful sense of duty inspired by his mother. A spiritual descendant of the founding father of the Jesuit missions, Père Julien Maunoir, Père Thomas was an enthusiast for all things Celtic, and preached in Breton at a time when knowledge of the language was a rarity among the educated. Théophile-Malo was a model pupil, always coming either first or second in class.

In 1760 the Breton Parliament expelled the Jesuits from Basse-Bretagne, partly for their political intrigues, and partly for their religious dogmatism, which disturbed the freethinkers among the politicians. Père Thomas retired to Paris, and Théophile-Malo left the Jesuit college. Now aged nearly seventeen, he returned home, to Carhaix and Kergoat. Here he spent three years or more in a restless, uncertain state of mind. Encouraged in dreams of glory by his mother, he read the exploits of Greek and Roman leaders in the classical authors, and also investigated the history of his native town. It might seem that he was drifting into the kind of learned dilettantism common in the eighteenth century. But his ambition for an army career had never left him, though he was twenty-three by the time he embarked on it. In the last decades of the Ancien Régime the French army was as fossilised as other aspects of French life. The only hope of rising to high rank was to go to the Ecole Militaire, in Paris; but Théophile-Malo was a bourgeois, a member of the Third Estate, and the Ecole Militaire was open only to members of the nobility. This exclusiveness was one major reason why the French army was comparatively unsuccessful during the eighteenth century, until the Revolution swept away the old caste system and opened the way to the officers who commanded Napoleon's victorious armies.

The only way of becoming an officer by the back door, so to speak, was to join the Musketeers; and Théophile-Malo prevailed on his uncle, the Jesuit Père Thomas, to use his influence on his behalf. Also the smallest scrap of nobility was better than none at all, and in March 1767 Théophile-Malo persuaded four of his old college friends to testify that he was a '*gentilhomme*' of Brittany, adding a 'de' to his surname of Corret for good measure. Armed with this '*attestation de noblesse*', Théophile-Malo set off for Paris. Here he found that his uncle, by devious means, had managed to get him admitted to the Black Musketeers of the King's Guard, which was the first stepping-stone to becoming a regular officer. He remained a Musketeer for only five months. In the summer of 1767 Colonel de Frémeur, commanding officer of the Angoumois Regiment, asked for Théophile-Malo to be transferred to his command. After some delays permission was granted, and on October 27 he took the oath of loyalty to the King before the War Commissioners, under the amplified name of Théophile-Malo Corret de Kerbauffret. His potential as a soldier must have been obvious, in spite of his complete lack of experience, as he got his commission as *sous-lieutanant* without paying for it—almost unheard of in those days.

He was posted immediately to the south, first to the Pyrenees, then eastward along the Mediterranean coast to Collioure, Perpignan and finally Marseilles. Here he was to stay for six years, until the spring of 1774. From Marseilles he wrote home complaining about his lack of money, saying that he had to sell his watch to buy his uniform and equipment, and commenting on the high rates of pay given to Germans and other foreign officers. A civil brawl was the only action that he saw during his time at Marseilles. One night at the theatre, in January 1774, an officer of the Angoumois was insulted by the audience in the pit. The next night a whole group of officers went to the theatre and were again insulted with the words 'Down with the uniform! Down with the white arses!' The officers drew their swords and the audience fled from the theatre, but on the intervention of the chief of police the play was resumed. When it was over, however, the officers found a mob of three thousand people milling around outside the theatre and had to force their way back to barracks, sword in hand. The only serious injury was to one of the theatre musicians, who broke a leg trying to get away from the uproar. Nevertheless, the Angoumois regiment was confined to barracks, and warrants were taken out against the thirteen officers concerned, Théophile-Malo among them. Shortly afterwards, the Angoumois were posted to Avignon, then to Montauban, in the Tarn-et-Garonne district, where they stayed until 1777. At their next station, Huningue, near Basle, Théophile-Malo was severely wounded in a duel. The cause is not known; but it must have been a foul swordstroke, as it penetrated his thigh and pierced his lower abdomen. As a result, he spent much of the autumn of 1778 taking the waters, and paying out a good deal of money on doctors. On his recovery, he volunteered to go to the United States to serve under Lafayette, but he was turned down.

By 1779 Théophile-Malo was thirty-five, still a lieutenant, and had not seen active service after nearly twelve years with the Angoumois regiment. As he had done in his youth at Carhaix, he read the classics and studied modern languages—English, Spanish, German and even Turkish. But such studies were always peripheral to his main ambition; and he was obviously not going to rise far in the army at the present rate of progress. The answer was to find some blue blood somewhere among his ancestry and to join the select band of the promotable nobility. Ferreting among the archives, he found that an ancestress, Adèle Corret, had been mistress of Duc Henry de Bouillon, Prince de la Tour d'Auvergne, at the beginning of the seventeenth century. So he prepared a detailed family tree proving the genealogy and sent it off to the reigning Duc Godefroy. In October 1779 he had his reply. Far from being indignant at this approach from an unknown and so far undistinguished junior officer, the Duke wrote Théophile-Malo a most affable letter. In it he confirmed the details of the claim, and allowed Théophile-Malo to take both his name and his arms (a tower and a gonfalon or flag, crossed with a bar for bastardy). Théophile-Malo heard the full confirmation of his claim when he was at Guingamp staying with his brother-in-law Limon de

Timeur. For his mother, now old and ailing, this was the culmination of her aristocratic ambitions; but she survived only a month or two and died in her son's arms early in 1780. Théophile-Malo spent the rest of his leave visiting the Duke, who kept semi-royal state in a great house in Normandy, and in trying to get official recognition for his transformation from Corret to La Tour d'Auvergne-Corret.

The following year a detachment of the Angoumois was sent to America, but La Tour d'Auvergne was not included. Instead, still plagued by his duelling wound, he took the waters at Baden-Baden and sold his house in Carhaix to raise the cash. Late in the year a long leave period fell due. Desperate to see some action, he volunteered to spend his leave on attachment to the joint Franco-Spanish expeditionary force sent to recapture Minorca from the English. In October 1781 he sailed from Toulon to Mahon, where the Duc de Crillon, commander-in-chief of the expeditionary force, made him one of his aides. Thus at an age when most junior officers would be thinking of retiring on a pension, La Tour d'Auvergne saw action for the first time. An official account of his exploits on Minorca runs as follows.

> Always in the most dangerous positions, Lieutenant de La Tour d'Auvergne astonished the Spaniards and the English by a hundred proofs of the most brilliant courage. He set alight an English frigate under cannon fire and musket bullets; he set fire to an ammunition dump in the midst of the enemy; while on reconnaissance, he repulsed a surprise English sortie, captured a junior officer and handed him over on the spot to his general. In a skirmish where the Catalans had repulsed the English, a Catalonian volunteer was lying wounded and helpless on the glacis. La Tour d'Auvergne returned alone in the midst of heavy fire, took the man on his shoulders and restored him to the ranks of the Catalans.

Any one of these exploits would have gained Théophile-Malo a medal in later centuries. But he had by-passed the Ministry of War in going to Minorca. The Minister, the Marquis de Ségur, was indignant; and La Tour d'Auvergne received a reprimand from the general in charge of the French forces. In January

1782 he was sent back to France, in spite of the support of the Duc de Crillon; and an interview with Ségur in Paris only made matters worse. He consoled himself by writing philosophically to his sister: 'What has happened to me doesn't surprise me at all. In whatever state to which one is called, if one wants to rise above the mediocre one must expect envy and persecution. That is the natural state of things. But I will not allow my setbacks to weaken the feelings I have always had for my honour and my duty.'

He returned to the Angoumois regiment, now stationed at Strasbourg. Here he studied hard, taking German lessons, drawing and painting, and working on his researches for his proposed book on Celtic origins. He also found time to study the art of fortification in the field. His requests for overseas service were regularly turned down by the Ministry. In 1784 the regiment was posted back to Collioure. Here Théophile-Malo was at last appointed Captain second class (*capitaine de second*), at the age of forty. The years were passing, with little enough achieved, and at the end of 1785 another long sabbatical leave came round. La Tour d'Auvergne was now seriously thinking of retiring. In view of the goodwill he had gained from the Spaniards during his brief period of service with them in Minorca, he decided to spend his leave in Spain. In Madrid he was fêted; he was presented at court, met the Infanta and all the grandees, and in May 1786 was awarded the Cross of Charles III by the King of Spain. An honour he appreciated more was being made a corresponding member of the Madrid Academy of History and Science, in recognition of his growing reputation as a student of comparative languages.

When the Revolution broke out in 1789, with the taking of the Bastille on July 14, the Angoumois regiment was at Bayonne, and La Tour d'Auvergne was on convalescent leave back in Brittany. There is little evidence that he took much notice of the Revolution in its early stages. He must surely have been divided in his loyalties. As a bourgeois who had come into conflict with ancient snobberies he must have been for '*liberté, égalité, fraternité*'; on the other hand, he had sworn his oath of loyalty to the King, and he was the strongest of traditionalists. His hopes for the future are made clear by a letter which he wrote to a high-ranking army friend, on his return to Bayonne in 1790: 'Although I was on the point of abandoning a career which has offered me nothing but heartache and disgust, my spirits have revived since your announcement that patriotism will at last be recognised as an entitlement to esteem and promotion.'

The officer caste saw itself threatened by the Revolution and was on the whole hostile to it. Many of them left France as soon as they could; but those who stayed found their old traditions undermined in a number of ways. By a law of January 1, 1791, regiments lost their names and were given numbers. The Angoumois became the 80th Infantry Regiment of the Line. Then in June the National Assembly made it obligatory for soldiers to swear loyalty to the Constitution rather than the King; the Angoumois, now the 80th, had to do this in April 1792. In June the colonel and fifteen officers of the 80th decided to emigrate and asked La Tour d'Auvergne to join them. He refused, no doubt feeling himself steadily more in sympathy with the aims of the new Republic. At this time the Chouans—the White Russians of their day, anti-Revolutionaries from the Vendée and much of Brittany—held the Morbihan and the southern part of the Côtes-du-Nord. Such was La Tour d'Auvergne's lack of sympathy with their fight for their principles that he referred to them as 'brigands', though many of them were ordinary peasants and townsmen from Basse-Bretagne, as he was himself.

By now he was no longer a plain infantry officer, but had been given the command of the grenadiers of the 80th. In the summer of 1792 he took part in the campaign against the Austrian army in the foothills of the French Alps, round Chambéry and the Mont Cénis Pass. In a suitably egalitarian and patriotic gesture, he did not take advantage of his right to have a horse, but fought on foot, surrendering his forage allowance so that the money could be used to pay for two more infantrymen from Finistère. This act of self-denial was widely publicised in the revolutionary press, and was the starting-point of the La Tour d'Auvergne legend. At the beginning of 1793 it was proposed that he should be made Colonel of the 20th Regiment, but he refused the promotion, preferring to stay with the 80th, which had been his 'family' for nearly thirty years.

In May 1793 France declared war on Spain, which meant

that La Tour d'Auvergne was fighting against many of his Spanish friends and former allies. Nevertheless he fought with his usual efficiency in the defence of Bayonne, and was put in charge of the camp arrangements for the 80th, which were in a deplorable state, without either a quartermaster or a surgeon. In July the post of Lieutenant-Colonel of the 80th became vacant; under the newly established referendum system by which regiments chose their own senior officers, La Tour d'Auvergne received an overwhelming majority of votes. Here again fate intervened, once more coming between Théophile-Malo and a senior command. The following month the old regiments were split up and reorganised into 'Demi-brigades', and La Tour d'Auvergne was assigned with his grenadiers to the 148th. He was posted to the front line, where, says Jaffrenou, 'sleeping on a truss of straw, never undressing, with his uniform in rags, his unconquerable spirit supported his body worn out by the labours of the military profession'. One of La Tour d'Auvergne's friends, recalling the Spanish campaign, described how 'at dawn you would see him, with a book, his pipe and his sabre, keeping the sentries on the alert and watching the movements of the enemy. During the fighting he would carry his old cloak, riddled with bullet holes, over his left arm. It was his banner to rally his men.'

La Tour d'Auvergne, now aged fifty, fought on into 1794. By this time he had lost most of his teeth, perhaps through scurvy, and could no longer eat the army biscuit which formed the French troops' staple food. After the summer's campaign, totally exhausted, he sought leave to retire from the army, to his birthplace at Carhaix. His commanding general wrote in glowing terms: 'I have witnessed the labours, the night watches and the hardships of La Tour d'Auvergne in the front line, and it is with sorrow that I note the exhaustion of his powers, which deprives us of a soldier whose experience and talents have made an immeasurable contribution to the brilliant successes we have achieved.' The Bayonne Representatives of the People gave their assent to his retirement. La Tour d'Auvergne said his farewells to his sorrowing grenadiers, packed his favourite classical authors (Caesar's *Gallic Wars*, Plutarch's *Lives* and the poems of Horace), and left Bayonne to return home. In spite of the rigours of the Spanish campaign, he had managed in

1792 to see through the press the first edition of the book that was to appear a few years later as *Origines Gauloises*, his main testament.

He went first overland to Bordeaux, and embarked there just before Christmas on a ship bound for Brest. But instead of the expected easy passage, the ship was caught in a violent winter storm, with a wind off the land which kept her in the open sea for nearly four weeks, and finally wrecked her on the rocks a few miles from Camaret, almost within sight of Brest. Crew and passengers came safely ashore, but they were immediately picked up by a cruising squadron of five English frigates and taken back to Bodmin. In Cornwall La Tour d'Auvergne felt completely at home. In the gentlemanly style in which eighteenth-century warfare was conducted, he was a prisoner on parole, and was even allowed to wear his uniform and keep his sword. He talked to Cornish-speakers, took copious notes of the similarities between their speech and that of the Welsh and the Bas-Bretons, rummaged around in public libraries, and sketched out the plan of a French-Celtic dictionary.

That the old soldier was far from submerged in the scholar is shown by an encounter that took place in the countryside round Bodmin. One day in October 1795 La Tour d'Auvergne was returning from a walk when he ran into a squad of English soldiers. Infuriated both by his French uniform and by the tricolour cockade in his hat, some of the soldiers attacked him and tried to snatch the cockade from him. Whereupon he drew his sword, stuck the cockade on the end of it, and shouted to the soldiers, in English, 'Come and take it!' Wisely, no doubt, in the face of this furious, toothless, sword-waving Frenchman, the English soldiers did not pursue the matter; but La Tour d'Auvergne was sufficiently incensed to put in a complaint to the local magistrate.

The following January he was exchanged for an English officer of similar rank, and went to Paris, where he set up house in the suburb of Passy. He continued with his Celtic researches, and used the force of his reputation to get things done for his fellow-Bretons, including improvements to the harbour at Audierne. Then followed one of the most extraordinary episodes of his career. In 1797 an old friend and mentor in Celtic matters, Jacques Le Brigant, retired and living in

Tréguier, asked him to use his influence to get his last surviving son out of the army. The only way La Tour d'Auvergne could do this was to find a replacement for the boy, and the best replacement he could think of was himself. In his letter to the Minister for War he was blunt about his infirmities. Asking that 'Citizen La Tour d'Auvergne-Corret' should be allowed to serve out his retirement attached to the infantry, he continued: 'The entire absence of his top teeth, and the fact that his lower ones only hang by a thread, means that he can no longer pronounce clearly enough to give orders. He only asks for the position of ordinary volunteer, and to relieve one of his brothers-in-arms.' He was assigned to the Rhine army and spent the rest of 1797 there. But in spite of this gesture, Le Brigant's son had to stay with the colours.

The next spring La Tour d'Auvergne visited his beloved Brittany for the last time, to make final arrangements for retirement to the village of Trémargat, near Carhaix. Here, in the manor-house of Lampoul-Izella, he had a room made ready with 'a large box-bed, a cupboard, a table, three wooden chairs, a spit and two firedogs'—everything in fact that an ordinary Breton would need. But he was never to enjoy the austere ease of retirement in the hills and woodlands around Trémargat. In April 1799 he rejoined the army as a volunteer, was promoted Captain First Class, and fought in Switzerland. In the autumn, at the end of the Swiss campaign, he was planning to return to Brittany for good, 'to see my fireside, to live in the cottage I still possess, and to choose my last resting-place near my cradle'. But once more Le Brigant intervened in La Tour d'Auvergne's plans, with yet another request: that an appeal should be made to Napoleon for the release of his son.

La Tour d'Auvergne did not write to Napoleon asking directly for the boy's release. Instead, he volunteered for a third term of duty as a replacement. On April 27, 1800, he received the following notice from Napoleon: 'Bonaparte, First Consul of the Republic, in reply to the proposal of the Minister of War, decrees: the Defender of the Fatherland La Tour d'Auvergne is named First Grenadier of the Armies of the Republic. He will be granted a sabre of honour.' This act of public recognition was a source of great embarrassment to Théophile-Malo, who was an essentially modest man. He insisted that he was not the '*premier*' grenadier, but merely the '*plus ancien*'. Also he was worried about losing the goodwill of his fellow-grenadiers through the imputation that he was in some way more courageous than they were. It is more than likely that the granting of the title was a propaganda move by Napoleon and his War Minister, Carnot. At any rate, Jaffrenou refers to the demoralised state of the French army at this moment in 1800: La Tour d'Auvergne was to be sent to the front as a morale-booster. He seems to have had presentiments that this campaign was to be his last, writing that 'my destiny is to die on a battlefield. This title of First Grenadier is my death warrant.'

In June he set out from Paris for Basle, and from there joined the grenadiers of the 46th Demi-brigade in the Rhine Palatinate, where France, Germany and Switzerland meet. From Dettingen on June 27 he sent home his last letter to an old friend, written 'seated on a drum and in haste. The grenadiers of the 46th, who form the advance guard, are at this moment about to advance, I think towards Ingolstadt. . . . I have received the most flattering welcome from all my brave brothers-in-arms, and from all the generals and officers of the army. My joy is at its height.' That evening, three columns of the French army, including two battalions of the 46th, attacked the Austrians. The commanding officer of the 46th, Colonel Forty, and La Tour d'Auvergne were both killed before Oberhausen, near Neuberg in Bavaria. The French general's report stated that 'the First Grenadier of France died from a lance thrust through the heart'; but autopsy revealed the heart intact. Death had come from the violence of a blow to the rib cage of a mortally exhausted man. The following day the general commanding the Army of the Rhine issued orders that, to honour La Tour d'Auvergne, 'first, the drums of the grenadier companies of the whole army will be covered with black crêpe for three days. Second, the name of La Tour d'Auvergne will be kept at the head of the roll-call of the 46th Demi-brigade, where he chose to serve. His vacancy will never be filled.' Before burial, the heart was removed from the body, embalmed, placed in a casket and hung from the standard of the 46th. Then La Tour d'Auvergne, Colonel Forty and two unknown soldiers were buried outside Oberhausen, and a monument was erected over them.

Stripped of the trappings of revolutionary figurehead and heroic single-minded soldier, is it possible to get more than a shadowy idea of what La Tour d'Auvergne was actually like? A plate at the front of the 1801 edition of his *Origines Gauloises* shows a face not without humour, with an aquiline nose, short upper lip and the beginnings of a double chin. In many ways he was not a typical man of the eighteenth century, but a throwback to the Middle Ages, a Templar or Knight of St John, a man without ties of family or property, religious, ascetic, patient in all the disappointments that marked his early career. There seem to have been no women in Théophile-Malo's life; though Jaffrenou mentions, without much conviction, a lifelong unfulfilled love for his sister-in-law, who became a nun. As for his apparent lack of ambition, it is strange that a man with such a talent for the art of war should have been content to advance no further than captain, even refusing a colonelcy when it was offered to him. Yet there have always been those who have preferred the role of brilliant subordinate to the often thankless task of leadership.

Nor is La Tour d'Auvergne's magnum opus—the *Origines Gauloises, celles des Plus Anciens Peuples de l'Europe, puisées dans leur Vraie Source*, to give it its full title—particularly revealing about its author's character. It is a worthy piece of late-eighteenth-century antiquarian research, pushing Celtic origins back to the ancient Scythians and beyond, and with an amazing number of languages quoted, from Catalan to Frisian and from Icelandic to Persian. There are occasional glimpses of La Tour d'Auvergne at work, as when he describes his investigations into the thickness of skulls of Bretons. Writing of an operation he witnessed at Bayonne on a Breton sailor who had fallen head first into the hold of his ship, he says that this man's skull was six times thicker than an ordinary skull. When the wound was opened up, 'not the slightest fracture was visible, not even a hairline crack'.

One myth about La Tour d'Auvergne, constantly repeated in accounts about him, is that he believed that Adam and Eve spoke Breton in the Garden of Eden. This would make him out to be a complete idiot, even by eighteenth-century antiquarian standards, and he was certainly far from that. Here is what he actually said in the *Origines Gauloises*: '*Eva* and *Adam*, these words seem to be purely Celtic. They are the first words that emerge from the mouths of Breton children, when they want to have their most pressing natural needs satisfied: with the word *eva* our children ask for drink, and with *adam* they ask for food.' To say that Breton has the words *adam* and *eva* for eat and drink is by no means the same as saying that Adam and Eve spoke Breton. The *Origines Gauloises* is rarely lyrical, but there is one passage where La Tour d'Auvergne links the Welsh and the Bretons in an inspiring outburst.

> Glory and love of country, the sublime exaltation of freedom —these emotions suited to inspire courage have often placed weapons in their hands, to decide whether they should live as free men or vegetate as slaves. . . . Many nations famous for their conquests and for reducing men to slavery have disappeared, swallowed up by other empires; and we have felt no sorrow for their passing. But we are moved by the misfortunes and fate of a peace-loving people, who, content with the sterile soil of their birth, with their forests and mountains marked out by nature as the last refuge of their freedom, have defended their own peace without ever seeking to violate or trouble that of others.

At Carhaix, La Tour d'Auvergne is commemorated by a heroic-looking statue in one of the main squares; the sides of the plinth are decorated with relief panels of his exploits. When I saw the statue, it was concealed by the caravans and dodgem-car tents of a travelling fair, but I finally ran it to earth behind a caravan filled with electronic equipment. The electrician pronounced it '*magnifique*', and indeed it is. More personal relics are kept in the Mairie, under a glass case, gothically shaped and gilded like a medieval reliquary—two buttons from La Tour d'Auvergne's uniform, a lock of his hair (brown, not grey or white as I would have expected), a canine tooth. When I remarked that it was all rather reminiscent of a dead saint, the official who showed me the relics said that the old grenadier was a kind of lay saint—'*un saint laïque, si vous voulez*'. And every year, on the anniversary of his death, Carhaix holds a miniature festival of a religious service followed by Breton games, to celebrate the most uncompromisingly Breton of her sons.

CHAPTER XIX

The German Occupation

ANYONE WHO HAS spent even an afternoon on the Breton coast will have noticed the inescapable relics of the German Occupation in the Second World War. Every curving beach has its grinning concrete gunslits at either end, sometimes with rusty rails for the guns to run on, and occasionally even with the dilapidated carcass of a gun. Among the heather and gorse of any clifftop you will find concrete platforms and rabbit warrens of tunnels cut into the rock, with here and there what appears to be a ruined cottage, but is actually a strongpoint cunningly camouflaged to look like part of the scenery. On Cap Fréhel I have found sloping ramps leading down to silos, which presumably were launching platforms for flying bombs or rockets; and everywhere these thousands of tons of concrete represent toil and application on a scale unmatched by more ancient landmarks. Churches and menhirs were set in place over centuries, or millennia; but these brutal relics of a barbarian invasion were built in a matter of months, as the new conquerors strove to make impregnable the seaward frontiers of the thousand-year Reich. Today here and there gun emplacements are being adapted as country homes, like the Martello towers along our own south coast, and they must be the most solid residences anywhere in the world. To get an idea of the fortress-like permanence of the gun emplacements you need go no further than the ring road outside Saint-Malo, where the procession of concrete domes still dominates the half-country, half-town of tumbledown farms and suburban super-markets.

After circumventing the Maginot Line in 1940 with contemptuous ease, it might seem surprising that the Germans put their trust in defences of such a conventional nature. In the event, the Atlantic Wall, of which the Brittany section formed a major part, led to an immense deployment of valuable troops spread thinly along hundreds of miles of coastline, with nothing to do, and constantly harassed by a population that grew more defiant, aggressive and well organised as the months and years went by. After the fall of France in June 1940, the prevailing French mood was one of dazed shock—an atmosphere hardly conducive to organised resistance. The nuclei of the later Resistance groups, in Brittany as in the rest of France, came from the members of the defeated French army, either escaped prisoners-of-war or disbanded army units.

Though the Germans must surely have been expecting some kind of organised opposition in other parts of France, one gets the impression that they were surprised and even somewhat hurt to encounter it in Brittany. For during the 1930s, and even before Hitler's accession to power in 1933, there had been contacts between the nationalists in Germany and the separatists in Brittany; and after the Nazis took control these links were strengthened. Among the more extreme Breton elements, the secret society Gwenn ha Du, which in 1932 was responsible for blowing up the controversial statue in Rennes depicting Brittany kneeling at the feet of France, was overtly pro-Nazi; and a leading Breton nationalist, Célestin Lainé, went so far as to found a Breton 'army', known as the Bezenn Perrot, for the purpose of expelling the French from Brittany. Misled by the closeness of such untypical contacts with Brittany, the Germans expected to be hailed as liberators releasing the Bretons from a bondage that had lasted since the Act of Union with France in 1532. But instead of a welcome of any kind, they found a resistance more closely knit and implacable than virtually anywhere else in France.

True to form, the German propaganda machine had provided all the ingredients for a successful brainwashing of an occupied area; but equally true to form it utterly failed to understand that, though a Breton disliked being told what to do by a Frenchman, he would categorically refuse to do what a German told him, even if that German offered him autonomy. And the Bretons' suspicion of the Germans' friendly advances were fully justified. In his book *The Germans in France*, Jacques Lorraine analyses the German attitude to racial minorities such as the Celts, and finds that in the long run they were marked down for the treatment meted out to the Jews—in other words, ultimate disappearance from the face of the New Europe. An autonomous Brittany might have existed for a while, but sooner or later it would have been assimilated and the country resettled by members of the 'master race'.

Lorraine describes the various ways in which the invaders tried to buy Breton complaisance. 'Breton officers and soldiers, when taken prisoner, were not sent to Germany; they remained on the spot, in improvised camps, where their mothers and wives could visit them; they had the option between freedom, if they adhered to the Autonomist movement, and captivity in Germany if they were adamant.' Only a month after the Occupation had started, a weekly separatist newspaper, called *L'Heure Bretonne*, was brought out under the German aegis. Here again Breton reactions had been completely misjudged. Instead of welcoming the paper now that the Breton hour had come, no one read it, and even the journalists who worked for it were too shamefaced to write under their own names but all used pseudonyms. Throughout Brittany, says Lorraine, 'people were not satisfied to boo newspaper-sellers, to hoot them down or to tear their papers; but they retaliated by singing the *Marseillaise*, by acclaiming France under the very eyes of the invaders whose bewilderment was almost too comical to behold'. In view of the obvious lack of enthusiasm for out-and-out separatism, the Germans abandoned it and opted for some kind of regionalism for Brittany, but this found no welcome either. They proposed to teach the Breton language in schools, which was one of the planks of the Breton resurgence; but the Bretons staunchly refused to accept the teaching of their language under German domination. Finally the Germans gave up this fruitless hearts-and-minds struggle, and treated Brittany no differently from the other occupied territories.

The most illuminating account I have come across of what it was actually like to be in Brittany when France fell and the Germans took over is not by a Breton, not even by anybody French, but by an American writer, Ida Treat. Married to a French merchant-navy captain, she lived on the Ile de Bréhat, at the northernmost tip of Brittany (though the island is unnamed, it is easy enough to identify); and her book *Rock of France*, written and published in the blackest days of the war, is a celebration of the unconquerable spirit of her adopted country. It meticulously chronicles the day-to-day life of the islanders, as the quiet pattern of their days is interrupted first by the distant rumours of war, then by the bewildered presence of French soldiers, ill-organised and ill-armed, and finally by the troops of the occupying power. Because of her American citizenship, Ida Treat managed to leave Brittany at the beginning of 1941, before the Resistance had taken on any well-organised form; but she depicts the gradual hardening of local attitudes to the invader that provided the broad basis from which the movement sprang.

At the outset, the Bretons of her island were as confused as everyone else by the events of Munich, the German invasions of Czechoslovakia and Poland, and the vacillation of politicians on both sides of the Channel. The unpreparedness of the French army in the 'phony war' of 1939–40—'*drôle de guerre*', the French called it—was terrifying. The troops sent to guard the island arrived in a pathetic state of unmilitary disarray, though no doubt it was not the crack troops who were posted to obscure corners of the Breton coast. 'Out in the lane the Sergeant's men had finished unloading the cart and sat smoking in the grass. Nearly all wore wooden sabots and their ordinary clothes, though some had added a vague military touch—a leg-band, a broad leather belt and here and there a *képi* (military cap). One little fellow had on a pair of stained and patched horizon-blue breeches, much too big, that bagged about his bare calves like plus-fours. Their uniforms, it seemed, were "somewhere on the way", together with their blankets and their cotton sleeping-bags.'

France's surrender in June was a traumatic experience for the islanders, who waited in trepidation for the invaders to appear. When they finally crossed over from the mainland, it was an anticlimax. In Ida Treat's case, the first signs of occupation came in the form of 'two blond Aryans, with boots like mirrors; they spoke beautiful French, were stiffly courteous, played with the dog, and made polite remarks about the view.' Her account of the way in which the Germans attempted to establish contact with the islanders shows how high-level orders to fraternise were translated into blundering reality by the troops in the field.

> In the village, people affirmed that the men in green were making efforts to be as unobnoxious as possible. Some had

even been known to buy butter at their own canteen for the family in whose house they were quartered. Children said the soldiers were always giving them candy. It appeared they had orders to establish 'friendly contacts' with the Bretons. They made use of a method that was directness itself. Village folk told us the soldiers walked into their houses with the aplomb of expected guests, sat down without being asked and stayed until they felt like leaving. As the 'host' spoke no German, they carried on conversations among themselves, or improved their French vocabulary by pointing at objects and demanding the French word for them. They were disconcertingly at home. . . . They beamed on the sullen Bretons, were ready to kiss every girl and drink brotherhood with every Frenchman.

These would-be friendly troops were the first wave of Germans—men in their late twenties and thirties, with memories of pre-Hitlerian years. They were followed by younger men of the Hitler Youth vintage, the hardline Nazis who believed implicitly in the Führer and the rightness of all his works. It was at this time that the Germans were nicknamed the Colorado beetles, the *doryphores* who laid the country waste. 'It was no idle epithet. They had stripped the land to the bone. The shops were empty, the cellars dry. In a rich dairy region butter, cheese and eggs had become rare, even rarer than they were in the Reich. What still was left to us they hunted out and devoured.' Yet paradoxically, as the Germans battened on the countryside and the Bretons prepared for a long ordeal by shortage and hunger, the realisation came to them that the invader was not invincible. On the island the troops prepared for the invasion of England, and were seasick. Months went by, and the expected easy victory never materialised; British planes dared to fly over France and bomb the Fatherland; and there were even cases of suicide among the depressed soldiers. The Bretons, says Ida Treat, 'had made an important discovery: stripped of its steel, the German mailed fist was only a flesh-and-blood hand after all'. Her book closes on this note of a faint glimmer of hope—a hope that was to inspire the Resistance movement in the bitter years ahead.

The Resistance proper began on June 18, 1940, four days

after the Germans entered Paris, and the day after Marshal Pétain surrendered. That evening de Gaulle made his famous broadcast appeal from London to his demoralised fellow-countrymen: 'Whatever happens, the flame of resistance must not and shall not be extinguished' ('*Quoi qu'il arrive, la flamme de la résistance ne doit pas s'éteindre et ne s'éteindra pas*'). The French response took two forms. Able-bodied men within striking distance of the coast made their way across the Channel and joined de Gaulle in England, to form the nucleus of the Free French forces; while those who were not prepared to cut all their ties but nevertheless wished to continue the struggle stayed behind and made the first tentative efforts towards setting up a Resistance organisation.

Those who left France mainly slipped away surreptitiously in small groups; but in contrast were the tough fishermen of the Ile de Sein, who left the island *en masse* immediately after de Gaulle's appeal. You can see Sein lying low on the water west of the Pointe du Raz—so low, in fact, that the houses look as though they are virtually afloat. In his monumental three-volume history, *La Bretagne dans la Guerre*, Hervé le Boterf describes this unprecedented mass exodus.

> What was most remarkable was not perhaps the fact that all the able-bodied men chose to go, but that they only took this decision after having calmly discussed it in public with the important men of the island. . . . Sein was without doubt the only village in France where the mayor, the priest, the teacher, the doctor and the president of the ex-servicemen's association met together in conclave to discuss the appeal of June 18 and to adopt a position dependent on that message. It was unanimously decided that each man should heed this call to voluntary mobilisation. On Sunday, June 23, at sermon-time during high mass, the *recteur* climbed the pulpit and proclaimed to the faithful: 'Today, my brethren, France appeals to you from London. Make sure that you answer her call (*Sachez lui répondre*).'

The first boat left the next evening, with fifty men aboard. The whole population of the island came to see them off, the *recteur* blessed them and the assembly sang the *Marseillaise*.

Then they slipped quietly across the Channel to Cornwall. Further boats followed two days later, bringing the number up to about 130. These extraordinary men, who had left parents, wives and children behind them on the island, found their way into the quotation books when de Gaulle reviewed the first Free French contingent of 500 men in the Empire Hall a fortnight or so later; seeing that one in every four came from the island, he made the classic comment '*Sein est donc le quart de la France*' ('So Sein is one quarter of France').

In the early days of the Occupation, when France was divided into occupied and unoccupied zones, the embryo Resistance had a comparatively easy time, as hunted members could always slip across the demarcation line with forged papers into the Vichy-controlled area, and either go into hiding or escape to England via Spain or Switzerland. But in November 1942 the Germans occupied the whole of France, and conditions changed abruptly. There was nowhere left in France for a hunted Resistance man to hide; and in 1943 the renegade French Milice (Militia) was set up, with one of its prime purposes to infiltrate Resistance units and betray their members to the Gestapo. However, the altered conditions of the Occupation and the increasing number of reprisals, far from discouraging the Resistance fighters, merely strengthened their opposition, and led them to tighten up their own organisation and make it more efficient. In the coastal regions, and in Brittany especially, a focus was given to their activities by the building of the Atlantic Wall, which was given priority by Hitler after a series of major conferences with his generals in August 1942. Hitler's idea was to prevent the creation of a second front in the West while he concentrated on defeating the Russians in the East. The vulnerability of the Atlantic seaboard to attack had been proved by the Allied Commando raid on Saint-Nazaire in March 1942; and all the resources of Teutonic efficiency went into the completion of the Wall. The task of getting together the hundreds of thousands of construction workers—not just from France but from the whole of Europe—was given to the Todt organisation, so called after an industrialist whose name has sinister connotations with the German *Tod*, meaning death. It is even rumoured—though it would no doubt be hotly denied in the areas concerned—that a number of Bretons from the south of the country made a fortune selling sand to the Germans to turn into concrete. The workers included a contingent of Moroccans, who, says Le Boterf, turned the dyke-intersected marshlands of Brittany's Grande Brière into an odd approximation to an African lake-dwellers' settlement.

The Atlantic Wall—something of a misnomer, as it was more a series of interlinked strongpoints than a continuous fortification—was one of the most staggering construction efforts of modern times. Le Boterf sees it as something novel in the field of large-scale fortification; and rightly, as it left the Maginot and Siegfried Lines far behind in the immensity of its scale. It represented, as he says, 'a new style of architecture, at the same time both cubist and military, whose basic elements were the bunker and the blockhouse. . . . The crops, still green, were cut and the fields mown to make way for wide ditches. Later on, an artificial vegetation of *chevaux de frise*, of concrete pyramids, of metal stakes and wooden posts—the famous "Rommel asparagus"—took the place of the rustling branches of the pines and birches. The granite rocks, which the ocean had not succeeded in broaching over the centuries, staggered under the impact of high explosive, like drunken louts coming out of a bar.' A strange choice for an outburst of near-lyricism, one might think; but the Atlantic Wall was in its way as remarkable an achievement as Hadrian's Wall, even perhaps as the Great Wall of China itself.

When it was completed, the Wall was garrisoned by between 300,000 and 350,000 men, with another 150,000 engaged in its supply and servicing. The harassment of men and materials offered enormous scope to the Resistance, who took full advantage of their opportunities. In common with their colleagues elsewhere in France, their activities were largely controlled from London, and were set in motion by clandestine code messages from the BBC. The co-ordinating body in London was the SOE (Special Operations Executive); while the Resistance itself was composed of two separate organisations, the FFI (French Forces of the Interior, or Forces Françaises de l'Intérieur), and the FTP (Francs-Tireurs et Partisans, *franc-tireur* literally meaning a 'free-shooter', after an irregular corps of infantry dating from the time of the

French Revolution). As in other countries, such as Yugoslavia, with an effective resistance movement split into various parts, the FFI and FTP did not always see eye to eye. The FFI regarded themselves as descendants of the Chouans, who had been against the Revolution and for King and Church; whereas the FTP were Communist-dominated and considered themselves a workers' army. On the whole the FFI were older and were led by naval and army officers, lawyers and other professional men. They were in favour of organisation, of hideouts in farms or woods, which were easier to control but also easier to discover. The FTP, on the other hand, were the true *maquis*, men of the open field and hedgerow, who would strike and then vanish without trace—guerrilla fighters of no fixed abode, who regarded the FFI as over-structured and inflexible in its approach to new conditions of warfare. No doubt also class ideology entered into the mutual suspicion of the two groups.

In addition to units devoted to harassment and sabotage, the Resistance ran a number of *réseaux d'évasion* (escape networks), whose task was to organise the 'rat-run' across the Channel of Allied airmen who had been shot down over enemy territory, or escaped from prisoner-of-war camps. Nowhere were the *réseaux* more resourceful than in the Guingamp and Saint-Brieuc area, with its hundreds of creeks and harbours facing across the Channel towards England. North of Plouha, half way up the Bay of Saint-Brieuc, a forbiddingly stony beach was the site of the most successful of all these secret operations. Now called the Plage Bonaparte, until 1944 it was known by the prosaic name of the Anse Cochat (Cochat Cove). It requires some effort of the imagination to visualise the beach in its war-time loneliness, as there is now a large car park behind it, and a tunnel has been burrowed through the rock to give easy access to the foreshore. An inscription at the mouth of the tunnel describes how, between January and August 1944, 135 Allied airmen shot down over France 'embarked in secret for England on dark nights'—airmen whose recovery at this crucial stage of the war was vitally important for the successful liberation of Europe. There is also a clifftop monument high up above the beach, a simple granite menhir inscribed '*A la Gloire de Tous les Réseaux d'Evasion*'. The rescue operation was given the code name Bonaparte, and the message that a lift-off would be taking place from the beach was transmitted by the BBC through the code sentence '*Bonjour à tous dans la maison d'Alphonse*'. On receipt of the message, the members of the escape network code-named Shelburn would collect a group of up to twenty-five airmen from the houses where they were hidden singly or in small groups and marshall them at a small cottage on the clifftop—the '*maison d'Alphonse*' of the message.

La Maison d'Alphonse is the title of a book by the French writer Rémy (Gilbert Renault), who was himself a leading figure in the Resistance movement and had his own escape network elsewhere in France. His book takes the form of a long series of linked interviews with the veterans of Shelburn, and conveys in a matter-of-fact, conversational way what it was actually like for the farmers and housewives, the priests and teachers who sheltered the airmen from one day to the next (*hébergeur* or *hébergeuse* was the name for those who gave asylum), and who risked almost certain torture and death at the hands of the Gestapo if they were caught, or even suspected. What emerges is the virtually hundred-per-cent backing for the Resistance in this corner of Brittany, and the seemingly casual way in which people would be asked to take in airmen for what might be a lengthy stay.

With the undercurrent of gossip that permeates village life, the *hébergeurs* found it hard to keep secret the fact that they were hiding someone under their roof; but in the whole of Rémy's long book there was only one traitor, who went by the ironically patriotic nickname of Roger le Légionnaire. Yet though there must have been countless opportunities for betrayal, the dour Bretons kept their own counsel. At times it became a matter of taking the local police into their confidence, as by virtue of their uniform they were working together with the Germans, if not actively for them; but here again confidence was never misplaced. The airmen often grew restive at their close confinement, perhaps in an attic or a barn, and the *hébergeurs* had their difficulties—with a couple of Poles, who had to have a bottle of brandy every day to keep them indoors, or with the Indian pilot who found time to acquire a *petite amie* when he was hiding in Gourin. The Abbé Boulbain, one of the Shelburn leaders, told Rémy of his sympathy with the problems of the Allied airmen.

> I had a lot of admiration for those lads, who had known the terror of being shot down and baling out over unknown country swarming with Germans, and who came to us after being hustled from one lodging to another, sometimes wounded. It's true that those who gave them asylum ran great risks, but the airmen needed great patience and trust, shut up in house after house, not knowing a word of our language for the most part, unable to answer ignorant passers-by who tried to engage them in conversation, uprooted from shelter to shelter, often taken into the woods without the possibility of any explanation.

Once the message had got through from the BBC that an operation was on for a particular night, there remained the difficulty of assembling the airmen and getting them down to the Plage Bonaparte—a difficulty made ten times worse when the message was followed after an interval by '*Denise, ta soeur est morte*', meaning that the operation had been cancelled. Each *réseau* man would have the job of rounding up two or three airmen and taking them to the rendezvous at the Maison d'Alphonse. There could be unexpected complications: when for example a giant American of six feet five had to be crammed into clothes made for a Breton farmer a foot shorter and ten inches more round the waist, and had then to be smuggled in broad daylight through fields and across roads constantly under patrol. Assuming that all had gone smoothly, the airmen would be shepherded through the minefield at the top of the cliff and down the steep path on to the beach, to wait for the dinghies to take them off. The Plage Bonaparte was not a safe place from which to signal the English corvette carrying out the operation, as the jutting Pointe de la Tour a little to the north was the site of a German outpost. So the French signalled that they were ready by means of a blue lamp in a cardboard tube, and made sure that the Germans could not see them by placing it inside a cave. Simultaneously a man hidden half-way up the cliff flashed the letters B (for Bonaparte) or H (as an alternative) out to sea.

The tense excitement of those vigils on the beach is brilliantly conveyed by one of the veterans Rémy interviewed.

> Job (Joseph Mainguy) and Tarzan (Pierre Huet) were in on all the operations. You remember, eh? The steady blue lamp at the bottom of the cliff far back in the cave, and you, Job, with the torch with which you flashed the letters B or H in Morse? The dinghies suddenly arriving, without anyone hearing them, with four English sailors in each? The password 'Dinan-Saint-Brieuc', and the sailors unloading weapons, food, cigarettes, jerrycans of petrol, tyres, all in big suitcases. The airmen leaving, sometimes slipping into your pocket a message to be read when you got back to the Maison d'Alphonse: 'Long live France! Trust in us! We'll be back!' The dinghies rowed off, making for freedom, but you had to head back towards the Germans, with your heavy loads, climbing the sheer cliff. At the top, it was the minefield again, the white rags to be picked up so that the patrols did not spot them during the day, while the corvette, waiting for the airmen two or three miles offshore, made for England. Do you know what the English called this operation, because it went so smoothly? The Channel bus service!

Life with the *réseau* had its lighter moments. There was, for example, the Guingamp dentist, a member of the Resistance, who experimented with various anaesthetics on his German patients until he hit on the drug now known as pentothal, the 'truth drug'. By using this on the local Gestapo commanding officer, he was able not only to find out the plans for forthcoming operations in the area, but also to get himself a pass (*Ausweis*) to travel freely around the countryside. But membership of any branch of the Resistance, either as organiser of escapes or as a fighter with the maquis, was for the most part a dogged, patient business, with the certainty of death, either by firing squad or the medieval method of decapitation, if you were caught. To minimise the risks from a captured Resistance member breaking down under torture, the various *réseaux* operated on the principle of '*cloisonnement*', or 'partitioning', which meant not only that one *réseau* knew next to nothing about the work of any other, but that members of the same *réseau* were only given the minimum amount of information to enable them to carry out their work. Rémy quotes from a document of the time that lays down guidelines for setting up a branch of the Armée Secrète (AS for short), the Resistance fighters' own name for themselves. After naming six officers, it goes on: 'It is taken as read that the NCOs alone will know the officers, and that the NCOs will only be known by the junior NCOs. Then comes the problem of recruitment, which is turning out to be easy. Certain people . . . can each bring in 50 to 60 men. They will be organised in districts. Contacts will be extended. . . . The whole business is spreading fast, and according to the officers the morale among the young men is tremendous (*l'esprit des jeunes est épatant*).'

And not only the *esprit des jeunes*: *La Maison d'Alphonse* breathes a spirit of triumphant conquest of enormous odds among young and old, men and women. Over and over again Rémy's interviews end with an affirmation that, in spite of everything, those were good times to be alive. In the words of Mme Cellarié, who at one time found herself looking after fourteen airmen: 'That was a period when you didn't laugh every day. But at least, you were alive! They could have asked anything of us!'

Apart from the organised *réseaux*, there were countless deeds of heroism carried out by ordinary sailors from every harbour of Brittany. In Camaret's Tour Vauban museum is a model of a fishing smack with a proud if slightly idiomatic inscription: 'Many allied airfighters, crashed in France during Second World War have been driven in Great Britain by the ship *Suzanne-Renée* and her valorious crew.' And the same story was repeated a thousand times along Brittany's rugged coastline.

From the start of the Occupation, acts of sabotage had been followed by reprisals, which grew more merciless as the war progressed and Germany's defeat was seen to be inevitable. The most notorious reprisal of the early days took place in October 1941, when forty-eight Bretons (twenty-one from Nantes and twenty-seven from Châteaubriant) were shot in reprisal for the killing of Colonel Holtz, the Nantes garrison commander. On an inside wall of the castle (now the *Sous-préfecture*) at Châteaubriant is a large inscribed stone stating that the bodies of the town's twenty-seven murdered hostages were laid there after death; while in Nantes the Cours des Cinquante Otages commemorates all forty-eight *maquisards*. (The number has been rounded up from forty-eight to fifty for simplicity's sake, I was told. But the tall copper monument beside the River Erdre has the correct tally of names carved at its foot.) Between 1941 and 1944 the mayors of five Breton towns were shot as hostages—those of Concarneau, Plomeur, Saint-Pol-de-Léon, Huelgoat and Lanriec. Quimper was a hotbed of Resistance activities, organised largely from one of the town's main schools, the Lycée La Tour d'Auvergne. Though the school was partly occupied by Germans, it managed to include among its unofficial extras such subjects as printing clandestine leaflets and blowing up railway lines. Many of the schoolboys took part in the Resistance, and a number of them were caught and shot out of hand during the final days of the Occupation. Fittingly enough, Quimper's main open space is now called the Place de la Résistance. Such street names can be multiplied a hundredfold in towns large and small, from the Rue des Fusillés in Rennes to the Place des Résistants et Fusillés in Le Faou.

From the beginning of 1944, as the preliminaries for Operation Overlord (code name for the Allied invasion of France) got under way, the Resistance stepped up its attacks, and the Germans intensified their reprisals. Not for nothing does Hervé le Boterf call his account of 1944 the Year of Blood (*L'Année du Sang*). His pages dealing with butcheries, beatings to death, rapes and mutilations by the Germans themselves, by the renegades of the Milice, and by Russians from Georgia fighting for the Germans, make numbing reading. The reprisal orders given to the German troops were threefold: to carry out immediate reprisals, even if the innocent were made to suffer; to arrest all civilians in the immediate area of an act of sabotage; and to burn the houses of suspects. Some of the barbarities listed by Le Boterf could only have been perpetrated by men who were literally insane. A sixteen-year-old baker's apprentice who made bread for the *maquisards* was thrown alive into his own oven; while eight Resistance fighters of Pluvigner had their legs and backbones broken with iron bars to the accompaniment of a dance played on the accordion. Such episodes might be regarded as occasional aberrations by panicky troops in the field. But the Germans also had their regular interrogation and execution centres for members of the Resistance, where mock trials were held to give a semblance of legality. Right up to their final defeat the Nazis refused to treat the *maquisards* as legitimate prisoners-of-war, even after they had taken their proper place as recognised members of the Allied forces. One such death centre was the citadel of Port-Louis, where excavations in 1945 brought to light three ditches containing the bodies of sixty-nine Resistance men, who had been tortured and mutilated before death.

In Brittany, as elsewhere in France, the Resistance came fully into the open two days before D-Day (June 6, 1944), known to the French as '*Le Jour J*'. On June 4 the *maquisards*—eventually they numbered over 30,000 in Brittany, opposed to 150,000 German troops—were unleashed by messages from the BBC. '*Il fait chaud à Suez*' ('It's warm in Suez') was the signal for overt sabotage; while '*Les dés sont sur le tapis*' ('The dice have been cast') was the order for all-out combat. The Bretons had their own ambiguous message, '*La flèche ne percera pas*' ('The arrow will not pierce'). The acts of sabotage carried out were in four categories. Most important was the so-called Plan Vert, which involved blowing up trains and railway lines. Plan Violet meant the destruction of telephone cables and installations above and below ground, Plan Bleu the disruption of electricity supplies, while Plan Tortue involved the sabotage of roads and road transport. In his masterly *Histoire de la Libération de la France* Robert Aron splits the Brittany campaign into five phases: the weeks before June 6, the mobilisation of the *maquis* from June 6 to 18, the Allied offensive from June 18 to August 2, the Allied advance and the Liberation proper from August 2 to 20, and the mopping-up period for the month or so after that.

On D-Day, according to Aron's figures, there were in Brittany about 19,500 combatant members of the Resistance, of whom about half were under arms. By the end of July the total had risen to about 31,500, of whom 13,750 were armed; while during the mopping-up period the number of armed *maquisards* rose to about 20,000. This was a sizeable army, and contributed enormously to the ease with which Patton and the American Third Army were able to liberate Brittany in August

—as opposed to Normandy, where resistance was spasmodic and on a small scale. The Morbihan was used as the 'guinea-pig' for the other Départements, to enable the Allies to discover how effective the *maquis* was likely to be; this meant that by D-Day there were 7,000 men mobilised in the Morbihan, seven times as many as in the next-door Département of Finistère. It was in the Morbihan that the first of the pitched battles between the Resistance and the Germans took place, at the village of Saint-Marcel, near Malestroit—a battle that Aron calls 'a sort of Resistance Dunkirk, where, after a heroic action, the battalions succeeded in extricating themselves under difficult conditions'. On receipt of the BBC's messages of June 4, 8,000 reservists were mobilised at Saint-Marcel. Identity cards were issued, armbands were handed out as there were no uniforms, and proper catering and vehicle-repair facilities were set up. Troops of the Free French army were parachuted in, among them the one-armed Colonel Bourgoin. When the Germans heard of his arrival, they are reputed to have arrested every one-armed man in the Morbihan in the hope of catching him, but not surprisingly they were unsuccessful. On June 18 the Germans counter-attacked, first with a patrol, then with a battalion, and finally with a whole division. The odds were too great for the *maquis*, who dispersed, after killing 560 Germans. The French lost 200 *maquisards* and fifty parachutists. There is a monument to the battle a short way from Saint-Marcel, an ugly stone memorial that looks like a bomb nose down beside a cornfield. The inscription has some discrepancy with the written sources; it refers to the 560 enemy dead but only gives forty-two as the total French losses.

A similar battle took place at much the same time in the Forêt de Saffré, between Nantes and Châteaubriant. The *maquis* was mobilised on June 15, and on June 28 the Germans attacked the camp, capturing thirty-five Resistance men, of whom twenty-seven were shot after a farcical trial. Their monument is well signposted as you drive along the N178. It stands solitary at the end of a lane, in a broad sweep of fields with woods away in the distance—a symbolic figure of France, being accoutred with sword, shield and helmet by the *maquisards*, while one of their dead comrades lies at her feet. Away to the north, the Côtes-du-Nord is full of small roadside monuments carved with the Cross of Lorraine and inscribed with anything upwards of half a dozen names. I came across a typical example on a tiny back road, in the depths of the countryside between Corlay and Guingamp, and got out of the car to read the inscription in a freezing spring shower. It was to the *maquis* of the village of Plésidy, which I later discovered was one of the most famous of all the Resistance groups—'an exemplary and disciplined unit', says the inscription. Thirteen of its members were killed on July 27, 1944, while inflicting 'bloody losses' ('*pertes sanglantes*') on the enemy forces.

Aron lists the impressive total of operations carried out between July 10 and August 4 in the Côtes-du-Nord: 2,500 Germans killed or wounded, 300 telephone and high-tension cables cut, 200 acts of sabotage to railway lines, forty derailments, fifty convoys ambushed and 200 vehicles captured, destruction of a fuel depot at Saint-Brieuc, thirty attacks on German observation posts, and finally the capture of Saint-Brieuc prison on August 3, and the freeing of thirty-two Frenchmen condemned to death by the Gestapo.

Apart from such large-scale parachute drops as those that preceded the battles of Saint-Marcel and Saffré, small parachute teams were sent over from England to link up with the Resistance units. Known as Jedburghs, or 'Jeds' for short, they consisted of three men: a French officer, an Allied officer, either British or American, and an NCO radio operator. About ninety such teams were dropped altogether. Their brief was to discourage the *maquis* from engaging in pitched battles with the Germans, persuading them to 'act brutally and by surprise, kill the maximum number of Boches, destroy the greatest amount of material possible, and vanish after capturing as much equipment as possible'. Besides the Jeds, Operational Groups (OGs) were also parachuted in—commandos consisting of thirty-two men, who could be split into two or four groups depending on what type of sabotage was involved.

After nearly two months of constant harassment by the Resistance and their Allied helpers, the Germans in Brittany were already half-way to defeat. It was this softening-up process that enabled Patton's troops to rampage across the country in the early days of August. On August 1 the Americans were still at Avranches; and in a characteristic gesture Patton bet

Montgomery that Brest—two hundred miles away—could be taken within five days. Patton's orders were brief and to the point: 'Take Brest!' An eyewitness quoted in the official American account, Martin Blumenson's *U.S. Army in World War II: Breakout and Pursuit*, conveys the exhilaration felt by the Americans as they rushed through Rennes (liberated on August 3) and on to central Brittany. 'The trucks were like a band of stage-coaches making a run through Indian country. We got used to keeping the wheels going, disregarding the snipers, and hoping we wouldn't get lost or hit.' Or as Blumenson puts it, 'A naturally headstrong crew became rambunctious in Brittany.' As for the *maquisards*, their feelings were summed up by one of their leaders: 'We have been rabbits, but we have become the hunters.'

The efficiency of the Resistance meant that Patton could divide his army into three parts, of which only one (the 8th Army Corps) was used in Brittany, while the other two corps struck south and east. His strategy was to by-pass the main pockets of German resistance in the ports of Saint-Malo, Brest, Lorient and Saint-Nazaire. This meant that the country as a whole was liberated at breakneck speed, with little damage, whereas the four ports were almost totally destroyed after weeks of siege. Patton himself was a tank man, a swashbuckling cavalryman by instinct; but his commander in the field, General Troy H. Middleton, was an infantryman and hence more cautious. The speed of the American advance, largely along the main roads, meant that the Germans were able to retreat along the minor roads unintercepted, and thus managed to get far more men through to the ports than they might otherwise have done. In addition, the American lines of communication were greatly overstretched. The siege of Brest was typical of the way in which Patton's lightning campaign got bogged down in its final stages. As a matter of timing, Patton only just lost his bet with Montgomery, since the Americans were within striking distance of Brest within six days; but the siege was to last six more weeks. The operation reads like a twentieth-century version of a medieval engagement, with tanks for armoured knights, bombs and rockets for cannon balls, and the flame-throwing Crocodiles for the blazing brands hurled against the enemy.

When the siege began, Brest had already suffered greatly from Allied bombings. The civilian population had dwindled to about 15,000, living in such houses as were still habitable, and after the siege had lasted a week they were evacuated during a truce—again reminiscent of the Middle Ages. The German garrison of 35,000 men was commanded by General Hermann Ramcke, a fanatical Nazi who ordered his men to fight to the death, on the direct instructions of Hitler, and who carried out instant reprisals against any Resistance suspects. Against him were 50,000 Americans under Middleton, and a sizeable contingent of Free French under Colonel Albert Eon. The difficulties of the siege were compounded by bad relations between the Americans and the French. At one point Colonel Eon complained to General Middleton that his men were demoralised by seeing the Americans 'systematically putting out of action artillery captured from the enemy, preventing our men, who are without shoes, from appropriating the boots of prisoners, and stuffing the German prisoners with food and renewing their footwear, while our own units were dying of hunger and walking barefoot through the gorse'. This was in reference to the storming of the summit of Menez-Hom, the dome-shaped mountain that guards the Crozon peninsula and was used by the Germans as an outwork of their defences of Brest. Relations reached their lowest ebb when the Americans bombed Telgruc, on the Crozon peninsula, by mistake, killing over a hundred people, including a number of *maquisards*. Colonel Eon sent a furious message to the effect that the Germans were obviously quite safe from American bombs, and would no doubt approve of this 'massacre of patriots'.

To such acrimonious undertones the siege went on, culminating in a week of attack from shells, bombs and rockets. Finally the Americans attacked the city and captured it on September 18, after bitter house-to-house fighting. Brest was a heap of unrecognisable rubble, and the installations of the greatest port in western France had been sabotaged by the Germans and put out of action for the rest of the war.

In the early days of the Liberation, after the American forces had moved on and before proper civilian government was re-established, the more unscrupulous *maquisards* took the opportunity to settle old scores. Naturally the members of the hated Milice were executed summarily; but the hostility felt for them spilled over and engulfed even moderate Breton nationalists. A French journalist (quoted by Meic Stephens in his *Linguistic Minorities in Western Europe*) wrote that 'it was enough to have danced in a Celtic society or to have followed a Breton language course to be considered as a dangerous extremist'. Even known Resistance fighters were executed or imprisoned. Members of the Bezenn Perrot, says Meic Stephens, went before the French firing squads 'unrepentant, convinced that France was the enemy for as long as it refused to recognise Brittany's right to live its own national life and believing to the end that in the war between France and Germany they had simply joined the losing side'. The bitterness of those confused weeks must surely have contributed greatly to the sense of persecution evinced by the nationalists in recent years.

After more than three decades one might suppose that the Bretons were beginning to forget their sufferings under the Occupation; and in view of the importance of the German tourist trade, it would no doubt be expedient for them to do so. Here and there it is happening, as I found when I revisited the Château de Bienassis, near Erquy, after a lapse of some years. Bienassis is a most peaceful little château, a place of pointed turrets and bees murmuring drowsily among the eaves—the last place one can envisage as a scene of horror. It was occupied by the Germans for two years, during which time they cut cut down many of the fine trees for fuel; and before leaving (for reasons unspecified, but presumably as a reprisal) they shot six local inhabitants in what is now the rose garden. The first time we went there, in 1959, the story was told in full; but on our return in the mid-sixties the episode was not mentioned. When we asked the guide why she had omitted it, she said it was not good for tourism. But such tactful editing of history is a rare occurrence. On a visit to the Côtes-du-Nord in the spring of 1977 I stopped to read a large wooden notice board, prominently placed by the side of the road, and freshly painted with the same message on both sides. A mile or so beyond Uzel, at the junction of the main road to Saint-Brieuc, is a stone monument with dozens of names on it, which the passing motorist might easily miss; and the notice board is to make sure that he does not do so. It reads as follows: 'Friend, do you hear (*Ami, entends-tu*)? This is Lorges, centre of Resistance for the Département, where 55 men of the Resistance, after torture, were murdered and buried in this wood by the Nazi hordes. In the night, freedom listens to us.' No euphemisms here: the Resistance men, '*après la torture, furent massacrés et enfouis dans ce bois par les hordes Nazies*'. Beside the notice, a stone points the way up a steep path—the Chemin des Martyrs—to the dark and brooding pine woods on the crest of the hill.

CHAPTER XX

Brière and Pays Bigouden

As THE AIRCRAFT banks before landing at Nantes Airport, it passes over what looks like a weed-grown stretch of runway on the north bank of the Loire. But give it a closer look, and you will see that what at first sight appears to be tarmac is in fact a dark expanse of water, and the grass tufts that seem to be poking through it are great clumps of reeds. This is the marshland of La Grande Brière, the strangest and most mysterious of all the hidden corners of Brittany. Though it is skirted by the motorway that runs between Nantes and Saint-Nazaire, you would never guess it; and the policy of keeping the Brière secret, except to those who deliberately seek it out, extends to the fact that you will look in vain for any road signs pointing you to it. These 7,000 hectares (17,500 acres) of water and reedbed constitute a delicately poised entity, threatened constantly by the incursions of the modern industrialised external world; and their management is a complex matter, involving not just ecology, but a knowledge of human nature and especially, as this is France, of political human nature.

The Marais de Grande Brière, to give it its proper name, lies at the heart of one of Brittany's two regional parks. The whole park, called the Parc Naturel Régional de Brière, covers 40,000 hectares (100,000 acres), and takes in a large number of villages and a considerable amount of farmland. As a matter of terminology, the French have two types of what we would loosely term 'national parks'. There are the Parcs Nationaux proper, of which there are seven, and which are financed entirely by the State. They have been created to preserve wild or little-inhabited areas for the benefit of scientists and tourists. The twenty-two Parcs Régionaux, on the other hand, are largely financed locally, with assistance from government sources. According to a leaflet prepared in connection with the Brière: 'They are not confined spaces subject to prohibitions, but are on the contrary inhabited areas where tourist development must be channelled in a harmonious way. No putting away in a glass case, but a dynamic and co-ordinated scheme of protection. No vetoes or prohibitions, rather an advisory capacity.'

Topographically speaking, the Brière forms the hinterland to the prosperous seaside town of La Baule, the docks and shipyards of Saint-Nazaire, and the oil refineries of Donges. It is thus rather as though the Norfolk Fens had been whisked away and set down somewhere near Southampton Water. Geologically, it lies between two rock faults, which run in a north-west to south-east direction: inland the Sillon de Bretagne, which stretches from the Vilaine to the Loire; and on the seaward side a smaller fault that cuts off the Brière from the salt marshes of Guérande and Le Croisic. In the course of aeons it has been raised and lowered above the sea; ancient fish have swum above it at one epoch, while mastodons have trampled over it at another. During successive ebbings of the sea prehistoric man, from Neanderthal to Neolithic, moved in before being washed out again, leaving cultural remains in the form of stone tools and weapons, and food refuse. Then came a layer of mud that preserved all these remains for the archaeologist; and finally the thick covering of peat that provided the staple industry of the Brière until this century.

The Brière's social organisation is unique in France. It is owned jointly by the 70,000 inhabitants of the twenty-one *communes* that surround it, ranging in size from the big towns of Saint-Nazaire and La Baule to villages like Saint-Lyphard and Saint-Joachim. This right of ownership is jealously guarded by the Briérons; its origins are lost in antiquity, but it received official sanction in 1462, in the form of letters patent from Duke François II of Brittany. Thirty years later the Duke's daughter, the great and much-loved Duchess Anne, confirmed the letters patent. If you talk to a Briéron and bring up the topic of ownership, as likely as not he will bring the Duchess into the conversation. The letters patent regulated the Briérons' main activities: fishing and hunting, and the cutting of peat and reeds. In the early days some kind of rough-and-ready organisation was all that was necessary; but by the nineteenth century the population had grown to the point where matters had to be regularised and made more formal. So in 1830 the Commission Syndicale was set up, with one representative (*syndic*) elected from each of the twenty-one *communes*, under a president chosen from the *syndics*. Nowadays the same situation applies, except that the *syndics* are elected every six years, at the time of the local government elections, and so the administration has become far more political. A *syndic*'s worthiness to serve is now less important than whether he is a Communist or a man of the Right, and the loss may well be the Brière's.

Like other fenmen, the Briérons have always been suspicious, mistrusting strangers and looking on the inhabitants of even the next-door village with a jaundiced eye. Even after many of the able-bodied men had begun to work in the shipyards at Saint-Nazaire, in about 1900, they would still come home in the evening and tend their cows, hunt or mend their fishing nets. Such traditional activities lasted until after the Second World War; and it is only recently that professional hunters have preferred to become guides to tourists who want a day's shooting, or a trip among the reeds in a punt. Peat has not been cut commercially since about 1950. When the possibility of the Parc Naturel was first mooted in the 1960s, the Briérons were mistrustful of the whole project, fearing that they would end up as strange animals in a tourist zoo. A fact-finding commission in 1968 did little to allay their fears. Mme Jarnet, the present Directeur of the park, told me that the Briérons had a 'fear in the pit of the stomach' ('*peur viscérale*') that their rights would be taken away—a fear that has haunted them down the centuries. In 1970 the park was officially established, with a long and elaborate charter (*Charte Constitutive et Statuts*), revised in 1977 in the light of experience. Like the medieval letters patent, the charter takes pains to point out that it is there to 'protect this marshland in its biological uniqueness and in its inalienable character of indivisible proprietorship' ('*son caractère inaliénable de propriété indivise*').

The day-to-day running of the Parc Naturel is carried on by a so-called Syndicat Mixte (not to be confused with the *syndics*, who continue the nineteenth-century administration of rights on the marsh). The Syndicat Mixte is run by a committee consisting of no fewer than forty-seven members, representing sixteen of the twenty-one *communes*, the Département of Loire-Atlantique, in which the Brière lies, and other bodies such as the Chamber of Commerce of Saint-Nazaire and the Chamber of Agriculture of Nantes. When one remembers that the Directeur is appointed by the Syndicat Mixte, and has not only to satisfy them but also the Briérons at large, not to mention running the park itself, he (or she, as is at present the case) needs the stamina of a marathon runner and the political skills of a Machiavelli.

The park is run from the little village of Fédrun, a short way off the road that skirts the eastern side of the Marais. It stands on one of the so-called 'islands' that are in fact small suburbs of Saint-Joachim, the main township of the Marais. The headquarters is in the Maison du Parc, a neat little building that has been converted from two tumbledown cottages. Unlike many Brière buildings, which were little more than single-room hovels, the Maison du Parc has an attic storey directly under the thatch. The roof is not lined in any way, and so the fluffy reed ends poke through into the upstairs offices, giving off a pleasantly sweet smell. Behind the Maison du Parc is another cottage that has been converted into a laboratory for the park's scientific staff; while also in Fédrun is the Auberge du Parc, where under the guidance of Mme Jarnet I ate a memorable Brière meal, whose main elements were *matelote d'anguille* (a kind of eel stew in a magnificently rich sauce), and *magrit de canard aux pommes* (duck fillets cooked with apples). Both eel and duck, needless to say, were straight off the marshes.

The Brière in general, and Fédrun in particular, were put on the French literary map by Alphonse de Châteaubriant's classic novel *La Brière*, first published in 1923. In part it is a Thomas Hardy-like work, in which character and landscape coalesce to form an immediately recognisable identity. But it is also well-researched history, in which one of the main strands is the search for copies of the letters patent of Duke François II, in response to the threat of industrialisation to the rights of the Briérons. Indeed, if you go to Fédrun, as I did, soon after reading *La Brière*, you get a curious sense of *déjà-vu*. Not only is the village still exactly as Châteaubriant described it (apart from the smartened-up cottages like the Maison du Parc), but the old eel-fisherman who takes tourists out in his punt is called Roger Aoustin, and Aoustin is the surname of the protagonist of the novel.

Châteaubriant's fearsome Aoustin is the *garde* of the Brière, whose job is to make sure that the Briérons cut turf only during one specified fortnight of the year and pay duty on each cubic metre—a job that needs a hard man, as his three predecessors have been murdered. Aoustin lives with a cowed wife, and a beautiful daughter, Théotiste, who has fallen in love with Jeanin, a young man from the despised village of Mayun, away to the north, whose inhabitants are basket-makers rather than fishermen and hunters. It is Aoustin who is commissioned by the *syndics* to find the letters patent, and who finally succeeds in doing so, in the hovel of an old mad woman. But Aoustin's implacable and unrelenting nature, which leads him to the documents, also leads him to the destruction of his own family. Théotiste is jailed after killing the child she has borne to Jeanin, returns home disgraced, goes mad and finally dies in Aoustin's punt out on the marsh; while Aoustin leaves wife and home, and has his hand blown off by Jeanin's gun, as he is returning from Nantes after depositing the precious documents there.

All this may sound melodramatic; and indeed *La Brière* is full of melodrama. But the old man is a fictional giant, a kind of King Lear of the marshland, whose nickname of Lucifer is not unfitting. And as the story progresses he becomes the physical embodiment of the Brière in a real sense, as he gets a craftsman to carve him a false hand of iron-hard bog oak from the peat—the wood known as *mortas*, which the Briérons used to extract for the beams of their cottages. After the *syndics* have deprived him of his duties as *garde*, on the grounds that a one-handed man cannot do the work, he comes before them triumphantly brandishing his formidable black hand. 'I defy you now to tell me,' he says, 'where the Brière ends and I I myself begin!' For Aoustin, 'the map of the world was divided firmly into two parts: the continents on one side, and the Brière on the other. Likewise there were two types of human being: the men from elsewhere, and his compatriots of the peat, the fierce sons of this black soil, born like him in a punt on an armful of straw.'

For centuries the sale of peat in Nantes was the chief source of external revenue for the Briérons. After cutting and drying, the coal-hard blocks would be loaded on to special boats—the *blins*, far larger than the marshman's normal *chaland* or punt, and carrying up to four tons or so. At the beginning of *La*

Brière Aoustin and the young man Jeanin are just returning from one such trip to the city; and the dark earth lends its sombre colour to much of the book. In a vivid passage Châteaubriant describes the frenzied activities of peat-cutting time, when the Briérons toiled from dawn to dusk with their T-shaped peat-knives (*salet* or *salais*), long-handled spades and carrying-baskets.

> The milling swarms settled down. Busy groups, whole battalions, attacked the ground. The peat knife was put to work. One slice after another, one cut after another: do it at once, the first minute and the last are of equal value, when you have only a week to finish, an uncertain future, and authority on your heels. Six centuries of free turf-cutting had gone to form the instinctive movements of those bodies and arms now circumscribed by the law of the present day. They hurled themselves on the treasure. Bearded men with darting eyes, women with calloused ankles in their coarse working garments worn under a pointed kerchief, girls with their pretty eyes shining below their mob-caps—in teams, in families, in clans, they settled to their fifty square feet and turned over the soil with its short grass, dug it, rummaged in it, carried off the strips of sward. Or, if the subsoil was worthless, giving peat that crumbled or a soup of peat and bog oak, they would leave that spot and start again elsewhere. Everywhere the topsoil was removed. A main trench was dug like a railway cutting. And in it men and women toiled together; for plenty of these strapping women—forty-year-old housewives, with their wedding-rings buried in the flesh of their fingers—knew better than anyone how to push home the peat-knife below the weight of their ample bodies. All along this main axis, in the black peat itself, the removal trench grew broader. The peat-knife made its vertical cuts; then the horizontal peat-spade finished the job and detached the turf, heavy and damp, for arms less strong to carry to the higher ground. The young boys pushed the wheelbarrows and made ready the peat-baskets. Apart from the very old, there was no one left behind in the villages. The whole ant-heap of the Brière was out on the turf pile, even the babies, who had been brought by their mothers and who lay

crying in reed-baskets laid on the ground, among the big tawny dogs with flecked eyes and smooth coats, which came and sniffed at them.

When Châteaubriant wrote his novel in the 1920s, the traditional life of the Brière, centred on peat-cutting, was still in full swing. But with the gradual running down of the industry the canals grew neglected and overgrown, and the water-free areas or *platières* where the Briérons pastured their animals have become invaded by the insidious reeds. One of the main subjects of study for the park's laboratory experts is how to stop the reeds from spreading, with the ultimate aim of bringing the ground back to grazing. Surprisingly this is not as difficult as might be thought. The old reeds are cut, and the park's seventy or so cattle and ten horses are allowed to graze on the young shoots. This weakens the reeds' root systems so that they can no longer grow, and within about three years the *platières* are back to grass once more. The park's most valuable acquisition of recent years has been a dredger to keep the main channels clear; though it has been estimated that ten dredgers would be needed to do the job properly.

The canal system is a comparatively simple one. The Marais is cut almost exactly in two halves by a large canal running due east-west, and each of these halves is divided in two by a diagonal canal, giving four 'quarters' of different shapes and sizes. These efficient, dead-straight canals were laid out in the last century, and dug entirely by muscle power. In addition to the main arteries, there are any number of *curées*, or smaller service canals, leading from the periphery of the Marais to its main axes. The layout of Fédrun is typical of the whole system. Round the 'island' on which it stands runs a *curée*, like a moat round a castle. Parallel with the *curée* is a fringe of houses right round the outer edge of the island, each backing on to the *curée* and with its own individual channel leading to it (the aquatic mentality of the Briérons is shown by the word for this channel, which is *seuil*, meaning 'threshold'). The central part of the island (the *gagnerie*) is given over to cultivation, and no trees are allowed to take up the precious space. Indeed, the only trees in evidence on the Marais are the water willows growing along the edge of the *curée*. Water was used for all transport purposes; the *chalands* and *blins* were the cars and lorries of the old Briérons, with the *seuils* as private parking areas and driveways.

The universal *chaland*, of which there are still plenty to be seen all over the Brière, is a small oval flat-bottomed boat, tarred against the weather. It is propelled by a punt-pole, though the young Briérons tend to prefer outboard motors. These poles are not the elegantly regular shafts of lazy afternoons on the Thames (any more than the *chalands* are 'punts' within the meaning of the act), but long poles of rough chestnut, cut by the boatman for his own use, with a Y-shaped fork at the working end to give a better purchase on the bed of the canal. In the old days the canals had firm beds, made of gravel brought down in the *blin* from Nantes after the peat cargo had been sold, but nowadays the beds are as neglected as the rest of the waterway system. The control the boatmen have over this unwieldy craft is astonishing. When I went out with Roger Aoustin there was a hard and cold wind blowing, with gusts of rain—so unpleasant, in fact, that he insisted that I put on an ancient sou'wester stowed under one of the seats. But whether the wind was ahead, on the beam or astern he was fully in control, even in the teeth of the wind on the wide expanse of the main canal. Of the once-rich bird life there seemed little trace, apart from the occasional duck and moorhen, a few plovers and a couple of buzzards hovering over the reedbeds in the distance. Perhaps it was the wrong time of the year, or—more likely—everything else had been shot.

The rehabilitation of the Brière is going to be a long and difficult task. But in spite of the obvious problems ahead, not to mention the pressures from road-building, quarrying and other lobbies, there is a feeling of hopefulness about the whole venture. Old walls are being repainted with whitewash, and old roofs re-thatched—though here again there have been difficulties. In certain villages thatch is now compulsory, which led to strong objections from some of the Briérons concerned, to whom thatch was a sign of poverty, while a slate roof meant prosperity. Slate was used on the so-called '*maisons de capitaines*', built by retired seadogs who had spent their lives in the navy and returned home to the Brière to enjoy their retirement. On the whole such conflicts have now been sorted out.

The park authorities themselves are leading the way in active renovation. A house in the hamlet of Rozé has been reconstructed and made into a small museum of Brière life; known as the Maison de l'Eclusier (Lock-Keeper's House), it stands on an island between two sluice-gates, at the point where salt water from a tributary of the Loire was kept separate from the fresh water of the Marais. In Camérun at the north end of the Marais an architect's workshop has been set up in two renovated cottages, where advice and help is given with building problems. Most ambitious of all the park's schemes has been the acquisition for reconstruction of a complete hamlet, Kerhinet, near Saint-Lyphard, over on the western side of the Marais. When I went there in 1977 one house had already been rebuilt and furnished in the traditional Briéron manner, with such features as a bed below a tent-like curtain hanging, and an artificial bridal crown of wax orange blossom—one of the cottage industries of the Brière girls, and one which incidentally in Châteaubriant's novel the girl Théotiste practised in the time of her disgrace. Eventually it is hoped that Kerhinet will include a working farm, a restaurant, and craftsmen working in the ancient skills of weaving and basket-making.

Every August the Briérons hold their own festival at Fédrun, in which the participants fool about on the water in a variety of aquatic contests, while the spectators sit on a hay-covered stretch of squelchy peat, unprotected from either the sun or the rain. Stalls at the back sell anything from cider to eel sandwiches, and there are live geese to be gambled for in a lottery. The games vary from a simple barrel race on the water to a complex ritual in which three punts are used for a kind of pig-in-the-middle. On the outer punts members of one team throw eggs to each other, while the man in the middle, from the opposing team, has to hit them with a paddle. If he misses and the egg is caught, it is ceremonially broken over the head of an opponent. The two sides in the games are Fédrun versus '*la Reste*'—not just the rest of the Brière, but the rest of the world. When I saw the games the name of Aoustin predominated in the Fédrun team, one member of which—so the commentator announced—had not left the island for two years. Incredible, but that is the Grande Brière for you.

The Brière is not particularly rich in legends; perhaps the

hard life and the watery flatness discouraged the higher flights of imagination. But Saint-Lyphard at least has one story, in which prehistory and Christianity meet and merge. Near the village, until about the middle of the last century, there stood a menhir known as the 'Split Stone' (Pierre Fendue), because of a great cleft down its length. Lyphard, so the story goes, was a widower who lived with his daughter on the edge of the Brière marshland. At that time a dragon was terrorising the countryside, and could only be satisfied by giving it a young girl to eat every month. Eventually the lot fell on Lyphard's daughter; but unlike the other Briérons, he was not prepared to sit back and let her be eaten. He resolved to attack the dragon, but before doing so tested out his sword on a nearby menhir, with a blow so hard that the blade sank right in. He needed so much strength to pull it out again that his fingerprints, as well as the cleft made by his sword, were left for ever on the side of the rock. Being a canny Briéron, he did not engage the dragon in open combat by day, but jumped on it while it was snoring in the moonlight and cut off its head. Not as sporting as St George and the Dragon, perhaps; but typical of the prudence and the family loyalty that form one aspect of the dour race of Brière marshmen.

The massive dockyards of Saint-Nazaire are only a few miles from the heart of the Brière, yet they seem to belong to another world. Nevertheless, Saint-Nazaire is a Brière *commune*, like any of the little villages, and it is linked to them by a shared quality of wateriness. I explored the deserted waterfront area one cold spring evening, walking across gigantic lock-gates, past monumental cogs and hawsers, to the monstrous submarine base built by the Germans in the Second World War—a squat concrete construction, blotched and streaked with rust, that looks as though it is hewn from a solid block of masonry hundreds of yards long and thirty feet high. As night falls you can see down the tunnels that lead into its centre, which is now used for innocuous purposes like cold storage. Not surprisingly, in view of its strength, the 'Base Sous-marine' survived the 120 air-raids and bombardments the town suffered during the war, especially at the time of the Liberation, when Saint-Nazaire was one of the pockets of resistance where the Germans held on until the end. Roughly nine-tenths of the town was totally destroyed; and the postwar Saint-Nazaire, built to a rigid grid pattern, is not a particularly interesting place. However, it is a summer resort as well as a shipbuilding and dockyard town, with a sandy beach backed by a double row of plane trees. At the southern end of the beach, beside the harbour pier, a rough granite column commemorates 'Operation Chariot'—the Commando raid of March 27–28, 1942. In the course of the raid the Anglo-Canadian troops managed to penetrate the harbour defences and do considerable damage; unfortunately, during the savage rearguard action that followed many civilians were killed. At the foot of the column are six columns of names, with about thirty names in each. A far more ancient menhir than this monument stands in the middle of the residential area of the town, in company with a dolmen of two uprights and a roofing-stone. The Stone Age thoroughly domesticated, in fact.

When I first saw the Saint-Nazaire dockyards in 1959, the *France* was in the process of being built, and her mighty hull dwarfed the whole town. In 1977 she was bought by a Saudi Arabian millionaire to turn into a hotel at anchor: so brief are the lives of the last of the ocean-going leviathans. Today Saint-Nazaire's chief pride is the graceful new bridge across the Loire: two pylons striped red-and-white, supporting the wide central span with fan-like arrangements of cables. The bridge charges a large toll, but it saves a long trip upstream to Nantes.

Twenty minutes or so to the west is the great sweep of La Baule's beach, unique among Brittany's major beaches in that it faces due south. Before you get there on the coast road you pass the little resort of Saint-Marc, unchanged since Monsieur Hulot took his holiday there a couple of decades ago. The Hôtel de la Plage, with its terrace overlooking the sand, is still there, as is the tiny cannon pointing out to sea to repel unwelcome invaders. All that is lacking is Jacques Tati's lugubrious face peering round a rock.

A few miles north of La Baule is the little walled town of Guérande, like a miniature northern Carcassonne. A medieval gatehouse leads to a pedestrianised shopping street—the only place where I have seen a silhouette artist carrying on his trade in the open air, snipping out excellent silhouettes in five minutes or so. Guérande owes its prosperity to salt, collected from the nearby salt marshes; the name of the town derives from the Breton 'Gwen Rann', meaning 'White District', and salt was already being produced in quantities in Gallo-Roman times. You can still buy fresh salt from the *marais salants* that fill the bay between Guérande and the Le Croisic peninsula. The *marais* are divided into small ponds, further subdivided by mud embankments; the sea water can be let into each small section by lifting a slate 'sluice-gate' a few inches across. As the salt dries, it is skimmed off with flat-sided rakes, and finally piled up in great heaps under sheets of black polythene—not the most beautiful additions to the strange flat landscape, but no doubt the most effective method of keeping the salt dry until the lorries come to take it away. Salt off the marshes, at about one franc a kilo, is one of the few real bargains left in Brittany.

At Piriac-sur-Mer, a pretty little harbour town near Guérande, we went to a *fest-noz* whose main attraction was a four-man group singing sea-shanties in the main square, to the accompaniment of gigantic slide projections of fishing scenes and seascapes. Afterwards we sat on the harbour drinking cider and looking at the ships' lights winking out at sea. It was one of those magical evenings that can only happen in Brittany.

At the other extremity of Brittany, to the west of Quimper, is a region whose traditions and individuality are as marked as those of the Brière. This is the Pays Bigouden, a windswept region of bright light and undistinguished villages, where the countrywomen still wear the tall white *coiffe* on their heads as a matter of course, and are to be seen, heads down like unicorns, spearing their way into the wind on bicycle or moped. The Pays Bigouden has ill-defined boundaries, but it can be said that it occupies most of the country's south-west extremity, excluding Audierne, the Pointe du Raz and the rugged Cap Sizun coast. It has its own capital in the small town of Pont l'Abbé, its own Land's End in the rocky Pointe de Penmarc'h, and its own literary testament in *Le Cheval d'Orgeuil*, the autobiography of Pierre-Jakez Hélias, who chronicles without sentimentality and with a mosaic-like wealth of detail the passing of his ancestral civilisation.

His village, Pouldreuzic, is right in the middle of the Pays

Bigouden, and is the sort of place you drive through without a second glance. Yet for all its dull appearance it was a microcosm of the old Brittany, and Hélias's account of his childhood and youth there in the years following the First World War is an insider's view of that vanished world. So great are his powers of recall that he almost convinces you he remembers the outbreak of the War, which took place when he was six months old. In the stifling heat of August 1914 his father and mother were working side by side in the fields, cutting the wheat with sickles.

> It was high time, as the over-ripe ears were ready to let the grain fall to the ground. It was all the fault of officialdom, which had ordered my father to do his annual month of military service at Vannes, in the artillery, at haymaking time. Since he had come home again, with a gloomy look on his face, the poor man had set to work with a will, knowing that his days of working the land were numbered. . . . Husband and wife recovered their breath, one beside the other, without saying a word. What was there to say? Their whole destiny lay before their eyes: the field from which they had to earn their daily bread; a mile away, towards the sea, the church tower of the village that was their capital city; in the shadow of the tower, a whitewashed cottage where a six-month-old baby lay unattended waiting for his mother's milk. . . . At five o'clock in the afternoon the bells of the parish church began to make such a row that everyone thought the bellringer had gone mad. In fact, the poor fellow was ringing the alarm for a fire that would last for more than four years and spread across the world.

The book takes its title from a remark made by the author's maternal grandfather, Alain Le Goff: 'Though I'm too poor to buy another horse, at least the Horse of Pride will always have a stall in my stable.' This grandfather, constantly preoccupied with keeping poverty at bay—'*La Chienne du Monde*', the Bitch of the World, was how the Bretons described their everlasting enemy—was the boy's guide to the richness of imagination and fantasy. He was a widower, and when Pierre-Jakez was little the two shared the same box-bed, where the old man peopled the darkness with the creatures of his invention while the boy's parents snored in the next *lit-clos* along the wall. Alain Le Goff inhabited the Breton-speaking universe of the Celtic imagination—very different from the French-speaking practicalities of school life and the outside world, as Hélias soon discovered. *Le Cheval d'Orgueil* is a kind of war book, whose battles are moral and mental rather than physical. On the language front it was French versus Breton; at school Republican and anti-religious (*Rouge*) against Church influence (*Blanc*); in the wider context the erosion of specifically Breton customs and ways of behaviour (*savoir-vivre*) in the wake of the First World War and the constantly growing number of tourists. But all such changes happened in the background, and were invisible most of the time behind the age-old tasks of tilling the fields, building and repairing houses, making sabots, attending *pardons*, getting drunk, buying and selling.

The centre of that life was the house, and the basis of the house was the earth floor, unchanged since the Middle Ages, no doubt since prehistoric times. When a floor was remade, the whole village took part. The flooring material was known as 'toad's clay' (*argile à crapaud*).

> Was it because of its greyish colour, its warty excrescences, or because the toad likes to live in the earth and the shade, whereas the frog prefers the water and the sun? Your guess is as good as mine. What I can tell you is that it was a mixture of sand, clay and ordinary earth, with a handful of ash now and then. Each householder had his own formula for making his floor. . . . The old layer of beaten earth was loosened with a pickaxe, loaded into a wheelbarrow and carted off, to make way for the new toad's clay, which had already been roughly mixed. Then began the dance of the sabots. My parents, our neighbours who had been asked to lend a hand, myself and my older friends all spent an hour or two treading the mixture, which had to be neither too hard nor too soft, until it became glutinous and slightly tacky. My father flattened the surface with a large wooden rammer and a strange little roller he had borrowed from somewhere. Filthy right up to my thighs, including the skin under my old dress (there was talk of putting me into trousers), I went off to eat a hunk of bread with enough pâté on it to make it slide down nicely.

Most of the cottages where Hélias and his friends grew up have either fallen down or been made into second homes. But this is the way the world is going, and Hélias is philosophically pessimistic about the outcome. He ends this massive book (it runs to almost 600 pages) with a grim little parable about a future world in which all the peasants have abandoned the country for the cities, where they work on the production line, live on synthetic food and drink, and play with their electronic toys. Whereas their employers buy up the abandoned homesteads, rediscover the joys of rusticity and real food, and sell the surplus at an immense profit to the uprooted peasants now living in the towns. 'Finally, so as to live without worry on their country estates, the new masters surrounded with barbed wire the hideous agglomerations where all the poor devils were herded together. They built watchtowers with machine-guns to prevent them from getting out. And when they were alone among themselves, protected from the common people, these aristocrats founded exclusive regional clubs whose members were forbidden to speak anything but Occitan, Basque or Breton.'

Fortunately this nightmare situation is still some way off, even by the standards of a prophet of doom. Meanwhile the women (and not just the old women) of the Pays Bigouden continue to starch their *coiffes* and set them foursquare to the wind. Like Breton church towers, they are pierced with holes to give the gales less purchase. The Bigouden *coiffe* is by far the most easily recognisable of the the dozens of shapes and sizes to be seen at gatherings like the Fêtes de Cornouaille. It has been growing steadily in height throughout this century, and is now standardised at precisely thirty-two centimetres (thirteen inches) tall. Rumour has it that Bigouden buses have their roofs made higher to allow for the *coiffe;* and it caused a certain amount of ill feeling in the early days of the cinema. A Bigouden woman out for a cycle ride will often protect her *coiffe* with a specially shaped plastic covering; or she may remove the tall superstructure and just wear the little black velvet base to which it is attached. The art of putting on the *coiffe* can only really be explained by a sequence of working diagrams. The first essential is for the wearer to have long hair, over which a small bonnet is fixed. The back hair is then swept forward, over the bonnet, and held in position on top of the head with a semicircular comb, tied round with a velvet ribbon. This provides the base for the topmost section, or *grande coiffe*, which needs regular starching if it is to keep its shape. Perhaps the *coiffe* has had its day, except for special occasions and as a magnet for tourists' cameras. Yet the fact that hundreds of girls still wear it at the big festivals, as part of a totality of costume and not just as a freak headdress, must mean that it is far more than a dead relic, 'destined for the chill immobility of the museum', as Hélias puts it.

Pont l'Abbé has a Bigouden museum in the large castle that dominates the main square of the town. But the essence of the Pays Bigouden lies further west, in the ruined splendours of the village of Penmarc'h, once a prosperous fishing port, and the wilderness of black rock that stretches out to sea beyond the Eckmühl lighthouse. The noble church of Penmarc'h has obviously seen better days; but those days were long ago, before the end of the sixteenth century, as in 1595 the town was sacked and has never really recovered. Its destroyer, Guy Eder de la Fontenelle, was the most savage of the guerrilla leaders thrown up by the religious wars that racked France at the end of the sixteenth century. Born in Brittany about 1574 and sent to Paris to be educated, La Fontenelle returned to his home country in 1589, still hardly more than a boy, and raised an army of thugs to terrorise the hill country round Carhaix. Ostensibly he was fighting for the Ligue—the League of fanatical Catholics which had been set up in opposition to the spread of Protestantism, and which was thus opposed to the Protestant King of France, Henri IV. But as Protestantism never made much headway among the strongly traditional Bretons, there was little for the Ligueurs to do in Brittany except plunder the country, which they did with the utmost savagery.

The Ligue's justification vanished when Henri IV became a Catholic in 1593, but La Fontenelle's depredations were only just beginning. Having made the inland region of Cornouaille into a wilderness, he then turned his attention to the coast. In 1595 he captured a small island (Ile Tristan) off Douarnenez, fortified it and made it his headquarters, emerging to plunder and sack Penmarc'h, Pont-Croix, and other towns and villages. In 1598 he made his submission to Henri IV, but in 1600 he was arrested and imprisoned. Two years later, after joining an abortive conspiracy, he was condemned to death and broken on the wheel in Paris. La Fontenelle was merely the worst of the many adventurers thrown up by the Wars of the League, during which the main European conflicts of the time spilled over into Brittany. In 1590 the Ligueurs were sent troops by Philip II of Spain, while the following year Queen Elizabeth sent a small expeditionary force to Paimpol to help the French King, who had not yet renounced his Protestantism. An important part of the Spanish plan was the capture of Brest, and as a preliminary they took and fortified the northernmost headland of the Crozon Peninsula, still called the Pointe des Espagnols. They were finally dislodged and defeated towards the end of 1594, after a six-week siege.

The miseries of the 1590s in Brittany were graphically described by a contemporary historian, Canon Jean Moreau, of Quimper. His history of the Ligue tells of the 'four scourges of God, by which he punished his people against whom he was angered: war, plague, famine and wild beasts. War brought famine, and then the plague to those who avoided the cruelty of the soldiers, or rather of the brigands, whom certain people managed to escape by hiding in hedges or rabbit warrens; but there was no escape from hunger, for no one had the freedom to return home, and if they did so they found nothing but bare walls, since everything had been carried off by the soldiers. So the poor people could only flee to the woods, where they languished for some days, eating barberries and other bitter wild fruits, and with no means of making a fire, through fear of being given away by the smoke. Thus they died in the parklands and ditches, where the wolves, finding them dead, grew so accustomed to human flesh that, in the aftermath, for a space of seven or eight years they would attack even armed men, and no one dared go out unaccompanied.' The wolves grew so cunning that the peasants believed them to be dead soldiers come back to life as werewolves.

Penmarc'h in its sleepy decay is far removed from such horrors. Below the lighthouse fishermen mend their nets, coiffed women gossip, and school-children hunt for the seashells that fill every rock pool of the reefs that stretch far out to sea at low tide. A couple of hundred yards from the lighthouse is a rock shaped like a horse's head, with mane and hair of seaweed. Is this the Penmarc'h (horse's head in Breton) after which the headland is named? No one seems to know. Near by is one of the prettiest of all the Breton chapels, the delightfully named Notre-Dame de la Joie, built on a small creek and a real seafarer's church. A little to the north, near Saint-Guénolé, is a small prehistoric museum marked by some dolmens in the garden.

In spring the fields beyond Penmarc'h are bright with daffodils and tulips, and in this Lincolnshire-like setting is possibly the oldest and certainly the most moving of the Breton *calvaires*. This is Notre-Dame de Tronoen, which needs some cunning navigation along back roads to find. Lichen-covered and gnawed for centuries by the strong sea wind off the Bay of Audierne, these figures of the Last Supper and Crucifixion have never felt the touch of the restorer's hand; while the chapel (kept locked) has a forlorn and neglected look about it. Among the carvings is one of a bare-breasted Virgin suckling the infant Jesus; unlike the similar carving at La Martyre, it has escaped the zeal of the mutilator.

The Pays Bigouden fades away between the village of Plozévet and the fishing port of Audierne. Its northern boundary may be regarded as the N784 road to Quimper, or the River Goyen, whose estuary divides Audierne neatly into two halves. Audierne looks prosperous enough, with a fine sweep of waterfront houses that look as though they had strayed from Ramsgate. But the reality is different, and has been well described by Ronald Millar in his splendid book on the Audierne tunny-fishermen, *A Time of Cherries*. He came to the fishing village of Sainte-Evette (Santez-Edwette in Breton) by chance, settled there, got to know the fishermen and finally, after an uphill struggle, succeeded in being taken on board a tunnyman not as an observer but as a member of the crew. He sailed on the *Jacques et René* in the 1974 season, which one might think was recent enough to indicate a still-prosperous industry. But the small Audierne boats are disappearing, ousted by the big deep-sea trawlers of the kind you can see round the coast at Douarnenez. So his book is a record, to use the old cliché, of a vanishing way of life. The ulcer-ridden *bosco* (first mate) Martial, who piled work on to the inexperienced Millar; the slow-moving cook Erry; Michel, the young *patron* of the boat;

Jean, who had once been a *patron* himself but had fallen on hard times—such characters will in a few years have made way for the new breed of big-ship sailors, indifferent to whether they are aboard a tunnyman or an oil-tanker.

Ronald Millar started with the great advantage of being an experienced yachtsman, with as much knowledge of the sea as any of his fellow-crewmen. But the tunny-fisherman needed more than straightforward seamanship. The fish were caught with a complex system of lines hung from *tangons*—booms fixed at an angle, one on either side of the boat. Each line had its own name and needed its own expertise; and much of *A Time of Cherries* is an account of hooks embedded in fingers, of hands burnt by fishing lines, and of near-disasters caused by misunderstandings of the *bosco*'s instructions.

The title is taken from a Breton proverb to the effect that if the cherries grow full and lush on the trees, it means that the water will be warm, and so the tunny will come north to the fishing-grounds. An attractively poetic proverb; but the tunny are being over-fished like everything else, and the cherries now ripen to little avail. *A Time of Cherries* depicts a world of gruelling discomfort and tempers wearing thin as the one job succeeds another, and such conditions are not much to the taste of the modern world. Yet though the tunnymen are doomed and the brightly painted *tangons* are being relegated to the loft, the disappearance of the old-style Breton fisherman will leave a gap in the wide variety of the world. 'Bull-necked, with strong short arms terminating in small hands fitted with steel hooks, he is built like a block, with no perceptible change in girth from the powerful, hunched shoulders to the short, slightly bowed legs.' So Millar describes him. For a few decades more these sailors will be seen growing old on the quayside, and then they will be gone, following the landlocked peasants of the remote countryside into oblivion.

From Audierne the road leads west to Brittany's Land's End, the Pointe du Raz. A tourist trap of vast car parks, knick-knack shops and crêperies, its turf has been worn away by the shoe-leather of hundreds of thousands of feet, not to mention the tyres of those who are too lazy to walk a quarter of a mile or so. Yet in spite of the crowds, the jagged rocks, falling away in splinters to the sea, contrive to keep their fierce grandeur.

Beyond the treacherous strait known as the Raz de Sein (*'raz'* is the same word as our own 'race') the Ile de Sein lies low on the horizon; and a little to the north is the Baie des Trépassés, the Bay of the Dead, named after the souls that embarked there for the Islands of the Blessed, or perhaps for the sailors who drowned in the swift current of the Raz. Probably the latter, as the most prominent man-made feature of the Pointe du Raz is the statue of Our Lady of Shipwrecks, Notre-Dame des Naufrages.

The Baie des Trépassés, as one would expect, is now the setting for a large hotel. But apart from that it is still a wild enough place, with cliffs on either side and an abundance of heather and gorse. In the 1870s it was a favourite sketching-spot for the inimitable Sarah Bernhardt, who when not acting her contemporaries off the stage or being showered with jewels by the crowned heads of Europe would come to Brittany to recuperate. One summer she stayed with Father Batifoulé of Audierne—a priest so fat that his table had to be cut away to allow for his stomach. In those days, she tells us in her memoirs, 'Brittany was wild, inhospitable, but as beautiful—perhaps more beautiful than at present, for it was not furrowed with roads; its green slopes were not dotted with small white villas; its inhabitants—the men—were not dressed in the abominable modern trousers, and the women did not wear miserable little hats with feathers.' But nostalgia apart, the old days had their disadvantages, as Bernhardt makes clear in her comic account of a painting excursion to the Baie des Trépassés.

> The first day there was nobody there. The second day a child came to look at us. The third day about ten children stood around asking for sous. I was foolish enough to give them some, and the following day there were twenty or thirty boys, some of them from sixteen to eighteen years old. Seeing near my easel something not particularly agreeable, I begged one of them to take it away and throw it in the sea, and for that I gave, I think, fifty centimes. When I came back the following day to finish my painting the whole population of the neighbouring village had chosen this place to relieve their corporal necessities, and as soon as I arrived the same boys, but in increased numbers, offered, if properly paid, to

take away what they had put there. I had the ugly band routed by Claude [her steward] and the lighthouse keeper, and as they took to throwing stones at us, I pointed my gun at the little group. They fled howling. Only two boys, of six and ten years of age, remained there. We did not take any notice of them, and I installed myself a little farther on, sheltered by a rock which kept the wind away. The two boys followed. Claude and the keeper Lucas were on the lookout to see that the band did not come back.

They were stooping down over the extreme point of the rock which was above our heads. They seemed peaceful, when suddenly my young maid jumped up: 'Horrors! Madame! Horrors! They are throwing lice down on us!' And in fact the two little good-for-nothings had been for the last hour searching for all the vermin they could find on themselves, and throwing it on us. I had the two little beggars caught, and they got a well-deserved correction.

Was the gun with which the Divine Sarah threatened the louse-ridden youth of Brittany her jewelled revolver which sold at Christie's in 1977 for £2,600? It would be a marvellously incongruous weapon if it were indeed so.

From 1886 Bernhardt had a regular summer retreat on Belle-Ile, off the Quiberon peninsula, where she bought and restored an old fortress—now called Fort Sarah Bernhardt—at the northern end of the island. Here, as Cornelia Otis Skinner tells us in her biography of the actress, she kept a household menagerie that included a wildcat and a boa-constrictor, entertained an endless stream of visitors, and used to go out at six in the morning to shoot duck or seagulls, accompanied by a small negro boy and two enormous mastiffs.

The northern coast of the Cornouaille peninsula is a rugged and inhospitable place, and for most of the way the road keeps well inland. However, what is bad for swimmers and sunbathers is good for seabirds; and Brittany's most important bird sanctuary has been set up at Cap Sizun, one of the wildest and most impressive stretches of the whole coastline. We spent one windy night there in the shelter of a disused quarry, looking out over a tremendous panorama of cliff and sea. The reserve was set up in the late 1950s, as a direct result of the threat to build a main road right along the top of the cliffs that now form the site of the reserve—a threat followed by a slaughter of seabirds perpetrated by tourists on a small offshore island. The most common birds to be seen there are herring gulls and cormorants; but there are also puffins, choughs, fulmars, razorbills and a host of other species. On a cold March day, in the course of a circuit of the clifftop walk, all I managed to see were herring gulls nesting and displaying on their slum-like ledges, and a few diving cormorants. But I do not claim to be much of an ornithologist.

From Cap Sizun it is not far as the cormorant flies to Douarnenez, which, the books tell us, is the fifth largest fishing port of France. A deep estuary cuts it off on the west from its lesser half, the town of Tréboul, which has its own attractive yacht harbour. Douarnenez' working centre is the Nouveau Port, built into the bay, with its massive storage areas and refrigerated warehouses. Most unusually, the town's shopping streets are piped for sound, as in Turkey or Yugoslavia, and you can buy your *baguettes* and *charcuterie* to the strains of Mozart and Vivaldi, no doubt chosen by some municipal music-lover. Offshore is the tree-covered Ile Tristan, where the villainous La Fontenelle had his stronghold. But the island's name has links with a time far earlier than the Wars of the League. For it is named after Tristan, the lover of Isolde, who is said to have been given it by King Mark. And the King himself supposedly had his palace at Douarnenez; though Cornishmen, and Wagner, would no doubt dispute this. However, Wagner's opera opens with the lovers sailing from Brittany to Cornwall; and Tristan's hereditary castle, called Kareol, was somewhere in Brittany.

Douarnenez itself has a strange name, which has given rise to various conjectures. One is that it derives from 'Tutuarn Enez', the Island of the hermit Tutuarn, who built himself a cell there in the sixth century. Or it may come from the Breton *Douar Nevez*, the New Land that appeared when King Gradlon's city of Ys was swallowed up by the sea. King Mark's own name may have a connection with Marc'h, the Breton for horse; and there has always been a strong link between sea gods such as Neptune and the cult of the horse. So are we perhaps back with some remote prehistoric cult which venerated the horse, and had its centre at Penmarc'h? Such conjectures are dangerous but alluring. At the end of La Villemarqué's poem on the sunken city of Ys, King Gradlon, his accursed daughter Dahut and the royal steed Morvarc'h (which means Sea-horse) are woven together into a mysterious tapestry of verse that sums up the haunting legend:

'Woodman, woodman, have you seen
Gradlon's fierce stallion, strong and keen,
galloping through this valley green?'
'King Gradlon's horse I did not mark,
But I heard, echoing through the dark,
trip trep trip trep, swift as a spark.'
'Fisherman, have you seen her comb
her golden hair beside the foam—
the girl who's made the sea her home?'
'I've seen the sea's pale child walk by,
I've heard her singing rise and die.
Her songs were sad as breaker's sigh.'

CHAPTER XXI

The Last Bretons?

IN 1836 THERE appeared the first and probably the most influential of the many books by Bretons mourning the lost glories of their country. Called *Les Derniers Bretons*, it was written by Emile Souvestre, who was born at Morlaix in 1804. In his Preface, Souvestre describes how angry he got with Parisians who ventured into Brittany with heads full of preconceptions, and returned with notebooks stuffed with wrong ideas, which they then proceeded to turn into books. He himself went to Paris in 1826, plunged into the literary life there, but returned mentally scarred to Brittany when a play he had written was a failure. *Les Derniers Bretons* was not only therapy for an author's wounded pride: it was a labour of love which took six years, and which he calls 'a complete picture of Breton psychology' ('*un tableau complet de Bretagne psychologique*'). But the word '*complet*' is misleading, as Souvestre dealt only with Breton-speaking Basse-Bretagne (Breizh-Izel), ignoring the French-speaking half and confining himself to the Départements of Finistère, Morbihan and the Côtes-du-Nord—the ancient bishoprics of Cornouaille, Vannes, Saint-Pol-de-Léon and Tréguier, whose fabric had been torn apart at the Revolution. Their inhabitants were his 'last Bretons'; and in a sense writers from La Villemarqué to Hélias have been writing about the 'last Bretons' ever since. Yet the Bretons somehow manage to survive, as each new generation uses the methods of its time to assert its identity.

At the present time this takes the form of the reassertion of the importance of the Breton language. Bretons look enviously north to Wales, where Welsh has a degree of recognition unimaginable in present-day Brittany. The revival of the ancient names of Dyfydd and Powys, Gwynedd and Clwyd, has no parallel in Brittany. You will search in vain for roadsigns that point to Roazon as well as Rennes, to Kemper as well as Quimper, and to Naoned as well as Nantes; although there has been a certain amount of daubing of French nameboards, similar to the Welsh green-paint campaign of the 1950s and 1960s. On the positive side, the Université de Haute Bretagne in Rennes has 500 students in its Breton department, and each year runs a crash-course in Breton which lasts for a week. Most towns have bookshops where you can buy teach-yourself guides, and there are flourishing correspondence courses in the Breton language. Yet it still remains a fringe subject, virtually unrecognised by official Paris-orientated education. As one of the six Celtic languages—the others are Welsh, Gaelic, Irish, Manx and Cornish—Breton has an ancient history stretching back far beyond upstarts like French and English. But a language, like the people who speak it, cannot live by history alone. The crisis of Breton is really two separate questions: first, to what extent is it a viable language for the modern world; and second, is a separate language essential for Brittany to retain its sense of identity?

The first of these questions has been thoroughly thrashed out by Jorj Gwegen, in *La Langue Bretonne Face à Ses Oppresseurs*, published in 1975. The title indicates the defiant stance from which the book is written: Breton is a stranger in a hostile world, the word '*oppresseur*' implying a deliberate and sustained attempt to crush the language, the oppressor being France over the last four and a half centuries. At the outset Gwegen reproduces a linguistic map of France, showing the extent to which other languages have predominated in the French 'Hexagon' down the years. Breton was at its greatest extent in the ninth century, when it spread across virtually the whole of Brittany (excluding Rennes and Nantes); three centuries later dialects of Occitan were spoken in the whole of the southern third of France, from Limousin and the Auvergne southwards; and there are today other minority languages in the Hexagon, such as Basque, Catalonian, Alsatian and Flemish. Of course, to say that a language has once existed in an area is not to say that it will necessarily continue to exist, otherwise Etrucsan would still no doubt be spoken in much of Italy. But the linguistic historians have a point; and one might regard the French authorities' hysterical outbursts against the modern tide of Franglais as a subconscious recognition of the fact that French itself may one day go the way of Occitan.

Gwegen chronicles the steady process of *francisation*, as the purposeful spread of the French language is called. After the union of France with Brittany in 1532 it was not long before *francisation* was under way. In 1539 François I made French the compulsory language on all legal documents, though the practice took almost a century to spread to Basse-Bretagne. While Brittany slumbered—as far as literature was concerned, though not orally—through the seventeenth and eighteenth centuries the process was comparatively slow; but the bureaucrats of the Revolution saw Breton as a barrier to unification. In 1794 their attitude was made plain by a member of the Committee of Public Safety, who said that 'federalism and superstition speak Bas-Breton; emigration and hatred of the Republic speak German; the counter-Revolution speaks Italian and fanaticism speaks Basque. Among a free people, the language must be one and the same for all.' The 'language of freedom' was naturally French; and the story of the nineteenth century from the point of view of the Breton language was of the imposition of French from outside—an imposition which Breton nationalists, both then and now, have seen as an aspect of colonialism, similar to the enforced *francisation* of French colonies in North Africa and the West Indies.

An altogether original and stimulating exhibition on one aspect of *francisation* was held at the Musée de Bretagne in Rennes in the summer of 1977. Called 'The Teachers and the Taught' ('Enseignants et Enseignés'), it was the first of its kind ever held in France—hardly surprising, as French attitudes did not emerge from it in a very good light. Its theme was most ambitious: to show, by means of documents and classroom artefacts, how education tried to mould the minds of an entire generation. To put it more precisely: How were the children of Brittany, which in the early nineteenth century was a forgotten and backward province, educated to be ready to fight for France at the outbreak of the First World War?

The turning-point in French education was the humiliating defeat of France by the Prussians in 1871. For the next forty years the tone was set by the need to inculcate a whole nation's children with the desire to avenge this humiliation, which had taken its most tangible form in the German annexation of Alsace and Lorraine. Only eleven years later, in March 1882,

Jules Ferry passed a law making primary education in France free, non-clerical and compulsory, and thus broke the stranglehold of the Church. At about the same time the militaristic organisations known as '*bataillons scolaires*' were set up, with the object of training 'children today, soldiers tomorrow'. Secularism and militarism were common to the whole of France; but Brittany posed special problems. The chief of these was that to many Breton children French was virtually an unknown language, which was a tremendous barrier to any form of standardised propaganda. The Government's attitude was summed up by the quotation: 'Whether one is Breton, Occitan or Basque, the words *Patrie* and *Nation* are always spelt in French'. French-speaking Breton children were subjected to the same propaganda. Per Denez, who is Professor of Breton at Rennes University, wrote to me that his father, along with other children in the Cancale district, was made to march up and down the school yard every morning chanting 'We will recapture Alsace and Lorraine' ('*Nous reprendrons l'Alsace et la Lorraine*').

Ironically enough, the Breton language was largely kept alive by the need for children to be taught their catechism, whether the school was secular or religious. A primary school regulation made for the Département of the Côtes-du-Nord in 1852 stated: 'French alone will be used in schools. Nevertheless, in those *communes* where only the Breton catechism is in use, the teacher will give instruction in that catechism.' Whether in Breton or French, the catechism was used to instil a proper sense of the fitness of things. One example, printed at Rennes in 1857, included the following: 'The 7th Commandment of God. Q: Who are those who take unjustly the goods of another? A: They are thieves, money-lenders, cheating merchants, and workers and servants who misuse their time.'

Yet for all its faults, the system did produce a major breakthrough in literacy. At the end of the eighteenth century, the highest proportion of literacy among men was in Finistère, at 35–40 per cent, compared with only 5–10 per cent in the Morbihan, the next-door Département. The figure for women was 5–10 per cent throughout Brittany. When one remembers that these figures represent merely those who could sign their names in the parish registers instead of making a mark, it is clear that the ability to read and write must have been virtually nil. (These figures need to be taken with a certain amount of caution, as they refer to literacy in French, rather than Breton. It is impossible to know how many people could read the popular religious books printed in Breton.) However, a century later literacy was almost universal. This was achieved by an army of teachers, turned out from the two Ecoles Normales in Rennes—the Ecole Normale des Instituteurs, founded in 1831, and its female counterpart the Ecole Normale des Institutrices, which did not come into being until 1885, over half a century later.

The position of the teacher in local life was summed up by a photograph showing the main building of a small Breton town, in which the Mairie, the classroom and the teacher's house formed a single complex. Such complexes were the anti-clerical focus of most towns and large villages in France, with the republican mayor and teacher allied against the forces of reaction represented by the Church. According to the philosophy of Jules Ferry, already mentioned, the *commune* with the mayor in charge was the basic cell from which the structure of the State was built, the school was there to shape ideas of civic duty and republicanism, while the teacher (who was often town clerk as well) was the agent whereby those ideas were formed. Of course, Church-run schools (*écoles libres*) continued side by side with the lay *écoles publiques*, and the social fabric was often split apart by their differences. The pupils of different schools would engage in running battles after hours, parents who sent their children to the lay schools might be pressurised by their employers to take them away and send them to Church schools, and in some churches sacraments were even refused to so-called 'republican' parents.

The two groups of children, lay and Church-educated—the '*deux jeunesses*'—were unified by the use of common textbooks that gave '*une certaine idée de la France*'. Chief of the unifying subjects were history and geography. As far as history was concerned, the aim was 'to make known the life and soul of the people of France down the centuries'—'the history of France for a Brittany without history', as the catalogue wryly commented. Typical of the geography books was *Le Tour de France par Deux Enfants*, first published in 1877 and still being published, which has sold $8\frac{1}{2}$ million copies down the years, and which teaches that France is 'the most beautiful country in the world, rich, unified, hard-working, destined to greatness by the activity of her sons, who owe this wonderful *patrie* a devotion that cannot be shared'. A devotion that led to the interpretation of the colours of the French flag as red for the blood the patriot sheds, white for his purity of heart, and blue for the vast French sky above him.

This is very much the educational background described by Pierre-Jakez Hélias in *Le Cheval d'Orgueil*—the fights between the children of Pouldreuzic village, Church *Blancs* against Republican *Rouges*, the prevention of Breton-speaking at school and its discouragement at home. Hélias and his friends suffered the humiliation of the *vache* or *symbole*—the sabot or other object that was hung as a mark of disgrace round the neck of a boy or girl caught talking Breton, and could only be got rid of by catching a fellow-pupil in the same sin and then reporting him or her to the teacher. As Machiavellian a way of making children ashamed of their native tongue as can be imagined. Hélias describes his problems when he went to the Lycée La Tour d'Auvergne in Quimper in the 1920s, after spending his early childhood speaking Breton.

> Everyone forgot that we were transplants, immigrants in spite of ourselves in a civilisation not our own. Not only were we still translating as best we might from our spoken language into book-French, but our whole way of life, our daily behaviour from getting up to going to bed, annoyed the others or made them laugh. Our country politeness seemed like stupidity to them, and we looked at their townee airs and graces with amazement. I learnt once and for all that the most miserable bourgeois thought himself superior to the noblest peasant—a misapprehension that is still with us. Besides, we were among the poorest of the students. For playing football in the yard, the others had leather shoes, but we had wooden sabots tied round the ankle with string. The string would break, the sabot would hurtle into a window, and the window would shatter with a crash. We had to pay, of course, which was a serious expense for some of us, and we were also treated to a lecture coupled with detention.

A century or more of such active discouragement of Breton has had its natural effect. Jorj Gwegen gives the depressing figure for all pupils actively studying the Breton language, as opposed to speaking it occasionally at home or at work: a total of between 8,000 and 10,000 including those learning by correspondence. The number of those able to speak the language (*bretonnants*) is less than half of the 1½ million inhabitants of Basse-Bretagne, the proportion being significantly linked to age. Thus of 705,000 in the 25–64 age group, 423,000 were *bretonnant*; whereas of 360,000 in the under-14 age group, only 18,000 spoke the language. These are 1974 figures, and no doubt the numbers are now more discouraging still. Gwegen is under no illusions.

> Useless to delude oneself: there is no longer a Breton-speaking community in the complete sense of the expression. . . . The Breton-speaking universe is submerged, attacked on all sides. Breton is not used at primary schools, for secondary education, for professional exams, or to become a civil servant. It is not used at the post office, at the bank, at the insurance agent, at the supermarket, at the shoe-shop, at the cake-shop, to buy a ticket to the cinema, or at the station to buy a ticket to Paris. . . . Apart from shutting myself away at home, stopping up my doors and windows, surrounding my garden with three rows of barbed wire and an electric fence, I cannot escape from the French-speaking tide that engulfs everything, with all the dykes thrown open.

Breton is still the working language for men in the fields and for fishermen. But the women have rejected it as a symbol of *ruralité*, whereas French signifies *urbanité*. Gwegen gives any amount of interviews with schoolchildren and students who have been made ashamed of speaking Breton themselves, who have felt humiliated when their parents have spoken Breton in front of school friends, who have been laughed at for their accents by *francisants*. But the chief reason for its decline is that it has no commercial value: it is not '*rentable*' in any way. Thus there are now two main classes of *bretonnants*: the elderly, who have been left behind in the march of progress, and the militants, mainly students, to whom it is a weapon in their separatist aims. Gwegen's solution is nothing less than the complete replacement of French by Breton as the primary language in the whole of Basse-Bretagne, that is, west of an imaginary line from Plouha on the Bay of Saint-Brieuc to Damgan on the estuary of the Vilaine. Breton should be taught both at the mother's knee and at school: '*Ar Brezhoneg er skol*' ('Breton at school') is his slogan. It should be a natural means of communication, not just another school subject. He contradicts the often-repeated saying that 'Breton is the language of the heart and French is the language of reason' by maintaining that Breton is quite capable of being the language of both head and heart. The final stage would be the abandonment of *francophone* Rennes or Nantes as the capital, and the setting up of a new capital somewhere near the linguistic frontier that separates the *bretonnants* from the *francisants*.

How this revolution will be achieved is scarcely touched on; but more improbable things have no doubt happened. Hélias takes a more hard-headed view of the future. Seeing that by the year 2000 there may be only 25,000 *bretonnants* left, he sees the task of himself and his contemporaries—the last generation who learnt Breton at their mother's knee—as 'making an inventory of the whole civilisation that is interpreted by that language'. He points out that there is really no such being as a *bretonnant*, since there are several Breton dialects, corresponding to the four ancient bishoprics used as his classification by Emile Souvestre. And he has a warning for those intellectuals who take to Breton after several generations' gap, with no direct contact with Breton-speakers, and use the language as one of a set of political attitudes. There are even those, he tells us, who forbid French to be spoken at home, thus imposing the *vache* stood on its head ('*la vache à l'envers*').

One of the main problems with the Breton revival is that there is no great Breton literature to turn back to: no equivalent of the mass of Welsh and Irish literature that has survived since the Middle Ages and earlier. The *Barzaz-Breiz* is really no substitute for the *Mabinogion*, or for the heroic deeds of Cu Chulainn and Conchobhar. In other words, if every Breton-speaker disappeared from the face of the earth tomorrow, would the writings of the nineteenth and twentieth centuries drive scholars to study the language? It seems unlikely. There is a saying '*Hep Brezhoneg, Breizh ebet*' ('Without Breton, no Brittany'); but it is equally true to say that without a Breton literature, there can be no Breton language, except on a spoken, person-to-person basis. This is perhaps why Breton popular music has such a strong appeal. Renewing the tradition of the ancient bards, Alan Stivell and his colleagues mix the Breton language with elements taken from old Breton music and the world of today's pop music, to produce something entirely new. One of Stivell's records, *Before Landing*, is the 1970s equivalent of the *Barzaz-Breiz*, giving a historical résumé of key events in the story of Brittany, with a strongly nationalistic and anti-French bias. Not surprisingly, Stivell is as successful in other Celtic countries as he is in his native land.

No one can spend any time in Brittany without noticing evidence of the desire for separatism, ranging from the mild tourist nationalism of BZH car stickers, through walls daubed with slogans for the FLB (Front pour la Libération de la Bretagne) to more serious incidents like the bomb explosion I witnessed in Quimper in 1976. Journals on sale cover the whole spectrum of the Left, from the fairly moderate *Le Peuple Breton*, which deals seriously with economic questions, to the anarchist *PDG*, standing for *Le Poing dans la Gueule* (*The Fist in the Face*), which is strongly pro-IRA, among other things, and calls for 'a fight to the death against the French state'. The classic grievances of Bretons down the ages were expressed in one issue I read of the *PDG*: 'Today Brittany is reduced to being a training-ground for the army of occupation, a laboratory for the sorcerer's apprentices of nuclear power, a tourist reserve, and a cheap reservoir of labour.' But all such protests have little effect on the centralising tendencies of France, which have remained unchanged through Louis XIV and Napoleon to the current succession of presidents.

As an outsider who has visited Brittany almost entirely as a tourist, it would be as impertinent for me to attempt to offer any solutions to the problems of Brittany *vis-à-vis* France as it would be for a Frenchman to give advice on Welsh devolution. Yet an outsider can sometimes see the difficulties more clearly than those actively engaged in the struggle on one side or the other. The first and main problem is that Brittany is permeated by France, not just linguistically, but culturally as well, in the widest sense of the term. Apart from the slate roofs on the houses, you might be anywhere in France: the same shops selling the same food and drink, the same clothes, the same total feeling of Frenchness. As far as the main administrative alteration of recent years is concerned, Loire-Atlantique is now well and truly separated from the other four Départements, and the clock is never put back once such a major change has taken place. In many ways, this may prove to be a blessing in disguise for Brittany, as the historic rivalry between Rennes and Nantes is now over once and for all, and Rennes has the opportunity to grow to a capital's moral stature. The fact that Brittany no longer includes the shipbuilding and other industries of Nantes and Saint-Nazaire need not be to its detriment, provided that other industry is encouraged. Here again tourism is a tremendous money-spinner; and the setting-up of the Parc Naturel Régional d'Armorique in the depressed hill areas of the country is a pointer to a possibly more prosperous future.

The wisest words on the whole subject were written some years ago by Morvan Lebesque, the great Nantes journalist who died in 1970 while attending a Breton cultural congress in Brazil. In his book *Comment Peut-on Etre Breton?*, he points out that the impact of the French centralist state on Brittany has led the separatists to envisage a Brittany cast in the same mould. 'To demand separatism is to return to the past: not to the Middle Ages, as fools maintain, but to the epoch of confined nation-states that came after and congealed the medieval fluidity; it is to confound ancient history with the new, to fail to recognise that this is the age of different cultures, to renew links with the mentality of siege warfare.' Lebesque envisages a federal evolution of France and Brittany alike, 'to harmonise the double demands of culture and economics', whereby for example Nantes could look towards both Brittany and the Pays de la Loire. 'For those who think as I do, Brittany is not a racial bloc but a consciousness and a will to exist (*une conscience et une volonté d'être*). In a federal structure, Bretons will continue to live outside Brittany and will not be any the less Breton. Non-Bretons will live in Brittany, and among them, as today, there will be those who are more consciously Breton than the Bretons themselves. . . . There will still be non-Breton officials and technicians in Brittany, but they will have to justify themselves before her and not before irresponsible Parisians. They will no longer exploit her people and assassinate her culture.'

I have spoken to Bretons who fear that their country is about to be turned by decree into a sterilised national park, empty for most of the year and inhabited full-time mainly by retired people who have gone there to enjoy the peace and quiet. And certainly no one would describe present-day Brittany as a humming hive of industrial enterprise. But below the outer trappings of seaside resorts and sandy beaches, of *calvaires* and folk festivals, of seafood and seaweed gatherers, there is an ancient strength and will to survive. When writing this book, I have found that every foray into Brittany, every hour reading some history or previously unknown poem or novel, has been a revelation of an undreamed-of richness and variety. I hope that it will not displease the friends I have made there by its superficiality: but how can one learn in a couple of years what it takes a lifetime to discover? At least it is written with some of the love that native Bretons feel for their land of rock and moorland, set like a granite buttress on the western edge of Europe. *Kenavo.*

BIBLIOGRAPHY

Abelard and Heloise. *Letters*. Translated by Betty Radice (Penguin, 1974)

Abjean, René. *La Musique Bretonne* (Jos Le Doaré, Châteaulin, 1975)

Aron, Robert. *Histoire de la Libération de la France* (Fayard, Paris, 1959)

Arrowsmith, Nancy. *A Field Guide to the Little People* (Macmillan, 1977)

Blackburn, Henry. *Breton Folk: an Artistic Tour in Brittany*. Illustrated by Randolph Caldecott (Sampson Low, 1880)

Blumenson, Martin, *U.S. Army in World War II: Breakout and Pursuit* (Washington, D.C., 1961)

Boudaille, Georges. *Gauguin* (Thames and Hudson, 1964)

Brantôme, Abbé de (Pierre de Bourdeilles). *Vies des Dames Illustres*

Bretagne Héraut d'Armes. *Récit des Funérailles d'Anne de Bretagne* (Paris, 1858)

Caesar, Julius. *The Conquest of Gaul*. Translated by S. A. Handford (Penguin)

Chardronnet, Joseph. *Histoire de Bretagne* (Nouvelles Editions Latines, 1965)

Chateaubriand, François-René de. *Mémoires d'Outre-Tombe* (2 vols, Brussels, 1849)

Châteaubriant, Alphonse de. *La Brière* (Bernard Grasset, 1923)

Clark, Eleanor. *The Oysters of Locmariaquer* (Secker and Warburg, 1965)

Corbière, Tristan. *Les Amours Jaunes* (Paris, 1903)

Costello, Louisa Stuart. *Memoirs of Anne, Duchess of Brittany* (London, 1855)

Daniel, Glyn. *Lascaux and Carnac* (Lutterworth Press, 1955)

De la Warr, Countess. *A Twice Crowned Queen: Anne of Brittany* (Eveleigh Nash, 1906)

Duguay-Trouin, René. *Vie de Monsieur Du Guay-Trouin, Ecrite de sa Main*. Edited by Henri Malo (Bossard, 1922)

Dupont, Etienne. *Les Corsaires Chez Eux* (pub. by the author, 1929)

Durtelle de Saint-Sauveur, E. *Histoire de Bretagne* (2 vols, Rennes, 1935)
Engen, Rodney K. *Randolph Caldecott* (Oresko Books, 1976)
Fawtier, Robert. *La Vie de Saint Samson* (Paris, 1912)
Flaubert, Gustave. *Par les Champs et par les Grèves* (Paris, 1929)
Gabory, Emile. *Le Meurtre de Gilles de Bretagne* (Paris, 1929)
Gauguin, Paul. *Avant et Après* (Paris, 1923)
Gauguin, Paul. *Lettres à sa Femme et à ses Amis* (Grasset, Paris, 1946)
Gregory of Tours. *History of the Franks.* Translated by Lewis Thorpe (Penguin, 1974)
Gwegen, Jorj. *La Langue Bretonne Face à ses Oppresseurs* (Nature et Bretagne, 1975)
Hélias, Pierre-Jakez. *Le Cheval d'Orgueil* (Plon, 1975)
Herm, Gerhard. *The Celts* (Weidenfeld and Nicolson, 1976)
Jackson, J. Hampden (editor). *A Short History of France* (Cambridge, 1974)
Jacob, Max. *Lettres, 1920–41.* Edited by S. J. Collier (Blackwell, 1966)
Jacob, Max. *Le Cornet à Dés* (Gallimard, 1954)
Jacob, Max. *Poèmes de Morven le Gaëlique* (Gallimard, 1953)
Jaffrenou, F. Taldir. *La Véritable Histoire de La Tour d'Auvergne-Corret* (Paris, 1928)
La Tour d'Auvergne-Corret, Théophile-Malo. *Origines Gauloises, celles des Plus Anciens Peuples d'Europe, Puisées dans leur Vraie Source* (1801)
La Villemarqué, Vicomte Hersart de. *Barzaz-Breiz, Chants Populaires de la Bretagne* (Paris, 1923)
La Villemarqué, Vicomte Hersart de. *Les Romans de la Table Ronde* (Paris, 1860)
Lebesque, Morvan. *Comment Peut-on Etre Breton?* (Editions du Seuil, 1970)
Le Boterf, Hervé. *La Bretagne dans la Guerre* (3 vols, Editions France-Empire, 1969, 1970, 1971)
Le Braz, Anatole. *La Légende de la Mort* (Editions Alpina, 1958)
Le Grand, Père Albert. *Vies des Saints de la Bretagne-Armorique* (Saint-Brieuc, 1837)
Le Mercier d'Erm, Camille (editor). *Les Bardes et Poètes Nationaux de la Bretagne Armoricaine* (Rennes, 1918)

Lorraine, Jacques. *The Germans in France* (Hutchinson, undated, *c.* 1945)

Mabinogion, The. Translated by Jeffrey Gantz (Penguin, 1976)

Millar, George. *Oyster River: One Summer on an Inland Sea* (Bodley Head, 1963)

Millar, Ronald. *A Time of Cherries: Sailing with the Breton Tunnymen* (Cassell, 1977)

Miln, James. *Excavations at Carnac: the Bossenno and the Mont Saint Michel* (David Douglas, Edinburgh, 1877)

Miln, James. *Excavations at Carnac: the Alignments of Kermario* (David Douglas, 1881)

Montigny, Etienne Mignot de. *Voyage en Bretagne, 1752* (Société d'Histoire et d'Archéologie de Bretagne, 1925)

Norman, C. B. *The Corsairs of France* (Sampson Low, 1887)

Rémy. *La Maison d'Alphonse* (Librairie Académique Perrin, 1968)

Renouard, Michel (editor). *Guide de Bretagne* (Ouest-France, 1976)

Russell of Liverpool, Lord. *The French Corsairs* (Robert Hale, 1970)

Sévigné, Madame de. *Lettres* (2 vols, Bibliothèque de la Pléiade, 1953, 1955)

Souvestre, Emile. *Les Derniers Bretons* (Paris, 1875)

Stephens, Meic. *Linguistic Minorities in Western Europe* (Gomer Press, 1976)

Surcouf, Robert. *Un Corsaire Malouin: Robert Surcouf* (Paris, 1890)

Taylor, Thomas. *The Life of St Samson of Dol* (S.P.C.K., 1925)

Tchou (editor). *Guide de la Bretagne Mystérieuse* (3 vols, Press Pocket, 1966)

Treat, Ida. *Rock of France* (Lindsay Drummond, 1942)

Trollope, T. Adolphus. *A Summer in Brittany* (2 vols, Henry Colburn, 1840)

Vercel, Roger, *Du Guesclin* (Paris, 1932)

Wilson, Geoffrey. *The Old Telegraphs* (Phillimore, 1976)

Young, Arthur. *Travels in France during the Years 1787, 1788, 1789* (George Bell and Sons, 1889)

Index

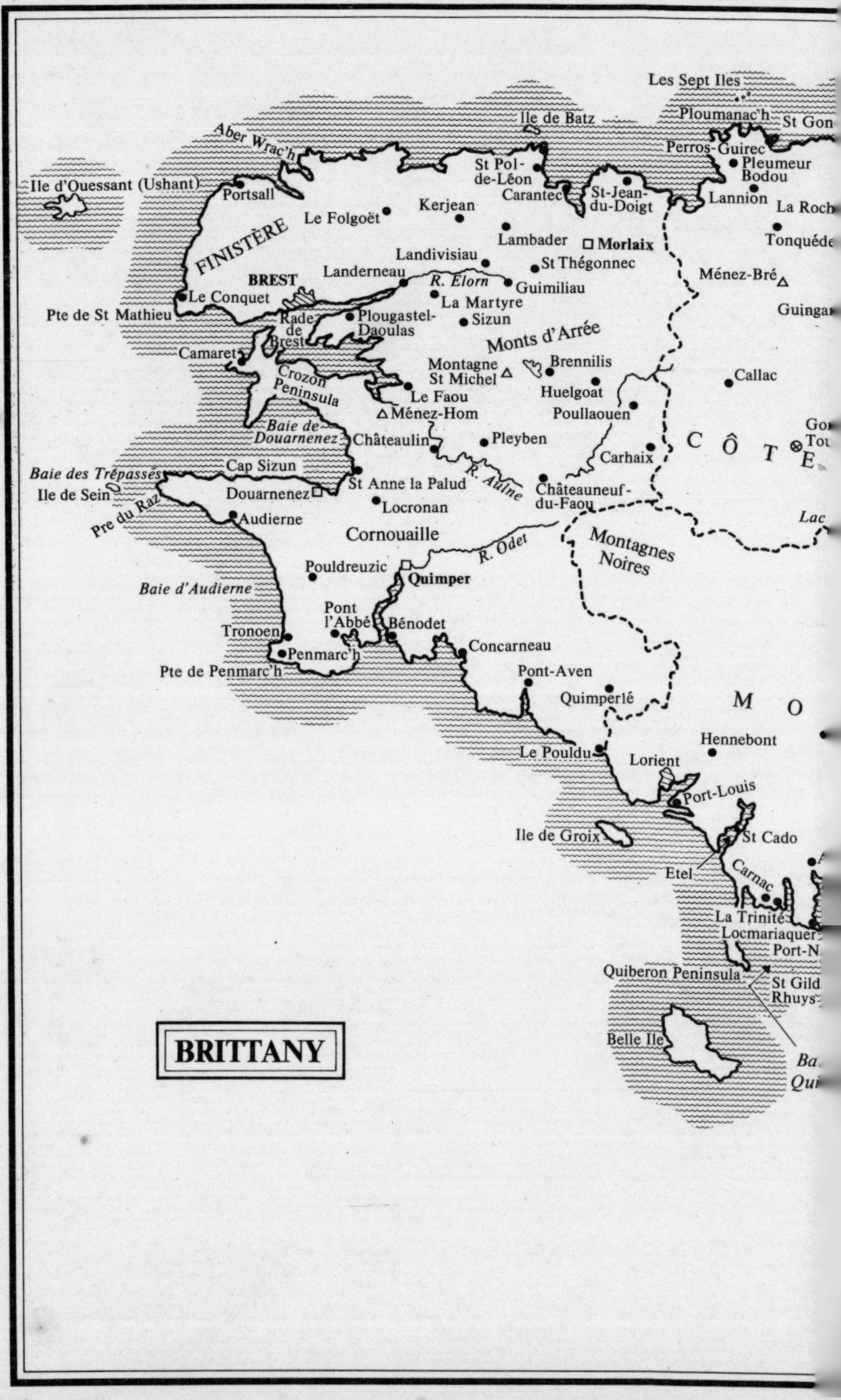
BRITTANY
FINISTÈRE
Les Sept Iles
Ile de Batz
Ploumanac'h
Aber Wrac'h
Perros-Guirec
Pleumeur Bodou
Ile d'Ouessant (Ushant)
Portsall
St Pol-de-Léon
Carantec
St-Jean-du-Doigt
Lannion
Le Folgoët
Kerjean
Lambader
Morlaix
Landivisiau
St Thégonnec
Ménez-Bré
BREST
Landerneau
R. Elorn
Guimiliau
Le Conquet
La Martyre
Pte de St Mathieu
Rade de Brest
Plougastel-Daoulas
Sizun
Monts d'Arrée
Camaret
Montagne St Michel
Brennilis
Callac
Crozon Peninsula
Le Faou
Huelgoat
Ménez-Hom
Poullaouen
Baie de Douarnenez
Châteaulin
Pleyben
Carhaix
CÔTE
Baie des Trépassés
Cap Sizun
R. Aulne
Ile de Sein
Douarnenez
St Anne la Palud
Châteauneuf-du-Faou
Pre du Raz
Locronan
Audierne
Cornouaille
Montagnes Noires
R. Odet
Pouldreuzic
Quimper
Baie d'Audierne
Pont l'Abbé
Bénodet
Tronoen
Concarneau
Penmarc'h
Pte de Penmarc'h
Pont-Aven
Quimperlé
MO
Hennebont
Le Pouldu
Lorient
Port-Louis
Ile de Groix
St Cado
Etel
Carnac
La Trinité
Locmariaquer
Quiberon Peninsula
Belle Ile